THE

GENERAL CATALOGUE

AND

EARLY ANNALS

OF

Union Theological Seminary

IN THE

CITY OF NEW-YORK.

1836–1876.

NEW-YORK:
No. 30 Clinton Place.
1876.

GENERAL

CATALOGUE

OF

UNION THEOLOGICAL SEMINARY

IN THE

CITY OF NEW-YORK.

1836–1876.

New-York:
S. W. GREEN, PRINTER, 16 AND 18 JACOB STREET.

1876.

Founded, January 18, 1836.

Instruction Commenced, December 5, 1836.

First Public Anniversary, July 11, 1838.

Seminary Building Opened, December 12, 1838.

Incorporated, March 17, 1839.

BOARD OF DIRECTORS.

PRESIDENTS.

Accessit.		Exit.
1836	*Rev. Thomas McAuley, D.D., LL.D.	1840
1840	*Richard Townley Haines	1840
1840	Rev. Samuel Hanson Cox, D.D., LL.D	1841
1841	*Richard Townley Haines	1870
1870	Charles Butler, LL.D	

VICE-PRESIDENTS.

1836	*Zechariah Lewis	1840
1841	Charles Butler, LL.D	1870
1870	Norman White	

RECORDERS.

1836	*Rev. Erskine Mason, D.D	1841
1841	*Rev. Henry Augustus Rowland, D.D	1843
1843	*Rev. James Woods McLane, D.D	1864
1864	Rev. Edwin Francis Hatfield, D.D	1874
1874	Ezra Munson Kingsley	

TREASURERS.

1836	*William Mills Halsted	1845
1845	*Anthony Post Halsey	1863
1863	Rev. Joseph Steele Gallagher	1874
1874	Ezra Munson Kingsley	

DIRECTORS.

1836	*Rev. Thomas McAuley, D.D., LL.D	1845
1836	*Rev. Henry White, D.D	1840
1836	*Rev. Thomas Harvey Skinner, D.D., LL.D	1848
1836	Rev. William Patton, D.D	1849
1836	*Rev. Erskine Mason, D.D	1851

Accessit.		Exit.
1836	*Rev. Ichabod Smith Spencer, D.D.	1849
1836	*Rev. Absalom Peters, D.D.	1842
1836	Rev. William Adams, D.D., LL.D.	
1836	Rev. Elijah Porter Barrows, D.D.	1837
1836	*Rev. Henry Augustus Rowland, D.D.	1845
1836	*Zechariah Lewis	1840
1836	*Micah Baldwin	1845
1836	Charles Butler, LL.D.	
1836	*John Nitchie	1838
1836	*Leonard Corning	1842
1836	*Abijah Fisher	1859
1836	*William Mills Halsted	1851
1836	*Caleb Oliver Halsted	1860
1836	*Fisher Howe	1871
1836	*Richard Townley Haines	1870
1836	*Joseph Otis	1844
1836	*Pelatiah Perit	1857
1836	*Cornelius Baker	1840
1836	*Knowles Taylor	1842
1837	*Rev. David Magie, D.D.	1840
1837	*Rev. Nathanael Emmons Johnson	1844
1837	*Rev. Ansel Doan Eddy, D.D.	1856
1837	Rev. Selah Burr Treat	1843
1837	Rev. Samuel Hanson Cox, D.D., LL.D.	1873
1838	*Anson Greene Phelps	1853
1840	*Rev. Albert Barnes	1870
1841	Rev. Asa Dodge Smith, D.D., LL.D.	1864
1841	David Leavitt	1846
1841	*Anthony Post Halsey	1863
1842	*James Colton Bliss, M.D.	1855
1842	*Rev. James Woods McLane, D.D.	1864
1844	*Rev. William Beale Lewis	1849
1844	Treadwell Ketcham	1850
1844	Cyrus Putnam Smith, Esq.	1848
1844	Rev. Horatio Nelson Brinsmade, D.D.	1851
1845	*Rev. Ebenezer Cheever	1846
1846	Rev. Edwin Francis Hatfield, D.D.	
1846	*Rev. Samuel Ware Fisher, D.D.	1848
1846	*David Hoadley	1873
1847	Francis Peoples Shoals	1850
1848	*John Center Baldwin	1870

Accessit.		Exit.
1848	*Rev. Jonathan Bailey Condit, D.D.	1851
1848	*Rev. Joseph Clay Stiles, D.D	1852
1849	Rev. Charles Henry Read, D.D	1850
1849	Rev. Samuel Thayer Spear, D.D	1860
1850	Rev. Jonathan French Stearns, D.D	
1850	Rev. Walter Hilliard Bidwell	1857
1851	*John Alfred Davenport	1855
1851	*Jasper Corning	1852
1852	Rev. George Lewis Prentiss, D.D	1873
1852	Rev. Joseph Fewsmith, D.D	
1852	Rev. Artemas Augustus Wood, D.D	1860
1852	*Rev. Alfred Elderkin Campbell, D.D	1859
1852	*James Boorman	1866
1852	*Anson Green Phelps, Jr	1858
1855	*Walter Scott Griffith	1870
1856	Hon. William Earle Dodge	
1856	Rev. James Patriot Wilson, D.D	
1856	Alfred Charles Post, M.D., LL.D	
1857	Norman White	
1857	*Rev. Joel Parker, D.D	1869
1859	*Rev. Walter Clarke, D.D	1861
1859	Salem Howe Wales	1867
1860	Rev. John Jenkins, D.D	1863
1860	William Agur Booth	
1860	Rev. Charles Seymour Robinson, D.D	1869
1860	Joseph Howland	1874
1861	Rev. Robert Russell Booth, D.D	
1863	Rev. Joseph Steele Gallagher	
1863	Hanson Kelly Corning	
1864	Rev. Samuel Thayer Spear, D.D	1869
1864	Rev. Thomas Samuel Hastings, D.D	
1866	John Crosby Brown	
1867	Daniel Willis James	
1868	Rev. Joseph Tuttle Duryea, D.D	1874
1869	Rev. John Hall, D.D	
1869	Rev. James Ormsbee Murray, D.D	
1870	Winthrop Sargent Gilman	1875
1870	Henry Day, Esq	
1870	John Taylor Johnston	
1871	Rev. Herrick Johnson, D.D	1873
1872	David Hunter McAlpin	

Accessit.			Exit.
1873		Rev. Marvin Richardson Vincent, D.D.	
1873		Rev. William Miller Paxton, D.D.	
1874		Rev. Zephaniah Moore Humphrey, D.D.	1875
1874		Ezra Munson Kingsley	
1875		Rev. Henry Darling, D.D.	
1875		Alexander Van Rensselaer	
1875		Rev. Charles Andrews Dickey, D.D.	

FINANCIAL AGENTS.

Accessit.			Exit.
1839	*	Rev. Gideon Noble Judd, D.D.	1841
1841	*	Rev. Timothy W. Lester	1842
1842	*	Rev. Absalom Peters, D.D.	1842
1843	*	Rev. Lubim Burton Rockwood	1850
1850		Rev. George Franklin Wiswell, D.D.	1852
1852		Rev. Joseph Steele Gallagher	1862
1864		Rev. Edwin Francis Hatfield, D.D.	1865
1870		Rev. Edwin Francis Hatfield, D.D.	1872

FACULTY.

PRESIDENTS.

Accessit.			Exit.
1836	*	Rev. Thomas McAuley, D.D., LL.D.	1840
1840	*	Rev. Joel Parker, D.D.	1842
1873		Rev. William Adams, D.D., LL.D.	

PROFESSORS.

SYSTEMATIC THEOLOGY.

Accessit.			Exit.
1836	*	Rev. Henry White, D.D.	1850
1851		Rev. James Patriot Wilson, D.D.	1853
1854		Rev. Henry Boynton Smith, D.D., LL.D.	1874
1874		Rev. Wm. Greenough Thayer Shedd, D.D., LL.D.	

PASTORAL THEOLOGY.

Accessit.		Exit.
1836	*Rev. Thomas McAuley, D.D., LL.D	1840

SACRED LITERATURE.

1837	*Rev. Edward Robinson, D.D., LL.D	1863
1863	Rev. Wm. Greenough Thayer Shedd, D.D., LL.D.	1874
1874	Rev. Philip Schaff, D.D., LL.D	

SACRED RHETORIC.

1840	*Rev. Joel Parker, D.D	1842
1873	Rev. William Adams, D.D., LL.D	

SACRED RHETORIC, PASTORAL THEOLOGY, AND CHURCH GOVERNMENT.

1848	*Rev. Thomas Harvey Skinner, D.D., LL.D	1871

CHURCH HISTORY.

1850	Rev. Henry Boynton Smith, D.D., LL.D	1854
1855	Rev. Roswell Dwight Hitchcock, D.D., LL.D	

THEOLOGICAL CYCLOPÆDIA AND CHRISTIAN SYMBOLISM.

1870	Rev. Philip Schaff, D.D., LL.D	1873

HEBREW AND THE COGNATE LANGUAGES.

1873	Rev. Philip Schaff, D.D., LL.D	1874
1875	Rev. Charles Augustus Briggs, D.D	

PASTORAL THEOLOGY, CHURCH POLITY, AND MISSION WORK.

1873	Rev. George Lewis Prentiss, D.D	

APOLOGETICS [EMERITUS].

1874	Rev. Henry Boynton Smith, D.D., LL.D	

INSTRUCTORS.

SACRED LITERATURE.

1836	*Rev. George Bush	1837
1837	*Rev. Ebenezer Burgess	1838
1838	*Robert Bridges Patton, Ph.D	1839
1838	*Isaac Nordheimer, Ph.D	1841
1843	*William Wadden Turner	1852
1852	Rev. Theron Holbrook Hawks, D.D	1853
1853	Rev. Charles Seely Dunning, D.D	1857

Accessit.		Exit.
1857	Rev. Elias Riggs, D.D., LL.D	1858
1858	*Henry Hamilton Hadley, A.M	1864
1864	Rev. Charles Casey Starbuck	1865
1865	Rev. Cornelius Van Alen Van Dyck, M.D., D.D.	1867
1867	Rev. John De Witt, D.D	1868
1867	Rev. George William Sheldon	1873
1873	Rev. Edward Read Burkhalter	1874

SYSTEMATIC THEOLOGY.

1869	Rev. Elijah Porter Barrows, D.D	1870

PASTORAL THEOLOGY.

1871	Rev. George Lewis Prentiss, D.D	1873

CHURCH POLITY.

1871	Rev. William Adams, D.D., LL.D	1872

SACRED RHETORIC.

1847	Rev. George Shepard, D.D	1848
1871	Rev. William Miller Paxton, D.D	1873

CHURCH HISTORY.

1847	Rev. Luther Halsey, D.D	1850
1853	Rev. Theron Holbrook Hawks, D.D	1854
1869	Rev. Philip Schaff, D.D., LL.D	1870

SACRED MUSIC.

1838	*Abner Jones	1840
1845	Edward Howe, Jr	1852
1852	George Frederick Root	1855
1854	*Lowell Mason, D.M	1855
1875	Theodore E. Perkins	1876

ELOCUTION.

1865	Stephen G. Peabody	1866
1866	Mark Bailey	1875

LECTURERS.

I. ON THE MORSE FOUNDATION.

1866 Arnold Guyot, Ph.D., LL.D.

"The First Chapter of Genesis."

Accessit.

1869 ARNOLD GUYOT, PH.D., LL.D.
"Man Primæval."

1875 JOHN WILLIAM DAWSON, LL.D., F.R.S.
"The Relation of Science to Revelation."

II. ON THE ELY FOUNDATION.

1867 REV. ALBERT BARNES.
"The Evidences of Christianity in the Nineteenth Century."

1871 REV. JAMES McCOSH, D.D., LL.D.
"Christianity and Positivism."

1874 REV. ANDREW PRESTON PEABODY, D.D., LL.D.
"Comparative Evidences of Science and Christianity."

III. ON THE PARKER FOUNDATION.

1871 WILLARD PARKER, M.D.
"Physical and Mental Hygiene."

1872 JAMES WOODS McLANE, M.D.
"Physical Health."

1873 DANIEL McMARTIN STIMSON, M.D.
"Physiology of Nutrition."

1874 DANIEL McMARTIN STIMSON, M.D.
"Physiology of Nutrition."

1875 DAVID TILDEN BROWN, M.D.
"Relations of Morbid Conditions of Body and Mind to Religious Experience."

1876 ISAAC RAY, M.D.
"Mental Hygiene with Special Reference to Pastoral Functions."

IV. SPECIAL COURSES.

1868 REV. RUFUS ANDERSON, D.D., LL.D.
"Missions."

1875 REV. RICHARD SALTER STORRS, D.D., LL.D.
"The Method of Preparation for Preaching."

Accessit.

1875 Rev. John Hall, D.D.
"Preaching."

1875 Hon. William Strong, LL.D.
"Relation of Civil Law to Ecclesiastical Polity, Property, and Discipline."

1876 Rev. William Mackergo Taylor, D.D.
"Theme and Range of the Pulpit."

1876 Rev. John Hall, D.D.
"Catechetics."

LIBRARIANS.

		Exit.
1839	Rev. Hermann Bokum............................	1841
1841	Rev. Edward Robinson, D.D., LL.D...............	1850
1850	Rev. Henry Boynton Smith, D.D., LL.D..........	

STUDENTS.

1837.

Amos Bordman Lambert ; b., South-Reading, Mass., June 6, 1810 ; U.N.Y., '34 ; P.T.S., '34–5 ; U.T.S., '36–7 ; Ord. (Presb.), Nov. 2, '37 ; Pas., Salem, Wash. Co., N.Y., '37–'65 ; Pas., Hoosick Falls, N.Y., '66–7 ; W.C., Salem, N.Y., '67 ; S.S., South-Hartford, N.Y., '67–'73 ; S.S., Rupert, Vt., 73——. D.D., U.N.Y., '54. 1.

1838.

Henry Belden ; b., Greenfield, Ct., April 9, 1813 ; U.C., '35 ; And. T.S., '35–6 ; P.T.S., '36–7 ; U.T.S., '37–8 ; Ord. (Presb.), May 2, '39 ; S.S., Gowanus (L.I.), N.Y., '38 ; Pas., Marlborough, N.Y., '39–'40 ; S.S., New Windsor, N.Y., '40–1 ; S.S., Washingtonville, N.Y., '41–4 ; Pas. (Cong.), Boonton, N.J., '44–6 ; Pas., Washingtonville, N.Y., '46–'52 ; Pas., N. York City, '52–6 ; C.M., Brooklyn, N.Y., '56–'66 ; W.C., New-Providence, N.J., '66–8 ; Pas., Parkville (L.I.), N.Y., '68–'71 ; Ev., do., '71–4 ; W.C. & Inv., do., '74——.

Samuel Robbins Brown ; b., Ellington, Ct., June 16, 1810 ; Y.C., '32 ; Prof., D. & D.I., N. York City, '32–5 ; Col.T.S., '36–7 ; U.T.S., '37–8 ; Ord. (Presb.), Oct. 14, '38 ; F.M., Hong Kong, China, '38–'46 ; W.C., N. York City, '47–9 ; Tea., Owasco, N.Y., '50–2 ; Pas. (R.D.), Sandbeach, N.Y., '52–8 ; F.M., Kanagawa, Japan, '59–'63 ; F.M., Yokohama, Japan, '62–7 ; U. States, '67–'70 ; F.M., Nagasaki, Japan, '70——. D.D., U.N.Y., '67.

Burtis Cunningham Megie ; b., New-York City, Dec. 4, 1813 ; U.N.Y., '35 ; And.T.S., '35–6 ; P.T.S., '36–7 ; U.T.S., '37–8 ; Ord. (Presb.), Oct. 31, '38 ; S.S., New-Paltz, N.Y., '38–9 ; S.S. & Pas., Dover, N.J., '39–'76 ; Pas., Pleasant Grove, N.J., '76——. D.D., U.N.Y., '75.

Alexander Olympus Peloubet ; b., Hudson, N. Y., May 28, 1810 ; U.N.Y., '35 ; Aub.T.S., '35–7 ; U.T.S., '37–8 ; Ord. (Cong.), ..., '39 ; S.S., Mount Hope, N.Y., '39–'40 ; S.S. (Presb.), Unionville, N.Y., '40–6 ; S.S., Lloyd, N.Y., '46–9 ; Pas., Circleville, N.Y., '50–9 ; Pas., Cairo, N.Y., '60–5 ; Pas., Mecklenburgh, N.Y., '65–'71 ; Pas., Five Corners, N.Y., '71–3 ; Pas., Mecklenburgh, N.Y., '73——.

*Thomas Sydenham Ward ; b., Bloomfield, N. J., Oct. 23, 1811 ; U.N.Y., '35 ; Aub.T.S., '35–7 ; U.T.S., '37–8 ; Ord. (Presb.), ..., '39 ; Pas., Hanover, N.J., '39–'42 ; W.C., Bloomfield, N.J., '43 ; S.S., Sparta, N.J., '44–6 ; W.C., Bloomfield, N.J., '46–'51 ; Pas., Carbondale, Pa., '51–'64 ; Died, do., Feb. 13, '64.

GEORGE INGERSOLL WOOD; b., Stamford, Ct., May 20, 1814; Y.C., '33; N.H.T.S., '35-6; U.T.S, '36-8; Ord. (Presb.), May 18, '40; Pas., Washington, D.C., '40-1; Pas., (Cong.), West-Hartford, Ct., 41-4; S.S., North-Branford, Ct., '44-'50; Pas. Ellington, Ct., '50-4; S.S., North-Branford, Ct., '55-8; Pas., Guilford, Ct., '58-'67; S.S., St. Cloud, Minn., '67-9; W.C., Ellington, Ct., '69——. 6.

AARON MERRICK COLTON; b., Georgia, Vt., Aug. 25, 1809; Y.C., '35; And.T.S., '35-7; U.T.S., '37-8; And.T.S., '38; Res. Lic., And.T.S., '38-'40; Ord. (Cong.), June 10, '40; Pas., Amherst, Mass., '40-'52; Pas., E. Hampton, Mass., '53——.

*ROBERT RANSOM KELLOGG; b., Hudson, N. Y., May 18, 1813; U.N.Y., '35; Aub.T.S., '35-6; U.T.S., '37-8; Ord. (Presb.), Dec. 5, '38; Pas., Brooklyn, N. Y., '39; Pas., Romeo, Mich., '40-8; Pas., Detroit, Mich., '48-'53; D. Sec., A. & F.C.U., Detroit, Mich., '53-5; Pas., Leroy, N. Y., '55-7; Pas., Lima, N. Y., '57-9; W.C., Elizabeth, N. J., '60; Pas., Milford, Pa., '61-6; Died, do., Sept. 25, '66.

*JAMES BENJAMIN TOWNSEND; b., Hebron, N. Y., Aug. 8, 1810; U.C., '35; Tea., Castleton, Vt., '35-6; Aub.T.S., '36-7; U.T.S., '37-8; Ord. (Presb.), Sep. .., '39; Tea., Knoxville, Tenn., '39-'40; S.S., Goochland Co., Va., '42-3; S.S., Paris and Florida, Mo., '43-4; Pas., St. Louis, Mo., '44-'50; Pas., Cincinnati, O., '50-2; W.C., do., '54; W.C., St. Louis, Mo., '52-7; W.C., Bloomington, Ill., '57-'65; Died, do., Jan. 27, '65. 3.

1839.

LUTHER HORN ANGIER; b., Southboro', Mass., Jan. 26, 1810; A.C., '33; U.T.S., '36-9; Ord. (Presb.), March 4, '40; Pas., Buffalo, N. Y., '40-5; S.S., Port Gibson, Miss., '47-8; S.S., Medford, Mass., '48-'50; Pas. (Cong.), Concord, Mass., '50-8; Pas., South-Malden, Mass., '59-'61; S.S., Sandwich, Mass., '63-4; S.S. & Pas., Rockport, Mass., '64-8; S.S., Edgartown, Mass.,'68-9; S.S., Litchfield, N. H., '70-1; Pas. (Presb.), South-Boston, Mass., '71-3; Pas., Parkersburgh, W. Va., '75——.

*WILLIAM BELDEN; b., Weston, Ct., Aug. 20, 1811; U.C., '35; U.T.S., '36-9; Res. Lic., '39-'40; Ord. (Presb.), ..., '40; Pas., Newark, N. J., '40-2; S.S., Milford, Pa., '43-4; Tea., N. York City, '45-'72; Died, Dover, N. J., June 18, '74.

WILLIAM BUSH BOND; b., West-Brookfield, Mass., Jan. 12, 1815; A.C., '35; L.T.S., '36-8; U.T.S., '38-9; Ord. (Cong.), Mar. 18, '40; Pas., Lee, Mass., '40-5; W.C., Stockbridge, Mass., '46-7; Pas., St. Johnsbury, Vt., '47-'58; S.S., Palmer, Mass., '65-'70; W.C., Chicago, Ill., '71; Pas., New-Braintree, Mass., '72——.

*JOSIAH ADDISON CARY; b., West-Brookfield, Mass., Mar. 29, 1813; A.C., '32; U.T.S., '36-9; Res. Lic., '39-'43; Ord. (Presb.), May 13, '44; Prof.

D. & D. Inst., N. York City, '32–'51; S.S. (R.D.), do., '51; Prin., D. & D.I., Columbus, O., '51–2; Died, do., Aug. 7, '52.

CHARLES CHAMBERLAIN; b., Holliston, Mass., Oct. 4, 1813; B.U., '36; And.T.S., '36–7; U.T.S., '38–9; Ord. (Cong.), July 8, '42; H. M., Ohio & Ind., '39–'41; Pas., Berkley, Mass., '42–4; S.S., Freetown, Mass., '45–7; S.S., Mendon, Mass., '47–'50; Pas., Auburn, Mass., '50–3; Pas., Ashford, Ct., '53–7; Pas., Eastford, Ct., '58–'67; S.S., Oxford, Ct., '67–9; S.S., Redding, Ct., '69–'71; S.S., Burlington, Ct., '71–4; S.S., East-Granby, Ct., '74——.

*PHILEMON ELMER COE; b., New-York City, June 20, 1815; C.N.J., '34; P.T.S., '34–6; U.T.S., '38–9; Ord. (Ep.), June 30, '43; Rec., Hammondsport, N. Y., '44; H.M., Medina & Royalton, N. Y., '45–'50; H.M., Stafford, N. Y., '50–1; Rec., Plainfield & Scotch Plains, N. J., '51–9; Rec., Westfield, N. J., '59–'73; Died, do., Dec. 20, '73.

CORNELIUS STADGE CONKLING; b., Northport (L.I.), N.Y., July 31, 1810; U.C., '36; U.T.S., '36–9; Res. Lic., '39–'40; Ord. (Presb.), Mar. 7, '40; Pas., Boonton, N.J., '40–4; S.S., West-Milford, N.J., '44–6; Pas., Mt. Pleasant, N.J., '46–'70; Supt. Pub. Instruction, Frenchtown, N.J., '70——.

JAMES SAMUEL EVANS; b., New-York City, ..., 1815; U.N.Y., '36; U.T.S., '36–9; Res. Lic., '40–1; Ord. (Presb.), June 12, '44; Tea., N. York City, '39–'43; Pas., Middletown (L.I.), N.Y., '44–9; Pas., Setauket (L.I.), N.Y., '50–'68; S.S., Chester, N.J., '70–'71; S.M., Brooklyn, N.Y., '71–4; P.M., do., '74–5; Pas., Newark (Woodside), N.J., '76——. D.D., U.N.Y., 57.

*SAMUEL WARE FISHER; b., Morristown, N.J., Ap. 5, 1814; Y.C., '35; P.T.S., '36–7; U.T.S., '37–9; Ord. (Presb.), Ap. .., '39; Pas., W. Bloomfield, N.J., '39–'43; Pas., Albany, N.Y., '43–6; Pas., Cincinnati, O., '47–'58; Prest. H.C., Clinton, N.Y., '58–'66; Pas., Utica, N.Y., '66–'74; Died, College Hill, O., Jan. 18, '74. Mod. Gen. Assem., '57; D.D., Mi.U., '52; LL.D., U.N.Y., '66.

ALEXANDER GULICK; b., New-York City, Ap. 9, 1814; P.T.S., '36–8; U.T.S., '38–9; Ord., (Presb.), May 10, '40; Pas., Mt. Pleasant, Greenville & Union, O., '40–3; Pas. (R.D.), Woodstock, N.Y., '45–'55; Pas., W. Hurley, N.Y., '55–'64; Pas. (Presb.), Bridgeville, Del., '64–7; Pas., Jasper, N.Y., '67–'73; S.S., Kingswood, W.Va., '74–5; W.C., Woodstock, N.Y., '75——.

JOHN GOODMAN HALL; b., Brooklyn, N.Y., Oct. 16, 1816; U.N.Y., '36; U.T.S., '36–9; Ord. (Cong.), Oct. 29, '39; S.S., New-Lebanon, N.Y., '39–'42; Pas., S. Egremont, Mass., '42–'50; Pas. Cherry Valley, N.Y., '50–7; Pas. (R.D.), Fort Plain, N.Y., '57–'63; S.S. (Presb.), Ravenna, O., '64–'73; W.C., Cleveland, O., '74——.

*JAMES HILDRETH; b., Brooklyn, N.Y., June 19, 1813; U.T.S., '37–9; U.S.Army, '39–'40; Ord. (Presb.), Mar. 10, '40; Pas., Haverstraw, N.Y., '40–7; S.S., Davenport, Io., '48–'50; Died, Savannah, Ill., July 20, '51.

*ISAAC FARWELL HOLTON; b., Westminster, Vt., Aug. 30, 1812; A.C., '36; U.T.S., '37–9; Ord. (Presb.), May 1, '60; Tea., N. York City, '39–'45; Prof., N.Y.C., '46–8; Trav. in S. America, '52–4; S.S., Meredith Bridge,

N. H., '55–6; Prof., M.C., '56–7; S.S., Lawrence, Ill., '58–'61; S.S., Alden, Ill., '61–2; S.S., Hill's Grove, Ill., '62–4; Ed., Boston, Mass., '65–7; Lit., Boston, Mass., '67–'74; Died, Everett, Mass., Jan. 25, '74.

*JAMES SHEPHERD JUDD; b., Cambridge, N.Y., ..., 1810; O.I., '37; U.T.S., '37–9; S.S., Bridgewater, N.Y., '40; Inv., Warrensburgh, N.Y., '40–5; Died, do., Jan. 8, '45.

*CHARLES KENMORE; b., Newton Ards, Ireland, ..., 1816; O.I., '37; U.T.S., '37–9; Ord. (Pres.), ..., '41; S.S., Kendall & Carlton, N.Y., '41–2; S.S., Churchville, N.Y., '42–3; S.S., Holland & Colden, N.Y., 46–8; S.S., Milton, N.Y., '48–9; S.S., Covington & Blossburgh, Pa., '49–'50; S S., Andover, N.Y., '51–3; S.S., Rose, N.Y., '54–5; S.S., Weston, N.Y., '55–6; S.S., Dyersville, Io., '57; S.S., Mt. Vernon, Ill., '57–8; Inv., Monticello, Miss., '58–9; Tea., Madison, Miss., ..——..; Tea., Greensburgh, La., ..——..; Tea., Fort Gaines, Ga., ..——..; Prof., Tallahassee, Fla., ..——'71; Died, Hornellsville, N.Y., June 15, '71.

*JEREMIAH SKIDMORE LORD; b., Jamaica (L.I.), N.Y., May 10, 1812; U.N.Y., '36; U.T.S., '36–9; Ord. (R.D.), Aug. 20, '39; Res. Grad., 39–'40; Pas., Montville, N.J., '39–'43; Pas., Griggstown, N.J., '43–7; Pas., N. York City (Harlem), '48–'69; Died, do., Ap. 2, '69. D.D., U.N.Y., '59.

DANIEL ELSTON MEGIE; b., New-York City, Feb. 9, 1808; U.T.S., '36–9; Res. Lic., '39–'40; Ord. (Presb.), Nov. 17, '40; Pas., Succasunna, N.J., '40–4; Pas., Boonton, N.J., '44–'72; W.C., Boonton, N.J., '72——.

BENJAMIN GILBERT RILEY; b., Middlefield, N.Y., Aug. 7, 1810; W.C., '34; And.T.S., '36–7; U.T.S., '37–9; Ord. (Presb.), Feb. 26, '40; Pas., Hartwick, N.Y., '39–'42; Pas., Livonia, N.Y., '43–'55; Tea., Lima, N.Y., '55–6; S.S., Horseheads, N.Y., '56–7; S.S., Lodi, Wis., '57–'63; S.S., Berlin, Wis., '63–4; S.M., Lodi, Wis., '64——.

JOSEPH ADDISON SAXTON; b., Tolland, Ct., Nov. 27, 1810; U.N.Y., '35; N.H.T.S., '36–8; U.T.S., '38–9; Ord. (Presb.), June 7, '43; S.S., Marlboro, Mass., '40; S.S., Harrisonburgh, Va., '40; S.S., Ware, Mass., '41; S.S., Washburnham, Mass., '42; Pas., Greenport (L.I.), N.Y., '43–5; S.S., New-River Parish, Ascension, La., '45–9; S.S., Plymouth, Ct., '49–'50; Pas. (Cong.), New-Hartford, Ct., '51–3; S.S., N. York City, '53; S.S., Fire-Place (L.I.), N.Y., '54; Tea., N. York City, '54–6; S.S., New-Preston, Ct., '56; S.S., Brookfield, Ct., '58; S.S., Fitchville, Ct., '59; Tea., Norwichtown, Ct., '59–'67; Tea., N. York City, '67–'70; Ag., do., '71; Prof., U.N.Y., do., '71——.

*PETER SNYDER; b., Schoharie, N.Y., Oct. 18, 1814; U.C., '36; P.T.S., '36–8; U.T.S., '38–9; Ord. (Presb.), Oct. 15, '40; S.S., Whippany, N.J., '40–2; S.S., New-Rochelle, N.Y., '42–4; Pas., Cairo, N.Y., '44–8; Pas., Watertown, N.Y., '48–'63; Died, do., Dec. 13, '63.

*FRANCIS WARRINER; b., Springfield, Mass., Nov. 20, 1804; A.C., '30; U.T.S., '39; Res. Lic., '39–'40; Ord. (Cong.), Oct. 26, '41; Pas., Chester, Mass., '41–7; W.C., Waterford, Vt., '48–'54; Pas., do., '54–'60; S.S., Chester Centre, Mass., '60–2; Tea., U.S.Navy, '62–5; Died, Chester, Mass., Ap. 22, '66.

21.

*John Edward Farwell; b., Ashby, Mass., Dec. 9, 1809; A.C., '36; And. T.S., '36–7; U.T.S., '37–8; And. T.S., '38–9; Ord. (Cong.), Oct. 30, '39; Oc. S., var. places, '39–'43; Pas., Rochester, N.H., '43–'52; S.S., Pelham, N.H., & var. places, '51–8; Died, Fitchburgh, Mass., Dec. 24, '58.

Barnabas Maynard Fay; b., Berlin, Mass., July 27, 1806; Y.C., '33; Prof., D. & D.I., N. York City, '33–8; U.T.S., '36–8; Ord. (Cong.), May 20, '40; Pas., Hardwick, Mass., '40–3; Tea., Durham, Ct., '43–4; Pas., Wilmington, Mass., '45–'50; Prof. Blind Asylum, Indianapolis, Ind., '50–4; Prof. D. & D. I., Flint, Mich., '54–'64; Banker, Saginaw, Mich., '64–9; W.C., Saratoga Springs, N.Y., '69——.

Jared Ware Fox; b., Sherburne, N.Y., Dec. 5, 1810; O.I., '37; U.T.S., '37–8; Ord. (Cong.), Oct. .., '39; S.S., Chili, N.Y., '40–4; S.S., Stone Church, N.Y., '44–7; S.S., Sherburne, N.Y., '47–'50; S.S., Preble, N.Y., '50–3; S.S., Churchville, N.Y., '53–5; S.S., Walworth, N.Y., '55–'60; Pas., Burlingame, & S.S., Ridgeway, Kan., '61–8; H.M., Ridgeway, Kan., '68——.

Horace Fraser; b., Steuben, N.Y., Feb. 9, 1808; U.N.Y., '37; U.T.S., '36–7; Aub. T.S., '38–'40; Ord. (Presb.), ..., '42; S.S., Branchport, N.Y., '42–7; S.S., Angelica, N.Y., '47–9; S.S., Branchport, N.Y., '49–'52; S.S., La Fayette, N.Y., '54–6; S.S., Canoga, N.Y., '57–9; W.C., do., '59–'63; S.S., Varick, N.Y., '64–'70; West-Town, N.Y., '70——.

Oris Fraser; b., Steuben, N.Y., Feb. 9, 1808; U.N.Y., '37; U.T.S., '36–7; Aub. T.S., '37–9; Ord. (Presb.), Feb. .., '41; S.S. & Pas., Bath, N.Y., '39–'43; S.S., Springfield & Brooklyn, Pa., '44–7; S.S., Rocky Stream & Eddytown, N.Y., '48–'62; Oc. S., Florida, N.Y., '63——.

*Jeremiah Jay Greenough; b., Bradford, Mass., Nov. 18, 1807; D.C., '28; And.T.S., '35–6; U.T.S., '36–8; Tea., N. York City, '39–'60; Died, Great Barrington, Mass., July 18, '60.

*Joseph Haven; b., North Dennis, Mass., Jan. 4, 1816; A.C., '33; U.T.S., '36–'7; And. T.S., '37–9; Ord. (Cong.), Nov. 6, '39; Pas., Ashland (Unionville), Mass., '39–'46; Pas., Brookline, Mass., '46–'50; Prof., A.C., Amherst, Mass., '50–8; Prof., C.T.S., Chicago, Ill., '58–'74; Died, do., May 23, '74. D.D., Ma. C., '59, & A.C., '62; LL.D., Ken. C., '72.

*Jedediah Vincent Huntington; b., New York City, Jan. 20, 1815; U.N.Y., '35; U.T.S., '36–7; Ord. (Ep.), Feb. 24, '42; S.S., Middlebury, Vt., '42; Trav., Europe, '42–8; S.S., N. York City, '48; Ed. (R.C.), Baltimore, Md., & St. Louis, Mo., '49–'56; Lit., N. York City, '56–'61; Died, Pau, France, Mar. 10, '62. M.D., U.Pa., '38.

*Samuel Moseley; b., Westfield, Mass., April .., 1809; Y.C., '36; N.H.T.S., '36–7; U.T.S., '37–8; N.H.T.S., '38–9; S.S., Ticonderoga, N.Y., ..——..; S.S., Burlington, Ct., ..——..; S.S., Middle Haddam, Ct., ..——..; Died, Hartford, Ct., Dec. 9, '45.

Charles Chauncy Shackford; b., Portsmouth, N.H., Sep. 26, 1815; Har. C., '35; U.T.S., '37–8; Ord. (Cong.), May 19, '41; Pas., South-Boston, Mass., '41–3; W.C., Burlington, Io., '44–6; Pas., (Unit.), Lynn, Mass., '46–'65; Tea., Boston, Mass., '65–'71; Prof., Corn. Univ., Ithaca, N.Y., '71——.

*Ransom Taylor; b., Smithfield, R.I., ..., 1807; U.N.Y., '35; Prof., D. & D.I., N. York City, '35–7; U.T.S., '36–8; Died, Augusta, Ga., Feb. 4, '38. 11.

1840.

Erasmus James Boyd; b., Hartwick, N.Y., Dec. 1, 1815; H.C., '37; L.T.S., '37–8; U.T.S., '38–40; Ord. (Presb.), Nov. 3, '42; S.S. & Pas., Brooklyn, Mich., '40–'50; Prof. & Pres't., Y. Lad. Coll. Ins., Monroe, Mich., '50——.

Charles Peck Bush; b., Brighton, N.Y., Nov. 11, 1813; N.H.T.S., '37–9; U.T.S., '39–40; Res. Lic., '40–1; Ord. (Presb.), Nov. 15, '41; Pas., N. York-City, '41–5; Pas. (Cong.), Norwich, Ct., '46–'56; Ed. & S.S., Chicago, Ill., '56–7; Pas., (Presb.), Beloit, Wis., '57–9; D. Sec., A.T.S. of B., N. York-City, '60–3; D. Sec., A.B.C.F.M., (Cong.), Rochester, N.Y., '63–'71; Gen. Ag., A.B.C.F.M., N. York City, '71. D.D., H.C., '67.

Edmund Fowler Dickinson; b., Granby, Mass., ..., 1813; U.C., '37; And. T.S., '37–8; U.T.S., '38–'40; Res. Lic., '40–1; Ord. (Cong.), May 17, '43; S.S., Conneaut, O., '43–'54; C.M., Chicago, Ill., '54——.

George Duffield; b., Carlisle, Pa., Sep. 12, 1816; Y.C., '37; U.T.S., '37–'40; Ord. (Presb.), Dec. 27, '40; Pas., Brooklyn, N.Y., '40–'7; Pas., Bloomfield, N.J., '47–'52; Pas., Philadelphia, Pa., '52–'61; Pas., Adrian, Mich., '61–5; Pas., Galesburgh, Ill., '65–9: Pas., Saginaw City, Mich., '69–'73; Ev., Ann Arbor, Mich., '74——. D.D., K.C., '72.

Chester Fitch; b., Berkshire Co., Mass., Feb. 14, 1808; W.C., '34; U.T.S., '37–'40; Ord. (Cong.), Jan. 27, '41; Pas., New-Marlboro', Mass., '41–52; Pas., Binghamton, N.Y., '53–8; Pas. (Presb.), N. York Mills, N.Y., '58–'68; S.S., Rockford, Ill., '68——.

Josiah Leonard; b., Kingsboro', N.Y., Ap. 15, 1816; U.C., '37; U.T.S., '37–'40; Ord. (Presb.), Oct. .., '40; Pas., Mexicoville, N.Y., '40–2; Pas., Oswego, N.Y., '42–5; Pas., Delhi, N.Y., '45–8; Pas., Malden, N.Y., '48–'56; Pas., Fulton, Ill., '56–'71; S.S., Clinton, Io., '72——.

*Francis Edmund Lord; b., East-Haddam, Ct., July .., 1811; U.C., '37; P.T.S., '37–8; U.T.S., '38–'40; Ord. (Presb.), Sep. 27, '42; S.S., Evans, N.Y., '41–2; Pas., Walworth, N.Y., '42–5; S.S. & Pas., Wayne, O., '45–'51; Pas. (Cong.), Olivet, Mich., '52–5; Died, do., ..., '55.

Hiram Slauson; b., Greenville, N. Y., Dec. 5, 1810; U.C., '37; U.T.S., '37–'40; Ord. (Cong.), Sep. 17, '40; Pas., Whitehall, N.Y., '40–2; Pas. (R.D.), Northumberland, N.Y., '43–'53; Pas., Port Jervis, N.Y., '53–7; Pas. (Cong.), Unionville, Ct., '57–8; S.S., E. Whitehall, N.Y., '58–'61; Pas. (R.D.), New-Salem & Clarksville, N.Y., '62–6; W.C., Whitehall, N.Y., '66——.

*James M. Smith; b., Jamaica (L.I.), N.Y., ..., 1810; M.D., N.Y., '32; P.T.S., 37–8; U.T.S., '38–'40; Ord. (Presb.), ..., '39; Pas., Upper Ten-Mile Creek & Mt. Nebo, Pa., '39–'43; S.S., Bethlehem & North-Branch, Pa., '43–4; Pas., Tarentum, Pa., '44–'53; W.C., Grand Spring, Wis., '53–4; Died, do., ..., '54.

GEORGE PALMER TYLER; b., Brattleboro, Vt., Dec. 10, 1809; Y.C., '36; U.T.S., '37–'40; Res. Lic., '40–1; Ord. (Presb.), June 2, '41; Pas., Lowville, N.Y., '41–'53; Pas. (Cong.), Brattleboro, Vt., '53–'69; S.S., Lansingburgh, N.Y., '69–'75; S.S., Troy, N.Y., '75——. D.D., M.C., '64. Address, Lansingburgh, N.Y.

EDMUND FREEMAN WALDO; b., Prattsburgh, N.Y., June 21, 1811; A.C., '37; U.T.S., '37–'40; Ord. (Presb.), Feb. .., '42; S.S., Huron, N.Y., '41–5; S.S., Allegan, Mich., '45–9; S.S., Wayland, Mich., '49–'52; S.S., Dowagiac, Mich., '52–6; S.S., Rochester, Mich., '56–7; S.S., Palmyra, Wis., '57–8; S.S., Jefferson, Wis., '58–'63; S.S., Pardeeville, Wis., '63–4; S.S., Linden, Mich., '65–'71; S.S., Tawas City, Mich., '71–4; S.S., Linden, Mich., '73; S.S., Huron, N.Y., '75——.

*FRANCIS CHANDLER WOODWORTH; b., Colchester, Ct., Feb. 12, 1813; O.I., '37; U.T.S., '37–'40; Ord. (Cong.), Oct. 28, '40; Pas., Fair-Haven, Vt., '40–2; Pas., S. Norwalk, Ct., '42–4; Ed., N. York City, '45–'59; Died, do., June 5, '59. 12.

DAVID ELY BARTLETT; b., East-Windsor, Ct., Sept. 29, 1805; Y.C., '28; Tea., D. & D.I., Hartford, Ct., 28–'32; Do., N.York City, '32–8; U.T.S., '37–8; Prin., D. & D.I., Va., '38–'40; Prof., D. & D.I., N. York City, '41–'52; Tea., Poughkeepsie, N.Y., '54–'60; Prof., D. & D.I., Hartford, Ct., '60——.

*ELIAS CLARK; b., Orange, Ct., July 12, 1814; U.C., '38; U.T.S., '38–9; N.H.T.S., '39–'40; Ord. (Cong.), Jan. 7, '51; S.S., Franklin, O., '49–'50; Pas., Egremont, Mass., '51–7; S.S., Rochester, Minn., '57–'60; S.S., Bellevue, Io., '61–4; S.S., Ottumwa, Io., '64–6; Died, West-Salem, Wis., Oct. 29, '66.

ROBERT CRAWFORD; b., Paisley, Scotland, Nov. 24, 1804; W.C., '36; P.T.S., '36–7; Tut., W.C., '37–8; U.T.S., '38–9; Res. Lic., '39–'40; Ord. (Cong.), Aug. 20, '40; Pas., North-Adams, Mass., '40–'55; Pas. (Presb.), Crookville, Pa., '55–7; Pas. (Cong.), Deerfield, Mass., '57——. D.D., J.C., '58.

WILLIAM HALL; b., New York City, March 16, 1812; U.N.Y., '35; U.T.S., '39–'40; S.S., Onondaga, N.Y., '40——..; Ord. (Cong.), Jan. 20, '48; Pas., Ludlow, Mass., '48——..; S.S., Milton, N.Y., ..——..; S.S., Austinburgh, O., ..——..; S.S., Oakland, N.Y., ..——..; S.S., Java, N.Y., ..——..; W.C., Elizabeth, N.J., ..——'75; W.C., N. York City, '75——.

STEDMAN WRIGHT HANKS; b., Mansfield, Ct., Sep. 6, 1811; A.C., '37; N.H.T.S., '37–8; U.T.S., '38–9; Ord. (Cong.), Mar. 20, '40; Pas., Lowell, Mass., '40–'53; D. Sec., A.S.F.S., Boston, Mass., '53——.

*EDWIN H. HAWLEY; b., Carlisle, N.Y., Oct. ...., 1811; U.C., '38; U.T.S., '38–9; N.T.I., '39–'40; Ord. (Bap.), ..., '41; Pas., Bedford, O., '41 ——..; Died, Painesville, Ohio, ..., 18...

*HENRY HAINES LOOMIS; b., Cooperstown, N.Y., Ap. 28, 1813; U.C., '37; T.T.S., '37–8; U.T.S., '38–9; N.H.T.S., '39–'40; S.S., Fulton, N.Y., '40–1; Died, do., Sep. 23, '41.

*Hezekiah Howard Loomis ; b., Cooperstown, N.Y., Ap. 28, 1813 ; U.C., '37 ; T.T.S., '37-8 ; U.T.S., '38-9 ; N.H.T.S., '39-'40 ; S.S., Lockport, N.Y., '40-1 ; Died, Cazenovia, N.Y., Jan. 6, '42.

*Charles Backus McLean ; b., Simsbury, Ct., Aug. 23, 1815 ; Y.C., '36 ; Tea., N. Stamford, Ct., '36-7 ; And.T.S., '37-8 ; U.T.S., '38-9 ; Ord. (Cong.), Feb. 7, '44 ; S.S. & Pas., Collinsville, Ct., '43-'66 ; W.C., Wethersfield, Ct., '66-'73 ; Died, do., Oct. 29, '73.

Matthew Meigs ; b., Albany, N.Y., Feb. 5, 1812 ; U.C., '36 ; U.T.S., '37-9 ; Prof., U.M., '39-'43 ; Ord. (Presb.), Oct. 13, '42 ; S.S., Pontiac, Mich., '43-4 ; Tea., Winchester, Va., '44-6 ; Prof., Del. C., '46-'50 ; Prest., do., '50-1 ; W.C., Pottstown, Pa., '51——. Ph.D., L.F.C., '68.

Robert Curtis Mills ; b., New York City, Feb. 6, 1819 ; U.N.Y., '37 ; U.T.S., '37-'40 ; N.T.I., '40 ; Res. Lic., U.T.S., '40-1 ; Ord. (Bap.), Mar. 17, '42 ; Pas., Colchester, Ct., '42-5 ; Pas., Springfield, Mass., '45-8 ; Pas., Salem, Mass., '48——. D.D., B.U., '61.

*Alexander Montgomery ; b., Westfield, N.Y., July 24, 1808 ; A.C., '37 ; And.T.S., '37-8 ; U.T.S., '38-9 ; Ord. (Cong.), July 23, '39 ; Pas. (Presb.), Maysville, N.Y., '39-'41 ; Prin., Westfield, N.Y., '41-6 ; Pas., Beaver Dam, Wis., '46-'50 ; Ag., A.T.S., Chicago, Ill., '50-5 ; D. Sec., A.B.C.F.M., Beloit, Wis., '55-7 ; W.C., do., '57-9 ; Died, do., Feb. 18, '59.

*Jonas De Forest Richards ; b., Hartford, Vt., Dec. 28, 1809 ; D.C., '36 ; Tut., Ma. C., '36-7 ; L.T.S., '37-8 ; U.T.S., '38-9 ; And.T.S., '39-'40 ; Ord. (Cong.), May 28, '41 ; Pas., Charlestown, N.H., '41-'51 ; Pas., Chester, Vt., '53-7 ; S.S., Weathersfield, Vt., '57-'62 ; W.C., Monroe, Mich., '63-6 ; Pas., Wethersfield, Vt., '66-7 ; Mem. of Senate, Ala., '68-'72 ; Prof., Ala. State Univ., '69-'72 ; Died, Mobile, Ala., Dec. 2, '72. LL.D., D.C., '65.

George Washington Schuyler ; b., Stillwater, N.Y., ..., 1810 ; U.T.S., '37-8 ; Law., ... ; Treas. N.Y. State, '63 ; Supt. Bank Dep., N.Y. State, '65 ; Mem. Leg. N.Y., '74.

*Jackson Smith ; b., Middletown, N.Y., Mar. ...., 1813 ; U.N.Y., '36 ; U.T.S., '36-8, '39-'40 ; N.T.I., '40 ; Ord. (Bap.), ..., '40 ; Pas., Lyons' Farms, N.J., '41-5 ; Pas., Penn's Neck, N.J., '46-8 ; Died, Middletown, N.J., ..., '46.

James Washington Wood ; b., Florida, N.Y., Oct. 25, 1813 ; L.F.C., '37 ; U.T.S., '37-9 ; Ord. (Presb.), Dec. 11, '39 ; Pas., Deckertown, N.J., '39-'45 ; Pas., Chester, N.Y., '45-'62 ; W.C., Easton, Pa., '62-5 ; Pas., Allentown, Pa., '65——. 16.

1841.

Erastus Smith Barnes ; b., Governeur ,N.Y., Sep. 26, 1810 ; A.C., '38 ; U.T.S., '38-'41 ; Ord. (Presb.), Sep. 23, '41 ; Pas., Martinsburgh, N.Y., '41-7 ; Pas., Chazy, N.Y., '47-'51 ; Pas., Booneville, N.Y., '51-6 ; S.S., Lyons' Falls & Port Leyden, N.Y., '56-9 ; Pas., Lenox, N.Y., '59-'60 ; S.S. (Cong.), Munnsville, N.Y., '60-9 ; S.S., Austinburgh, O., '69-'70 ; S.S., Monroeville, O., '70-1 ; S.S., Unionville and N. Madison, O., '71-5 ; S.S., Poynette and Lowville, Wis., '75——.

*JESSE KENDALL BRAGG ; b., Royalston, Mass., Oct. 11, 1811 ; A.C., '38 ; U.T.S., '38–'41 ; Ord. (Cong.), Oct. 19, '42 ; Pas., Middleboro' (Lakeville), Mass., '42–'52 ; Pas., Brookfield, Mass., '52–9 ; S.S., Sandwich, Mass., '61–2 ; Ed., Boston, Mass., ..——.. ; S.S., N. Wrentham, Mass., '69–'71 ; S.S., Norfolk, Mass., '71–4 ; Died, do., June 14, '74.

JOHN LIDDEL CHAPMAN ; b., Ash Grove, n. Clones, Ireland, Feb. 17, 1812 ; U.T.S., '38–'41 , Ord. (R.D.), Nov. 16, '42 ; Pas., Clintonville, N.J., '42–9 ; Tea., do., '49–'64 ; S.S., Irving, Kan., '64–8 ; S.S., Troy, Kan., '69–'71 ; Prof., Brooklyn, N.Y., '72——. Residence, Irvington, N.J.

*HERVEY SMITH DALE ; b., Danvers, Mass., ..., 1812 ; B.U., '34 ; U.T.S., '38–'41 ; Ord. (Bapt.), ..., '41 ; Pas., Newport, O., '41–'51 ; Pas., Lebanon, O., '52–6 ; Ag., W.B. Ed. Soc., Cincinnati, O., '56–7 ; Died, do., ..., '57.

JOSIAH GARDNER DAVIS ; b., Concord, Mass., Feb. 23, 1815 ; Y.C., '36 ; And.T.S., '38–9 ; U.T.S., '39–'41 ; Ord. (Cong.), May 22, '44 ; Pas., Amherst, N.H., '44——. D.D., D.C., '66.

*GEORGE GEMMEL ; b., Stamford, N.Y., Sep. 3, 1812 ; O.I., '38 ; U.T.S., '38–'41 ; Ord. (Cong.), Jan. 6, '42 ; S.S., Buffalo Grove & Grand Detour, Ill., '41–3 ; S.S., Byron, Ill., '43–'56 ; S.S., Spring Grove, Io., '56–9 ; H.M., Quasqueton, Io., and vicinity, '59–'64 ; Died; do., July 11, '64.

JAMES LYNE SEABURY GRANDIN ; b., Papakating, N.J., Ap. 17, 1804 ; U.T.S., '38–41 ; Ord. (M.E.), Aug. 29, '47 ; S.S., Angelica, N.Y., '41–2 ; Tea. & S.S., Honeoye Falls, N.Y., '42–3 ; S.S., Westfield, Pa., '43–4 ; S.S., Tioga and Lawrenceville, Pa., '44–5 ; Pas., Southport & Jackson, N.Y., '45–6 ; Pas., Springfield, Pa., '46–8 ; Pas., Loyalsock, Pa., '48–'50 ; Pas., Bethel, N.Y., '50–1 ; Pas., Henrietta, N.Y., '51–2 ; Pas., Canadice, N.Y., '52–4 ; Pas., Groveland, N.Y., '54–5 ; Pas., Ridge, N.Y., '55–7 ; Pas., Coke's Chapel & Bristol, N.Y., '57–8 ; Pas., Springwater, N.Y., '58–'60 ; Pas., Enfield, N.Y., '60–2 ; Pas., Orange, N.Y., '62–3 ; Pas., Baldwin, N.Y., '63–5 ; Pas., Merchantville, N.Y., '65–6 ; Superan., '66–'71 ; Ag. Am. Peace Soc., '71——. Address, Elmira, N.Y.

*MILO JUDSON HICKOK ; b., New-Haven, Vt., Aug. 22, 1809 ; M.C., '35 ; Prof., Del. C., '35–8 ; U.T.S., '38–'41 ; Tut., M.C., '40 ; Ord. (Cong.), May 4, '42 ; Tut., Ma.C. & Pas., Harmar, O., '42–4 ; S.S. (Presb.), Utica, N.Y., '44–5 ; Pas., Rochester, N.Y., '45–'54 ; S.S., Montreal, C.E., '54–5 ; Pas., Scranton, Pa., '55–'68 ; Inv., Marietta, O., '68–73 ; Died, do., July 19, '73. D.D., C.N.J., '61.

SILAS JESSUP ; b., Palmyra, N.Y., May 23, 1813 ; Wab.C., '38 ; U.T.S., '38–'41 ; Ord. (Presb.), May .., '45 ; S.S., Oregon City, Ill., '42–3 ; S.S., Albany, Ill., '43–6 ; S.S., Elkhorn Grove, Ill., '46–'56 ; S.S., East Paw Paw, Ill., '55–7 ; Inv., Rockton, Ill., '58–'74 ; Do., Polo, Ill., '74–6 ; Do., Rockton, Ill., '76——.

JOHN MILLS JOHNSON ; b., Morristown, N.J., July 27, 1815 ; C.N.J., '35 ; U.T.S., '38–'41 ; Ord. (Presb.), Oct. 19, '41 ; S.S. & Pas., Hanover, N.J., '41–9 ; Ag., A.T.S., '49 ; Inv., Morristown, N.J., '49–'55 ; Pas., Hanover, N.J., '55–'68 ; S.S., Vandalia, Ill., '68–'72 ; Pas., Neoga, Ill., '73——.

*TIMOTHY W. LESTER ; b., Marlborough, N.Y., Oct. 19, 1810 ; U.T.S.,

'38–'41 ; Fin. Ag., U.T.S., Vicinity of N. York City, '41–2 ; Died, Chester, N.Y., Ap. 5, '42.

MICHAEL FREDERICK LIEBENAU ; b., New-York City, March 1, 1813 ; U.N.Y., '39 ; U.T.S., '38–'41 ; Ord. (Presb.), Oct. 28, '41 ; Pas., New-Paltz Landing (now Highland), N.Y., '41–6 ; Pas., Paterson, N.J., '46–'50 , Pas., Highland, N.Y., '50–'67 ; Pas. (R.D.), Dashville Falls, N.Y., '67–8 ; Pas., Rosendale, N.Y., '68——.

WILLIAM ANDREW MANDELL ; b., Hardwick, Mass., ..., 1811 ; A.C., '38 ; U.T.S., '38–'41 ; Ord. (Presb.), Ap.21, '42 ; Pas., Bridgeton, N.J., '42–4 ; C.M., Philadelphia, Pa., '44–5 ; Pas., Dartmouth, Mass., '46–'54 ; Pas., Lunenburgh, Mass., '56–'65. W.C., do., '65–8 ; W.C., Cambridgeport, Mass., '68——.

*JAMES MCCHAIN ; b., New-York City, Feb. 4, 1819 ; Y.C., '38 ; U.T.S., '38–'41 ; Ord. (Presb.), Jan. 18, '43 ; Pas., Franklin, N.Y., '43–5 ; Pas., Abingdon, Va., '46–'69 ; Died, do., March 1, '69.

*MILES TOMLINSON MERWIN ; b., Milford, Ct., June 15, 1802 ; Y.C., '28 ; Tea., New-Haven, Ct., N.York City, & Brooklyn, N.Y., '28–'39 ; U.T.S., '39–'41 ; P.T.S., '41–2 ; Ord. (Presb.), ..., '46 ; S.S., Erie Co., Pa., '42–5 ; Pas., Irvine, & S.S., Sugar Grove, Pa., '45–9 , Pas. & S.S., Clearfield, Pike & Bradford, Pa., '49–'54 ; S.S., Toms River, N.J., '54–5 ; W.C., Marianna, Fla., '55–7 ; W.C., New-Haven, Ct., '57–8 ; W.C., & S.S., Phila., Pa., '58–'63 ; Died, New-Haven, Ct., Ap. 13, '65.

*GEORGE MONILAWS ; b., New-York City, Dec. 16, 1813 ; U.C., '39 ; U.T.S., '39–'41 ; Ord. (Presb.), Ap. 10, '42 ; S.S., Somers, N.Y., '42–5 ; S.S., Apalachicola, Fla., '46–7 ; Pas., Somers, N.Y., '47–8 ; Died, do., Ap. 6, '48.

JOSEPH HENRY MYERS ; b., Waterford, N.Y., ..., 1817 ; U.Vt., '37 ; U.T.S., '38–'41 ; Ord. (Cong.), Oct. .., '43 ; S.S. & Pas., East-Poultney, Vt., '42–6 ; Pas. (Presb.), Knoxville, Tenn., '47–'51 ; Prof., U.E.T., '49–'51 ; S.S., St. Augustine, Fla., '52–7 ; S.S., Plainfield, N.J., '57–9 ; S.S., St. Augustine, Fla., '59–'61 ; Tea., Monticello, Miss., '61–4 ; Tea., Savannah, Ga., '64–5 ; Tea., Bergen Point, N.J., '65–6 ; Pas., Milton, N.Y., '67–'76 ; Pas., Fernandina, Fla., '76——. D.D., U.Vt., '58.

JOEL EDSON ROCKWELL ; b., Salisbury, Vt., May 4, 1816 ; A.C., '37 ; U.T.S., '37–8, '39–'41 ; Ord. (Presb.), Oct. 13, '41 ; Pas., Valatie, N.Y., '41–7 ; Pas., Wilmington, Del., '47–'51 ; Pas., Brooklyn, N.Y., '51–'68 ; Pas., Edgewater (S.I.), N.Y., '68——. D.D., Jef. C., '59.

ALEXANDER TROTTER ; b., Edinburgh, Scotland, Sept. 5, 1810 ; O.C., '38 ; U.T.S., '39–'41 ; Ord. (Presb.), July 11, '43 ; S.S., Drummondtown, Va., '41–2 ; S.S., Jackson & Albion, Mich., '42–3 ; S.S., Battle Creek, Mich., '44–6 ; Ag., A.P.S., '47–'50 ; Pas., Hunter, N.Y., '50–3 ; Pas., Centreville, N.Y., '55–8 ; Pas., Livingstonville, N.Y., '58–'63 ; S.S., Vassar, Mich., '63–6 ; Ed., do., '69——.

HORACE WINSLOW ; b., Enfield, Mass., May 18, 1814 ; H.C., '39 ; Aub.T.S., '38–'40 ; U.T.S., '40–1 ; Ord. (Presb.), May 25, '42 ; Pas., New-Windsor, N.Y., '42–3 ; Pas., Lansingburgh, N.Y., '43–5 ; Pas. (Cong.), Rockville, Ct., '45–'52 ; Pas., New-Britain, Ct., '52–8 ; Pas., Great Barrington, Mass., '58–'62 ; Ch., U.S.Army, '62 ; Pas., Binghamton, N.Y., '63–8 ; Pas., Willimantic, Ct., '69——. 20.

*Robert Atkinson; b., Ballina, Ireland, ..., 1813; M.D., Dublin, '33; U.T.S., '38-'40; And.T.S., '40-1; S.S., Taunton, Mass., '41-2; Died, N. York City, June .., '42.

Hermann Bokum; b., Königsberg, Prussia, Jan. 2, 1807; Ger. Tea., Har.C., '35-8; U.T.S., '38-'40; Ord. (Ger. Ref.), ..., '40; Pas., Columbia, Pa., '40-9; Pas., Cincinnati, O., '49-'55; Ev., Knoxville, Tenn., '55-'61; Ch., U.S. Army, '62-5; S.S., Atlanta, Ga., '66-72; C.M., Phila., Pa., '73——.

Moses Woodruff Dodd; b., Bloomfield, N.J., Nov. 11, 1814; C.N.J., '37; P.T.S., '37-8; U.T.S., '38-9; Publisher, N. York City, '39——.

*James Drummond; b., Bristol, Me., Ap. .., 1815; B.C., '36; Tea., Newcastle, Me., '36-8; U.T.S., '38-9; B.T.S., '39-'41; Ord. (Cong.), Oct. 12, '42; S.S. & Pas., Lewiston Falls, Me., '42-'58; Pas., Springfield, Mass., '58-'61; Died, Lynn, Mass., Nov. 29, '61.

Justin Field; b., Northfield, Mass., ..., 1816; A.C., '35; U.T.S., '38-9; And.T.S., '39-'40; Ord. (Ep.), ..., '46; W.C., Roxbury, Mass., '43-5; Rec., Stockbridge, Mass., '46-'50; Rec., Great Barrington, Mass., '50-2; Rec., Medford, Mass., '52-'62; Rec., Lenox, Mass., '62——.

Stephen Symonds Foster; b., Canterbury, N.H., Nov. 17, 1809; D.C., '38; U.T.S., '38-9; Anti-Slavery and Temperance Lecturer, '39——. Address, Worcester, Mass.

Henry Laurens Hammond; b., Smyrna, N.Y., Feb. 14, 1815; O.C., '38; U.T.S., '39-'40; And.T.S., '40-1; Ord. (Cong.), Dec. 8, '41; S.S., Kingston, Mass., '41-2; S.S. (Presb.), Homer, Mich., '42-4; S.S. (Cong.), Detroit, Mich., '44-7; S.S., Morrisville, N.Y., '48-'50; Pas., Grand Rapids, Mich., 50-6; Ag. & Ed., Chicago, Ill., '56-'61; S.S., Princeton, Ill., '61-2; Treas., C.T.S., Chicago, Ill., '62-'72; Trade, do., '72——.

*William Augustus Meigs Hand; b., Berlin, Ct., ..., 1817; W.U., '36; Studied Law. '36-7; U.T.S., '38-9; Died Cromwell, Ct., May 17, '39.

James Sebastian Hamilton Henderson; b., Frederick Co., Md., Sep. 26, 1815; U.T.S., '38-9; P.T.S., '39-'41; Ord. (Presb.), Dec. 18, '41; S.S., Smyrna, Tenn., '41-3; S.S., Augusta, Ky., '43-'52; S.S. & Pas., Big Spring, Pa., '52-'62; S.S., Middlebrook, Md., '63——.

*Thomas David Hoover; b., Washington, D.C., ..., 1817; Cn. C., '38; U.T.S., '38-'40; P.T.S., '40-1; Ord. (Presb.), ..., '41; S.S. & Pas., Harper's Ferry, Va., '41-5; Tea., Darien, Ga., '45-9; W.C., N. York City, '50-2; Tea., Princeton, N.J., '53-7; Pas., Cranbury, N.J., '57-'67; Died, Cincinnati, O., May 22, '67.

Charles Kellogg; b., Hudson, N.Y., ..., 1816; U.N.Y., '39; U.T.S., '39-'40; And.T.S., '40-1; Ord. (Cong.), Nov. 10, '41; S.S., Richmond, Mich., '41-6; S.S., Almont, Mich., '46-'56; Trade, Detroit, Mich., '57——.

Anson McLoud; b., Hartland, Ct., ..., 1814; Y.C., '38; U.T.S., '39-'40; P.T.S., '40-1; Ord. (Cong.), Dec. 8, '41; Pas., Topsfield, Mass., '41——.

*Jonathan Bryan Marshall; b., Milford, Ct., July 9, 1817; A.C., '38; U.T.S., '38-9; Died, ..., .., ..., '61.

*JOSHUA LELAND MAYNARD; b., Montville, Ct., Nov. 21, 1813; U.T.S., '39–'40; Ord. (Cong.), Jan. 14, '41; Pas., Cornwall, Ct., '41–'52; Pas., E. Douglas, Mass., '52–'64; Pas., Plainfield, Ct., '63–5; Pas., Williston, Vt., '64–'73; Died, do., Ap. 24, '73.

*OLIVER WILLIAM NORTON; b., Canandaigua, N.Y., Dec. 9, 1812; U.T.S., '38–9; Ord. (Cong.), Nov. 10, '40; S.S., Angelica, N.Y., '39–'40; S.S., Castile, N.Y., '40–2; S.S. (Presb.), Rockford, Ill., '40–4; S.S., Roscoe, Ill., '44; S.S., Sycamore, Ill., '47; S.S., Jefferson, Wis., '48–9; C.M., N. York City, '50; S.S., Ashville, N.Y., '51; S.S., Stanhope, N.J., '52–3; S.S., Ararat & Gibson, Pa., '54–6; S.S., Springfield, Pa., '59–'60; S.S., Brooklyn, Mich., '62–5; S.S., Somerset, Mich., '65–7; W.C., Litchfield, Mich., '68–'73; Died, Quincy, Ill., Oct. 27, '73.

CHARLES MOSES OAKLEY; b., New-York City, July 2, 1815; U.T.S., '38–9; Ord. (Presb.), Oct. 25, '42; S.S., Nyack, N. Y., '41–2; Pas., Millville, N.J., '43–6; Pas., Port Richmond, Pa., '46–7; Pas., Fox Hill, N.J., '47–'51; Pas., N. Germantown, N.J., '47–'51; S.S., Melville (L.I.), N.Y., '53–'66; S.S., Amagansett (L.I.), N.Y., '67——.

WHITMAN PECK; b., Greenwich, Ct., May 16, 1815; Y.C., '38; U.T.S., '38–'40; And.T.S., '40–1; Ord. (Presb.), Oct. 23, '44; S.S., Erving & S. Orange, Mass., '41–2; Pas., Genoa, N.Y., '41–9; S.S., North-Branford, Ct., '51–5; W.C. & Tea., Greenwich, Ct., '54–'61; Tea., Ridgefield, Ct., '62–4; Tea., Fishkill, N.Y., '65–9; Tea., New-Haven, Ct., '69——.

JOHN D. PERRYMAN; b., White Co., Tenn., ..., 1811; N.U., '35; U.T.S., '38–'40; Trade, N. York City, ..——

FRANKLIN AUGUSTUS SPENCER; b., Westmoreland, N.Y., Dec. 24, 1811; O.I., '38; U.T.S., '38–'40; Ord. (Presb.), June 8, '42; S.S. (Cong.), Westmoreland, N.Y., '41–'50; Pas., do., '50–3; Pas., New-Hartford, Ct., '53–'63; Pas., Terryville, Ct., '63–5; S.S. (Presb.), Fulton, N.Y., '65; Sec., N.Y. State Temp. Soc., '65–9; W.C. & Oc. S., Clinton, N.Y., '69——.

FRANCIS WILLIAM UPHAM; b., Rochester, N.H., ..., 1817; B.C., '37, U.T.S., '38–'41; Phys., N. York City; Prof., Rutgers Inst., ..——.

LORIN VERY; b., Danville, Vt., ..., 1813; U.N.Y., '38; U.T.S., '38–9; Tea., N. York City, '39—— 21.

1842.

JAMES AIKEN; b., Goffstown, N.H., Nov. 14, 1810; D.C., '39; U.T.S., '39–'42; Ord. (Cong.), Aug. 30, '43; Pas., Hollis, N.H., '43–8; Pas., Gloucester, Mass., '48–'52; Pas., Putney, Vt., '54–7; Pas., Hanover, Mass., '57–'69; S.S., North-Carver, Mass., '69–'70; S.S., Dracut, Mass., '70–1; W.C., Charlestown, Mass., '72–3; S.S., North-Falmouth, Mass., '73——. Address, Charlestown, Mass.

JAMES MACWHORTER BRUEN; b., Newark, N.J., July 30, 1818; U.Pa., '39; U.T.S., '39–'42; Ord. (Presb.), July 1, '45; S.S., New-Brunswick, N.J., '44–5; Pas., New-Windsor, N.Y., '45–8; W.C., Newark, N.J., '48–9; S.S., &

Pas. (R.D.), Clintonville, N.J., '49–'52; W.C. & Ev., Irvington, N.J., '52——.

CHARLES HENRY AUGUSTUS BULKLEY; b., Charleston, S.C., Dec. 22, 1819; U.N.Y., '39; U.T.S., '39–'42; Ord. (Presb.), Nov. 17, '42; Pas., N. Brunswick, N.J., '42–3; H.M., Janesville, Wis., '43–5; Pas., Mt. Morris, N.Y., '47–'50; S.S. (R.D.), Ithaca, N.Y., '50–2; S.S. (Cong.), Winsted, Ct., '53–8; S.S., Paterson, N.J., '59–'61; Ch., U.S.Army, '61–3; Pas., Owego, N.Y., '65–7; Ch., Y.M.C.A., Brooklyn, N.Y., '67–8; Pas. (Presb.), Malone, N.Y., '68–'75; Prof., Boston, Mass., '75——.

*ABEL BENJAMIN BURKE; b., Woodstock, Ct., Feb. 13, 1816; D.C., '38; U.T.S., '39–'42; S.S., Jacksonville, Fla., '42–6; Tea., Alexandria, Ga., '46–7; Died, do., May 11, '47.

AARON LUCIUS CHAPIN; b., Hartford, Ct., Feb. 6, 1817; Y.C., '37; Tea., Baltimore, Md., '37–8; Prof., D. & D.I., N.Y., & Stud., U.T.S., '39–'42; Ord. (Presb.), Jan. 24, '44; Pas., Milwaukee, Wis, '44–'50; Prest., Bel. C., Beloit, Wis., '50——. D.D., W.C., '53.

CHARLES FREDERICK DIVER; b., Philadelphia, Pa., Dec. 15, 1812; Jef.C., '39; U.T.S., '39–'42; Ord. (Presb.), Oct. 22, '44; Pas., Providence, Pa., '44–7; S.S., Hublersburgh & Spring Mills, Pa., '47–'51; Pas., Waterford, Pa., '51–2; Pas., Cedarville, N.J., '52–'61; W.C., do., '61–2; Ch., Phila., Pa., '62——.

HORACE EATON; b., Sutton, N.H., Oct. 7, 1810; D.C., '39; U.T.S., '39–'42; Ord. (Presb.), June 21, '43; Pas., N. York City, '43–9; Pas., Palmyra, N.Y., '49——. D.D., D.C., '69.

CHARLES GILLETTE; b., Halifax, Vt., Oct. 17, 1815; A.C., '39; U.T.S., '39–'42; Res. Lic., '42–3; Ord. (Presb.), June 26, '45; S.S. & Pas., Granville, N.Y., '44–7; Pas., Fort Covington, N.Y., '48–'58; S.S., Milford, N.Y., '58–'70; S.S., Westford, N.Y., '70–1; S.S. & Pas., Mannsville, N.Y., '71–4; S.S., Redcreek, N.Y., '74——.

BENJAMIN MOORE GOLDSMITH; b., Mattituck (L.I.), N.Y., Feb. 16, 1817; U.N.Y., '38; U.T.S., '39–'42; Ord. (Presb.), Feb., 25, '45; S.S., Southport, N.Y., '42–5; Pas., do., '45–9; S.S., Bellona, N.Y., '49–'52; Pas., do., '52——.

EDWARD HOPPER; b., New-York City, Feb. 17, 1816; U.N.Y., '39; U.T.S., '39–'42; Ord. (Presb.), Oct. .., '43; Pas., Greenville, N.Y., '42–'51; Pas., Sag-Harbor (L.I.), N.Y., '52–8; W.C., N. York City, '59–'64; S.S., Plainfield, N.J., '65–9; Pas., N. York City, '69——. D.D., L.F.C., '71.

WILLARD MINOR HOYT; b., Walton, N.Y., Dec. 9, 1812; U.N.Y., '39; U.T.S., '39–'42; Ord. (Presb.), Feb. 9, '43; Pas., Nineveh, N.Y., '43–'66; Pas., Chaumont, N.Y., '66–8; Pas., Middleton, Wis., '68——.

*CHARLES KENDALL; b., Westminster, Mass., Feb. 14, 1813; A.C., '39; U.T.S., '39–'42; Ord. (Cong.), Aug. .., '42; Pas., Bernardston, Mass., '42–'54; Tea., Mercersburgh, Va., '55; S.S., S. Royalston, Mass., '55–6; S.S., Petersham, Mass., '55–9; S.S., Auburn, Mass., '59–'66; S.S., Windham, N.Y., '66–'73; Died, do., March 19, '73.

Daniel Decius Tompkins McLaughlin; b., New-York City, Oct. 18, 1812; Y.C., '34; Tea., N.York City, '34–'43; Ord. (Presb.), Ap. 16, '46; S.S., New-Windsor, N.Y., '44; S.S., Somers, N.Y., '45–6, '48–'56; Pas. (Cong.), Sharon, Ct., '58–'65; W.C., do., '65; Pas., Morris, Ct., '66–'71; S.S., Monterey, Mass., '73–5; S.S., Torrington, Ct., '75——. Address, Litchfield, Ct.

William Weston Patton; b., New-York City, Oct. 19, 1821; U.N.Y., '39; U.T.S., '39–'42; Ord. (Cong.), Jan. 18, '43; Pas., Boston, Mass., '43–5; Pas., Hartford, Ct., '46–'57; Pas., Chicago, Ill., '57–'67; Ed., do., '67——. D.D., I.A.U., '62.

Joseph Peckham; b., Bolton, Mass., Ap. 23, 1816; A.C., '37; And.T.S., '37–8; U.T.S., '39–'42; Ord. (Cong.), Nov. 30, '42; Pas., Kingston, Mass., '42–'56; S.S., ..., Minn., '56–9; S.S., Plymouth, Mass., '59; S.S., Kingston, Mass., '60——.

John Wainwright Ray; b., Norwich, N.Y., ..., 1813; A.C., '39; U.T.S., '39–'40; Aub.T.S., '40–1; U.T.S., '41–2; Ord. (Presb.), Nov. 16, '42; Pas., Glenn's Falls, N.Y., '42–5; S.S., Norwich, Ct., '45–6; As. Sec., A.E.S., N. York City, '46–7; S.S., Oswego, N.Y., '47–8; Pas., Clyde, N.Y., '48–9; Ag., A.T.S., S. Ala., '49–'51; S.S., Danville, N.Y., '51–2; S.S., Plainfield, Mich., '52–3; Pas., Rockville, Ct., '53–5; S.S., Avon Springs, Minn., '55–7; Law, Kansas, '58–'60; Col. U.S.Army, '60——. .; Rec. (Ep.), Tecumseh, Mich., '65——. .; . ., Rochester, N.Y., . .——.

*Moses Robinson; b., Burlington, Vt., Ap. 26, 1815; M.C., '39; U.T.S., '39–'42; Ord. (Presb.), ..., '43; S.S., Livonia, Ind., '43–4; S.S., Brownston, Ind., '44–5; S.S., Westfield, O., '45–7; Pas., Enosburgh, Vt., '47–'51; S.S., Newport, Vt., '51–4; S.S., Iowa City, Io., '55; S.S., Waterloo, Io., '55–6; S.S., Steamboat Rock, Io., '56–'65; Died, do., Sep. 2, '65.

*Cyrus Egbert Rosenkrans; b., Wallpack, N.J., Mar. 12, 1809; A.C., '37; U.T.S., '39–'42; Ord. (Presb.), Feb. 16, '43; Pas., Troy, Wis., '42–4; S.S., E. Troy, Wis., '44–9; Pas., Columbus, Wis., '49–'59; S.S., Otsego & Hampden, Wis., '59–'60; Died, Columbus, Wis., Feb. 8, '61.

*Joseph Rosenkrans; b., Wallpack, N.J., Nov. 13, 1812; U.C., '39; U.T.S., '39–'42; Ord. (Presb.), Feb. 15, '43; Pas., Bethlehem, N.Y., '43–5; S.S., Newport, N.Y., '45–8; S.S., Dunnsville. N.Y., '49–'51; S.S., Martinsburgh, N.Y., '51–3; Pas., Onondaga Valley, N.Y., '52–6, Pas., Romulus, N.Y., '56–'61; S.S., Onondaga Valley, N.Y., '61–3; Died, do., June 19, '63.

*Henry Ostrander Schermerhorn; b., Prattsville, N.Y., June 20, 1815; U.T.S., '39–'42; Res. Lic., '42–4; Ord. (Presb.), Jan. 8, '45; S.S. & Pas., Ticonderoga, N.Y., '44–7; Tea., N.York City, '47–9; Pas. (Cong.), do., '49–'54; Died, Utica, N.Y., Sep. 23, '54.

Raymond Hoyt Seely; b., Norwalk, Ct., Feb. 19, 1812; U.N.Y., '39; U.T.S., '39–'42; Res. Lic., '42–3; Ord. (Cong.), July 5, '43; Pas., Bristol, Ct., '43–9; Pas., Springfield, Mass., '49–'58; Ch., Paris, France, '58–9; Pas., Haverhill, Mass., '60——. D.D., U.N.Y., '64.

Henry Seymour; b., Hadley, Mass., Oct. 20, 1816; A.C., '38; U.T.S., '39–'42; Ord. (Cong.), March, 1, '43; Pas., Deerfield, Mass., '43–9; Pas., East-Hawley, Mass., '49–'66; W.C., do., '66–'70; S.S.. do., '70——.

STEPHEN MONTFORT VAIL; b., Union-Vale, N.Y., ..., 1818; B.C., '38; U.T.S., '39-'42; Ord. (M.E.), May .., '46; Pas., Fishkill, N.Y., '42-4; Pas., Sharon, Ct., '44-6; Pas., Pine Plains, N. Y., '46-7; Prin. of Sem., Pennington, N.J., '47-9; Prof., Bib. Inst., Concord, N.H., '49-'68; Superan., '68——. D.D., G.C., '56.

SAMUEL JESSUP WHITE; b., Durham, N.Y., March 7, 1815; W.C., '39; U.T.S., '39-'42; Ord. (Presb.), Oct. 9, '42; S.S., Yorktown, N.Y., '42-3; Pas., Franklin, N.Y., '43-'51; S.S., Cannonsville, N.Y., '52-'60; Pas., Gilbertsville, N.Y., '60-8; Pas., Walton, N.Y., '68-'75; Pas. (Cong.), Cornwall, Ct., '75——. D.D., W.C., '74. 24.

---

*ABIJAH PRATT BEEBE; b., Jackson, N.Y., ..., 1813; O.I., '37; U.T.S., '39-'40; Ord. (Presb.), May 2, '43; S.S. & Pas., Oriskany, N.Y., '42-5; Inv., N.Y. Mills, N.Y., '45-8; do., Elgin, Ill., '48-9; Died, Rome, N.Y., Sep. 6, '49.

ALLEN HENRY BROWN; b., New-York City, Sep. 23, 1820; C.C., '39; U.T.S., '39-'40; P.T.S., '40-2; Ord. (Presb.), Jan. 5, '48; Ag., A.T.S., '44-6; S.S., May's Landing, N.J., '47-'60; Presb. M., Absecon, N.J., '60-'74; Syn.M., Camden, N.J., '74——.

RICHARD ABRAHAM CHALKER; b., Saybrook, Ct., Nov. 16, 1817; U.T.S., '39-'40; Ord. (M.E.), June 15, '44; S.S., Amenia, N.Y., '40-1; S.S., Johnsville, N.Y., '41-2; Pas., Hyde Park & Milan, N.Y., '42-3; Pas., Farmington, Ct., '43-4; Pas., Hyde Park, N.Y., '44-6; Pas., Sing Sing, N.Y., '46-8; Pas., Peekskill, N.Y., '48-'50; Pas., Saugerties, N.Y., '50-1; Pas., N. York City, '51-3; Pas., Poughkeepsie, N.Y., '53-4; Pas., Kingston, N.Y., '54-6; Pas., Chester, N.Y., '56-7; Pas., New-Brunswick, N.J., '57-9; Pas., Bordentown, N.J., '59-'61; Pas., Salem, N.J., '61-'3; Pas., Pennington, N.J., '63-5; Pas., Mount Holly, N.J., '65-7; Pas., Camden, N.J., '67-'70; Pas., Red Bank, N.J., '70-3; Pas., New-Brunswick, N.J., '73-5; Pas., Lambertville, N.J., '75——.

EPHRAIM DEYOE; b., Austerlitz, N.Y., Dec. 18, 1814; U.C., '39; U.T.S., '39-'40; Ord. (Ev. Lu.), Sep. 19, '43; S.S., Woodstock, N.Y., '40-3; Pas., Ghent, N.Y., '43-6; Pas., German Valley, N.J., '46-'58; Pas., Saddle River, N.J., '58——.

*JAMES PINKERTON FISHER; b., Londonderry, N.H., Jan. 1, 1813; U.C.,'39; U.T.S., '39-'41; Ord. (Presb.), ...'45; Tea., Philadelphia, Pa., & Ag., A.T.S., '41-5; S.S., Glen, N.Y., '45-6; S.S., West-Galway, N.Y., '46-7; Ag., A.B.C.F.M., Schenectady, N.Y., '47-'51; S.S. & Pas., Johnstown, N.Y., '51-'60; S.S., Buffalo, N.Y., '61-2; Ag., U.S.C.C., Washington, D.C., '63-5; Died, Little Britain, N.Y., Aug. 30, '65.

*ASHBEL FULLER; b., Kent, Ct., July 26, 1817; U.C., '38; U.T.S., '39-'40; Tea., Kent, Ct., '40-'73; Died, do., Jan. 4, '73.

*WILLIAM OSMAN GORHAM; b., Hardwich, Mass., Sep. 9, 1814; A.C., '38; U.T.S., '39; Ord. (Ep.), ..., ..; Died, Athol, Mass., Nov. 7, '69.

*ALONZO HAYES; b., Barrington, N.H., Aug. 10, 1810; D.C., '39; Tea., Washington, D.C., '39-'40; U.T.S., '40-1; And. T.S., '41-2; Ord. (Cong.), May 24, '43; Pas, W. Barnstable, Mass., '43-'50; S.S. & Pas., Dublin, N.H.,

'50-3; Agr., Alexandria Co., Va., '53-7; Died, Hall's Cross Roads, July 15, '57.

*WILLIAM P. HOTCHKISS; b., Hartford, Ct., ..., 1818; O.I., '39; U.T.S., '39-'40; Ord. (Cong.), May 11, '43; S.S., Concord, Mich., '41-3; S.S., Centerville, Mich., '43-4; Inv., '43-'61; Died, S. Francisco, Cal., ..., ..

TIMOTHY BLOOMFIELD JERVIS; b., Rome, N.Y., ..., 1809; U.T.S., '40-1; Aub. T.S., '41-2; U.T.S., '42-3; Ord. (Presb.), July 12, '43; S.S., Oriskany, N.Y., '44-5; S.S., Unadilla, N.Y., '45-6; Pas., Richfield-Spa, N.Y., '47-'53; S.S., Oakfield, N.Y., '53-5; S.S., Newport, N.Y., '56-9; S.S., Oriskany, N.Y., '59-'64; S.S., Burr Oak, Mich., '65-6; S.S., Pine Island, Minn., '66-9 W.C. & Col., Woodbridge, N.J., '69-'72; Pas., Aspinwall, Pa., '72——.

WILLIAM M. JONES; b., Catskill, N.Y., ..., 1803; M.D., ..., '28; U.T.S., '41.

JOHN WICKLIFFE LANE; b., Homer, N.Y., May 7, 1815; U.T.S., '39-'40; Ord. (Presb.), Ap. .., '49; S.S., Wilson, N.Y., '42-4; S.S., Olean, N.Y., '47-'50; S.S., Corfu (Pembroke), N.Y., '50-3; S.S., Centerville, N.Y., '53-'69; S.S., Rushford, N.Y., '69——.

JOHN WESLEY LINDSAY; b., Barre, Vt., Aug. 20, 1820; W.U., '40; U.T.S., '40-1; Ord. (M. E.), May 15, '46; S.S., New-Paltz & Plattekill, N.Y., '43-5; Pas., Lenox, Mass., '45-7; Tut., W.U., Middletown, Ct., '47-8; Prof., W.U., do., '48-'60; Pas., N. York City, '60-4; Prest., G.C., Lima, N.Y., '64-8; Prof. Boston Univ., '68. D.D., W.U., '63——.

GILBERT HAMILTON LITTLEJOHN; b., Herkimer Co., Mich., ..., 1815; O.I., '39; U.T.S., '40-1; Trade, Whitesboro, N.Y.; do., N. York City; R.R. Sup., Cleveland, O.; do., ..., Ill., '54——.

CHARLES ELIPHALET LORD; b., Portsmouth, N.H., Feb. 11, 1817; D.C., '38; Tea., So. Berwick, Me., '38-9; do., Kingston, N.C., '39-'40; U.T.S., '39-'41; N.H.T.S., '41-2; Aub. T.S., '42-3; Ord. (Presb.), May 8, '44; Pas., Niles, Mich., '44-7; S.S., Evansville, Ind., '48-9; S.S. (Cong.), Stratham & New Market, N.H., '50-2; S.S., Westbrook, Me., '52-3; S.S., C. Elizth., Me., '53-6; Pas., Mt. Vernon, N.H., '57-'61; Coll. Pas., South-Easton, Mass., '63-7; Pas., Chester, Vt., '67-9; S.S. (Presb.), Beverly, N.J., '69-'70; W.C., Boston, Mass., '70-3; Prof., Lay Coll., Brooklyn, N.Y., '73-4; S.S., Boston, Mass., '74-5; S.S., Pelham Manor, N.Y., '75——. D.D., E.T.U., '73.

CHESTER SMITH LYMAN; b., Manchester, Ct., Jan. 13, 1814; Y.C., '37; Tea., Ellington, Ct., '38-9; U.T.S., '39-'40; N.H.T.S., '40-2; Ord. (Cong.), Feb. 15, '43; Pas., New-Britain, Ct., '43-5; Inv. & Tea., Sand. Islds., '45-7; Inv., Cal., '47-'50; Lit., New-Haven, Ct., '50-8; Prof., Y.C., New-Haven, Ct., '58——.

WILLIAM MULFORD MARTIN; b., Rahway, N.J., June 29, 1813; U.N.Y., '37; U.T.S., '39-'41; Prin., H. School, Brooklyn, N.Y., '42-'52; Ord. (Presb.), Ap. 3, '52; Pas., Woodbridge, N.J., '52-'63; S.S., Columbia, Cal., '63-4; S.S., Virginia City, Nev., '64-7; Ch., Y.M.C.A., Brooklyn, N.Y., '68——.

*JOSEPH PENNELL; b., Brunswick, Me., Nov. 7, 1811; B.C., '39; U.T.S., '39; Chemist, S. Norwalk Ct., ..—— '68; Died, do., Sep. 3, '68.

FREDERICK TRENCK PERKINS; b., Sanbornton, N.H., Aug. 16, 1811; Y.C., '39; U.T.S., '39–'40; N.H.T.S., '40–2; Ord. (Cong.), Jan. 11, '43; Pas., E. Cambridge, Mass., '43–'51; Pas., Manchester, Ct., '51–6; Pas., Williamsburgh, Mass., '57–'60; Pas., Galesburgh, Ill., '60–8; S.S., Hartford, Ct., '70–2; S.S., Naugatuck, Ct., '72–5; S.S., Tilton & Northfield, N.H., '75——.

JOHN HANCOCK PETTINGELL; b., Manchester, Vt., ..., 1815; Y.C., '37; Prof., D. & D.I., N.York City, '37–'43; U.T.S., '39–'41; Ord. (Cong.), Dec. 6, '43; S.S., South-Dennis, Mass., '43–9; Pas., Saybrook, Ct., '49–'50; D. Sec., A.B.C.F.M., Albany, N.Y., '53–6; Trav., Europe and Asia, '56–7; D. Sec., A.B.C.F.M., Albany, N.Y., '57–'60; Pas., Saxonville, Mass., '60–3; Pas., Westbrook, Ct., '63–6; Sea. Ch., Antwerp, Belgium, '66–'71; W.C., Brooklyn, N.Y., '72——,

*ZENAS MONTAGUE PHELPS; b., West-Hampton, Mass., ..., 1811; W.C., '39; U.T.S., '39–'41; Tea., Sing Sing, N.Y., ..——..; Tea., Riverdale, N.Y., ..——..; Died, ..., '72.

*ALMON BRADLEY PRATT; b., North-Cornwall, Ct., June 3, 1812; U.T.S., '39–'41; Ord. (Cong.), Ap. 13, '52; Pas., Genesee & Vienna, Mich., '51–'65; S.S., Flint, Mich., '67–9; Tea., Berea, Ky., '69–'73; S.S., Camp Creek, Neb., '73–5; Died, do., Dec. 28, '75.

JOHN MORRISON REID; b., New-York City, May 30, 1820; U.N.Y., '39; U.T.S., '39–'41; Ord. (M. E.), May 15, '43; S.S., Wolcotville, Ct., '44–6; Pas., Bakerville, Ct., '46–7; Pas., Jamaica (L.I.), N.Y., '47–9; Pas., Birmingham, Ct., '49–'51; Pas., Middletown, Ct., '51–2; Tut., W.U., Middletown, Ct., '52–3; Pas., N. York City, '53–5; Pas., Brooklyn, N.Y., '55–7; Pas., Bridgeport & Fairfield, Ct., '57–8; Prest., G.C., Granville, O., '58–'64; Ed., Cincinnati, O., '64–8; Ed., Chicago, Ill., '68–'72; Cor. Sec., Miss. Soc., M.E. Ch., N. York City, '72——. D.D., U.N.Y., '58.

JAMES CHAPMAN SMITH; b., Middleville (L.I.), N.Y., March 17, 1810; U.T.S., '39–'41; Ord. (Presb.), Dec. 21, '41; S.S., Cutchogue (L.I.), N.Y., '42–5; S.S. & Pas., Pompey Centre, N.Y., '45–'51; S.S., Oran, N.Y., '51–2; S.S., Oneida Lake, N.Y., '52–6; Pas., Summer Hill, N.Y., '56–'60; S.S., Red Creek, N.Y., '60–4; S.S., Romulus, N.Y., '64–8; S.S., Newfield, N.Y., '68–'74; S.S., Marathon & Texas Valley, N.Y., '75——.

*ERASTUS CARTER SPOONER; b., Brandon, Vt., July 18, 1815; M '39; U.T.S., '39–'41; Tea., Brandon, Vt., '41; Died, do., Dec. 11, '41.

BENJAMIN FRANKLIN STEAD; b., Pittsburgh, Pa., Feb. 22, 1815; U.N.Y., '39; U.T.S., '39–'41; Ord. (Presb.), Feb. 22, '42; Pas., Philadelphia (Bridesburgh), Pa., '42–'52; Pas., Astoria (L.I.), N.Y., '52——. D.D., U.N.Y., '65.

ANDREW LEETE STONE; b., Oxford, Ct., Nov. 25, 1815; Y.C., '37; Tea., Uxbridge, Mass., '37–8; Prof., D. & D.I., N. York City, '38–'41; U.T.S., '39–'41; And.T.S., '41–2; Sec., S.S.U., Philadelphia, Pa., '42–4; Ord. (Cong.), Sep. 3, '44; Pas., Middletown, Ct., '44–9; Pas., Boston, Mass., '49–'66; Pas., San Francisco, Cal., '66——. D.D., A.C., '61.

EDWARD STRONG; b., Somers, Ct., Oct. 25, 1813; Y.C., '38; U.T.S., '39–'40; Tut., Y.C., '40–2; Ord. (Cong.), Dec. 14, '42; Pas., New-Haven, Ct.,

'42–'62; S.S., Kalamazoo, Mich., '64; Pas., Pittsfield, Mass., '65–'71; Pas., Boston (W. Roxbury), Mass., '72——. D.D., H.C., '64.

JACOB VAN NOSTRAND; b., New-York City, Feb. 27, 1814; U.N.Y., '38; U.T.S., '39–'41; Prof., D. & D.I., N. York City, '38–'57; Prest., D. & D.I., Austin, Texas, '57——.

HIRAM WHEELER; b., Schoharie, N.Y., ..., 1808; U.C., '40; U.T.S., '39–'40; Ord. (Ev. Lu.), ... ; Pas., Claverack, N.Y., '53——..; Pas., Sharon Springs, N.Y., '59——..; Pas., Middletown, N.Y., ..——.

EPHRAIM MUNROE WRIGHT; b., Northampton, Mass., ..., 1816; W.C., '39; U.T.S., '39; N.H.T.S., '40–1; Tea., East-Hampton, Mass., '44–9; Sec. of State, Mass., '53–5; Ord. (Cong.), July 3, '61; Pas., Bethlehem, Ct., '61–5; Pas., Terryville, Ct., '65–'70; Tea., East-Hampton, Mass., '70——.

ABRAHAM TEATOR YOUNG; b., Carlisle, N.Y., May 10, 1806; U.C., '39; U.T.S., '39–'40; P.T.S., '40–2; Ord. (Presb.), Sep. 20, '43; Pas., E. Aurora, N.Y., '43–7; Pas., Warsaw, N.Y., '47–'50; Pas., E. Bethany, N.Y., '50–6; S.S., Charlotte, N.Y., '56–9; Pas., Sackett's Harbor, N.Y., '59–'64; S.S., Oak's Corners, N.Y., '64——. 32.

1843.

RICHARD HARRISON BULL; b., New-York City, Sep. 28, 1817; U.N.Y., '39; U.T.S., '39–'41, '42–3; Tea., N. York City, '43–'54; Prof., U.N.Y., do., '54——.

WILLIAM AVERY CLIFT; b., Griswold, Ct, Sep. 12, 1817; A.C., '39; U.T.S., '40–3; Ord. (Cong.), Dec. 18, '44; Pas., Stonington, Ct., '44–'64; Ag., N. York City, '64–7; S.S. & Pas., Stonington (Mystic Bridge), Ct., '67——.

WILLIAM THOMAS DOUBLEDAY; b., Binghamton, N.Y., March 28, 1818; Y.C., '38; U.T.S., '39–'41, '42–3; Ord. (Presb.), March 3, '47; S.S., Bainbridge, N.Y., '43–5; S.S., Truxton, N.Y., '46–9; S.S., Gilbertsville, N.Y., '50–'60; Pas., Delhi, N.Y., '60–2; Pas. (Cong.), Goshen, Ct., '64–'71; W.C. & Inv., Vineland, N.J., '71——.

HENRY BOND ELLIOTT; b., Woodstock, N.Y., June 21, 1823; U.N.Y., '40; U.T.S., '40–2; And. T.S., '42–3; U.T.S., '43; Ord. (Cong.), May 24, '44; S.S., Alexandria, N.J., '44; Pas., Waterbury, Ct., '45–'51; S.S., Springfield, Mass., '52–4; Pas., Brooklyn (E.D.), N.Y., '54; Pas., Stamford, Ct., '55–7; Pas., Columbus, O., '58–'60; W.C., Brooklyn, N.Y., '61–3; W.C., N. York City, '63–5; S.S., Poughkeepsie, N.Y., '65–6; S.S., New-Canaan, Ct., '66–9; S.S., Litchfield, Ct., '70–3; S.S., Stonington, Ct., '74——.

NATHANIEL ELMER; b., Wantage, N.J., Jan. 31, 1816; U.C. '40; U.T.S., '40–3; Ord. (Presb.), Oct. ...., '44; S.S., Stanhope, N.J., '43–5; S.S., Circleville, N.Y., '45–7; S.S., Factoryville, N.Y., '48–'50; S.S., Waverly, N.Y., '51–7; Pas., E. Manlius, N.Y., '57–8; Pas., E. Avon, N.Y., '58–'62; S.S., Stone Church, N.Y., '62–6; W.C., Leroy, N.Y., '66–7; W.C., Deckertown, N.J., '67–8; S.S., Middletown, N.Y., '68–'70; S.S., Belmont, N.Y., '70–4; S.S., Emporium, Pa., '74——.

SAMUEL HAIGHT HALL; b., Geneva, N.Y., May 15, 1819; U.C., '37; U.T.S., '40-3; Ord. (Presb.), Jan. 29, '45; S.S., Tallmadge, O., '44; Pas., Marshall, Mich., '45-'53; Pas., Syracuse, N.Y., '53-6; Pas., Owego, N.Y., '56-'64; Com., A.B.S., N. Orleans, La., '64-5; Sec., A.S.F.S., N. York City, '65——. D.D., Ing. U., '61.

*GEORGE KERR; b., Carrickfergus, Ireland, Dec. 18, 1812; W.C., '39; U.T.S., '40-3; Ord. (R. D.), ..., '43; Pas., Conesville, N.Y., '43-6; Prin. Acad., Franklin, N.Y., '46-'60; Prest. State Ag. Coll., Ovid, N.Y., '61; Prin. Acad., Watertown, N.Y,, '62-5; Do., Cooperstown, N.Y., '65-7; Died, do., March, 27, '67. LL.D., H.C., '52.

HENRY DEARING LATHAM; b., Newburgh, N.Y., Sep. 30, 1812; U.T.S., '40-3; Ord. (M. E.), May 19, '47; S.S., Essex, Ct., '43-4; S.S., Fair Haven, Ct., '45; S.S., Madison, Ct., '46-7; Pas., Riverhead (L.I.), N.Y., '48; Pas., Brooklyn, N.Y., '49-'53; W.C., '53-4; Pas., W. Granby, Ct., '54-5; Pas., Colebrook River, Ct., '56-7; Pas., Westport & Poplar Plains, Ct., '58-9; Pas., Windsor & Windsor Locks, Ct., '60-1; Pas., Essex & Saybrook, Ct., '62-3; Pas., Northport & Centreport (L.I.), N.Y., '64-6; Pas., Milford, Ct., '68-'70; Pas., Madison, Ct., '71; Pas., N. Wilton, Ct., '72; Pas., Newtown, Ct., '73; W.C., do., '74; Pas., Higganum, Ct., '75-6.

*JOHN LEWIS; b., Walpole, Mass., July 19, 1817; D.C., '40; U.T.S., '40-3; Ord. (Cong.), May 6, '44; S.S., Fairplay & New-Diggings, Wis., '43-4; S.S., New-Diggings, Wis., '45-7; Pas. (Presb.), Platteville, Wis., '48-'60; Died, do., Sep. 2, '60.

*THOMAS HICKS MUDGE; b., Orrington, Me., Sep. 27, 1815; W.U., '40; N.T.I., '40-2; U.T.S., '42-3; Ord. (M.E.), Ap. 30, '47; Pas., Brookfield, Mass., '43-4; Pas., Leominster, Mass., '44-6; Pas., Grafton (Farmansville), Mass., '46-8; Pas., Weston, Mass., '48-'50; Pas., Natick & Needham, Mass., '50-1; Pas., S. Hadley Falls, Mass., '51-2; Pas., Spencer, Mass., '52-3; Pas., Walpole, Mass., '53-5; Pas., Rockbottom, Mass., '55-6; Tea., Ellington, Ct., '56-7; Prof. McK.C., Lebanon, Ill., '57-8; Pas., Waterloo, Ill., '58; Pas., St. Louis, Mo., '59-'60; Pas., Ironton, Mo., '60-1; Pas., Independence, Mo., '61-2; Pas., Manhattan, Kan., '61-2; Prof., Baker Univ., Baldwin City, Mo., '62; Died, do., July 24, '62.

GEORGE FRANCIS NEEDHAM; b., Boston, Mass., Feb. 7, 1816; W.U., '40; U.T.S., '40-'3; Ord. (Ind. Meth.), ..., ..; S.S., Providence, R.I., '43; Pas., Athol & Needham, Mass., '44; Pas., Buffalo, N.Y., '45; Pas., East Solon, N.Y., '46; Inv., Kalamazoo, Mich., '47-'50; Tea., Rochester, N.Y., '50-7; Trade, Buffalo, N.Y., '58-'61; Ch. Sanitary Com., Wash., D.C., '61-2; Clerk, U.S. Treas. Dep., do., '63——.

ORIN FOWLER OTIS; b., Colchester, Ct., May 8, 1811; Y.C., '40; U.T.S., '40-3; Ord. (Cong.), Mar. 11, '47; S.S. & Pas., Chepachet, R.I., '44-'64; Miss., Providence, R.I., '65.

*SAMUEL L. PITCHER; b., Phila., Pa., ..., 1817; C.N.J., '40; U.T.S., '40-3; S.S., Springfield X Roads, Pa., '43-4; Died, do., ..., '44.

WILLIAM KING PLATT; b., New-York City, Aug. 17, 1817; U.C., '40; U.T.S., '40-3; Ord. (Presb.), June 13, '44; Pas., Milton, N.Y., '44-7; S.S.,

Orangeville, N.Y., '48–9; S.S., Sweden, N.Y., '49–'55; S.S., Fairport, N.Y., '55–7; Pas., Somers, N.Y., '57–'64; Pas., Hector, N.Y., '64–9; S.S., Ludlowville, N.Y., '69——.

WILLIAM PORTER; b., Lee, Mass., Jan. 10, 1820; W.C., '39; And.T.S., '40–1; U.T.S., '41–3; Ord. (Cong.), Aug. 25, '47; W.C., and Inv., Florida & Georgia, '43–'50; Tea., Marietta, O., '50–2; Prof., Bel.C., Beloit, Wis., '52——.

EDWARD ERASTUS RANKIN; b., Newark, N.J., May 15, 1820; Y.C., '40; U.T.S., '40–3; Ord. (Presb.), April 23, '44; Pas., Springfield, N.J., '44–'50; Pas., New-York City, '50–'63; S.S., Newark, N.J., '64–5; Pas. (Cong.), Fairfield, Ct., '66——. D.D., R.C., '63.

*LUBIM BURTON ROCKWOOD; b., Wilton, N.H., Ap. 8, 1816; D.C., '39; And.T.S., '40–1; U.T.S., '41–3; Ord. (Presb.), April 18, '45; Fin. Ag., U.T.S., '43–'50; Coll. Pas. (Cong.), Rocky Hill, Ct., '50–8; D. Sec., A.T.S. (of N.Y.), Boston, Mass., '59–'72; Died, do., May 7, '72.

JOHN WILLIAM SCHERMERHORN; b., Prattsville, N.Y., Jan. 26, 1812; U.C., '36; U.T.S., '39–'41, '42–3; Res. Lic., '43–4; Tea., N. York City, '44–'52; W.C., N. York City, '53——.

HENRY MARTYN SCUDDER; b., Panditeripo, Ceylon, Feb. 5, 1822; U.N.Y., '40; U.T.S., '40–3; Ord. (Presb.), Nov. 12, '43; F.M., Madras, India, '44–'51; F.M., Arcot, India, '51–'63; Pas. (R.D.), Jersey City, N.J., '64–5; Pas. (Presb.), San Francisco, Cal., '65–'71; Pas. (Cong.), Brooklyn, N.Y., '71——. M.D., U.N.Y., '53; D.D., R.C., '59.

THOMAS JAMES SHEPHERD; b., Clarke Co., Va., Ap. 25, 1818; Cn. C., '39; U.T.S., '40–3; Ord. (Presb.), Oct. 5, '43; Pas., Lisbon, Md., '44–'52; Pas., Philadelphia, Pa., '52——. D.D., Cn. C., '65.

THOMAS HARVEY SKINNER; b., Philadelphia, Pa., Oct. 6, 1820; U.N.Y., '40; U.T.S., '40–2; And.T.S., '42–3; U.T.S., '43; Ord. (Presb.), Dec. 8, '43; Pas., Paterson, N.J., '43–6; Pas., N. York City, '46–'55; Pas., Honesdale, Pa., '56–9; Pas. (R.D.), Stapleton (S.I.), N.Y., '59–'68; Pas. (Presb.), Fort Wayne, Ind., '68–'71; Pas., Cincinnati, O., '71——. D.D., C.N.J., '67.

JUDSON BURR STODDARD; b., Pawlet, Vt., ..., 1813; U.C., '40; U.T.S., '40–3; Ord. (Cong.), May 16, '44; S.S., Yorktown, N.Y., '43–4; Pas., Sherman, Ct., '44–'54; Inv., '54–5; Pas., S. Windsor, Ct., '55–'63; S.S., Philadelphia, Pa., '63; S.S. (Presb.), Croton Falls, N.Y., '63–5; S.S. (Cong.), So. Meriden, Ct., '65–8; Pas., Essex (Centrebrook), Ct., '69–'75; W.C., do., '75——.

GEORGE BENJAMIN UTTER; b., Plainfield, N.Y., Feb. 4, 1819; O.I., '40; U.T.S., '40–3; Ord. (7th Day Bap.), June 5, '43; Ed., N. York City, '44–'61; Ed., Westerly, R.I., '61——.

ELIPHALET WHITTLESEY; b., Salisbury, Ct., July 13, 1816; W.C., '40; U.T.S., '40–3; Ord. (Cong.), Sep. 27, '43; F.M., Maui, S. Islds., '44–'54; Inv., Hammonton, N.J., '54——. 24.

JOHN BOYD ALLEN; b., Sturbridge, Mass., ..., 1814; U.C., '40; U.T.S., '40–1; E.W.T.S., '41–3; Ord. (Presb.), March .., '46; S.S., Covington, Pa., '45–'50 ; Pas., Gustavus, O., '50–6 ; Pas., Brooklyn, O., '56–'67 ; W.C., Cleveland, O., '67–'70 : S.S., Clinton, Mo., '70–3 ; W.C., do., '73——.

WILLIAM RHODES BAGNALL; b., Boston, Mass., July 17, 1819; W.U., '40 ; U.T.S., '40–2 ; Ord. (M.E.), April 30, '47 ; Tut., W.U., '42–6 ; S.S., Walpole, Mass., '44–5 ; Pas., Northampton, Mass., '46–7 ; Prin. Acad., E. Greenwich, R.I., '47–9 ; Pas., Holliston, Mass., '49–'50 ; Pas., Southbridge, Mass., '50–2 ; Pas., Shrewsbury, Mass., '52–4 ; Pas., Malden, Mass., '54–6 ; Pas., Charlestown, Mass., '56–8 ; Pas., Boston, Mass., '58–9 : Pas., Chelsea, Mass., '59–'60, Manuf. & Mercht., Malden, Mass., '60——.

JOSEPH BARTLETT; b., Salisbury, N.H., Jan. 26, 1816; D.C., '35; Tea., Andover, Mass., '37–8 ; Tutor, D.C., '38–'41 ; And.T.S., '40–1 ; U.T.S., '41–2 ; And.T.S., '42–3 ; Ord. (Cong.), Oct. 7, '47 ; S.S., Waterville, Me., '46–7 ; Pas., Buxton, Me., '47–'67 ; W.C., Andover, Mass., '67–8 ; S.S., South-New-Market, N.H., '69——.

*HORACE THOMPSON BLAKE ; b., Worcester, Mass., ..., 1819; A.C., '38 ; U.T.S., '40–1 ; Died, Worthington, Mass., June 2, '41.

*ISAAC GEORGE HUBBS; b., ... (L.I.), N.Y., ..., 1813; C.N.J., '40 ; U.T.S., '40–1 ; Tea., N. York City, '41–'62 ; Ag., A.M.A., N. Orleans, La., '63–5 ; Tea., N. York City, '65–'73 ; Died, do., Feb. .., '73.

JOSEPH T. LEE ; b., Charleston, S.C., ..., 1811; Ch. C., '30; U.T.S., '40–1.

WILLIAM HENDERSON MCCARER; b., Philadelphia, Pa., ..., 1814; Jef. C., '38 ; U.T.S., '40–2 ; Ord. (Presb.), Oct. .., '43 ; Pas., W. Nantmeal, Pa., '43–9 ; S.S. & Pas., Evansville, Ind., '49——.

*JAMES PIERRE MORANGE ; b., Montreal, Can., ..., 1818; U.C., '40 ; U.T.S., '40–1 ; Law, N. York City, '41–7 ; Died, do., Jan. 14, '47.

THOMAS GILBERT OSBORN; b., Riverhead (L.I.), N.Y., Oct. 15, 1820; W.U., '40 ; U.T.S., '41 ; Law Student, Har. C., '41–3 ; Ord. (M.E.), June 21, '48 ; S.S., Southampton (L.I.), N.Y., '44–6 ; Pas., Bridgehampton (L.I.), N.Y., '46–8 ; Pas., Patchogue (L.I.), N.Y., '48–'50 ; W.C., '50–1 ; Pas., Birmingham, Ct., '51–3 ; Pas., Bridgeport, Ct., '53–5 ; Pas., Waterbury, Ct., '55–7 ; Pas., N. York City, '57–'61 ; Pas., Brooklyn, N.Y., '61–2 ; Pas., New-Haven, Ct., '62–3 ; P. Elder, Bridgeport, Ct., '64–5 ; W.C., New-Haven, Ct., '65–6 ; Pas., Riverhead (L.I.), N.Y., '67–9 ; P. Elder, Birmingham, Ct., '69–'70 ; Do., Norwalk, Ct., '70–3 ; Pas., Port Chester, N.Y., '73–5 ; W.C., Norwalk, Ct., '75——.

JOHN FRANCIS PINGRY; b., Newburyport, Mass., Sep. 26, 1818; D.C., '36 ; U.T.S., '40–1 ; Ord. (Presb.), June 28, '42 ; Pas., Fishkill, N.Y., '42–6 ; Tea., do., '46–'53 ; Tea. & Pas., Newark (Roseville), N.J., '53–'60 ; Tea., Elizabeth, N.J., '61——. Ph.D., C.N.J., '68.

HARRIS RIGHTER; b., Pine Plains, N.Y., ..., 1810; U.C., '31; U.T.S., '40–1 ; Ord. (Cong.), Sep. 28, '42 ; Pas., S. Middletown, N.Y., '42–6 ; W.C., Oyster Bay (L.I.), N.Y., '47–'53 ; W.C., Newark, N.J., '53——.

ALDEN BURRILL ROBBINS; b., Salem, Mass., Feb. 18, 1817; A.C., '39 ; And.T.S., '40–1 ; U.T.S., '41–2 ; And.T.S., '42–3 ; Ord. (Cong.), Sept, 20,'43 ; S.S. & Pas., Muscatine, Iowa, '43——. D.D., A.C., '68.

Ambrose Spencer Rogers; b., Cornwall, Ct., May 21, 1815; U.C., '40; U.T.S., '40-1; Tea., Cornwall, Ct., '41; Do., New-Milford, Ct., '42——..; Do., Cornwall, Ct., .. ——

William Salter; b., Brooklyn, N.Y., Nov. 17, 1821; U.N.Y., '40; U.T.S., '40-2; And. T.S., '42-3; Ord. (Cong.), Nov. 5, '43; H.M., Makoqueta, Iowa, '43-6; Pas., Burlington, Iowa, '46——. D.D., Io. U., '64.

Peter D. Schory; b., Berne, Switz., ..., 1811; C.N.J., '40; U.T.S., '40-1; And.T.S., '41-3; Ord. (G.R.), ..., '43; Pas., New-Holland & New-Providence, Pa., '43-8; Pas., Upper & Lower Mt. Bethel, Pa., '49-'54; Pas., Lancaster, O., '56-'62; W.C., do., '62——.

Byron Sunderland; b., Shoreham, Vt., Nov. 22, 1819; M.C., '38; U.T.S., '41-3; Ord. (Presb.), Nov. 13, '43; S.S., Alexander, N.Y., '43; Pas., Batavia, N.Y., '43-'51; S.S., Syracuse, N.Y., '51-2; Pas., Washington, D.C., '53——. Ch., U.S. Sen., '61-4; Do., '73——. Ch., A. & F.C.U., Paris, France, '64-5. D.D., M.C., '55.

*William A. Thompson; b., Monson, Mass., ..., 1811; U.N.Y., '40; U.T.S., '40-2; N.H.T.S., '42-3; Ord. (Cong.), ...; S.S., Troy, Bloomfield & Fox, Io., '43-5; S.S., Fairfield, Io., '45-'50; S.S., Port Byron, '50-2; Drowned, Mendocia Slough, Ill., May 3, '52.

*Albert Gallatin Upham; b., Rochester, N.H., July 10, 1819; B.C., '40; U.T.S., '40-1; M.D., Vt. Med. Acad., '42; Prof., do., Castleton, Vt., '42-4; Studied Med., Paris, France, '42-4; Phys., Boston, '44-7; Died, do., June 16, '47.

*George Stayley Van Cleef; b., New-York City, June 28, 1817; C.C., '37; U.T.S., '40-2; And.T.S., '42-3; Res. Lic., '44-5; S.S., Sandy Hill, N.Y., '45; S.S., Bridport, Vt., '46; Insane, '46-'63; Died, N. York City, Nov. 29, '63. 19.

1844.

Samuel Howe Allen; b., Belchertown, Mass., Feb. 20, 1819; A.C., '41; U.T.S., '41-4; Ord. (Cong.), April 22, '46; Pas., Windsor Locks, Ct., '46-'62; W.C., do., '62——.

George Washington Barrows; b., Bridport, Vt., Feb. 22, 1817; U.T.S., '41-4; Ord. (Cong.), Jan. 28, '45; Pas., Salisbury, Vt., '45-'63; Pas., Elizabethtown, N.Y., '63——.

Elijah Hayward Bonney; b., Hadley, Mass., Nov. 4, 1816; A.C., '39; U.T.S., '41-4; Ord. (Cong.), Feb. 25, '47; S.S., Bennington, Vt., '45-6; S.S. & Pas., Pawlet, Vt., '46-'53; S.S., Bellows Falls, Vt., '53-4; S.S., Plainfield, Mass., '54-5; S.S., Albion, N.Y., '55; S.S. (Presb.), Vernon Centre, N.Y., '55-'72; S.S., Lenox, N.Y., '72-5; S.S., Somerset, N.Y., '76——.

*George Atherton Davis; b., Lunenburgh, Vt., Jan. 3, 1813; D.C., '38; Tea., ..., Md., '39-'41; U.T.S., '41-4; Ord. (Presb.), April, .., '45; S.S. & Pas., Hanover C. H., Va., '43-6; Died, do., Oct. 9, '46.

William Cowper Foster; b., Hanover, N.H., July 8, 1815; D.C., '41; U.T.S., '41-4; Res. Lic., N.H.T.S., '44-5; Ord. (Cong.), Oct. 13, '47; S.S.,

Westboro, Mass., '46-7; Pas., Cuyahoga Falls, O., '47-9; Pas., Boston, Mass., '49-'51; Pas., Lawrence, Mass., '52-7; S.S., Chicago, Ill., '57-8; S.S. & Pas., North-Becket, Mass., '60-3; W.C., Wilbraham, Mass., '63-'70; S.S., Civil Bend., Io., '70 2; W.C., Middletown, Ct., '73——.

*EZRA HALL GILLETT; b., Colchester, Ct., July 5, 1823; Y.C., '41; U.T.S., '41-4; Res. Lic., '44-5; Ord. (Presb.), April 16, '45; Pas., Harlem, N.Y., '45-'70; Prof., U.N.Y., N. York City, '70-5; Died, do., Sept. 2, '75. D.D., H.C., '64.

CHARLES HAWLEY; b., Catskill, N.Y., Aug. 19, 1819; W.C., '40; U.T.S., '41-4; Ord. (Presb.), Jan. 29, '45; Pas., New-Rochelle, N.Y., '45-8; Pas., Lyons, N.Y., '48-'57; Pas., Auburn, N.Y., '57——. D.D., H.C., '61.

*HARRISON OTIS HOWLAND; b., W. Brookfield, Mass., Jan. 25, 1813; A.C., '41; U.T.S., '41-4; Res. Lic., '44-5; Ord. (Presb.), Dec. 23, '46; Pas., Ashland, N.Y., '46-'50; S.S. & Pas. (Cong.), Warner, N.H., '53-7; Pas., Chester, N.H., '57-'62; Pas. (Presb.), Girard, Pa., '64-8; S.S., Ellington, N.Y., '69-'72; Died, Kinderhook, N.Y., Feb. 13, '72.

*JAMES HOYT; b., Greenfield, N.Y., Oct. 7, 1817; U.C., '40; U.T.S., '41-4; Res. Lic., '44-5; Ord. (Presb.), April 12, '46; S.S., Harlem, N.Y., '44; S.S., Stanwich, Ct., '45; Pas., Tuskegee, Ala., '46-9; Pres., Talladega, Ala., '49-'53; S.S. (Cong.), Stamford, Ct., '53-5; S.S., New-London, Ct., '55; Pas. (Presb.), Orange, N.J., '56-'66; Died, do., Dec. 16, '66.

ZERAH TAYLOR HOYT; b., Greenfield, N.Y., Dec. 3, 1812; U.C., '40; U.T.S., '41-4; Ord. (Presb.), Feb. 17, '46; S.S., W. Greenfield, N.Y., '44-5; S.S., Stanwich, Ct., '45; S.S., Hastings, Mich., '45-'55; S.S., S. Greenfield, N.Y., '55——.

FREDERICK FRELINGHUYSEN JUDD; b., Bloomfield, N.J., May 18, 1821; C.N.J., '39; U.T.S., '41-4; Ord. (Presb.), May 18, '59; Tea., Berkshire, N.Y., '47-'59; Pas., Parsippany, N.J., '59-'63; S.S., Catskill, N.Y., '63-4; S.S., Hunter, N.Y., '65-9; S.S., Port Henry, N.Y., '70-3; Inv., '73——.

AMOS EDWARD LAWRENCE; b., Geneseo, N. Y., June 25, 1812; Y.C., '40; U.T.S., '41-4; Ord. (Presb.), June 25, '48; Clk., A.H.M.S., N. York City, '44-8; Pas., Cutchogue (L.I.), N.Y., '48-'51; Pas. (Cong.), Southbury, Ct., '51-'60; Pas., Lancaster, Mass., '60-5; W.C., Coldwater, Mich., '65-6; S.S., Housatonic, Mass., '66-9; S.S., South Lee, '70-1; S.S., Stockbridge, Mass., '73-4; W.C., Newton-Centre, Mass., '74——.

*NATHANIEL CLARK LOCKE; b., Salem, N.J., June 1, 1816; M.C., '38; Tea., Loundesboro, Vt., '38-'41; U.T.S., '41, 2-4; Ord. (Presb.), Oct. .., '45; H.M., Eastville, Va., '44-6; Pas., Brooklyn, N.Y., '47-'50; Pas., Hempstead (L.I.), N.Y., '52-'60; Died, do., July 21, '62. D.D., U. Ala., '58.

SAMUEL JUNIUS PARKER; b., Danby, N.Y., May 8, 1819; A.C., '41; U.T.S., '41-4; S.S., Ramapo, N.Y., '45-6; S.S., Geneva, N.Y., '46-7; S.S., Clyde, N.Y., '47-8; S.S., Volney, N.Y., '48-'51; Tea. and Med. Stu., Ithaca, N.Y., '52-4; Phys. and Ch., Mobile, Ala., '55-7; Phys., Ithaca, N.Y., '57——.

EDWARD J. VAIL; b.,...., .., ..., 1811; U.N.Y., 1841; U.T.S., '41-4; Ord. (Presb.),...., '45; S.S., Oriskany, N.Y., '45-6; W.C., Brooklyn, N.Y., '46-7; S.S., Jamesville, N.Y., '47-8; Pas., Babylon (L.I.), N.Y.,

'48–'51; Uniontown, Cal., '51–4; W.C., San Francisco, Cal., '54–7; W.C., Crescent City, Cal., '57–'61 ; W.C., San Francisco, Cal., '61——.

LEVI FAY WALDO; b., Prattsburgh, N.Y., Jan. 28, 1817; U.C., '40; U.T.S., '41–4; Ord. (Cong.), July 9, '44; Pas., Poughkeepsie, N.Y., '44–'54 ; Pas., N. Brookfield, Mass., '54–6; Prin., Kewanee, Ill., '56–7 ; Pas., Buda & Milo, Ill., '58–9; Pas., Lasalle, Ill., '59–'61 ; Pas. and Prin., Allegan, Mich., '61–5; Pas., Lowell, Mich., '65–6; Pas., Quincy, Ill., '66–8; Pas., Oneida, Ill., '68–'70; Pas., Beardstown, Ill., '70–2; Pas., Lowell, Mich., '72–4; Pas., Pentwater, Mich., '74–5; Pas., Frankfort, Mich., '75——.

JOHN WARD; b., Bloomfield, N. J., ..., 1818; U.N.Y., '41; U.T.S., '41–4; Ord. (Presb.), Mar. .., '45; Pas., Stanhope, N.J., '45–8; W.C., Bloomfield, N.J., '48–9; Pas., Clyde, N.Y., '49–'55; Ag., Utica, N.Y., '55–7; W.C., Phila., Pa., '57–8; Pas., do., '58–'60; W.C., Newark, N.J., '60–2; S.S., Freedom Plains, N.Y., '63–7 ; W.C., Bloomfield, N.J., '68–'72 ; Pas., Montgomery, N.Y., '73–5 ; W.C., Bloomfield, N.J., '75——.

*CHARLES DABNEY WHARTON; b., Richmond, Va., ..., 1818 ; U.Va., '39; U.T.S., '41–4; S.S., Leesville, Va., '44–5; Died, do., ..., '45.

LIVINGSTON WILLARD; b., Albany, N.Y., Aug. 7, 1816; U.C., '42 ; U.T.S., '41–4; Ord. (R.D.), Dec. 3, '44; S.S. and Pas., Galway, N.Y., '44–7; S.S., Haverstraw, N.Y., '48–9; W.C., N. York City, '50; S.S., do., '51; Pas. (Cong.), N. Stamford, Ct., '52–6; Pas. (Presb.), Sparta, N.J., '56–'60; Pas., Port Jervis, N.Y., '60–2; S.S., Sparta, N.J., '62–3; Pas, Marshall, Mich., '63–9; W.C., Yonkers, N.Y., '70–2; W.C., N. York City, '72——.

GEORGE FRANKLIN WISWELL; b., Whitehall, N. Y., May 29, 1817 ; U.T.S., '41–4; Ord. (Presb.), June 18, '45; Pas., Southold (L.I.), N.Y., '45–'51; Fin. Sec., U.T.S., '51–2; Pas., Peekskill, N.Y., '53–6; Pas., Wilmington, Del., '56–'67; Pas., Philadelphia, Pa., '67——. D.D., H.C., '66. 20.

---

*EPHRAIM TUCKER BARSTOW; b., Jewell City, Ct., Sep. 12, 1814; Y.C., '41; U.T.S., '41–2; Died, Rochester, N.Y., May 21, '45.

*JAMES FANNING; b., Franklinville (L.I.), N.Y., ..., 1817; U.C., '40; U.T.S., '41–2; Tea., N. York City, '43–'63; Died, do., March 9, '63.

PATTERSON FLETCHER; b., Harrisonburgh, Va., March 18, 1816; Wash.C.Va., '40; U.T.S., '41–3; Ord. (Presb.), Ap. .., '44; Pas., Elk Branch, Jeff. Co., Va., '44——..; S.S., Middleburgh, Va., ..——..; Pas., Richmond, Va., ..——..; Pas., Loch Willow, Augusta Co., Va., '67–'75 ; S.S., Lebanon, Va., '75——.

WILLIAM CLARK FRENCH; b., Livonia, N.Y., June 3, 1818; Ken.C., '41; U.T.S., '41–3; Ord. (Ep.), Dec. 25, '46; Rec., Granville, O., '46–'50; Rec., Delaware, O., '50–2; Rec., Worthington, O., '52–4; Rec., Ironton, O., '54–8; Rec., Oberlin, O., '58–'73; As. Min., Cleveland, O., '74——; Ed., 'Stand. of the Cross," '68——; D.D., Ken.C., '75.

WILLIAM T. FRENCH; b., Culpepper Co., Va., ..., 1814; U.T.S., '42.

*Thomas Ewing Hathaway; b., Homer, N.Y., ..., 1811; H.C., '41; U.T.S., '41; Tea., N. York City, ..——..; Tea., Chicago, Ill., ..——, '50; Died, do., June 13, '50.

Henry Hickok; b., Bethel, Ct., Jan. 10, 1819; U.T.S., '41–3; Ord. (M.E.), Aug. .., '47; Pas., Starkey & Barrington, N.Y., '43–4; Pas., Lockport, N.Y., '44–5; Pas., Brockport, N.Y., '45–6; Pas., Penfield, N.Y., '46–7; F.M., Fuh Chau, China, '47–9; Pas., Palmyra, N.Y., '49–'51; Pas., Elmira, N.Y., '51–3; Pas., Rochester, N.Y., '53–4; Pas., Elmira, N.Y., '54–6; S.S., (Presb.), Wampsville, N.Y., '56–9; S.S., Vernon, N.Y., '59–'63; S.S., Sackett's Harbor, N.Y., '65——.

John Hume Kedzie; b., Bovina, N.Y., Sep. 8, 1815; O.C., '41; U.T.S., '42–3; N.H.T.S., '43–4; Law, Chicago, Ill., '47——.

Saurin Eliot Lane; b., West-Suffield, Ct., ..., 1818; U.C., '41; U.T.S., '41–3; Ord. (Presb.), Oct. 22, '45; Pas., Galway, N.Y., '47–'62; Pas., Carmel, N.Y., '63——..; S.S., Point Pleasant, W. Va., '74——.

Sabin McKinney; b., Binghamton, N.Y., March 7, 1816; A.C., '41; U.T.S., '41–2; Aub. T.S., '42–3; Ord. (Presb.), Ap. 16, '45; S.S., Bath, N.Y., '44–5; S.S., Greenwich, N.Y., '45–7; Pas., Fredonia, N.Y., '47–'51; S.S., Franklin, Pa., '52–4; Ag., A. & F.C.U., E. Bloomfield, N.Y., '54–5; Pas., Bergen, N.Y., '55–7; Inv. & Mer., Binghamton, N.Y., '57——.

Benjamin Franklin Parsons; b., Wiscasset, Me., June 21, 1820; B.C., '41; U.T.S., '41–2; B.T.S., '44–6; Ord. (Cong.), Jan. 12, '47; S.S., Watertown, Ill., '46–7; S.S. & Pas., Waukegan, Ill., '47–'52; Pas., Dover, N.H., '53–'61; Pas., Nashua, N.H., '61–7; S.S., Boston, Mass., '68–9; W.C., Derry, N.H., '69–'73; S.S., Woonsocket, R.I., '74——.

*William Henry Porter; b., Rye, N.H., Sep. 19, 1817; Y.C., '41; U.T.S., '41–2; N.H.T.S., '42–3; Ord. (Presb.) Oct. 29, '45; Pas., Litchfield, N.H., '45–9; W.C., Cambridge, Mass., '51–'61; Died, Roxbury, Mass., May 26, '61.

Abraham T. Seely; b., Milford, Pa., ..., 1815; U.C., '41; U.T.S., '41–2.

*Ephraim Tenney; b., Dummerston, Vt., Nov. 12, 1813; W.C., '41; U.T.S., '41–2; Died, Brooklyn, N.Y., March 8, '42.

James N. Tompkins; b., ..., ..., 1818; U.N.Y., '39; U.T.S., '41.

Henry W. Willoughby; b., Hollis, N.H., ..., 1817; U.T.S., '41.

16.

1845.

Jacob Jackson Abbott; b., Groton, Vt., July 17, 1813; D.C., '39; Tut., D.C., '41–3; U.T.S., '43–5; Ord. (Cong.), Aug. 27, '45; Pas., Bennington, Vt., '45–7; Ag., A.T.S., Car. & Ga., 47–8; S.S., Hollis, N.H., '48–9; Pas., Uxbridge, Mass., '50–'64; S,S., Northbridge (Whitinsville), Mass., '64–5; Pas., Yarmouth, Me., '65——.

Samuel Wordsworth Bailey; b., Little Compton, R.I., July 28, 1810; Y.C., '39; U.T.S., '44–5; Ord. (Cong.), May .., '49; S.S., Greenpoint (L.I.),

N.Y., '46–7; S.S., Waymart & Prompton, Pa., '47–8; S.S., Pittsburgh, Pa., '48–9; S.S., W. Springfield, Mass., '49–'50; S.S., Cold Spring, N.Y., '50–2; S.S., N. York City, '52–'60; Oc. S., do., '60–'70; Oc. S., Boston, Mass., '71–5; Oc. S., N. York City, '76——.

FREDERICK GORHAM CLARK; b., Waterbury, Ct., Dec. 13, 1819; U.N.Y., '42; U.T.S., '45; Ord. (Presb.), Dec. 29, '45; S.S., Greenwich, Ct., '45–6; Pas., Astoria (L.I.), N.Y., '46–'52; Pas., N. York City, '52–'67; Pas. (Cong.), Greenwich, Ct., '67–'71; Pas., Brooklyn, N.Y., '74–5; W.C., N. York City, N.Y., '75——. D.D., U.N.Y., '64.

REES CADWGAN EVANS; b., London, Eng., Jan. 15, 1815; Jef. C., '42; U.T.S., '42–5; Ord. (Presb.), Jan. 8, '46; Pas., Lewiston, N.Y., '46; C.M., (Ep.), Philadelphia, Pa., '48–'53; Rec., Doylestown, Pa., '54–5; S.S. & Rec., Philadelphia, Pa., '55–72; Miss., Gloucester, N.J., '73——.

HENRY CLAY FISH; b., Halifax, Vt., Jan. 27, 1820; U.T.S., '42–5; Ord. (Bap.), June 26, '45; Pas., Somerville, N.J., '45–'51; Pas., Newark, N.J., '51——. D.D., U.R., '58.

*WILLIAM FORREST, JR.; b., New-York City, ..., 1821; C.C., '40; U.T.S., '42–5; Res. Lic., P.T.S., '45–6; Tea., N.Y., '46–8; S.S., Milford, Pa., '48–9; Tea., N. York City, '49–'56; Died, do., Feb. .., '56.

TIMOTHY HILL; b., Mason, N.H., June 30, 1819; D.C., '42; U.T.S., '42–5; Ord. (Presb.), Oct. 22, '46; S.S., St. Charles, Mo., '46–'51; S.S., St. Louis, Mo., '52–'61; S.M., do., '60–1; S.S., Rosamond, Ill., '61–2; S.S., Shelbyville, Ill., '63–5; S.S., Kansas City, Mo., '65–8; D. Sec., Board of Home Miss., Kansas City, Mo., '68——. D.D., High U., '73.

EDWARD HOWE; b., Portland, Me., ..., 1820; B.C., '41; U.T.S., '42–5; Tea. of Music, U.T.S., '45–'52; Do., N. York City, '52——

*HORATIO STOCKTON HOWELL; b., Ewing, N.J., Aug. 14, 1820; U.T.S., '42–5; Ord. (Presb.), Jan. 15, '46; Pas., E. Whiteland, Pa., '46–9; Pas., Elkton, Md., '49–'53; S.S., Del. Water Gap, Pa., '53–'61; Ch., U. S. Army, '61–3; Killed, Gettysburgh, Pa., July 1, '63.

WILLIAM WARE HOWLAND; b., W. Brookfield, Mass., Feb. 25, 1817; A.C., '41; U.T.S., '42–5; Ord. (Cong.), Oct. 14, '45; F.M., Batticotta, Ceylon, '46——..; F.M., Tillipally, Jafna, Ceylon, ..——.

*SAMUEL HURLBUT; b., Charlotte, Vt., Nov. 26, 1816; M.C., '39; Tea., Castleton, Vt., '39–'42; U.T.S., '42–5; Ord. (Cong.), June 2, '47; S.S., Lodi, N.J., '45–6; S.S. & Pas., New-Haven, Vt., '46–'56; Died, do., Dec. 2, '56.

JOSEPH PAUL LESTRADE; b., Philadelphia, Pa., Ap. 22, 1817; U. Pa., '41; U.T.S., '42–5; Ord. (Presb.), ..., '48; H.M., Bedford Co., Va., '48–'50; C.M., N. York City, '50–4; Pas., Hunter, N.Y., '54–9; C.M., N. York City, '59–'68; Ev., do., '68——.

*JOSEPH MCKEE; b., ..., Ireland, ..., 1805; Bft. C., '29; U.T.S., '44–5; Ord. (Presb.), May 25, '48; Tea., N. York City, '45–7; S.S., do., '47–8; Pas., Peekskill, N.Y., '48–'52; Pas. (R.D.), N. York City, '52–8; Tea., do., '59; Tea., Newark, N.J., '60–3; Died, do., Aug. 10, '63.

WILLIAM HULL MEGIE; b., New-York City, Sep. 13, 1817; U.N.Y., '39; U.T.S., '43–5; Ord. (Presb.), ..., '50; S.S., N. Stamford, Ct., '46–9;

S.S., Williamstown, N.Y., '50; S.S., Sparta, N.J., '51; S.S., W. Milford, N.J., '52–5; S.S., Junius, N.Y., '55–'66; S.S., West-Fayette, N.Y., '66–9; S.S., Newfoundland, N.J., '69–'74; S.S., Paterson, N.J., '75; Tea., Jersey City, N.J., '76——.

HENRY OSBORN; b., Cairo, N.Y., May 18, 1821; W.C., '42; U.T.S., '42–5; Ord. (Presb.), Nov. 12, '46; S.S., Tallahassee, Fla., '45–6; Pas., Hunter, N.Y., '46–9; Tea., Windsor, N.Y., '49–'51; S.S., New-Milford, Pa., '52–6; Tea., Elmira, N.Y., '56–7; Tea., Chester, N.Y., '58–9; S.S., Circleville, N.Y., '59–'66; S.S., Decatur, O., '66–'70; W.C., Leavenworth, Kan., '71–3; S.S., Tonganoxie, Kan., '73——.

HENRY STAFFORD OSBORN; b., Philadelphia, Pa., Aug. 17, 1823; U. Pa., '41; U.T.S., '42–5; Ord. (Presb.), June .., '46; S.S., Coventry, R.I., '45–6; Pas., Hanover C.H., Va., '46–9; Pas., Richmond, Va., '49–'53; Pas., Liberty, Va., '53–8; S.S., Salem, Va., '58–9; Pas., Belvidere, N.J., '59–'66; Prof., L.F. Coll., Easton, Pa., '66–'70; S.S., Oxford, O., '70–1; Prof., do., '71–3; S.S., do., '73——. LL.D., L.F.C., '64.

*NOAH FORD PACKARD; b., Abingdon, Mass., ..., 1815; B.U., '42; U.T.S., '42–5; S.S., Cranston, R.I., '45–6; S.S., Stanwich, Ct., '46; S.S., N. Orleans, La., '46–7; Died, do., Sep. 3, '47.

CHARLES PEABODY; b., Newport, N.H., Nov. 8, 1816; D.C., '39; Tea., Concord, N.H., & New-Bedford, Mass., '39–'42; U.T.S., '42–5; Ord. (Cong.), Sep. 15, '45; D. Sec., A.T.S., St. Louis, Mo., '45–'61; Supt., Soldiers' Home, do., '61–'73; D. Sec., A.T.S., Chicago, Ill., '73——.

WINTHROP HENRY PHELPS; b., Albany, N.Y., March 1, 1818; U.N.Y., '42; U.T.S., '42–5; Ord. (Cong.), Feb. 9, '48; S.S., Greenfield, N.Y., '45–6; S.S., Hillsdale, N.Y., '46–9; S.S. & Pas., Stockbridge (Curtisville) Mass., '49–'54; S.S. & Pas., Monterey, Mass., '54–'61; S.S., Riverton, Ct., '61–3; Ch., U.S. Army, '63–5; W.C., So. Egremont, Mass., '66——.

SAMUEL SANDFORD POTTER; b., New-Providence, N.J., Sep. 25, 1814; U.N.Y., '42; U.T.S., '42–5; Ord. (Presb.), May 26, '46; S.S., Scienceville, N.Y., '45–7; S.S., Newark, N.J., '47–'50; Pas., Lawrenceburgh, Ind., '50–6; Tea., Glendale, O., '56–'63; Tea., New-Albany, Ind., '65——..; Tea., Centreville, Ind., ——..'70; Ed., Cincinnati, O., '70——.

BENJAMIN J. RELYEA; b., Plattekill, N.Y., Sep. 11, 1819; U.T.S., '42–5; Ord. (Presb.), May 27, '46; S.S., Delhi & Pittsburgh, Ind., '45–7; S.S. (Cong.), N. Scituate, R.I., '48–'50; Pas., Fall River, Mass., '50–6; S.S. & Ed., Brooklyn, N.Y., '57–'61; Pas., Westport (Green's Farms), Ct., '61——.

ALONZO BERRY RICH; b., Grand Isle, Vt., Nov. 10, 1814; U. Vt., '42; U.T.S., '42–5; Ord. (Presb.), Feb. 18, '46; S.S., Mt. Pleasant, N.J., '45; S.S., Deckertown, N.J., '46–8; Pas. (Cong.), Stanwich, Ct., '48–'52; Pas., Beverly; Mass., '52–'67; D. Sec., Coll. & Theo. Soc., West, '67–'70; Pas., West-Lebanon, N.H., '71——. D.D., U.Vt., '68.

*SOCRATES SMITH; b., Henniker, N.H., June 16, 1814; D.C., '42; U.T.S., '42–5; Ord. (Presb.), Nov. 23, '45; S.S., Beardstown, Ill., '45–6; S.S., Panther Creek, Ill., '46–9; Tea., Greenville, Ill., '50–3; H.M., Jerseyville,

Ill., '53–5; S.S., Troy, Ill., '55–9; W.C., Greenville, Ill., '59–'69; Died, do., ..., '69.

*Frederick Merrick Starkweather; b., Northampton, Mass., Sep. 5, 1820; A.C., '41; U.T.S., '42–5; S.S., Springfield, N.J., '46; S.S., Chester, Mass., '47; W.C., Northampton, Mass., '48–9; Tea., Baltimore, Md., '50; Died, Northampton, Mass., March 13, '51.

Rufus Porter Wells; b., Whately, Mass., Feb. 4, 1818; A.C., '42; E.W.T.S., '42–3; U.T.S., '43–5; Ord. (Presb.), Sep. 26, '46; S.S. & Pas., Jonesborough, Tenn., '45–'62; S.S., Prairie du Sac, Wis., '63–4; S.S., Thorntown & Bethel, Ind., '64–5; S.S., Knoxville, Tenn., '65–6; S.S., Gilbertville, Mass., '66–9; Pas., Southampton, Mass., '69–'74; S.S., Mason, N.H., '74——.

Shepard Wells; b., Crown Point, N.Y., Ap. 13, 1818; I.C., '40; U.T.S., '40–1, '43–5; Ord. (Cong.), Sep. .., '45; D. Sec., A.T.S., Columbia, Tenn., '45–'60; Ag., U.S.C.C., St. Louis, Mo., '62–5; Prest., Y.M.C.A., St. Louis, Mo., '65–'70; Ev., St. Louis, Mo., '70——. 26.

Lauren Armsby; b., Northbridge, Mass., Jan. 16, 1817; A.C., '42; U.T.S., '42–3; And.T.S., '43–5; Ord. (Cong.), May 27, '46; S.S., Pittstown, Me., '45–6; Pas., Chester, N.H., '46–'56; Pas., Faribault, Minn., '56–'64; Ch., U.S.Army, '64–5; S.S., Candia, N.H., '65–'71; S.S., Mound City, Kan., '70–3; S.S., Council Grove, Kan., '73——.

Thomas S. Arthur; b., Abbeville, S.C., ..., 1822; R.M.C., '42; U.T.S., '42–4; Ord. (Ep.), ..., '45; Rec., Greenville, S.C., '45–'67.

*Joseph H. Babcock; b., Dover, N.H., ..., 1821; U.T.S., '43–4; Ord. (Presb.), ..., '45; S.S., Portland, Ind., '45–7; S.S., New-Corydon, Ind., '47–8; Died, do., March 15, '48.

Simon Barrows; b., Monson, Mass., Ap. 28, 1811; D.C., '42; U.T.S., '42–3; Tea., New-Bedford, Mass., '45–6; Tea., Dorchester, Mass., '46–'51; Lit. Work, Athol, Mass., '52–3; Ord. (Cong.), Jan. .., '55; Pas., Tipton, Ill., '55–6; Ag., Davenport, Io., '56–'66; S.S., Quincy, Io., '67–'70; S.S., Weeping Water, Neb., '70–4; S.S., Osceola, Neb., '74——.

*John Cromwell; b., New-York City, Dec. 22, 1820; U.N.Y., '42; U.T.S., '42–4; Tea., N. York City, '44–6; Ord. (Presb.), ..., '46; Pas., Wilmington, O., '46; Died, do., Oct. 5, '46.

Henry Darling; b., Reading, Pa., Dec. 27, 1823; A.C., '42; U.T.S., '42–3; Aub.T.S., '43–5; Ord. (Presb.), Dec. 30, '46; Pas., Hudson, N.Y., '46–'53; Pas., Philadelphia, Pa., '53–'61; Inv., do., '61–3; Pas., Albany, N.Y., '64——. D.D., U.C., '60.

Luke Dorland; b., Wooster, O., Feb. 11, 1815; M.C., '41; U.T.S., '42–3; P.T.S., '43–4; Ord. (Presb.), Sep. 8, '47; H.M., Platte Co., Mo., '45–6; Pas., Ontario & Lexington, O., '46–'55; S.S., Mt. Salem & Eagle Creek., O., '55–'60; S.S., Columbia City, Ind., '60–2; S.S., Belleville & Waterford, O., '62–6; S.S. & Tea., Concord, N.C., '67——.

DIVIE BETHUNE DUFFIELD; b., Carlisle, Pa., Aug. 29, 1821; Studied Law, Y.C.,'42; U.T.S., '42–3; Law, Detroit, Mich., '44——. A.B., Y.C., '57.

SAMUEL WITT EATON; b., Framingham, Mass., Dec. 25, 1820; Y.C., '42; U.T.S., '42–3; N.H.T.S., '43–5; Ord. (Cong.), Jan. 28, '48; S.S., Montgomery, Mass., '45–6; S.S., Lancaster & Big Platte, Wis., '47——. Ch., U.S.Army, '62–5.

SAMUEL WARE FISHER; b., Northampton, Mass., ..., 1818; W.C., '41; U.T.S., '42–3; Tea., Northampton, Mass., ..——.

DANIEL DELAVAN FROST; b., Carmel, N.Y., ..., 1812; W.C., '40; U.T.S., '42–4; Ord. (Cong.), Dec. 29, '47; Pas., Redding, Ct., '47–'57; Pas., W. Stockbridge, Mass., '57–'62; W.C., New-Fairfield, Ct., '62–5; S.S., Litchfield, Mich., '65–'73; S.S., Le Mars, Io., '73——.

JAMES MASON HOPPIN; b., Providence, R.I., Jan. 17, 1820; Y.C., '40; U.T.S., '42–4; And.T.S., '44–5; Ord. (Cong.), March 27, '50; Pas., Salem, Mass., '50–'61; Prof., Y.C., New-Haven, Ct., '61——. D.D., K.C., '70.

WILLIAM SOLOMON LEAVITT; b., Putney, Vt., Jan. 26, 1822; Y.C., '40; U.T.S., '42–4; Ord. (Cong.), Dec. 3, '45; Pas., Newton, Mass., '45–'53; Pas. (Presb.), Hudson, N.Y., '53–'67; Pas. (Cong.), Northampton, Mass., '67——.

AARON LADNER LINDSLEY; b., Troy, N.Y., March 4, 1817; U.T.S., '42–4; P.T.S., '44–5; Ord. (Presb.), May 8, '46; Pas., Waukesha, Wis., '46–'51; H.M., Ozaukee, Wis., '51–2; Pas., South-Salem, N.Y., '52–'68; Pas., Portland, Oregon, '68——. D.D., U.N.Y., '68.

JAMES LITTLE; b., Middletown, N.Y., Nov. 3, 1818; W.C., '41; U.T.S., '42–3; Trade, Middletown, N.Y., '43——.

*HENRY GILBERT LIVINGSTON; b., Coxsackie, N.Y., Feb. 3, 1821; W.C., '40; U.T.S., '42–4; Ord. (Presb.), Aug. .., '45; S.S. & Pas., Carmel, N.Y., '44–9; Pas. (R.D.), Philadelphia, Pa., '49–'54; Prin., Carmel, N.Y., '54–5; Died, Carmel, N.Y., Jan. 27, '55.

CHARLES FRENCH LOW; b., Concord, N.H., Jan. 14, 1819; D.C., '42; U.T.S., '42–3; And.T.S., '43–5; Studied Law, Concord, N.H., '45–6; Do., N. York City, '46–7; U.S.Army, '47–9; Law, Jamestown, Cal., ..——.

WILLIAM OTTINGER, b., Springfield, Pa., Ap. 12, 1812; Jef. C., '41; U.T.S., '42–4; Ord. (Presb.), ..., '45; S.S., Fairton & Cedarville, N.J., '44; S.S., Unionville, Pa., '45; S.S., Monument, Mass., '46–7; S.S., Opequan & Cedar Creek, Va., '47–9; S.S., Unadilla & Otego, N.Y., '50; S.S., Mt. Kean & Edinborough, Pa., '51; S.S., Belle Valley, Pa., '52; S.S., Titusville & Cherry Tree, Pa., '53–4; Tea., Kossuth, Io., '55–6; Tea., Grandview, Io., '57; S.S., Swedes' Point & Boonsboro, Io., '58; Tea., Millington, Md., '60; Tea., Newark, Del., '61; Tea., Germantown, Pa., '61–'74; W.C., do., '74——.

*WILLIAM WALLACE PAGE; b., Albany, N.Y., July .., 1818; U.C., '42; U.T.S., '42–3; Ord. (Cong.), ..., '54; S.S., Scipio, N.Y., '51–2; S.S., Union Springs, N.Y., '52–3; Pas., Kent, Ct., '53–4; S.S., Ridgebury, Ct., '56–7; S.S., Rough Creek, Va., '58–9; S.S., Guilderland, N.Y., '62–5; S.S., Troy, N.Y., '65–7; W.C., Troy, N.Y., '67–'71; Died, do., Dec. 30, '71.

WHEELOCK HENDEE PARMLY; b., Braintree, Vt., July 27, 1816; C.C., '42; U.T.S., '42–3; H.T.S., '43–4; Ord. (Bap.), April 19, '46; As. Pas., Clinton, La., '45–7; Pas., Shelbourne Falls, Mass., '47–'50; Pas., Burlington, N.J., '50–4; Pas., Jersey City, N.J., '54——. D.D., M.U., '67.

BENJAMIN THOMAS PHILLIPS; b., New-York City, Jan. 9, 1820; C.N.J., '42; U.T.S., '42–3; P.T.S., '43–4; Ord. (Presb.), Dec. 18, '44; Pas., May's Landing, N.J., '44–5; H.M. & S.S., N. York City, '46–8; Pas., Rondout, N.Y., '48–'62; Ch., U.S.Army, Newburgh, N.Y., '63–5; Supt., Home, Phila., Pa., '66–'71; S.S., Windham, N.Y., '71–3; Pas., Manchester, N.J., '73——.

*NATHANIEL EDWARDS PIERSON; b., Madison, N.J., Jan. 7, 1814; W.C., '41; U.T.S., '42–4; Ord. (Cong.), July 11, '44; S.S., N. Stamford, Ct., '44–5; S.S., Sparta, N.J., '46–'50; Pas. (Presb.), Unionville, N.Y., '50–7; Pas., Horseheads, N.Y., '57–'61; Ch., U.S.Army, '62; Pas., Ridgebury, N.Y., '63–9; Pas., Escanaba, Mich., '69–'72; Died, do., May 19, '72.

CHARLES RICHARDS; b., Darien, Ct., Dec. 9, 1814; U.C., '41; And.T.S., '42–3; U.T.S., '43–4; Ord. (Presb.), May 25, '47; S.S., Lakeville, N.Y., '45–9; SS., Hector, N.Y., '49–51; S.S., Rensselaerville, N.Y., '51–5; S.S., Monroeville, O., '55–8; S.S., Maumee City, O., '58–'68; S.S., Pardeeville, Wis., '68–'73; W.C., do., '73——.

JOHN COTTON TERRETT; b., Stonington, Ct., July 5, 1809; W.C., '33; U.T.S., '42–5; Ord. (Cong.), Aug. 13, '45; S.S., South-Middletown, N.Y., '45–6; Tea., N.Y.C., '47–'51; Trade & Agric., Sharon, Ct., '47——.

JOHN R. YOUNG; b., Marlboro, N.Y., Oct. 17, 1820; U.C., '42; U.T.S., '42–5; Ord. (Presb.), June .., '47; Pas., Phelps, N.Y., '47–9; S.S., Painted Post, N.Y., '49–'52; S.S., Baldwinsville, N.Y., '52–6; S.S., Cortland, N.Y., '56–7; S.S., Keeseville, N.Y., '57–8; Pas., Plattsburgh, N.Y., '58–'63; W.C., Mamaroneck, N.Y., '63–5; W.C., Newport, R.I., '65–6; Pas., Greenbush, N.Y., '66–8; S.S., Albany, N.Y., '68–'70; S.S., Clyde, N.Y., '71–3; S.S., Newark, N.Y., '73–4; S.S., Tecumseh, Mich., '74–6; W.C., Albany, N.Y., '76. 25.

1846.

EDWIN THEODORE BRANTLY; b., Conecuh Co., Ala., Sep. 13, 1820; U.E.T., '43; U.T.S., '43–6; Ord. (Presb.), May 19, '49; S.S., Marshall Co., Tenn., '49; S.S., Giles Co., Tenn., '49–'51; S.S., Rutherford & Wilson Cos., Tenn., '51–6; S.S., Greenville, Tenn., '57–'61; Tea. & S.S., Cherry Valley, Wilson Co., Tenn., '62–'73; S.S. Nashville, Tenn., '74——.

EDWARD BALDWIN BRUEN; b., Newark, N.J., July 17, 1823; U. Pa., '42; P.T.S., '43–5; U.T.S., '45–6; Ord. (Presb.), June 25, '48; S.S. & Pas., Phila., Pa., '46–'57; W.C., '57–9; S.S., do., '59–'61; W.C., do., '61–4; S.S., do., '64–8; W.C. & Ev., do., '68–'73; S.S., do., '74–6; Pas., do., '76——.

AUGUSTUS WOODRUFF COWLES; b., Geneva, N.Y., ..., 1810; U.C., '41; U.T.S., '43–6; Ord. (Presb.), Feb. 16, '47; Pas., Brockport, N.Y., '47–'56; Prest., Fem. Coll., Elmira, N.Y., '56——. D.D., Ing. U., '58.

*WILLIAM DEMPSEY; b., Amenia, N.Y., ..., 1819; U.T.S., '43–6;

Res. Lic., '46–7; Tea., W.R.C., '47–'50; Ord. (Presb.), ..., '52; S.S., Plymouth, O., '50; S.S., Chester, O., '51; Pas., do., '52–6; S.S., Middlebury, O., '57–'63; S.S., Medina, O., '63–4; Died, do., May 18, '64.

*Charles Currier Durgin; b., Gilmanton, N.H., Aug. 5, 1815; Gil. T.S., '43–4; U.T.S., '45–6; S.S., Somers, N.Y., '46; Res. Lic., '47–8; S.S., Allendale, R.I., '48–9; W.C., Gilmanton, N.H., '49–'51; S.S., Hillsboro Centre, N.H., '51–2; S.S., Epsom, N.H., '52; W.C., Manchester, N.H., '52–6; Died, do., Nov. 21, '56.

Amasa Stetson Freeman; b., Boston, Mass., Oct. 6, 1823; U.N.Y., '43; U.T.S., '43–6; Ord. (Presb.), Ap. 14, '47; S.S. & Pas., Haverstraw, N.Y., '46——.

*Matthew Davidson Gordon; b., Blantyre, Scotland, Dec. 10, 1812; M.C., '40; Ag., '40–2; U.T.S., '42–3; Tut., M.C., '43–4; U.T.S., '44–6; Ord. (Presb.), Oct. 7, '46; Ch. & Warden, Sing Sing, N.Y., '46–8; S.S., Cairo, N.Y., '48–9; Pas., Hollis, N.H., '49–'52; Prin., Groton, Mass., '51–2; Tea., Barhamville, S.C., '52–3; Died, Hoosick Falls, N.Y., Aug. 21, '53.

Alfred Hudson Guernsey; b., Brandon, Vt., May 12, 1824; O.I., '40; U.T.S., '41–3, '45–6; Lit. & Ed., N. York City, '46——.

Eurotas Parmelee Hastings; b., Clinton, N.Y., Ap. 17, 1821; H.C., '42; U.T.S., '43–6; Ord. (Cong.), Oct. 6, '46; F.M., Batticotta, Ceylon, '47–'57; F.M., Manepy, Ceylon, '58——.

Samuel James Jones; b., ..., .., ..., 18..; U.N.Y., '43; U.T.S., '43–6; Ord. (Presb.), ..., '52; S.S., Cincinnati, O., '46–'52; S.S., Oakhill, O., '52–4; S.S., Oakhill & Madison, O., '54–6; S.S., Bangor, Wis., '57–9; S.S., Wesleyville, Pa., '61–2; W.C., ..., .., ——.

Samuel Penniman Leeds; b., New-York City, Nov. 15, 1824; U.N.Y., '43; U.T.S., '43–6; Res. Lic., '46–7; Ord. (Cong.), June 18, '51; S.S. & Pas., Cuyahoga Falls, O., '49–'55; As. Min., Philadelphia, Pa., '55–7; Ev., N. York City, New-Haven, Ct., & Stamford, Ct., '57–'60; S.S. & Pas., Hanover, N.H., '60——. D.D., D.C., '70.

Charles Edmond Lindsley; b., Middlebury, Vt., Ap. 12, 1818; Ma. C., '40; L.T.S., '42–4; U.T.S., '45–6; Res. Lic., '46–8; Ord. (Presb.), June 28, '50; S.S. & Pas., New-Rochelle, N.Y., '49–'59; S.S. & Pas. (Cong.), Southport, Ct., '59–'69; S.S., New-Rochelle, N.Y., '69–'71; W.C., do., '71–3; Tea., Pelham, N.Y., '73——.

Joseph Hamilton Martin; b., Jeff. Co., Tenn., Aug. 11, 1825; U.E.T., '41; U.T.S., '43–6; Ord. (Presb.), Oct. 24, '48; Sea. Ch., N. Orleans, La., '46–8; Pas., Huntsville, Ala., '48–9; S.S., Madisonville, Tenn., '49–'51; S.S., Knoxville, Tenn., '51–'64; S.S., York Co., S.C., '64–7; S.S., Wytheville, Va., '67–9; S.S., Mossy Creek, and vicinity, Tenn., '69–'73; Pas., Atlanta, Ga., '73——.

Edwin R. McGregor; b., New-York City, ..., 18..; U.N.Y., '43; U.T.S., '43–6; Ord. (Presb.), ..., '48; S.S., Poughkeepsie, N.Y., '46–8; Pas., Wappinger's Falls, N.Y., '48–9; Ed. & Sec., Am. Jews' Soc., N. York City, '49–'54; S.S. (R.D.), do., '55; W.C., Steubenville, O., '56; Pas., New-Lisbon, O., '56–7; Deposed, '58.

*John Blackburn Meek; b., Knox Co., Tenn., Sep. 24, 1821; Mv. C., '45; U.T.S., '44-6; Ord. (Presb.), Ap. 27, '47; S.S. & Pas., Athens, Tenn., '46-8; Died, do., Oct. 18, '48.

David Clark Meeker; b., Newark, N.J., Feb. 21, 1819; U.N.Y., '43; U.T.S., '43-6; Ord. (Presb.), June 29, '47: S.S., Plymouth, Ind., '46-8; S.S., Lima, Ind., '48-'50; Pas., Fairton, N.J., '50-5; S.S., Darby, Pa., '55-7; S.S., N. Hardiston, N.J., '57-'60; Pas., West-Nantmeal, Pa., '60-8; Pas., Dauphin, Pa., '68——.

Jacob Harris Patton; b., Fayette Co., Pa., ..., 1812; Jef. C., '39; U.T.S., '43-6; Tea., N. York City, '46——.

*John Peck; b., Greenwich, Ct., July 30, 1814; W.R.C., '42; W.R.T.S., '43-5; U.T.S., '45-6; Ord. (Presb.), Jan. 14, '48; H.M., Greenville, Ind., '46-'51; H.M., Momence & Rockville, Ill., '52-5; S.S., Marathon, N.Y., '56-'69; S.S., Traverse des Sioux, Minn., '60-5; Ag., Paterson, N.J., '66-8; Died, do., Nov. 24, '68.

*William Lyman Richards; b., Lahaina, Maui, S.I., Dec. 3, 1823; Jef. C., '41; Tea., Woodington, Va., '41-2; U.T.S., '43-6; Res. Lic., '46-7; Ord. (Presb.), Oct. 14, '47; F.M., Fuh Chau, China, '48-'51; Died, at sea, near St. Helena, So. Atl., June 5, '51.

Collingwood Rutherford; b., New Castle, Eng., Aug. 21, 1817; U.T.S., '43-6; Ord. (M.E.), May 21, '55; Pas., Princeton, N.J., '47-8; Pas., Rockaway, N.J., '48-9; Tea., Hempstead (L.I.), N.Y., '49-'53; Pas., Southampton (L.I.), N.Y., '53-5; Pas., New-Hartford, Ct., '55-6; Pas., E. Granby, Ct., '56-8; Pas., W. Suffield, Ct., '58-9; Pas., Haddam, Ct., '59-'60; Pas., Westbrook, Ct., '60-1; Tea., Fordham, N.Y., '61-8; Agr., ..., Mo., '68-'70; Prin., ..., Io., '70-2; Prin., N. York City, '72——.

Charles Noyes Todd; b., Rowley, Mass., Oct. 25, 1812; A.C., '39; Tea., Baltimore, Md., '39-'40; U.T.S., '41-3, '45-6; Tea., N. York City, '40-4; Res. Lic., And.T.S., '46-7; Tea. & S.S., Rowley, Mass., '47-9; Prin., Honesdale, Pa., '49-'54; Prin., Indianapolis, Ind., '54-'61; Trade, do., '63——.

David Torrey; b., Bethany, Pa., Nov. 13, 1818; A.C., '43; And.T.S., '43-4; U.T.S., '44-6; Tut., A.C., '46-7; Ord. (Presb.), Jan. 29, '50; Pas., Delhi, N.Y., '49-'60; Pas., Ithaca, N.Y., '60-4; P.E., Ann Arbor, Mich., '65-6; W.C., Honesdale, Pa., '66-9; Pas., Cazenovia, N.Y., '69——. D.D., H.C., '62.

George Miller Tuthill; b., Wading River (L.I.), N.Y., Oct. 31, 1818; A.C., '39; U.T.S., '43-6; Ord. (Presb.), Ap. 22, '47; S.S., St. Louis, Mo., '47-9; S.S., Monticello, Ill., '49-'51; S.S., Kalamazoo, Mich., '51; Pas. (Cong.), St. Clair, Mich., '51-8; S.S., Pontiac, Mich., '58-'65; Pas., Ashtabula, O., '65-7; S.S., St. John's, Mich., '67-'71; Dis. Supt., A.B.S., Kalamazoo, Mich., '71——.

William Henry Willcox; b., New-York City, Jan. 28, 1821; U.N.Y., '43; U.T.S., '43-6; Res. Lic., '46-7; Ord. (Cong.), Mar. 5, '51; Pas., Kennebunk, Me., '52-7; Pas., Reading, Mass., '57——. 24.

John Guest Atterbury; b., Baltimore, Md., Feb. 7, 1811; Y.C., '31; U.T.S., '43-4; Ord. (Presb.), July 23, '45; Pas., Flint, Mich., '45-'51; Pas., New-Albany, Ind., '51-'66; Sec., Presb. Ed. Com., N. York City, '68-'70; Pas., Detroit, Mich., '72-4; W.C., do., '74——. D.D., Ma. C., '63.

William Barrows; b., New-Braintree, Mass., Sep. 19, 1815; A.C., '40; U.T.S., '43-5; Ord. (Cong.), Sep. 4, '45; Pas., Norton, Mass, '45-'50; Pas., Grantville, Mass., '50-5; Pas., Reading, Mass., '56-'69; Sec., Cong. Pub. Soc., Boston, Mass., '69-'73; Sec., Mass. H.M. Soc., do., '73——. D.D., A.C., '67.

William Pratt Breed; b., New-York City, ..., 1816; U.N.Y., '43; U.T.S., '43-4; P.T.S., '44-6; Ord. (Presb.), Dec. 16, '47; Pas., Steubenville, O., '47-'56; Pas., Philadelphia, Pa., '56——. D.D., U.N.Y., '64.

*James Jennison Giles; b., Gloversville, N.Y., Jan. 9, 1816; U.C., '43; U.T.S., '43-4; P.T.S., '44-6; Died, Kingsboro, N.Y., Oct. 10, '46.

Henry Martyn Goodwin; b., Hartford, Ct., June 8, 1820; Y.C., '40; U.T.S., '43-5; N.H.T.S., '45-6; Ord. (Cong.), Feb. 19, '51; Pas., Rockford, Ill., '50-'72; W.C., Olivet, Mich., '73——.

Edwin Ruthven Hodgman; b., Camden, Me., Oct. 21, 1819; D.C., '43; And.T.S., '43-4; U.T.S., '44-5; And.T.S., '45-6; Ord. (Cong.), May 17, '49; S.S., Belmont, Me., '46-7; S.S., Orford East, N.H., '48-'50; Pas., Lunenburgh, Mass., '52-6; Pas., Lynnfield Centre, Mass., '56-8; W.C., Townsend, Mass., '58-9; S.S., Westford, Mass., '59-'64; Ev., do., '65-'75; S.S., do., (Forge Village), '75——.

*John Smith Kelley; b., Middletown, Ct., June 26, 1821; Y.C., '40; Tea., Haddam, Ct., '40-1; Tut., W.U., '41-3; U.T.S., '43-4; Died, N. York City, Dec. 29, '44.

Charles King McHarg; b., Albany, N.Y., March 18, 1823; U.C., '42; U.T.S., '43-5; N.H.T.S., '45-6; Ord. (Presb.), Feb. 27, '49; S.S., Clarkson, N.Y., '46-8; Pas., Cooperstown, N.Y., '48-'50; Pas., Syracuse, N.Y., '50-1; S.S., Fly Creek, N.Y., '52-4; Pas., Irvington, N.Y., '54-'64; Pas., Cooperstown, N.Y., '65-'70; S.S., Fly Creek, N.Y., '71-3, '74——.

William H. Mathews; b., Powhatan Co., Va., ..., 1816; U.T.S., '44-5; Ord. (Presb.), ..., '47; H.M., Franklin Co., Va., '45-7; S.S. & Pas., Leesville & Otter, Va., '47—— ..; Pas., Pittsylvania C.H., Va., .. ——.

Charles Carroll Parker; b., Underhill, Vt., Sept. 26, 1814; U.Vt., '41; U.T.S., '43-4; Tea., Burlington, Vt., '44-7; Ord. (Cong.), Oct. 4, '48; Pas., Tinmouth, Vt., '48-'54; S.S. & Pas., Waterbury, Vt., '54-'67; S.S., Buxton Centre, Me., '67-8; Pas., Gorham, Me., '68-'71; Pas. (Presb.), Parsippany, N.J., '72——. D.D., U.Vt., '69.

Nehemiah Pruden Pierce; b., Enfield, Ct., Aug. 28, 1817; A.C., '42; U.T.S., '43-5; Ord. (Presb.), Ap. 30, '46; S.S., Whippany, N.J., '45-'50; Pas. (R.D.), Brooklyn, N.Y., '51-'74; W.C. & Inv., do., '74——. D.D., R.C., '71.

*Solomon Dwight Pitkin; b., Amherst, Mass., June 20, 1822; A.C., '43; U.T.S., '43-5; N.H.T.S., '45-6; Ord. (Presb.), ..., '47; S.S., New-

Diggings & Benton, Wis., '47-8 ; S.S. & Pas., Battle Creek, Mich., '49-'57 ; Trade, Kansas City, Mo., '57-8 ; Died, Woodbridge, N.J., Sep. 30, '58.

LUDLOW DAY POTTER ; b., New-Providence, N.J., Jan. 3, 1823 ; C.N.J., '41 ; U.T.S., '43-4 ; P.T.S., '44-6 ; Ord. (Presb.), Nov. 12, '48 ; S.S., Brookville, Ind., '47-'50 ; Pas., Brookville & Matamora, Ind., '50-3 ; Prin., Dunlapsville, Ind., '53-5 ; Prof. Gl. C., Glendale, O., '56-'65 ; Prest., do., '65——. D.D., Han. C., '73.

FRANCIS GREENLEAF PRATT ; b., Middleboro, Mass., Jan. 30, 1821 ; A.C., '40 ; U.T.S., '43-5 ; And.T.S., '45-6 ; Ord. (Cong.), Oct. 19, '49 ; Pas., S. Malden, Mass., '49-'57 ; S.S., Peacedale, R.I., '60-1. W.C., E. Middleboro, Mass., '62——.

ADDISON VAN COURT SCHENCK ; b., New-Brunswick, N. J., ..., 1820 ; C.N.J., '43 ; U.T.S., '43-4 ; P.T.S., '44-6 ; Ord. (Presb.), June 28, '50 ; S.S. & Pas., Lexington, Mo., '49-'54 ; Tea., do., '54-6 ; Pas., St. Joseph, Mo., '56-8 ; S.S., St. Charles, Mo., '58-'60 ; Prest. Fem. Coll., do., '60-3 ; Prof. Wtm. C., Fulton, Mo., '63-6 ; Pas., Bedford, Pa., '66-8 ; Pas., Philadelphia, Pa., '68——.

*CORTLANDT WILLKINS SHATTUCK ; b., Groton, Mass., Sept. 23, 1816 ; D.C., '40 ; Tea., at South, '40-3 ; U.T.S., '43-6 ; And.T.S., '46 ; S.S., Charlestown, Mass., '46 ; Died, Groton, Mass., Oct. 13, '47.

ANDREW J. STEVENSON ; b., ..., Scotland, ..., 1816 ; Ep.T.S., '43-4 ; U.T.S., '44-5. Returned to Scotland.

*JOHN ADAM WALKER ; b., Lenox, Mass., Jan. 7, 1821 ; W.C., '40 ; And.T.S., '42-3 ; U.T.S., '43-4 ; Tut., W.C., '44-5 ; U.T.S., '45-6 ; Law, Lenox, Mass., '49-'53 ; Do., Pittsfield, Mass., '53-'64 ; Died, do., May 24, '64. 18.

1847.

ROBERT AIKMAN ; b., New-York City, June 29, 1816 ; Y.C., '43 ; U.T.S., '44-7 ; Ord. (Cong.), Nov. 11, '47 ; S.S., Washingtonville, R.I., '47-'50 ; As. Pas. (Presb.), Troy, N.Y., '50-2 ; Pas., Elizabeth, N.J., '52-'69 ; Pas., Madison, N.J., '69——. D.D., C.N.J., '75.

NATHAN S. ALLER ; b., Clinton, N.J., July 22, 1819 ; U.T.S., '44-7 ; Ord. (Presb.), ..., '48 ; S.S., Jeffersonville, Pa., '47-'50 ; Pas. (G.R.), Pleasantville, Pa., '50-'70 ; Pas. (Presb.), Mount Pleasant, N.J., '70——.

ROBERT C. ANDERSON ; b., Prince Edward Co., Va., ..., 1823 ; H.S.C., '43 ; U.T.S., '44-7 ; Ord. (Presb.), ..., '52 ; S.S., Appomattox, Va., '47-'51 ; S.S., Irisburgh, Va., '51—— .. ; S.S., Martinsville, Va., .. ——.

MARSHALL BULLARD ANGIER ; b., Southborough, Mass., Mar. 22, 1819 ; Y.C., '44 ; U.T.S., '44-7 ; Res. Lic., P.T.S., '48 ; Ord. (Cong.), June 8, '53 ; S.S., Worcester, Mass., '48 ; S.S., Orange, Mass., '48-'51 ; S.S. & Pas., Hopkinton, N.H., '51-'60 ; Pas., Dorchester, Mass., '60-3 ; Pas., Sturbridge, Mass., '63-8 ; Pas., Haydenville, Mass., '68-'74 ; Pas., Ipswich, Mass., '74——.

GEORGE BOWEN ; b., Middlebury, Vt., Ap. 30, 1816 ; U.T.S., '44-7 ; Ord. (Presb.), July 4, '47 ; F.M., Bombay, India, '47——.

Edwin Adolphus Bulkley; b., Charleston, S.C., Jan. 25, 1826; Y.C., '44; U.T.S., '44–7; Ord. (Presb.), Oct. 11, '47; Pas. (Cong.), Geneva, N.Y., '47–'50; Pas., Groton, Mass., '50–'64; Pas. (Presb.), Plattsburgh, N.Y., '64——. D.D., U.Vt., '68.

Charles Whittlesey Camp; b., New-Preston, Ct., Oct. 7, 1821; Y.C., '44; U.T.S., '44–7; Ord. (Cong.), Jan. 28, '48; S.S., Genesee & Palmyra, Wis., '47–8; S.S., Genesee, Wis., '48–'53; Pas., Sheboygan, Wis., '53–'64; Pas., Fond du Lac, Wis, '64–8; Pas., Waukesha, Wis., '68——.

*Joseph Gallup Cochran; b., Springville, N.Y., Feb. 5, 1817; A.C., '42; U.T.S., '44–7; Ord. (Presb.), June 10, '47; F.M., Seir, Persia, '47–'65; U. States, '65–7; F.M., Seir, Persia, '67–'71; Died, Oroomiah, do., Nov. 2, '71.

James Geddes Craighead; b., New-Carlisle, Pa., March 5, 1823; Del.C., '44; U.T.S., '44–7; Ord. (Presb.), Oct. 11, '47; S.S., Watertown, Wis., '47–9; Pas., Northumberland, Pa., '50–4; W.C., N. York City, '54–5; P.E., Ovid, N.Y., '55; Ed., N. York City, '56–'70; Inv. & Travelling, '70–6; Sec., Presb. His. Soc., Philadelphia, Pa., '76——. D.D., Mv.C., '71.

*Seneca Cummings; b., Antrim, N.H., May 16, 1817; D.C., '44; L.T.S., '44–6; U.T.S., '46–7; Ord. (Cong.), Sept. 30, '47; F.M.. Fuh Chau, China, '48–'55; U. States, '55–6; Died, New-Ipswich, N.H., Aug. 12, '56.

Alfred Henry Dashiell; b., Elk Ridge, Md., Jan. 9, 1824; Del. C., '43; U.T.S., '45–7; Ord. (Presb.), Dec. 20, '47; S.S., Rock Hill, Mo., '47–9; W.C., N. York City, '49–'50; Pas. (Cong.), Stockbridge, Mass., '50–'60; S.S., do. (Curtisville), '60–3; Ch., U. S. Army, '63–5; Pas. (Presb.), Bricksburgh, N.J., '67——.

*Halsey Dunning; b., Wantage, N.J., July 3, 1818; U.N.Y., '42; U.T.S., '44–7; Ord. (Presb.), Oct. 17, '47; Ch., Sing-Sing, N.Y., '47; S.S., Richmond, Va., '48–'54; Pas., Baltimore, Md., '54–'69; Died, do., Jan. 11, '69.

*William R. Durnett; b., Montreal, C.W., Jan. 15, 1817; U.T.S., '44–7; Ord. (Presb.), Oct. 13, '47; Pas., Delaware City, Del., '47–'51; S.S., Cedarville, N.J., '51–2; Pas., Philadelphia, Pa., '52–4; Died, Craneville, N.J., Sep. 10, '54.

Samuel Goodrich Dwight; b., Northampton, Mass., Jan. 18, 1815; U.T.S., '44–7; Ord. (Presb.), Oct. 17, '47; F.M. & Tea., Molokai, S. Islds., '47——.

*Joshua Edwards Ford; b., Ogdensburgh, N.Y., Aug. 3, 1825; W.C., '44; U.T.S., '44–7; Ord. (Presb.), Sept. 26, '47; F.M., Aleppo, Syria, '48–'54; F.M., Beirut, Syria, '55–8; F.M., Sidon, Syria, '58–'65; U. States, '65–6; Died, Geneseo, Ill., Ap. 3, '66.

Amzi Whitfield Freeman; b., South-Orange, N.J., June 10, 1821; C.N.J., '43; U.T.S., '44–7; Ord. (Presb.), Sep. 26, '49; S.S. & Pas., Covington, Ind., '47–'52; S.S., Fort Wayne, Ind., '52–4; S.S. & Pas., Aurora, Ind., '54——.

Robert Gray; b., Richmond, Va., June 6, 1819; U.T.S., '44–7; Ord. (Presb.), Aug. 25, '48; S.S., Franklin Co., Va., '47–'57; Pas., Woodstock, Va.,

'57-9; W.C., do., '59-'66; Pas., New-Dublin, Va., '66-'72; W.C., do., '72-3; S.S., Spring Hill, Tenn., '73——.

*JAMES MONROE KIMBALL; b., Eastport, Me., Mar. 19, 1822; U.N.Y., '44; U.T.S., '44-7; Ord. (Presb.), Ap. 9, '48; Pas. Portsmouth, Va., '47-9; Died, Washington, D.C., Mar. 2, '49.

*HENRY KINNEY; b., Amenia, N.Y., Oct. 1, 1816; Y.C., '44; U.T.S., '44-7; Ord. (Presb.), Sep. 6, '47; F.M., Hawaii, S. Islds., '47-'54; Died, Sonora, Cal., Sep. 24, '54.

JAMES MCGREADY MCLEAN; b., Green Co., Ala., Feb. 13, 1821; Mi. C., '45; U.T.S., '44-6, '46-7; Ord. (Presb.), July 11, '48; S.S., Marion, Miss., '47-8; S.S., Lexington, Miss., '48-'51; S.S., Greenwood, Miss., '51-3; S.S. & Pas., Mobile, Ala., '53-'63; Tea. & Ev., Fayetteville, Ala., '63-9; Pas., Oxford, Ala., '69——.

HENRY MATHEWS; b., Bloomsburgh, Md., Nov. 25, 1824; U.T.S., '44-7; Ord. (Presb.), '48; S.S., Ann Arundel Co., Md., '47-8; Pas., Woodstock, Md., '48-'51; W.C., Baltimore, Md., '51-2; Pas., Shepherdstown, Va., '53-'65; Pas., Elkton, Md., '65-'71; Pas., Randallstown, Md., '72-4; Tea., Mathews' Store, Md., '74-6; W.C., Baltimore, Md., '76——.

CYRUS TAGGART MILLS; b., Paris, N.Y., May 4, 1819; W.C., '44; U.T.S., '44-7; Ord. (Presb.), Feb. 2, '48; F.M., Batticotta, Ceylon, India, '49-'55; S.S., Berkshire, N.Y., '56-8; Prest., Oahu Coll., S. Islds., '60-4; W.C., Ware, Mass., '64-5; Ag., A.B.C.F.M., San Francisco, Cal., '65; Prin., Brooklyn, Cal., '65——. D.D., W.C., '70.

*WILLIAM OLMSTEAD; b., Colchester, Ct., Jan. 5, 1821; E.W.T.S., '44-5; U.T.S., '45-7; Ord. (Cong.), Ap. 11, '49; S.S., Brooklyn, N.Y., '47-8; S.S., Mason Village, N.H., '48-'51; Died, Colchester, Ct., June 6, '51.

HENRY ELIJAH PARKER; b., Keene, N.H., Ap. 17, 1821; D.C., '41; Tut., D.C., '43-4; U.T.S., '44-7; Ord. (Cong.), Mar. 13, '49; S.S., Eastport, Me., '47-'50; S.S. & Pas., Concord, N.H., '50-'66; Prof., D.C., Hanover, N.H., '66——. Ch., U.S.Army, '61-3.

*THOMAS H. PARISH; b., Gallatin, Tenn., Feb. 16, 1826; U.T.S., '44-7; Ord. (Presb.), ..., '47; S.S., Gallatin, Tenn., '47-9; Died, do., ..., '49.

BENJAMIN F. PETERS; b., Richmond, Va., ..., 1818; U.T.S., '44-7; Ord. (Presb.), ..., '48; S.S., Eastville, Va., '47-8; S.S., Richmond, Va., '48-'51; S.S., Mindon, La., '52-4; S.S., Red Bluff, La., '54-8; S.S., Reachie, La., '58-9; H.M., Gordo, Ala., '60——..; W.C., Fayetteville, Ala., ..——.

JOHN SAILOR; b., Carlisle, Pa., Nov. 2, 1823; L.T.S., '44-5; U.T.S., '45-7; Ord. (Presb.), June 28, '48; S.S., Nelson, Pa., '47-9; S.S., Campbell, N.Y., '49-'50; Pas., Warren, Pa., '50-5; Pas., Mich. City, Ind., '55-'63; Ch., State Prison, do., '61-3; Pas. (Cong.), Niles, Mich., '63-5; Pas. (Presb.), Allegan, Mich., '65-'75; Pas. (Cong.), do., '75——.

MATSON MEIER SMITH; b., New-York City, Ap. 4, 1826; C.C., '43; U.T.S., '44-7; Ord. (Presb.), Oct. 23, '49; Pas., Ovid, N.Y., '49-'50; Pas. (Cong.), Brookline, Mass., '51-9; Pas., Bridgeport, Ct., '59-'65; Rec. (Ep.), Newark,

N.J., '66–'71; Rec., Hartford, Ct., '72–6; Prof., Ep. Div. School, Philadelphia, Pa., '76——. D.D., C.C., '63.

GEORGE IRA TAYLOR; b., Northumberland, N.Y., Aug. 25, 1813; U.C., '43; U.T.S., '44–7; Ord. (Presb.), Oct. .., '49; S.S., Schroon & W. Moriah, N.Y., '48–9; Pas., Kingsbury, N.Y., '49–'51; Pas., Charlton, N.Y., '51–4; S.S., Winchester, Miss., '54–6; S.S., Lawrenceburgh, Ind., '56–'65; S.S., Middletown, O., '65–8; Pas., Malta, N.Y., '68–'73; Pas. (R.D.), Watervliet, N.Y., '73——.

TOWNSEND ELIJAH TAYLOR; b., La Grange, N.Y., July 18, 1818; M.C., '44; U.T.S., '44–7; Ord. (Presb.), Oct. .., '47; Sea. Ch., Lahaina, S. Islds., '47–'52; Pas., Honolulu, S. Islds., '53–5; W.C., do., '55–7; Sea. Ch., Kailua, S. Islds., '58–9; S.S., Honolulu, S. Islds., '59–'60; S.S., Columbia, Cal., '60–2; S.S., Petaluma, Cal., '62–5; D. Sec., P.C.H.M., San Francisco, Cal., '65——.

*GEORGE UHLER; b., Carlisle, Pa., Aug. 7, 1813; U.N.Y., '44; U.T.S., '44–7; Ord. (Presb.), Oct. 17, '47; S.S., Bloomingdale, N.Y., '47–8; S.S., Centerville, R.I., '48–9; Pas. (Cong.), Greenville, R.I., '49–'52; S.S., Harrisville, R.I., '52–4; Pas., Curtisville, Mass., '55–'64; W.C., do., '64–9; Died, ...

THOMAS ALLEN WEED; b., North-Stamford, Ct., Oct. 15, 1817; O.C., '43; U.T.S., '44–7; Ord. (Presb.), June 8, '48; Pas., Mexico, N.Y., '47–'70; S.S. & Pas., Wheatland, N.Y., '70——.

WILLIAM WOOD; b., Henniker, N.H., Dec. 2, 1818; D.C., '42; Tea., S. Weare, N.H., '42; Tea., Peru, N.Y., '43; U.T.S., '44–7; Ord. (Cong.), July 8, '47; F.M., Satara, Ind., '47–'62; U. States, '62–4; F.M., Satara, Ind., '64–'74.

*JOHN J. ZIELIE; b., Schoharie, N.Y., Sep. 4, 1819; U.C., '44; U.T.S., '44–7; Died, Schoharie, N.Y., Sept. .., '47.

JOHN HENRY ZIVLEY; b., Shelbyville, Tenn., Oct. 29, 1824; L.T.S., '44–5; U.T.S., '45–7; Ord. (Presb.), Ap. .., '48; S.S., Midway, Ky., '47–9; Pas., Huntsville, Ala., '49–'51; S.S., Austin, Texas, '51–3; Ev., Texas, '53——. 35.

---

*ENOCH HASKIN CASWELL; b., Middletown, Vt., March 25, 1818; M.C., '43; Tea., Bridport, Vt., '43–4; And.T.S., '44–5; U.T.S., '45–6; And.T.S., '46–7; Ord. (Cong.), June 28, '48; Pas., Salisbury, N.H., '48–9; S.S., Stockbridge, Vt., '49–'50; S.S., Barnet, Vt., '51–4; Tea., Bristol, N.H., '56; S.S., Loudon, N.H., '56–7; S.S., Hookset, N.H., '58–'60; S.S., Bennington, N.H., '61–3; Died, do., Nov. 11, '63.

*SAMUEL MILLS CONANT; b., Brandon, Vt., Nov. 22, 1820; M.C., '44; U.T.S., '44–5; Tea., Brooklyn, N.Y., '46–8; Law, Brandon, Vt., '49–'55; Died, do., Sep. 25, '55.

JESSE WOOD DENISON; b., Berne, N.Y., Ap. 9, 1818; U.C., '44; U.T.S., '44–5; N.W.B.T.S., '45–6; Ord. (Bap.), June 17, '46; Pas., Up. Alton, Ill., '46–7; Pas., Rock Island, Ill., '47–'51; Tea., do., '51–3; Pas., Brimfield, Ill., '53–4; Tea., Carrollton & Keokuk, Ill., '54–5; Pas., Denison, Io., '56–'63; Mem. of Io. Leg., '59–'61; Trade, Denison, Io., '61——.

WALTER PRICE DOE; b., Wilton, N.Y., Mar. 30, 1813; U.T.S., '44–6; And.T.S., '46–7; Ord. (Cong.), Nov. 10, '47; S.S., Greenville, R.I., '47–9; S.S. (R.D.), Gansevoort (L.I.), N.Y., '51–3; S.S. (Cong.), Mendon, Mass., '54–5; S.S., W. Stockbridge, Mass., '55–6; W.C., Providence, R.I., '56; S.S., Moreau, N.Y., '56–7; S.S., Rehoboth, Mass., '57–9; W.C., Providence, R.I., N. York City, & Saratoga, N.Y., '59——. Address, Providence, R.I.

DAVID AMBLER HOLBROOK; b., Whitesboro, N.Y., Jan. 8, 1820; H.C., '44; U.T.S., '44–6; Tut., H.C., '46–'50; Tea., Brooklyn, N.Y., '50–2; Tea., Clinton, N.Y., '52–'65; Tea., Adams, N.Y., '65; Tea., Sing Sing, N.Y., '66——. Ph.D., H.C., '71.

*GEORGE WASHINGTON KIMBALL; b., Eastport, Me., March 19, 1822; U.N.Y., '44; U.T.S., '44–6; U.S. Consul, St. Helena, S. Atl., '48–'60; Died, do., June 19, '60.

JOSEPH RICH MANN; b., New-York City, Jan. 17, 1822; C.C., '39; U.T.S., '44–5; P.T.S., '45–7; Ord. (Presb.), Oct. 22, '48; Pas., N. York City, '48–'58; S.S., do., '59–'61; Pas., Princeton, N.J., '61–4; W.C., do., '64–7; Pas., Kingston, N.J., '67–'73; W.C., Princeton, N.J., '73——. D.D., C.N.J., '62.

*SAMUEL DEXTER MARSH; b., Ware, Mass., Nov. 28, 1817; Y.C., '44 U.T.S., '44–6; N.H.T.S., '46–7; Ord. (Cong.), Sep. 9, '47; F.M., Umlazi, S. Af., '48–'53; Died, Itafamasi, S. Af., Dec. 11, '53.

*JOHN HOAR MORSE; b., Andover, Vt., ..., 1821; U.Vt., '42; U.T.S., '44; Died, N. York City, Nov. 19, '44.

EDWARD WARREN OSGOOD; b., Springfield, Mass., ..., 1823; A.C., '44; U.T.S., '44–5; Banker, San Francisco, Cal., ..——..; .., Jamaica Plains, Mass., ..——..; .., Germany, ..——.

ROYAL PARKINSON; b., Columbia, N.H., Nov. 8, 1815; D.C., '42; U.T.S., '44–6; And.T.S., '46–7; Ord. (Cong.), Oct. 18, '48; S.S. & Pas., Cape Elizth., Me., '47–'51; S.S., Windham, Vt., '52–5; Pas., W. Falmouth, Me., '55–7; S.S., Sandwich, N.H., '58–'61; S.S. & Pas., Hartford, Vt., '61–3; S.S., Randolph, Vt., '63–4; Ch., U. S. Army, '64–5; S.S., N. Brookfield, Vt., '65–6; S.S., Milton, Vt., '66–9; S.S., Temple, N.H., '70–2; W.C., Washington, D.C., '72——.

*WILLIAM STEDMAN PECK; b., Greensboro', Ala., Dec. 29, 1822; Y.C., '43; U.T.S., '44–6; Ord. (Presb.), June 25, '48; Pas., Livingston, Ala., '48–9; Died, Rome, Ga., Sep. 10, '49.

*MARTIN SHAW PIXLEY; b., Plainfield, Mass., June 26, 1820; W.C., '44; U.T.S., '44–6; Tea., Del. C., '46–7; Died, Plainfield, Mass., Sep. 29, '48.

GERRIT LANSING ROOF; b., Canajoharie, N.Y., Sep. 8, 1811; U.C., '31; Law, '33–'45; U.T.S., '45; Ord. (R.D.), Dec. 1, '46; Pas., Glen & Auriesville, N.Y., '46–'50; Pas., Port Jackson, N.Y., '50–5; Pas., W. Troy, N.Y., '54–'65; Pas. (Presb.), Lowville, N.Y., '65——.

*HOHANNES DER SAHAGYAN; b., ..., Turkey, ..., 1808; U.T.S., '44–5; Ord. (Cong.), May 16, '49; Pas., Ada Bazar, Turkey, '49; Pas., Scutari, Turkey, ..——..; Pas., Nicomedia, Turkey, ..——'65; Died, do., Feb. .., '65.

15.

1848.

ANDREW ABRAHAM; b., Florida, N.Y., Oct. 12, 1818; U.C., '44; U.T.S., '45–8; Ord. (Presb.), Oct. 13, '48; F.M., Mapumulo, S. Af., '49–'74; U. States, '74–5; F.M., Mapumulo, S. Af., '75——.

CHARLES MOODY ATKINSON; b., Newburyport, Mass., June 17, 1819; A.C., '44; U.T.S., '45–8; Ord. (Presb.), Feb. .., '49; S.S., Grenada, Miss., '48–9; S.S., Carrollton, Miss., '49–'52; Syn. Ag., ..., Miss., '52; S.S., Canton, Miss., '53–'68; S.S., Concord, Madison Co., Miss., '68–'71; S.S., Vaiden, Miss., '71–4; S.S., Durant, Miss., '74——. D.D., Kg. C., '75.

JACOB BEST; b., Livingston, N.Y., Feb. 3, 1823; W.C., '44; U.T.S., '45–8; Ord. (Presb.), Dec. 6, '48; F.M., Gaboon, W. Af., '49–'61; S.S., Prompton & Waymart, Pa., '64–'75; S.S., Brooklyn, Pa., '75——.

JOHN D. CARNES; b., New-York City, ..., 1816; U.T.S., '45–8; Ord. (Cong.), ..., '50; S.S., Ridgefield & Napoleon, O., '48–9; S S., Algonac, Mich., '50——.

*GEORGE CLARK; b., Lenox, Mass., Ap. 24, 1822; W.C., '43; Tea., Tallahassee, Fla., '43–5; U.T.S., '45–8; Ord. (Presb.), '49; Pas., St. Louis, Mo., '48–9; Tea., Tallahassee, Fla., '49–'50; Died, do., Dec. 24, '50.

OLIVER CRANE; b., West-Bloomfield, N.J., July 12, 1822; Y.C., '45; And.T.S., '45–7; U.T.S., '47–8; Ord. (Presb.), June 18, '48; F.M., Broosa, Turkey, '49–'50; F.M., Aintab, Syria, '51–3; Pas., Huron, N.Y., '54–7; Pas., Waverly, N.Y., '57–'60; F.M., Adrianople, Turkey, '60–3; Pas., Carbondale, Pa., '64–'70; F.M., Aintab, Turkey, '70–4; W.C., Morristown, N.J., '74——. M.D., Ec. Med. Coll., N.Y., '67.

*JAMES PERRINE CUTLER; b., Morristown, N.J., Oct. .., 1823; Y.C., '43; Law Student, '44; U.T.S., '45–8; Insane Asylum, Trenton, N.J., '49–'51; Died, do., Sep. 25, '51.

*RICHARD SALTER STORRS DICKINSON; b., Longmeadow, Mass., Ap. 3, 1824; A.C., '44; Aub.T.S., '45–7; U.T.S., '47–8; Ord. (Presb.), March 28, '49; Pas., N. York City, '49–'51; S.S., Phila., Pa., '53–5; Ch., A. & F.C.U., Paris, France, '56; Died, Edinburgh, Scotland, Aug. 28, '56.

ALEXANDER BURRITT DILLEY; b., Hanover, Pa., March 17, 1823; W.C., '43; U.T.S., '43–4, '45–8; Ord. (Cong), ..., '49; Pas., Benton's Port, Io., '49–'51; S.S., Bangor, N.Y., '52–'64; Ch., U.S. Army, '64–5; S.S., Rodman, N.Y., '66–'72; W.C., Watertown, N.Y., '73–5; S.S., Greene, N.Y., '76——.

*EDWARD MILLS DODD; b., Bloomfield, N.J., June 22, 1824; C.N.J., '44; Tea., '44–5; U.T.S., '45–8; Ord. (Presb.), June .., '48; F.M., Salonica, Turkey, '49–'52; U. States, '52–5; F.M., Smyrna, Asia, '55–'63; F.M., Marsovan, Asia, '63–5; Died, do., Aug. 19, '65.

JOHN WALDO DOUGLAS; b., Trenton, N.Y., Ap. 4, 1818; Y.C., '40; U.T.S., '44–6, '47–8; Ord. (Presb.), Nov. 29, '48; S.S., San Francisco, Cal., '48–9; S.S., San José, Cal., '49–'50; H.M., Los Angeles, Cal., '51–2; Ed., San Francisco, Cal., '52–5; W.C., San Francisco, Cal., '56–7; W.C., Ithaca, N.Y., '58–'60; W.C., Trenton, N.Y., '61——

CHARLES ALGERNON DOWNS; b., South-Norwalk, Ct., May 21, 1823; U.N.Y., '45; U.T.S., '45–8; Ord. (Cong.), May 1, '49; Pas., Lebanon, N.H., '49–'73; W.C., do., '73——.

JOHN WELCH DULLES; b., Philadelphia, Pa., Nov. 4, 1823; Y.C., '44; U.T.S., '45–8; Ord. (Presb.), Oct. 2, '48; F.M., Madras, India, '48–'53; Sec., A.S.S.U., Philadelphia, Pa., '53–7; Sec., P.P.C., do., '57–'70; Ed. Sec., P.B. Pub., do., '70——. D.D., C.N.J., '72.

ISRAEL EDSON DWINELL; b., Calais, Vt., Oct. 24, 1820; U.Vt., '43; U.T.S., '45–8; Ord. (Cong.), Nov. 22, '49; S.S., Rock Island, Ill., '48–9; S.S. & C. Pas., Salem, Mass., '49–'63; S.S. & Pas., Sacramento, Cal., '63——. D.D., U.Vt., '64.

CORNELIUS EARLE; b., New-York City, July 11, 1823; U.N.Y., '45; U.T.S., '45–8; Ord. (Presb.), Dec. 7, '48; Pas., Unionville, Pa., '48–'52; Pas., Catasaqua, Pa., '53——.

LUTHER CALVIN HALLOCK; b., Smithtown (L.I.), N.Y., May 23, 1818; L.T.S., '45–6; U.T.S., '46–8; Ord. (Cong.), Dec. 8, '48; S.S., Wading River (L.I.), N.Y., '48–'52; C.M., Charleston, S.C., '52–3; H.M., St. John's Isld., S.C., '54–5; S.S., Comac (L.I.), N.Y., '56–7; S.S., New-Village (L.I.), N.Y., '57–8; Inv., Wading River (L.I.), N.Y., '58–'63; Inv., Miller's Place (L.I.), N.Y., '63–5; Inv., Rocky Point (L.I.), N.Y., '66——.

RUFUS KING; b., Freehold, N.Y., ..., 1821; U.C., '44; U.T.S., '45–8; Ord. (Cong.), ..., '50; Pas., Amesbury, Mass., '50–3; Pas. (Presb.), Jamestown, N.Y., '55–'60; Tea., do., '60——,

SAMUEL YOUNG LUM; b., New-Providence, N.J., May 6, 1821; U.T.S., '45–8; Ord. (Cong.), Nov. 19, '51; S.S., Newark, N.J., '48–9; Travel in Cal., '49–'50; Pas., S. Middletown, N.Y., '51–4; S.S., Lawrence, Kansas, '54–7; Ag., A.H.M.S., Kansas, '57–8; W.C., Lawrence, Kansas, '59–'61; S.S., Rehoboth, Mass., '62–4; S.S., Madison, N.Y., '64–5; S.S., Groton, N.Y., '65–7; S.S., Lodi, N.J., '67–9; Supt, A.B.S., Lawrence, Kan., '69–'75; S.S., Mannsville, N.Y., '75——.

WILLIAM HORACE MARBLE; b., Winchester, N.H., Feb. 13, 1822; Gil. T.S., '45–6; U.T.S., '46–8; Ord. (Cong.), Sept. 11, '50; S.S., Winchester, N.H., '48; S.S., Chesterfield, N.H., '49–'51; S.S. & Pas. (Presb.), Columbus, O., '51–6; S.S. & Pas. (Cong.), Oshkosh, Wis., '56–'62; Ch., U.S.Army, '62–3; S.S., Waupun, Wis., '63–5; S.S., Waterloo, Io., '65–9; S.S., Prairie du Chien, Wis., '70–1; S.S., Grundy Centre, Io., '71——.

DAVID MURDOCH; b., Glasgow, Scotland, March 22, 1823; U.C., '45; U.T.S., '45–8; Ord. (Cong.), Sep. 18, '50; Pas., New-Milford, Ct., '50–'69; Pas., New-Haven, Ct., '69–'74; W.C., do., '74——. D.D., U.C., '67.

CHARLES PARKER; b., New-Haven, Ct., July 15, 1816; U.T.S., '45–8; Ord. (Cong.), Nov. 5, '48; S.S., Pleasant Valley, West, N.Y., '48–9; S.S., Ramapo, N.Y., '49–'50; S.S., N. York City, '50–1; S.S., West-Hoboken, N.J., '51–3; S.S. & Pas. (R.D.), Hoboken, N.J., '54–7; Pas., Bergen Point, N.J., '58–'60; S.S. (Presb.), Irving, Kansas, '61–5; Oc. S., Irving, Kan., '65–'73; Pas. (R.D.), Hoboken, N.J., '74——.

*Alexander Hamilton Parkins; b., Winchester, Va., Oct. 1, 1825; Del.C., '45; U.T.S., '45-8; Ed., Berryville, Va., '49-'61; Conf. Army, '61; Died, Manassas, Va., Aug. 6, '61.

Justin Wright Parsons; b., Westhampton, Mass., ..., 1824; W.C., '45; U.T.S., '45-8; Ord. (Presb.), Dec. 26, '49; F.M., Thessalonica, Turkey, '50-4; F.M., Smyrna, Asia, '54-7; F.M., Baghchijik, Turkey, '57-'60; F.M., Nicomedia, Asia, '61——.

Hamilton Wilcox Pierson; b., Bergen, N.Y., Sep. 22, 1817; U.C., '43; U.T.S., '45-8; Inv., Trav., '48-9; Ord. (Presb.), Nov. 13, '53; Ag., A.B.S., Hayti, W. Ind., '49-'50; Ag., A.B.C.F.M., N. York City, & Trav., '50-3; Ag., A.B.S., Louisville, Ky., '53-8; Prest., Cumb. C., Princeton, Ky., '58-'61; Ag., A.T.S., Washington, D.C., '61-2; Sec. of U.S.C.C., Toledo, O., & Tea. in Va., '63-5; Inv., Trav., & Lecturing, '65-'75; Inv., Cal., '75-6; Do., Bergen, N.Y., '76——. D.D., U.C., '60.

Samuel Sawyer; b., Goshen, N.Y., June 20, 1823; C.N.J., '42; U.T.S., '45-8; Ord. (Presb.), Sept. 29, '49; S.S. & Prof., Rogersville, Tenn., '48-'57; S.S. & Prest., Ind. Coll., Marion, Ind., '57-'61; Ch., U.S. Army, '61-4; Ag., P.C.H.M., Knoxville, Tenn., '64-6; Ag., Mv. Coll., '66-8; S.S., Chillicothe & Wheeling, Mo., '68-'72; S.S., E. St. Louis, Ill., '72-3; Pas., Pleasant Grove, N.J., '73-6; W.C., do., '76——.

Stephen Chester Strong; b., Northampton, Mass., Jan. 22, 1824; W.C., '45; U.T.S., '45-8; Ord. (Cong.), Ap. 12, '54; Pas., Southampton, Mass., '54-9; Pas., Gorham, Me., '60-7; S.S., South Natick, Mass., '68-'71; W.C., do., '71——.

Joseph Emerson Swallow; b., Nashua, N.H., Ap. 21, 1817; D.C., '43; Tea., '43-5; And.T.S., '45-6; U.T.S., '46-8; Ord. (Cong.), July 18, '48; Pas., Greenport, N.Y., '48-'50; Pas., Wilmington, Mass., '51-6; Pas., Nantucket, Mass., '56-8; S.S., Stoneham, Mass., '58-9; Pas., Southampton, Mass., '59-'62; S.S., Burlington, Mass., '63-7; Pas., Groton, Ct., '67-'70; S.S., South Canaan, Ct., '70-3; S.S., Alford, Mass., '73——.

Edward Brown Walsworth; b., Cleveland, O., ..., 1818; U.C., '44; Aub.T.S., '45-7; U.T.S., '47-8; Ord. (Presb.), Sep. 27, '48; Pas., E. Avon, N.Y., '48-'52; Pas., Marysville, Cal., '52-'61; S.S., Oakland, Cal., '61-4; Prest., Fem. Coll., do., '64-'72; Pas., Albion, N.Y., '73——. D.D., ..., '67.

Samuel Hopkins Willey; b., Compton, N.H., March 11, 1821; D.C., '45; U.T.S., '45-8; Ord. (Presb.), Nov. 30, '48; H.M., Monterey, Cal., '48-'50; Pas., San Francisco, Cal., '50-'62; V. Prest., Cal. C., Oakland, Cal., '62-'70; Pas. (Cong.), Santa Cruz, Cal., '70——. D.D., D.C., '75. 29.

---

*Joseph Whiting Browning; b., Belpre, O., Oct. 8, 1820; Ma.C., '44; L.T.S., '45-6; U.T.S., '46-7; Died, N. York City, Ap. 9, '47.

William Anderson Crawford; b., Woodstock, Va., Feb. 20, 1825; Del.C., '44; U.T.S., '45-6; Ord. (Presb.), May .., '58; Prin., Woodstock, Va., '48-'54; Prof., Del.C., '54-8; S.S. & Ev., Fairfax Co., Va., '58-'66; Ch., Conf.

Army, '62–4; S.S. & Ev., Fred. Co., Va., '66——. Residence, n. Winchester, Va., '61——.

*SILAS WILBER DEUEL; b., Duanesburgh, N.Y., Jan. 25, 1822; U.C., '45; U.T.S., '45–6; Died, Esperance, N.Y., Jan. 27, '48.

FRANCIS FOWLER; b., Worcester, Mass., ..., 1822; U.Vt., '43; U.T.S., '45–6; Tea., Worcester, Mass., ..——

EDWARD WHITING GILMAN; b., Norwich, Ct., Feb. 11, 1823; Y.C., '43; U.T.S., '45–7; N.H.T.S., '47–8; Ord. (Cong.), Dec. 4, '49; Tut., Y.C., '47–9; Pas., Lockport, N.Y., '49–'56; Pas., Cambridgeport, Mass., '56–8; Pas., Bangor, Me., '59–'63; Pas., Stonington, Ct., '64–'71; Sec., A.B.S., N. York City, '71——. D.D., Y.C., '74.

*JAMES HIPKINS McNEILL; b., Fayetteville, N.C., May 23, 1825; Del.C., '44; U.T.S., '45–7; P.T.S., '47–8; Ord. (Presb.), ..., '49; S.S. & Pas., Pittsboro, N.C., '48–'53; Sec., A.B.S., N. York City, '53–'61; Ed., Fayetteville, N.C., '61–3; Conf. Army, '63–5; Killed, Petersburgh, Va., Mar. 31, '65.

SILAS GOODYEAR RANDALL; b., Weybridge, Vt., July 26, 1819; M.C., '45; U.T.S., '45–6; And.T.S., '46–8; Ord. (Presb.), June .., '50, S.S., Roscoe, Ill., '48–'50; S.S., Essex, N.Y., '50–2; Inv., Elgin, Mich., '53–4; Do., Rockford, Ill., '54; Do., Chicago, Ill., '55; Do., Rockford, Ill., '56—— ..; Do. & Trade, Providence, R.I., .. ——.

WILLIAM EBENEZER TYLER; b., S. Weymouth, Mass., Ap. 20, 1822; A.C., '44; U.T.S., '45–7; Tea., D. & D.I., Columbus, O., '53–'60; Agric., Auburndale, Mass., '60——.

JOHN ELIAS WHITEHEAD; b., New-York City, ..., 1823; R.C., '44; U.T.S., '45; Tea., N. York City, '45——. M.D., Coll. P. & S., N.Y.C., '64. 9.

1849.

WILLIAM AIKMAN; b., New-York City, Aug. 12, 1824; U.N.Y., '46; U.T.S., '46–9; Ord. (Presb.), Dec. 26, '49; Pas., Newark, N.J., '49–'57; Pas., Wilmington, Del., '57–'69; Pas., N. York City, '69–'72; Pas., Detroit, Mich., '72——. D.D., U.N.Y., '69.

*ISAAC HENRY BRAYTON; b., Deerfield, N.Y., Nov. 29, 1821; H.C., '46; U.T.S., '46–9; Ord. (Presb.), Jan. 18, '50; S.S. & Pas., San José, Cal., '50–3; Ag., San Francisco, Cal., '53–4; Ed., do., '54—— ..; Pas., Marysville, Cal., ..——'60; Prof., Cal. C., Oakland, Cal., '60–9; Died, Nevada City, Cal., Ap. 12, '69.

ROBERT CAMPBELL; b., Kemper Co., Miss., ..., 1822; Mi. C., '46; U.T.S., '46–9; Ord. (Presb.), ..., '52; S.S., Vicksburgh, Miss., '49–'51; S.S., Monticello, Miss., '51–3; S.S., Trinity, La., '54–7; Tea., do., '57——

NATHAN COLTON CHAPIN; b., Hartford, Ct., Sep. 20, 1823; Y.C., '44; U.T.S., '46–9; Ord. (Cong.), Nov. 2, '51; S.S., Milwaukee, Wis., '49–'51; S.S., Watertown, Wis., '51–3; S.S., Kenosha, Wis., '54–7; Pas., La Crosse, Wis., '57–'71; S.S., Faribault, Wis., '72–4; Pas., Rochester, Minn., '74——.

ALEXANDER CROCKER CHILDS; b., Nantucket, Mass., Aug. 31, 1823; Y.C., '45; U.T.S., '46–9; Ord. (Cong.), May 18, '53; S.S., Elizabeth, Ill., '49–'50; S.S., Oswego, Ill., '50–1; S.S. & Pas., E. Falmouth, Mass., '52–5; Pas., Amesbury, Mass., '56–8: S.S., W. Rehoboth, '60–2; S.S., Chatham, Mass., '62–5; S.S., Wenham, Mass., '67–8; Pas., West-Charleston, Vt., '69–'72; S.S., Sharon, Ct., '72–4; S.S., Orfordville, N.H., '75——.

GEORGE WHITEFIELD COAN; b., Bergen, N.Y., Dec. 30, 1817; W.C., '46; U.T.S., '46–9; Ord. (Presb.), June 6, '49; F.M., Oroomiah, Persia, '49–'62; U. States, '62–4; F.M., Oroomiah, Persia, '64–'74. Residence, Niles, Mich., '74——.

CHARLES FANNING; b., New-York City, July 22, 1822; U.N.Y., '45; U.T.S., '46–9; Res. Lic., N.H.T.S., '49–'50; Ord. (Presb.), Oct. 23, '50; Pas., Belvidere, Ill., '50–2; Trade, N. York City, '53——.

HORACE W. FINCH; b., Finchville, N.Y., March 21, 1821; U.N.Y., '46; U.T.S., '46–9; Ord. (Cong.), Sep. .., '52; S.S., Danby, Vt., '49–'52; S.S., E. Whitehall, N.Y., '52–6; S.S., Spencertown, N.Y., '56–7; S.S., Canton, N.Y., '57–8; Pas. (R.D.), Greenport, N.Y., '57–'60; Agric., E. Whitehall, N.Y., '60——.

GEORGE DE FOREST FOLSOM; b., Bricksport, Me., July 26, 1822; Y.C., '45; N.H.T.S., '46–7; U.T.S., '47–9; Ord. (Cong.), July 16, '50; Pas., (Presb.), Elbridge, N.Y., '50–2; Pas. (Cong.), N. York City, '53–4; Pas., Springfield, Mass., '55–'60; Pas., Fair Haven, Ct., '62–8; S.S., Northford, Ct., '69——.

CHARLES HEDGES FORCE; b., Morristown, N.J., Oct. 22, 1823; U.N.Y., '46; U.T.S., '46–9; Ord. (Presb.), Nov. 22, '49; S.S. (Cong.), Central Falls, R.I., '49–'50; S.S., (Presb.), Unadilla, N.Y., '51–5; S.S. & Pas., S. Ottawa, Ill., '56–'67; S.S., Farm Ridge, Ill.; '68; S.S., Waltham, Ill., '69; Inv., Ottawa, Ill., '69——.

FISK HARMON; b., Bennington, Vt., Feb. 12, 1813; U.T.S., '45–6, '47–9; Ord. (Cong.), July 9, '50; Pas., Hebron, N.Y., '49–'51; S.S., Fall River, Mass., '52; Ag., N. York City, '53; S.S. (Presb.), Pittstown & Johnsonville, N.Y., '53–4; S.S., Lisbon, Wis., '54–6; S.S., Panora, Io., '56–8; Pas., Swede Point, Io., '58–'65; W.C., do., '65——.

GEORGE WINFRED HERVEY; b., South-Durham, N.Y., Nov. 28, 1821; Cn.C., '47; N.T.I., '46–7; U.T.S., '47–9; Ord. (Bap.), Ap. .., '50; Pas., Upper Middletown, Ct., '49–'51; Pas., Hudson, N.Y., '51–8; Pas., Canton, Mass., '58–'60; Lit., N. York City, '60——.

*EDMUND DYER HOLT; b., Fairfax, Vt., Sep. 20, 1818; A.C., '46; U.T.S., '46–9; Ord. (Presb.), May 28, '50; S.S., Rock Island, Ill., '49–'52; Pas., Montrose, Io., '52–6; S.S., Chatfield, Minn., '56–'65; Died, do., June 11, '65.

WILLIAM EDWARD HOLYOKE; b., Marietta, O., Sep. 19, 1821; K.C., '46; U.T.S., '46–9; Ord. (Cong.), Dec. 18, '52; S.S. & Pas., Farmington, Ill., '51–4; Pas., Elgin, Ill., '54–8; S.S. & Pas., Polo, Ill., '58–'65; S.S., Bunker Hill., Ill., '65–8; Pas., Chicago, Ill., '68–'74; Oc. S., do., '74——.

JACOB AUGUSTINE HOOD; b., Marblehead, Mass., May 5, 1822; D.C., '44; U.T.S., '46–9; Ord. (Cong.), Jan. 2, '50; Pas., Middleton, Mass., '50–4;

Pas., Pittsfield, N.H., '54–'62 ; S.S., Loudon, N.H., '62–7 ; Pas. (Presb.), Maroa, Ill., '67–'75 ; Pas., Columbus, Neb., '75——.

*CHARLES LIVINGSTONE ; b., Blantyre, Scotland, ... , 18 . . ; O.C., '45 ; O.T.S., '46–7 ; U.T.S., '47–9 ; Ord. (Cong.), Oct. 15, '51; S.S., Williston, Vt., '49–'51 ; Pas., Plympton, Mass., '51–5 ; S.S., Matapoisett, Mass., '55–9 ; Explorer, E. Af., '59–'65 ; Scotland, '66–'71 ; Br. Consul, Fernando Po, W. Af., '72–4 ; Died, do., ... , '74.

*JONATHAN LYONS ; b., Armagh, Ireland, Mar. 19, 1816 ; U.T.S., '46–9 ; Ord. (Presb.), Ap. . . , '50 ; H.M., Salem, Va., '50 ; S.S., Athens, Tenn., '51 ; Ag., A.B.S., Madisonville, Tenn., '52–4 ; Do., Greenville, Tenn., '54–7 ; Do., Benton, Tenn., '57 ; S.S. & Pas., Jeffersonville, Va., '57—— . . ; S.S., Tazewell C.H., Va., . .——'76 ; Died, do., ... , '76.

DWIGHT WHITNEY MARSH ; b., Dalton, Mass., Nov. 5, 1823 ; W.C., '42 ; And.T.S., '46–7 ; U.T.S., '47–9 ; Ord. (Cong.), Oct. 2, '49 ; F.M., Mosul, Turkey, '50–'60 ; S.S., Hinsdale, Mass., '61–2 ; Prin., Rochester, N.Y., '63–7 ; Pas., Godfrey, Ill., '67–8 ; Prin., Rochester, N.Y., '68–9 ; Pas., Whitney's Point, N.Y., '69–'71 ; Pas., Owego, N.Y., '71——. D.D., W.C., '75.

JAMES MORTON ; b., Loudon, Scotland, Feb. 7, 1818 ; Y.C., '45 ; U.T.S., '47–9 ; Ord. (Presb.), Jan. 12, '51 ; S.S., Turin, N.Y., '50–4 ; S.S., Del. City, Del., '54–9 ; S.S., N. York City, '60–1 ; S.S., Tremont, N.Y., '61–3 ; S.S., Galesburgh, Ill., '64 ; Trade, N. York City, '65——.

ISAAC NEWTON NAFF ; b., Franklin Co., Va., Oct. 6, 1817 ; U.T.S., '46–9 ; Ord. (Presb.), June 8, '51 ; S.S., Eastville, Va., '49–'50 ; S.S., Jeffersonville, Va., '50–7 ; Pas., Draper's Valley, Va., '57–'73 ; Pas., Dublin, Va., '73——.

GURDON WHEELER NOYES ; b., Stonington, Ct., Aug. 13, 1818 ; A.C., '46 ; U.T.S., '46–9 ; Ord. (Presb.), Dec. 19, '49 ; Pas., Portsmouth, Va., '49–'51 ; Pas. (Cong.), Cornwall, Vt., '52–4 ; S.S. & As. Pas., New-Haven, Ct., '54–'61 ; Pas., Fair Haven, Ct., '61–9 ; Pas., Woodbury, Ct., '69——.

ISAAC LEWIS PEET ; b., Hartford, Ct., Dec. 4, 1824 ; Y.C., '45 ; U.T.S., '46–9 ; Prof., D. & D.I., N. York City, '45——. LL.D., Col. C., '72.

ISRAEL BRYANT SMITH ; b., Huntington (L.I.), N.Y., Sep. 12, 1822 ; U.N.Y., '46 ; U.T.S., '46–9 ; Ord. (Presb.), July 12, '51 ; S.S., E. Hampton (L.I.), N.Y., '49–'50 ; S.S., Fresh Pond (L.I.), N.Y., '51–6 ; S.S., Mt. Pleasant & Uniondale, Pa., '57–'60 ; S.S., Northport (L.I.), N.Y., '60–'72 ; S.S., Greenlawn (L.I.), N.Y., '72——.

WILLIAM CLARK ULYAT ; b., Lutton, Lincolnshire, Eng., Jan. 15, 1823 ; U.N.Y., '46 ; U.T.S., '46–9 ; Ord. (Bap.), ... , '50 ; S.S., Princeton, N.J., '49–'53 ; Pas. & Ed., Norwalk, Ct., '53–7 ; Pas., Hudson, N.Y., '58–'62 ; Ed., N. York City, '63——'71 ; Pas. & Ed., Princeton, N.J., '71——.

JOSEPH CLINTON WHITNEY ; b., Springfield, Vt., Ap. 14, 1818 ; O.C., '45 ; U.T.S., '46–9 ; Ord. (Presb.), May 28, '50 ; S.S., Stillwater, Minn., '49–'53 ; Pas., Minneapolis, Minn., '53–7 ; S.S., Forest City, Minn., '58–'61 ; U.S. Army, Minneapolis, Minn., '62–5 ; Trade, do., '66——. 25.

CLEMENT EDSON BABB; b., Pittston, Pa., Aug. 19, 1822; Di.C., '40; U.T.S., '46-7; L.T.S., '47-9; Ord. (Presb.), Ap. .., '48; Pas., Indianapolis, Ind., '48-'52; Ed., Cincinnati, O., '53-'63; Pas., College Hill, O., '64-5; Ed., Cincinnati, O., '65-'73; Do., San José, Cal., '73-4; Do., Oakland, Cal., '74-6; Do., San Francisco, Cal., '76——. D.D., Ma.C., '70.

BRONSON BURTON BEARDSLEY; b., Trumbull, Ct., Sept. 8, 1817; Trade, Bridgeport, Ct., '35-'45; U.T.S., '46-7; Ord. (Cong.), Oct. 8, '50; S.S., White Plains, N.Y., '49-'50; H.M., Arkansas, '50-1; C.M., Hartford, Ct., '52-3; S.S., Shirley, Mass., '53-9; C.M., Hartford, Ct., '59-'60; Inv., Bridgeport, Ct., '60——. A.B., Y.C., '51.

JONATHAN KELSEY BURR; b., Middletown, Ct., Sep. 21, 1825; W.U., '45; U.T.S., '46-7; Ord., (M.E.), Ap. 12, '52; S.S., Rome & Wantage, N.J., '48-9; S.S., Milford, N.J., '49-'51; Pas., Orange, N.J., '51-3; Pas., Burlington, N.J., '53-5; Pas., Hoboken, N.J., '55-7; Pas., Trenton, N.J., '57-8; Pas., Newark, N.J., '58-'60; Pas., Orange, N.J., '60-2; Pas., Paterson, N.J., '62-4; Pas., Hoboken, N.J., '64-7; Pas., Newark, N.J., '67-'70; Pas., Morristown, N.J., '70-3; Pas., Hoboken, N.J., '73-6; Pas., ..., '76——.

JAMES GLENTWORTH BUTLER; b., Brooklyn, N.Y., Aug. 3, 1821; U.T.S., '46-7; N.H.T.S., '47-9; Res. Lic., do., '49-'50; Ord. (Presb.), Dec. 2, '52; Pas., West-Phila., Pa., '52-'68; Sec., A. & F.C.U., N. York City, '68-'71; Pas., Brooklyn (E.D.), N.Y., '71-3; W.C., Brooklyn, N.Y., '74——. D.D., H.C., '64.

*JOSEPH C. CHAMBERLAIN; b., Newark, Del., ..., 1826; Del.C, '44; U.T.S., '46; Died, N. York City, Nov. 9, '46.

HENRY PERRIN COON; b., Taghkanick, N.Y., ... 1822; W.C., '44; U.T.S., '46-7; P.T.S., '47; M.D., Univ., Pa., '49; Physician, Taghkanick, N.Y., '50——.

*GEORGE WASHINGTON DUNMORE; b., Rush, Pa., Oct. 5, 1820; U.N.Y., '46; U.T.S., '46-8; B.T.S., '48-9; Ord. (Cong.), Feb. .., '50; F.M., Aintab, Syria, '51; F.M., Diarbekr, Turkey, '51-4; F.M., Arabkir, Turkey, '54-5; F.M., Kharpoot, Turkey, '55-7; F.M., Erzeroom, Asia, '58-'60; Ch., U.S.Army, '61-2; Killed, in battle, St. Anguille Creek, Ark., Aug. 3, '62.

EZRA W. GOODRICH; b., Whitesboro, N.Y., ..., 1822; U.C., '46; U.T.S., '46-9.

MARSHALL HENSHAW; b., Bethany, Pa., Oct. 3, 1820; A.C., '45; U.T.S., '46-7; Tut., A.C., '47-9; Ord. (Cong.), Feb. .., '49; Prin., Derry, N.H., '49-'53; Prin., Byfield, Mass., '53-9; Prof., R.C., '59-'63; Prin., Williston Sem., E. Hampton, Mass., '63——. LL.D., U.N.Y., '63; D.D., A.C., '72.

*JOHN HOWARD; b., Richmond, Va., ..., 1819; U.T.S., '46-9; Ord. (Presb.), ..., '53; S.S., Richmond, Va., '49-'53; S.S., P. Edward C.H., Va., '54-5; S.S., Woodstock, Va., '55-6; Died, do., Feb. 27, '57.

ZEPHANIAH MOORE HUMPHREY; b., Amherst, Mass., Aug. 30, 1824; A.C., '43; U.T.S., '46-7; And.T.S., '47-9; Ord. (Presb.), Oct. .., '50; Pas., Racine, Wis., '50-6; Pas. (Cong.), Milwaukee, Wis., '56-9; Pas. (Presb.), Chicago, Ill., '59-'68; Pas., Philadelphia, Pa., '68-'75; Prof., Lane Theo. Sem., Cincinnati, O., '75——. D.D., U.Chic., '64; Mod., Gen. Ass., Presb. Chh., '71.

*Richard G. E. Humphreys; b., Dublin, Ireland, Aug. 17, 1821; U.N.Y., '46; U.T.S., '46–9; Ord. (Cong.), ..., '52; S.S. (Presb.), Cairo, N.Y., '51–2; W.C., N. York City, '53–'69; Died, do., Sep. 26, '69.

Lewis Jessup; b., Minisink, N.Y., May 30, 1821; U.T.S., '46–8; B.T.S., '48–9; Ord. (Cong.), Nov. 19, '51; Pas., Northfield, Ct., '51–4; Pas., S. Glastonbury, Ct., '55–6; Pas., Millbury, Mass., '56–'61; S.S., Lisbon, Ct., '62–4; S.S., Jewett City, Ct., '64–6; S.S., S. Adams, Mass., '67–'71; S.S., New-Haven, N.Y., '72–4; S.S., La Fayette, N.Y., '75——.

*George McNeill; b., Fayetteville, N.C., Sep. 4, 1827; Del.C., '46; U.T.S., '46–7; P.T.S., '47–9; Ord. (Presb.), ..., '53; S.S., Ashboro, N.C., '49–'54; S.S., Washington, N.C., '54–5; Prin., Oscola, Fla., '55–6; Prin., Fayettville, N.C., '56–7; Ed., do., '57–'63; Died, do., Aug. 18, '61.

John Tallmadge Marsh; b., Dec. 17, 1825; Y.C., '45; U.T.S., '46–7; And.T.S., '48–'50; Ord. (Cong.), Sep. 14, '53; H.M., Wis., '51–2; S.S., Rock Island, Ill., '52–3; Pas., Peoria, Ill., '53–5; S.S., Le Claire, Io., '55–6; S.S., Fort Howard, Wis., '56–8; S.S., Sheboygan Falls, Wis., '58–'60; S.S., Hartland, Wis., '60–2; S.S., New-Lisbon & Quincy, Wis., '62–3; U.S.Army, '63–6; S.S., Harpersfield, N.Y., '67–'71; Pas., New-Haven, N.Y., '71–2; S.S., Black Creek, N.Y., '73–4; S.S., Crown Point, N.Y., '74——.

Emmons Thompson Mockridge; b., Newark, N.J., ..., 1817; W.C., '46; U.T.S., '46–7; Trade, '48——.

*Henry Abeel Nitchie; b., New-York City, Aug. 13, 1817; U.T.S., '46–7. Not Ord. Died, N. York City, Jan. 17, '70.

Austin N. Parkhurst; b., New-York City, ..., 1822; U.N.Y., '46; U.T.S., '46–7.

John Chester Phelps; b., New-York City, ..., 1813; U.T.S., '46–8.

*John J. Robinson; b., Washington, Ga., ..., 1822; U.E.T., '45; U.T.S., '46–8; Ord. (Presb.), ..., '50; S.S., Maryville, Tenn., '50–1; Prof., Mv. C., do., '52–'61; Ch., Conf. Army, '62–5; S.S., Rogersville, Tenn., '66; Died, do., Aug. .., '66.

*William Lyman Silcox; b., Paterson, N.J., Feb. 28, 1820; W.C., '44; U.T.S., '46–8; Died, N. York City, Ap. 6, '48.

Joseph Gilliard Williamson; b., Philadelphia, Pa., Nov. 17, 1824; Del. C., '46; U.T.S., '46–8; P.T.S., '48–9; Ord. (Presb.), Nov. 21, '49; Pas., Bethlehem, N.J., '49——. Address, Sidney, N.J. 22.

1850.

Francis Eben Meriam Bacheler; b., Douglas, Mass., July 8, 1818; B.U., '47; U.T.S., '47–'50; Ord. (Cong.), May 16, '54; S.S. & Pas., Brooklyn, N.Y., '51–7; Pas., Patchogue (L.I.), N.Y., '58–9; S.S., Killingly (Dayville), Ct., '59–'62; W.C., Lebanon, Ct., '62–3; Pas., Sparta, N.J., '64–'70; S.S. (Cong.), Killingsly, (Dayville), Ct., '71——.

JOHN BRADSHAW; b., Potsdam, N.Y., ..., 1812; M.C., '39; Tea., Addison Co., Vt., '39–'41; Tea., Ft. Covington, N.Y., '41–3; Tea., Ogdensburgh, N.Y., '43–8; U.T.S., '49–'50; Ord. (Presb.), Oct. .., '51; S.S., Elizabethtown, N.Y., '50–3; Pas., Crown Point, N.Y., '53–'66; Ag., N. York City, '66–8; S.S., Middlebury, Vt., '69; S.S., Mooers, N.Y., '69–'71; Pas. (Cong.), Chicago, Ill., '71–5; W.C., do. '75——.

UZAL WADE CONDIT; b., Genoa, N.Y., Aug. 18, 1815; W.C., '47; U.T.S., '47–'50; Ord. (Cong.), Oct. 24, '50; Pas., Lynnfield Centre, Mass., '50–5; Pas., Deerfield, N.H., '55–'62; Pas., Salisbury, N.H., '64–9; W.C., Swedesborough, N.J., '69–'70; Pas. (Presb.), Oscola, Pa., '70–2; Pas., Jacksonville, Pa., '72–4; Tea., Easton, Pa., '74——.

ANDREW CLARK DENISON; b., Hampton, Ct., June 27, 1822; Y.C., '47; E.W.T.S., '47–9; U.T.S., '49–'50; Res. Lic., N.H.T.S., '50–1; Ord. (Cong.), Mar. 4, '51; C. Pas., Leicester, Mass., '51–6; Tea., Boston, Mass., '56–8; S.S., Westchester, Ct., '58–'61; Pas., Portland, Ct., '61–7; Tea., Charlotte, N.C., '68; S.S., Middlefield, Ct., '68——.

WILLIAM WOODBRIDGE EDDY; b., Jacksonville, Ill., ..., 1826; W.C., '45; U.T.S., '47–'50; Res. Lic., '50–1; Ord. (Presb.), Sep. 18, '51; F.M., Aleppo, Syria, '51–4; F.M., Beirut, Syria, '54–7; F.M., Sidon, Syria, '57——. D.D., ..., '74.

ASA ELMORE EVEREST; b., Peru, N.Y., Dec. 28, 1820; M.C., '47; U.T.S., '47–'50; Ord. (Cong.), Sep. 8, '50; S.S., Brooklyn, N.Y., '50–1; W.C., do., '51–2; W.C., Peru, N.Y., '51–8; S.S., Masonville, N.Y., '58–9; S.S. (Presb.), Mooers, N.Y. ,'59–'64; Ch., U.S. Army, '64–5; W.C., Peru, N.Y., '65–6; S.S., Sparland, Ill., '66–7; S.S., Ridgefield, Ill., '67–8; S.S., Thornton, Ill., '68–'70; Pas., Ludlow, Ill., '70——.

STEPHEN SYDNEY GOODMAN; b., New-York City, ..., 1822; U.N.Y., '47; U.T.S., '47–'50; Ord. (Presb.), July .., '51; S.S., Brooklyn, N.Y., '51–2; S.S., Oriskany, N.Y., '52–4; Pas., Milford, N.Y., '54–8; S.S., Unadilla, N.Y., '58–'66; Pas., W. Milford, N.Y., '66——.

RICHARD HALL; b., Cornish, N.H., Aug. 6, 1817; D.C., '47; U.T.S., '47–'50; Ord. (Cong.), Aug. 8, '50; S.S., Pt. Douglas, Minn., '50–6; Ag., A.H.M.S., St. Paul, Minn., '56——.

WHEELOCK NYE HARVEY; b., Jamestown, N.Y., April 15, 1825; U.N.Y., '44; U.T.S., '47–50; Ord. (Cong.), May 18, '53; Pas., Bethel, Ct., '53–8; Pas., Milford, Ct., '58–'62; Pas., Wilton, Ct., '62–7; Trade, N. York City, '68——.

JOHN HAWKS; b., Deerfield, Mass., Jan. 22, 1823; A.C., '47; U.T.S., '47–'50; Ord. (Presb.), Aug. 28, '51; S.S., Newport, Montezuma, & Toronto, Ind., '55–6; S.S., Kirtland, O., '56–7; S.S., Perrysville, Ind., '58–9; S.S., Rockville, Ind., '59–'60; Oc.S., do., '60——.

SIMEON SPAFFORD HUGHSON; b., Chester, N.J., March 27, 1823; O.C., '47; U.T.S., '47–'50; Ord. (Cong.), Aug. 20, '50; S.S., Walworth, N.Y., '50–2; S.S., Penn Yan, N.Y., '52–4; Pas., Rushville, N.Y., '54–'64; S.S., Newark, N.J., '65–'74; S.S., Patchogue (L.I.), N.Y., '74——.

WILLIAM H. LOCKWOOD; b., Brooklyn, N.Y., ..., 1824; U.N.Y., '47: U.T.S., '47-'50; Ord. (Presb.), ..., '52; S.S. & Pas., Coventryville, N.Y., '51-7; S.S., Lowville, N.Y., '57-'64; S.S., Eau Claire, Wis., '64——.

*HUGH SNEED MCELROY; b., Lebanon, Ky., July 26, 1828; Cr.C., '47; U.T.S., '47-'50; Ord. (Presb.), Oct. .., '50; S.S., Midway, Ky., '50-5; S.S., McAfee, Ky., '55; S.S. & Pas., Detroit, Mich., '55-7; Died, do., Dec. 24, '57.

PETER J. H. MYERS; b., Frankfort, N.Y., July 22, 1821; M.C., '47; U.T.S., '47-'50; Ord. (Presb.), ..., '50; S.S., Clinton, N.Y., '50-2; S.S., Middlebury, Vt., '52-3; W.C., Mooers, N.Y., '53; Pas., Haverstraw, N.Y., '54-9; C.M., Brooklyn, N.Y., '60-3; Ch., do., '64; Pas., Dandridge, Tenn., '65-7; C.M., Brooklyn, N.Y., '68——.

EMERY HARKNESS PAGE; b., Brooklyn, N.Y., ..., 1818; B.U., '47; U.T.S., '47-'50; Ord. (Bap.), ..., '50; Pas., Charlestown, Mass., '50-8; Pas., Brooklyn, N.Y., '59——.

WILSON PHRANER; b., Jamaica (L.I.), N.Y., Aug. 29, 1822; U.N.Y., '47; U.T.S., '47-'50; Ord. (Presb.), Oct. 28, '51; Pas., Sing Sing, N.Y., '51——.

EPAMINONDAS JAMES PIERCE; b., Philadelphia, Pa., Oct. 24, 1823; D.C., '45; Law Student, Philadelphia, Pa., '45-6; U.T.S., '47-'50; Ord. (Presb.), ..., '50; F.M., Gaboon, W. Af., '51-'60; W.C., Philadelphia, Pa., '60-3; S.S., Del. Water Gap, Pa., '63-5; S.S., W. Philadelphia, Pa., '65-6; S.S., Del. Water Gap, Pa., '66-9; S.S., Philadelphia, Pa., '70-1; Pas., Farmingdale, N.J., '71——.

LEWIS HUBBARD REID; b., Charlestown, N.H., March 2, 1825; Y.C., '47; U.T.S., '47-'50; Ord. (Presb.), Dec. 4, '50; Pas., Fayetteville, N.Y., '50-'61; Pas., Syracuse, N.Y., '61-8; Pas., Chicago, Ill., '68-'74; S.S. (Cong.), Canaan, Ct., '74——.

*SAMUEL ANDLEY RHEA; b., Blountville, Tenn., Jan. 23, 1827; U.E.T., '47; U.T.S., '47-'50; Ord. (Presb.), Feb. 2, '51; F.M., Gawar, Persia, '51-8; F.M., Seir, Persia, '58-9; U. States, '59-'60; F.M., Seir, Persia, '60-1; F.M., Oroomiah, Persia, '61-5; Died, near do., Sep. 2, '65.

GEORGE GABY RICE; b., Enosburgh, Vt., Sep. 22, 1819; U.Vt., '45; U.T.S., '47-'50; Ord. (Cong.), Jan. 29, '51; S.S., Fairfield, Io., '50-1; S.S., Council Bluffs, Io., '51-9; S.S., Hiawatha & Albany, Kan., '59-'67; W.C., Council Bluffs, Io., '67——.

*HENRY EDWIN RUGGLES; b., Newbury, Vt., Nov. 27, 1822; D.C., '45; Tea., Lyndon, Vt., '45-6; Tea., Hoosick Falls, N.Y., '46-8; U.T.S., '48-'50; C.M., N. York City, '50; S.S., St. Louis, Mo., '51; Ord. (Presb.), Ap. 13, '51; Pas., St. Charles, Mo., '51-2; Pas. (Cong.), Eaton Village, N.Y., '53-6; Died, Newbury, Vt., Dec. 24, '56.

CHARLES SECCOMBE; b., Salem, Mass., June 10, 1817; D.C., '47; U.T.S., '48-'50; Ord. (Cong.), Aug. 8, '50; S.S. & Pas., Falls of St. Anthony, Minn., '50-'66; Ag., Northfield, Minn., '66-7; S.S., Zumbrota, Minn., '67; Prof., Northfield, Minn., '68-'71; S.S., Francestown, N.H., '71-3; H.M. & Pas., Strahmburgh, Neb., '73——.

FRANKLIN GOLDTHWAITE SHERRILL; b., Homer, N.Y., Nov. 1, 1826; U.N.Y., '46· U.T.S., '46-7, '48-'50; Ord. (Presb.), Oct. 13, '50; S.S., Ceresco &

Ripon, Wis., '50–3; S.S. (Cong.), Caledonia & Oak Creek, Wis., '53–8; S.S., Fulton, Wis., '58–'61; S.S., Oak Creek, Wis., '61–4; W.C., Milwaukee, Wis., '64–5; S.S., Richmond, Mass., '65–7; S.S., California, Mo., '67——.

EDWIN GRAHAM SMITH; b., Williamstown, Vt., March 20, 1821; K.C., '46; L.T.S., '47–9; U.T.S., '49–'50; Ord. (Cong.), Nov. 7, '50; S.S., Dover, Ill., '50–6; S.S., Tremont & Morton, Ill., '57–'65; Ag. & Sup., A.B.S., Morrison, Ill., '65——.

NAHUM IGNACE STEINER; b., Bohemia, Aug. 6, 1829; U.T.S., '47–'50; Ag., A.S.M.C.J., N. York City, '50–4; Miss., London, Eng., '55–6; Miss., N. York City, '56——.

SETH BRADLEY STONE; b., New-York City, ..., 1817; Y.C., '42; U.T.S., '47–'50; Ord. (Presb.), ..., '50; F.M., Ifafa, Zulu, S. Africa, '51–'75; U. States, '75——.

GUY CHANDLER STRONG; b., Pawlet, Vt., Jan. 22, 1822; M.C., '47; U.T.S., '47–'50; Ord. (Cong.), Nov. 23, '53; S.S., Moira, N.Y., '50–4; S.S., E. Poultney, Vt., '54–6; S.S., Grandville, Mich., '56–'60; S.S., Sharon, Mich., '60–5; S.S., Ceresco, Mich., '66–7; S.S., South-Boston, Mich., '67–'73; S.S., Lodi, Ill., '73——.

WICKS SMITH TITUS; b., Victory, N.Y., June 23, 1820; U.C., '48; U.T.S., '48–'50; Ord. (M.E.), June 4, '54; S.S., Bergen, N.J., '51; S.S., Milltown, N.J., '52; Tea., Pennington, N.J., '53; Tea., Fulton, N.Y., '54; Pas., Ogdensburgh, N.Y., '54–6; Pas., Canton, N.Y., '56–7; Pas., Watertown, N.Y., '57–9; Pas., Camden, N.Y., '59–'61; Pas., Weedsport, N.Y., '61–3; Pas., Mexico, N.Y., '63–4; Pas., Geddes, N.Y., '64–5; Pas., Lowville, N.Y., '65–7; Pas., Wolcott, N.Y., '67–9; Pas., Hamilton, N.Y., '69–'71; Pas., Vernon, N.Y., '71–2; Pas., Winfield, N.Y., '72–4; Pas., Ames & Sprout Brook, N.Y., '74——.

JAMES WALKER; b., Deerfield, N.Y., Ap. 14, 1820; A.C., '44; U.T.S., '47–'50; Ord. (Presb.), Ap. 20, '53; S.S., Waynesville & Granville, Ill., '50–1; S.S., Garden Plain, Clyde & Unionville, Ill., '51–8; S.S., Eckford & Tekonsha, Mich., '58–'64; W.C., Marshall, Mich, '65–9; S.S. & Pas., Pewamo, Mich., '69–'74; S.S., Greenwood, Mich., '74——.

JAMES HENRY WARREN; b., Chippewa Co., Mich., Sep. 7, 1819; K.C., '47; U.T.S., '47–'50; Ord. (Cong.), Sep. 8, '50; S.S., San Francisco, Cal., '50–1; Pas., Nevada City, Cal., '51–8; Ed., San Francisco, Cal., '58–'62; S.S., San Mateo, Cal., '62–4; Supt., A.H.M.S., San Francisco, Cal., '65——. 30.

---

*CHARLES LUTHER ADAMS; b., Lysander, N.Y., ..., 1820; H.C., '47; U.T.S., '47–8; Aub.T.S., '48–'50; Ord. (Cong.), ..., '50; S.S., Neenah, Wis., '50–2; Died, do., Oct. 23, '52.

JOHN ELIOT BENTON; b., Guilford, Ct., ..., 1821; U.N.Y., '47; U.T.S., '47–9; N.H.T.S., '49–'50; Ord. (Cong.), ..., '51; S.S., Mission Dolores, Cal., '51–8; S.S., Folsom, Cal., '59–'69; S.S., Oakland, Cal., '71——.

CHARLES LORING BRACE; b., Litchfield, Ct., June 19, 1826; Y.C., '46;

N.H.T.S., '47–8; U.T.S., '48–9; Europe, '50–2; Sec., C.A.S., N. York City, '53——.

Edwin Johnson; b., Plymouth, Ct., Dec. 1, 1826; Y.C., '46; U.T.S., '47–9; N.H.T.S., '49–'50; Ord. (Cong.), June 6, '51; S.S., Milford, Ct., '50–1; Pas., Jacksonville, Ill., '51–9; Pas., Boston, Mass., '59–'61; Pas., Bangor, Me., '61–5; S.S. & Pas., Baltimore, Md., '65–9; Pas., Bridgeport, Ct., '70——.

Nathaniel Baker Klink; b., New-Scotland, N.Y., Feb. 25, 1823; U.C., '47; U.T.S., '47–8; P.T.S., '48–'50; Ord. (Presb.), Feb. 13, '54; S.S., Oneida Valley, N.Y., '51–2; S.S., W. Galway, N.Y., '52–3; Pas., Balston Spa, N.Y., '53–4; Pas., Fairmount, N.J., '55–9; S.S., Sacramento, Cal., '60–1; S.S., Vallejo, Cal., '62——.

John H. Meacham; b., Albany, N.Y., ..., 1826; U.C., '47; U.T.S., '47–8; Tea., Buffalo, N.Y., '48——.

*Homer Bartlett Morgan; b., Watertown, N.Y., May 31, 1827; H.C., '47; U.T.S., '47–8; Tea., '48–9; Aub.T.S., '49–'51; Ord. (Presb.), July 9, '51; F.M., Salonica, Turkey, '52–3; F.M., Smyrna, Asia, '53–6; F.M., Antioch, Syria, '57–'65; Died, Smyrna, Asia, Aug. 26, '65.

Alfred Plant; b., Clinton, Mass., Mar. 2, 1821; Y.C., '47; U.T.S., '47–8; N.H.T.S., '48–'50; Oc.S., St. Louis, Mo., Keosauqua, Ia., & Collinsville, Ill., '50–4; Agric., St. Louis, Mo., '54——. Address, Webster Grove, Mo.

Aaron Potter; b., West-Troy, N.Y., ..., 1820; U.C., '42; U.T.S., '47–8; H.T.S., '48–'50; Ord. (Bap.), ..., '50.

Josiah Addison Priest; b., Albany, N.Y., Ap. 28, 1822; H.C., '47; U.T.S., '47–8; Ord. (Presb.), June 25, '51; Pas., Cooperstown, N.Y., '51–5; Pas., Homer, N.Y., '55–8; Pas., W. Bloomfield (Montclair), N.J., '58–'61; Europe, '61–2; S.S., Cooperstown, N.Y., '64; Pas., Gloversville, N.Y., '64–8; Pas., Quincy, Ill., '68–'75; Pas., Newton, N.J., '75——. D.D., H.C., '72.

Edward C. Robb; b., Gallatin, Tenn., ..., 1820; N.U., '41; Physician, ..., '42–7; U.T.S., '47–8; P.T.S., '48; Phys., ..——

Thomas Henderson Rouse; b., Pittstown, N.Y., ..., 1820; W.C., '47; E.W.T.S., '47–9; U.T.S., '49–'50; E.W.T.S., '50; Ord. (Cong.), June 18, '54; S.S., Feeding Hills, Mass., '50; S.S. & Pas., Poquonnock, Ct., '51–7; Pas., Jamestown, N.Y., '57–'68; Tea., Benicia, Cal., '69; S.S., San Mateo, Cal., '70——.

Henry Russel Smith; b., Morris, N.Y., Dec. 27, 1822; U.C., '44; U.T.S., '47–8; P.T.S., '48–9; Ord. (Presb.), Ap. .., '50; S.S., Leesburgh, Va., '49–'67; S.S. & Prest., Huntsville, Ala., '67–'74; S.S., Walnut Grove & Beaver Creek, Wash. Co., Va., '74——.

James Hewit Trowbridge; b., Plattsburgh, N.Y., May 27, 1820; M.C., '47; U.T.S., '47–9; N.H.T.S., '49–'50; Ord. (Presb.), Nov. .., '50; Pas., Haverstraw, N.Y., '50–4; Pas., Marshall, Mich., '54–6; Pas., Dubuque, Io., '56–'62; Pas., Chicago, Ill., '62–5; W.C., Chicago, Ill., '65; Sec., P.C.H.M., Chicago, Ill., '65–'70; W.C. & Ed., Riverside, Chicago, Ill., '70——.

*William Wardlaw; b., Fayetteville, Tenn., Nov. 26, 1823; Ja.C., '46; U.T.S., '47–8; Died, Shelbyville, Tenn., Jan. 19, '49. 15.

1851.

William Pratt Barker; b., South-Wales, N.Y., Feb. 18, 1822; U.N.Y., '48; U.T.S., '48-'51; Med. Coll., N.Y., '51-3; Ord. (Presb.), May 4, '53; F.M., Satara, India, '51-8; F.M., Khokar, India, '58-'65; U. States, '66; F.M., Rutnagiri, India, '67——.

*Daniel Bond; b., Adams, N.Y., Sep. 1, 1826; H.C., '48; Aub.T.S., '48-'50; U.T.S., '50-1; Res. Lic., '51-2; Ord. (Presb.), June 29, '52; Pas., Peekskill, N.Y., '52; Died, do., Aug. 20, '52.

Edgar Warner Clarke; b., Milton, N.Y., May 29, 1825; W.C., '48; U.T.S., '48-'51; Ord. (Presb.), Dec. 9, '52; S.S. & Pas., North-Evans, N.Y., '52-6; Pas., Medina, N.Y., '56-'62; Prin., Milton, N.Y., '62-9; S.S., Canterbury, N.Y., '69-'72; S.S. (Cong.), Sterling, Ill., '72-4; Prin., Richview, Ill., '74——.

Eli Corwin; b., Walkill, N.Y., Oct. 30, 1824; W.C., '48; U.T.S., '48-'51; Ord. (Presb.), June 22, '51; Sea. Ch., San Francisco, Cal., '51-2; Pas., San José, Cal., '52-8; S.S. & Pas., Honolulu, S. Islds., '58——. D.D., W.C., '71.

Lewis Gano; b., Bethlehem, N.J., ..., 1821; U.T.S., '48-'51; Res. Lic., '51-2; Ord. (Presb.), Mar. 7, '55; Tea., Woodstock, Ct., '51; Trav., Europe, '51-2; S.S., Bethlehem, N.J., '52-3; Pas., Whitehall, N.Y., '54-6; S.S., Davenport, Io., '56-7; S.S., Albany, Ill., '57-8; W.C., Chicago, Ill., '58-9; Deposed, June 29, '60; Law, '61-5; Stocks, N. York City, '65——.

*Admatha Grout; b., Newfane, Vt., Feb. 19, 1817; D.C., '45; Tea., Vt. & Md., '45-8; U.T.S., '48-'51; Inv., W. Brattleboro, Vt., '51-5; Inv., Osawatomie, Kan., '55; Died, do., Sep. 6, '55.

Thomas Samuel Hastings; b., New-York City, Aug. 28, 1827; H.C., '48; U.T.S., '48-'51; Res. Lic., '51-2; Ord. (Presb.), July 5, '52; Pas., Mendham, N.J., '52-6; Pas., N. York City, '56——. D.D., U.N.Y., '65.

Theron Holbrook Hawks; b., Charlemont, Mass., Oct. 24, 1821; W.C., '44; U.T.S., '48-'51; Res. Lic., '51-2; Ord. (Cong.), Mar. 7, '55; Pas., W. Springfield, Mass., '55-6; Pas. (Presb.), Cleveland, O., '61-7; Pas. (Cong.), Marietta, O., '69——. D.D., W.C., '64.

Louis Palemon Ledoux; b., Opelousas, La., June 8, 1822; A.C., '48; U.T.S., '48-'51; Ord. (Presb.), June 22, '51; S.S., Newport, Ky., '52; Pas., Monroe, Mich., '53-5; Pas., Richmond, Va., '55-8; Pas. & Tea., Cornwall Landing, N.Y., '58——. D.D., Ind. U., '61.

*Arunah Hall Lilly; b., Castle Creek, N.Y., March 15, 1819; W.C., '48; U.T.S., '48-9; And.T.S., '49-'50; U.T.S., '50-1; Ord. (Presb.), Oct. 10, '51; S.S., Craneville, N.J., '51-3; S.S., Centreville, N.Y., '53-5; S.S., Sherman, N.Y., '55-6; Pas., Silver Creek, N.Y., '56-9; S.S., E. Palmyra, '59-'70; S.S., Marysville, Kan., '71; S.S. & Pas., Troy, Kan., '71-5; Died, do., Aug. 13, '75.

Samuel Wallace Phelps; b., Ridgefield, Ct., Sep. 10, 1820; U.N.Y.,

'48; U.T.S., '48-'51; Ord. (Cong.), June 28, '54; H.M., N.W., Ill., '51-2; S.S., Lee Centre, Ill., '52-'68; Inv., do., '68——.

SANFORD WASHBURN ROE; b., Brooklyn, N.Y., Dec. 22, 1826; U.N.Y., '47; U.T.S., '48-'51; Ord. (Presb.), Ap. 15, '51; S.S., N. Bergen, N.J., '51-2; Pas., Cairo, N.Y., '52-'60; Pas., Jamestown, N.Y., '60-5; W.C., do., '65-6; Pas. (R.D.), Germantown, N.Y., '66-8; W.C., do., '68-9; Pas., Middleburgh, N.Y., '70——. D.D., U.N.Y., '73.

*EDWARD FREDERICK ROSS; b., New-York City, Feb. 12, 1826; U.C., '48; And.T.S., '48-'50; U.T.S., '50-1; Ord. (Cong.), Sep. 26, '51; Pas., Morrisania, N.Y., '51-4; W.C., Poughkeepsie, N.Y., '54-5; Died, Pleasant Valley, N.Y., Feb. 22, '55.

JOSEPH ROWELL; b., Clermont, N.H., ..., 1820; Y.C., 48; U.T.S., '48-'51; Ord. (Cong.), Oct. 12, '51; Sea. Ch., Panama, New-Granada, '52-6; Do., Aspinwall, N.G., '56-8; Do., San Francisco, Cal., '58-9; Pas., San Francisco, Cal., '59——.

JAMES SINCLAIR; b., Lakeville, N.Y., ..., 1823; U.N.Y., '48; U.T.S., '48-'51; Ord. (Presb.), Nov. 13, '51; S.S. & Pas., Cutchogue (L.I.), N.Y., '51-'61; S.S., Boiling Spring, N.J., '61-2; S.S., Croton Falls, N.Y., '62-4; W.C., Harlem, N.Y., '64-5; Pas., Smithtown Branch (L.I.), N.Y., '65——.

*JOSEPH WALWORTH SUTPHEN; b., Sweden, N.Y., ..., 1825; H.C., '47; U.T.S., '48-'51; Ord. (Presb.), Nov. 7, '51; F.M., Marsovan, Turkey, '51-2; Died, do., Oct. 9, '52.

LYMAN WESLEY WALSWORTH; b., Adams, N.Y., March 13, 1821; O.C., '48; U.T.S., '49-'51; Ord. (M.E.), May 13, '55; S.S., Lattintown, N.Y., '51-2; S.S., Deposit, N.Y., '52-4; Pas., Newburgh, N.Y., '54-6; Pas., Dobbs' Ferry, N.Y., '56-8; Pas., Pine Plains, N.Y., '58-'60; Pas., Marlboro & Lattintown, N.Y., '60-2; Pas., Hillsdale, N.Y., '62-4; Pas., Lee, Mass., '64-7; Pas., Great Barrington, Mass., '67-'70; Pas., Dobbs' Ferry, N.Y., '70-3; Pas., Hancock, N.Y., '73-6.

EPHER WHITAKER; b., Fairfield, N.J., March 27, 1820; Del.C., '47; U.T.S., '48-'51; Ord. (Presb.), Sep. 10, '51; Pas., Southold (L.I.), N.Y., '51——.

AARON ROBERTS WOLFE; b., Mendham, N.J., Sep. 6, 1821; W.C., '44; U.T.S., '44-5; Tea., '45-8; U.T.S., '48-'51; Ord. (Presb.), Nov. .., '53; Prin., Tallahassee, Fla., & S.S., Iamonia, Fla., '53-5; Tea., N. York City, '55-8; S.S., Parsippany, N.J., '58-9; Prin., Montclair, N.J., '59-'72; W.C., do., '72——. 19.

---

*AUSTIN ARNOLD; b., Haddam, Ct., ..., 1821; Y.C., '48; U.T.S., '48-9; Law, San Francisco, Cal., '49-'50; Died, do., ..., '50.

*MYRON BARRETT; b., North-East, N.Y., Sep. 9, 1816; Y.C., '44; Tea., Columbus, O., '44-8; U.T.S., '48-'50; P.T.S., '50-1; Ord. (Presb.), Mar. 9, '52; S.S., Pontiac, Mich., '51-2; S.S., Detroit, Mich., '52-3; Pas., Newton, N.J, '54-9; S.S., Stroudsburgh, N.J., '60-1; S.S., New-Haven, Ct., '63-4; S.S.,

White Plains, N.Y., '65; W.C., Newton, N.J., '65–6; S.S., Andover, N.J., '67–8; Oc.S., Newton, N.J., '69–'76; Died, do., May 8, '76.

*Jacob Edgerton Blakely; b., Pawlet, Vt., June 9, 1820; M.C., '44; Tea., '44–8; U.T.S., '48–9; Aub.T.S., '49–'51; Ord. (Cong.), Mar. 9, '53; Pas., E. Pultney, Vt., '53–4; Died, do., May 6, '54.

Charles Duryee Buck; b., Knox, N.Y., Aug. 24, 1826; W.C., '45; U.T.S., '48–9; Ord. (R.D.), ..., '61; S.S. & Pas., Peekskill, N.Y., '51–'71; Pas., Hoboken, N.J., '71–4; S.S. (Presb.), Weekawken, N.J., '74——.

Matthias Day; b., Mansfield, O., May 11, 1824; O.C., '48; U.T.S., '48–9; Manuf., Mansfield, O., '50——.

Hannibal Goodwin; b., Ulysses, N.Y., ..., 1823; U.C., '48; U.T.S., '48–9; Ord. (Ep.), June 29, '51; S.S., Allentown, Pa., '51–3; Rec., Bordentown, N.J., '53–8; Rec., San Francisco, Cal., '58–'62; Rec., Napa, Cal., '63–4; Rec., San Francisco, Cal., '64——..; Rec., Newark, N.J., ..——.

Robert Gray; b., Albany, N.Y., ..., 1822; U.T.S., '48–9; Lit., N. York City, ..——.

William Brooks Greene; b., Nantucket, Mass., Nov. 8, 1823; Y.C., '45; U.T.S., '48–9; N.H.T.S., '49–51; Ord. (Cong.), Nov. 15, '55; Pas., Waterville, Me., '55–9; S.S., Needham, Mass., '59–'73; S.S., Scituate, Mass., '73——.

Francis Augustine Howe; b., Pepperell, Mass., ..., 1827; A.C., '48; U.T.S.. '48–9; M.D., Har. C., '54; Physician, Newburyport, Mass., '54——.

Richard Goodell Keyes; b., Watertown, N.Y., Jan. 6, 1826; H.C., '48; U.T.S., '48–9; Aub.T.S., '49–'51; Ord. (Cong.), Sep. 29, '52; S.S., (Presb.), Westford, N.Y., '53–4; S.S., Painted Post, N.Y., '54–6; S.S., Dexter & Brownsville, N.Y., '57–'60; S.S., Evansville, N.Y., '61; S.S., Burrville, N.Y., '63–4; W.C., Watertown, N.Y., '65——.

Daniel Brayton Lyon; b., Edinburgh, N.Y., ..., 1820; U.C., 47; U.T.S., '48–9; Aub. T.S., '49–'51; Ord. (Ep.); H.M., Saginaw, Mich., '52–8; H.M., Ionia, Mich., '59–'63; H.M., Ripon, Wis., '64——.

*Daniel Temple Noyes; b., Boston, Mass., ..., 1824; Y.C., '47; U.T.S., '48–9; And.T.S., '49–'51; Ord. (Cong.), Feb. 16, '53; Pas., Dorchester, Mass., '53–5; S.S., Prairie du Sac, Wis., '55–8; S.S., Spring Green, Wis., '58–'61; U.S.Army, '61–2; Killed, Corinth, Miss., Oct. 4, '62.

*Alexander Fisher Olmsted; b., Chapel Hill, N.C., Dec. 20, 1822; Y.C., '44; N.H.T.S., '46–7; U.T.S., '48–9; Ass. Prof., Univ., Ala., '49; Phil. Dep., Y.C., '49, '51–3; Died, New-Haven, Ct., May 5, '53.

*Andrew Tully Pratt; b., Black Rock, N.Y., Feb. 22, 1826; Y.C., '47; U.T.S., '48–9; N.H.T.S., '49–'51; M.D., Col. Phys. & Surg., N.Y., '52; Ord. (Cong.), Aug. 8, '52; F.M., Aintab, Syria, '53–8; F.M., Aleppo, Syria, '58–'60; F.M., Antioch, Syria, '61–2; F.M., Aleppo, Syria, '62–3; F.M., Marash, Syria, '63–8; Ed., Constantinople, Turkey, '68–'72; Died, do., Dec. 5, '72.

*George Soule; b., Willington, Ct., Oct. 12, 1823; A.C., '47; Tea., '47–8; E.W.T.S., '48–9; U.T.S., '49–'50; E.W.T.S., '50–1; Ord. (Cong.), Oct. 18, '55; S.S., Ashford, Ct., '51–2; S.S. & Pas., Hampton, Ct., '53–67; Died, do., Oct. 4, '67.

Giles Buckingham Willcox; b., New-York City, Aug. 7, 1826; Y.C., '48; U.T.S., '48–9; N.H.T.S., '49–'50; And.T.S., '50–1; Ord. (Cong.), June 15, '53; Pas., Fitchburgh, Mass., '53–6; Pas., Lawrence, Mass., '56–9; Pas., New-London, Ct., '59–'69; Pas., Jersey City, N.J., '69——. 16.

1852.

John William Bailey; b., Marlboro, N. Y., Mar. 26, 1822; W.C., '49; U.T.S., '49–'52; Ord. (Presb.), Dec. 9, '52; Pas. Galesburgh, Ill., '52–7; Prof., K.C., do., '57–'63; S.S., Bloomington, Ill., '64–7; Prof. & Prest., Carlinville, Ill., '67–'76. D.D., W. C., '69.

Charles Washington Baird; b., Princeton, N.J., Aug. 28, 1828; U.N.Y., '48; U.T.S., '49–'52; Ord. (Presb.), Oct. 4, '53; Ch., Rome, It., '52–4; Ag., A. & F.C.U., N. York City, '54–5; W.C., do., '55–9; Pas. (R.D.), S. Brooklyn, N.Y., '59–'61. Pas. (Presb.), Rye, N.Y., '61——. D.D., U.N.Y., '76.

*Jasper Newton Ball; b., Hebron, N.H., Ap. 19, 1826; D.C., '49; U.T.S., '49–'52; Ord. (Cong.), June 30, '53; F.M., Cesarea, Syria, '53–6; F.M., Yoggat, Turkey, '56–'61; S.S. (Presb.), Oconto, Wis., '62–4; S.S., Grand Rapids, Wis., '64–6; F.M., ..., W. Turkey, '66–9; Died, Grand Rapids, Wis., Mar. 9, '70.

James Leonard Corning; b., Albany, N.Y., Aug. 21, 1828; U.N.Y., '49; U.T.S., '49–'50; N.H.T.S., '50–1; U.T.S., '51–2; Ord. (Cong.), June 22, '52; S.S., Quinebaug, Ct., '52–3; Pas. (Presb.), Stamford, Ct., '53–6; Pas., Buffalo, N.Y., '57–'60; Pas., Milwaukee, Wis., '60–1; S.S. (Cong.), Woodstock, Ct., '61–2; Pas., Poughkeepsie, N.Y., '63–9; W.C., Vevay, Switzerland, '69——.

Edward Toppin Doane; b., Staten Island, N.Y., May 30, 1820; I.C., '49; U.T.S., '49–'52; Ord. (Presb.), Feb. 26, '54; F.M., Ebon Isld., Micronesia, '53–'75; F.M., Kobe, Japan, '75——.

Charles Seely Dunning; b., Walkill, N.Y., Jan. 31, 1827; W.C., '48; U.T.S., '49–'52; Ord. (Presb.), Nov. 8, '58; S.S., Binghamton, N.Y., '52–3; Tut., U.T.S., '53–7; Pas., Franklin, N.Y., '58–'61; Pas., Honesdale, Pa., '61——. D.D., L.F.C., '71.

Homer Northrop Dunning; b., Brookfield, Ct., July 17, 1827; Y.C., '48; U.T.S., '49–'52; Ord. (Cong.), Dec. 2, '52; Pas., Gloversville, N.Y., '52–'66; Pas., So. Norwalk, Ct., '66——.

Levi Wells Hart; b., New-Britain, Ct., June 7, 1825; Y.C., '46; Tea., '46–9; U.T.S., '49–'52; Tea., Yonkers, N.Y., '52; Tea., Brooklyn, N.Y., '52–6; Prof., New-Britain, Ct., '56; Tea., Brooklyn, N.Y., '57——.

*Thomas D. Hudson; b., Pulaski Co., Va., ..., 1824; W.C.Va., '49;

U.T.S., '49–'52; Ord. (Presb.), ..., '53; S.S., Newbern, Va., '53–5; Died, Wythe Co., Va., July 15, '55.

THOMAS JEFFERSON LAMAR; b., Jefferson Co., Tenn., Nov. 21, 1826; Mv.C., '48; U.T.S., '49–'52; Ord. (Presb.), May .., '54; H.M., Weston, Mo., '52–5; Tea., Savannah, Mo., '55–7; Prof., Mv.C., '57–'61; S.S., Maryville, Tenn., '61–6; Prof., Mv.C., do., '66——.

ELIJAH DOUGLAS MURPHY; b., Potsdam, N.Y., Feb. 1, 1818; U.N.Y., '49; U.T.S., '49–'52; Ord. (Presb.), May 4, '53; C.M., Brooklyn, N.Y., '53–4; S.S. (Cong.), Centerbrook, Ct., '54–5; S.S., Indian Orchard, Mass., '56–8; Pas., Avon, Ct., '58–'64; U.S.C.Com., '64; Pas. (Presb.), N. York City, '64——.

CHARLES FREDERICK MUSSEY; b., Hanover, N.H., Jan. 26, 1826; D.C., '48; L.T.S., '48–9; And.T.S., '49–'51; U.T.S., '51–2; Halle, Germany, '52–3; Ord. (Cong.), Mar. 26, '54; S.S., McConnellsville, O., '54–5; Pas. (Presb.), Westfield, N.Y., '55–'61; Pas., Batavia, N.Y., '61–9; Pas., Blue Rapids, Kan., '70——. D.D., High.U., '75.

OSCAR NEWTON; b., Madison Co., Miss., Oct. 19, 1830; Mi.C., '49; U.T.S., '49–'52; Ord. (Presb.) Aug. 2, '58; Tea., Jackson, Miss., '52–6; Tea., Summit, Miss., '57–9; Tea., Crystal Springs, Miss., '60——.

*EDWARD PEET; b., Hartford, Ct., May 28, 1826; U.N.Y., '47; U.T.S., '49–'52; Prof., D. & D. Inst., N. York City, '48–'62; Died, do., Jan. 27, '62.

EDGAR MORRISON RICHARDSON; b., Camden Co., N.C., Jan. 12, 1828; Mi.C., '49; U.T.S., '49–'52; Ord. (Presb.), ..., '53; S.S., Grenada, Miss., '53–'68; Pas., Memphis, Tenn., '69——.

*JAMES MONROE RICHARDSON; b., Carroll Co., Miss., ..., 1829; Mi.C., '49; U.T.S., '49–'52; Ord. (Presb.), ..., '53; S.S., Marion, Miss., '52–8; Tea., Enterprise, Miss., '58–'60; S.S., Flower's Place, Miss., '60–1; Conf. Army, '62–4; Killed in battle, ..., Ga., '64.

JOHN ALONZO SEYMOUR; b., Ridgefield, O., June 21, 1827; A.C., '49; U.T.S., '49–'52; Ord. (Cong.), Jan. 2, '55; S.S. & Pas., Kent, O., '52–6; S.S. & Pas., South Glastenbury, Ct., '56–'62; Pas., Enfield, Mass., '62–7; D. Sec., A.T.S., Cleveland, O., '67–'71; D. Supt., P.B.Pub., do., '71——.

JAMES REDFIELD SMITH; b., Delhi, N.Y., ..., 1819; U.T.S., '49–'52; Ord. (Presb.), May .., '53; S.S., Edgington, Ill., '53–4; S.S., Elizabeth & Plum River, Ill., '54–'62; S.S., Elizabeth, Ill., '62–4; W.C., Pleasant Corners, Ill., '64; S.S., Elizabeth, Ill., '65–6; S.S., Winslow, Ill., '67–9; W.C., Plum River, Ill., '69——.

WILLIAM SPOONER SMITH; b., Leverett, Mass., July 10, 1821; A.C., '48; U.T.S., '49–'52; Ord. (Cong.), Ap. 27, '54; S.S., Prompton & Bethany, Pa., '52–3; Pas., N. York City, '54–6; S.S., Stratham, N.H., '57–9; Pas., Guilford, Ct., '59–'65; W.C., Needham (Grantville), Mass., '65–6; W.C., W. Newton (Auburndale), Mass., '66——.

ELIJAH WOODWARD STODDARD; b., Coventryville, N.Y., Ap. 23, 1820; A.C., '49; U.T.S., '49–'52; Ord. (Presb.), July 11, '52; S.S., Hawley, Pa., '52–5; Pas., Amenia, N.Y., '55–'60; Pas., Angelica, N.Y., '60–4; Pas., Succasunna, N.J., '64——.

GEORGE PHILLIPS TINDALL; b., Lawrenceville, N.J., Ap. 29, 1822; U.M., '49; U.T.S., '49–'52; Ord. (Presb.), Ap. .., '53; Pas., Dayton, O., '53–7; Pas., Indianapolis, Ind., '57–'63; Pas., Ypsilanti, Mich., '63–'75; Pas., Flint, Mich., '75——.

*FREDERICK WHITNEY WILLIAMS; b., Kingston, N.J., July 22, 1829; U.N.Y., '49; U.T.S., '49–'52; Ord. (Cong.), Feb. 8, '54; Pas., New-Canaan, Ct., '54–'61; Trav., Europe, '61; S.S., Orient (L.I.), N.Y., '62; S.S., Black Rock, Ct., '63–'70; Europe, '71–5; Died, Rome, Italy, Ap. 3, '75. 22.

---

*WILLIAM WILDMAN CUMBERLAND; b., Elizabeth, N.J., ..., 1821; Ma.C., '46; U.T.S., '49–'51; Not Ord.; Mechanic, Jersey City, N.J.; Died, ..., ..., '61.

WILLIAM COWPER DICKINSON; b., Longmeadow, Mass., Jan. 26, 1827; A.C., '48; U.T.S., '49–'51; Tut., A.C., '51–2; And.T.S., '52–3; Ord. (Cong.), Ap. 12, '54; Pas., Middleboro, Mass., '54–6; S.S., Wilmington, Del., '56; S.S., Gloucester, Mass., '56–7; Pas., Kenosha, Wis., '58–9; Pas. (Presb.), Lake Forest, Ill., '59–'67; Pas., Battle Creek, Mich., '70–2; Pas., La Fayette, Ind., '72——.

HENRY KINGMAN EDSON; b., Hadley, Mass., Oct. 5, 1822; A.C., '44; Tea., '44–9; U.T.S., '49; S.S., Westhampton, Mass., '52; Prin., Denmark, Io., '52——.

JUNIUS LORIN HATCH; b., Warwick, Mass., ..., 1825; A.C., '49; U.T.S., '49–'50; Ord. (Cong.), ..., '53; S.S., Gloucester, Mass., '53–5; S.S., Brooklyn, N.Y., '55–'60; S.S. (Unit.), Concord, N.H., '64—— ..; S.S., Santa Clara, Cal., .. ——.

*HENRY CONDICT HEDGES; b., Newark, N.J., ..., 1828; Y.C., '48; U.T.S., '49–'50; Trade, N. York City, '51–9; Died, Newark, N.J., ..., '59.

ISAAC NEWTON HILL; b., New-Paltz, N.Y., May 19, 1828; M.U., '49; U.T.S., '49–'50; Ord. (Bap.), Sept. 10, '50; Pas., Cross River, N.Y., ...; Pas., Dover Plains, N.Y., ...; Pas., Albany, N.Y., ...; Pas., Bridgeport, Ct., ..., '57; Pas., Elizabeth, N.J., '57–9; Pas., New-Market, N.J., '59–'65; Pas., Jerseyville, Ill., '65——; Pas., Macomb, Ill., ...; Pas., South-Dover, N.Y., .. ——; P.O.Ad., Wing's Station, Dutchess Co., N.Y.

*JAMES BARBER HOWARD; b., Pittsfield, Mass., ..., 1824; W.C., '49; U.T.S., '49–'50; And.T.S., '51–2; Ord. (Cong.), Dec. 12, '54; Pas., Rockport, Me., '54–5; Died, Pittsfield, Mass., Jan. 16, '56.

*JOSEPH HURLBUT, Jr.; b., New-York City, Feb. 19, 1828; Y.C., '49; U.T.S., '49–'50; Tut., Bel. C., Beloit, Wis., '50–1; And.T.S., '51–2; Tut., Y.C., New-Haven, Ct., '52–4; Died, Paris, France, July 4, '55.

*JOHN FRELINGHUYSEN JUDD; b., Catskill, N.Y., ..., 1825; U.N.Y., '44; Tea., '44–9; U.T.S., '49–'50; Tea., Berkshire, N.Y., '50–2; Inv., do., '52–9; Died, do., Feb. 12, '59.

*JOHN MCNULTY; b., Killalla, Ireland, June 29, 1829; Belf.C., '49; Nbg.T.S., '49-'50; U.T.S., '50-1; P.T.S., '51-2; Ord. (Presb.), Feb. 24, '54; S.S., Donaldson, Pa., '52-3; H.M., Richmond City, Wis., '53-4; S.S., Dekorra, Wis., '54-'61; Died, do., May 15, '61.

JOHN NEWBANKS; b., Chazy, N.Y., Aug. 30, 1824; W.C., '49; U.T.S., '49-'50; Aub.T.S., '50-2; Ord. (Presb.), ..., '53; Pas., Chester, N.Y., '53-5; Lun. Asylum, '55-'60, and Marshall Infirmary, Troy, N.Y., '60——.

JOSIAH WILCOX NORTH; b., Berlin, Ct., Feb. 10, 1827; H.C., '48; U.T.S., '49-'50; N.H.T.S., '50-2; Ord. (Cong.), Sept. 22, '52; S.S., Geneseo, Ill., '52-4; S.S., Como, Ill., '55-6; W.C., Middletown, Ct., '56——.

HENRY JOHNSON PATRICK; b., Warren, Mass., Sept. 20, 1827; A.C., '48; U.T.S., '49-'51; And.T.S., '52; Ord. (Cong.), Nov. 16, '54; Pas., Bedford, Mass., '54-'60; Pas., W. Newton, Mass., '60——.

THOMAS RUGGLES GOLD PECK; b., Whitesboro, N.Y., ..., 1831; U.C., '48; U.T.S., '49-'51; Trav., Europe, '52-3; As. Ed., N. York City, '53-4; Ord. (R.D.), ..., '54; Pas., Richmond (S.I.), N.Y., '54-9; Pas., Charleston, S.C., '59-'64; Pas., Hastings-upon-Hudson, N.Y., '65——.

ISAAC OLIVER SLOAN; b., Philadelphia, Pa., ..., 1821; Jef.C., '42; U.T.S., '49-'50; Ord. (Presb.), ..., '56; S.S., ..., .., '52-6; Pas., Talleysville, Va., '56——..; S.S., Marine, Minn., '67-9; S.S., Belle Plaine, Minn., '69-'74; S.S., Bismarck, D. T., '74——.

DAVID HAVEN THAYER; b., Nunda, N.Y., ..., 1825; U.C., '49; U.T.S., '49-'50; N.H.T.S., '50-2; Ord. (Cong.), Jan. 5, '53; Pas., Mt. Carmel, Ct., '53-'66; Pas., E. Windsor, Ct., '66——.

*CORNELIUS WILLIAMS TOLLES; b., Newark, N.J., ..., 1828; C.N.J., '48; U.T.S., '49-'51; Lit., Newark, N.J., '51-'61; U.S.Army, '61-4; Died, of wounds, near Winchester, Va., Nov. 7, '64.

GEORGE SPAFFORD WOODHULL; b., New-York City, July 25, 1829; U.N.Y., '48; U.T.S., '49-'50; P.T.S., '50-2; Ord. (Presb.), May 18, '53; S.S. & Pas., Point Pleasant, W. Va., '53-'61; Ch., U. S. Army, '61-4; S.S. (Cong.), Tinmouth, Vt., '65-8; S.S., Cambridge, Wis., '69-'71; Prin., Flemington, N.J., '71-4; Pas. (Presb.), Marinette, Wis., '75——. 18.

1853.

CARSON WILLIAM ADAMS; b., Wilmington, Del., Nov. 29, 1825; D.C., '50; U.T.S., '50-3; Ord. (Presb.), June 26, '53; Pas., Pole Creek & Salem Chh., Va., '54-7; Pas., Thompsonville, Ct., '57-'68; S.S., Red Mills, N.Y., '68-'71; Pas., Waterville, N.Y., '71-4; Pas., N. York City (West-Farms), '76——.

PETER MASON BARTLETT; b., Salisbury, Ct., Feb. 6, 1820; W.C., '50; U.T.S., '50-3; Ord. (Cong.), Aug. .., '53; Ag., A.T.S., S.W. Ohio, Cincinnati, O., '53-4; Pas. (Presb.), Circleville, O., '54-7; Pas., Lansingburgh, N.Y., '57-'60; S.S., Flushing (L.I.), N.Y., '60-1; Ch., U.S.Army, '62-4; S.S., Williamstown, Mass., '64-6; Pas., Windsor Locks, Ct., '66-8; Prest. Mv.C., Maryville, Tenn., '69——. D.D., D.C., '72.

ELIAS LEVI BOING; b., New-York City, Oct. 31, 1824; U.N.Y., 50; U.T.S., '50-3; Ord. (Presb.), Sep. 1, '53; F.M., Choctaws, Ind. Terr., '53-4; S.S. (Cong.), Almont, Mich., '55; S.S. (Presb.), Durham, N.Y., '56-'64; Pas., Angelica, N.Y., '64-8; Ag., P.C.H.M., '68-'71; Pas., Federalsburgh, Md., '72——.

*JOHN HENRY BRODT; b., Troy, N.Y., July 2, 1827; U.T.S., '50-3; Res. Lic., '53-4; Ord. (Presb.), June 29, '54; H.M. & S.S., Columbia, Cal., '54-5; Ed., San Francisco, Cal., '56; Pas. (Cong.), Petaluma, Cal., '58-'62; S.S. (Presb.), Maryville, Cal., '62-4; S.S., San Francisco, Cal., '64; S.S., Salem, N.Y., '65-7; Pas. (Cong.), Brooklyn, N.Y., '67-'72; W.C., Dansville, N.Y., '73-5; Died, do., Sep. 8, '75.

LEVI PARSONS CRAWFORD; b., Lincoln Co., Tenn., May 20, 1823; I.C., '48; U.T.S., '50-3; Ord. (Presb.), June 23, '53; Ag., A.S.S.U., Ill., '53-6; Pas., Sandwich & Somonauk, Ill., '56-'65; Ch., U.S.Army, '62; Pas., Somonauk, Ill., '65-'70; Pas., Lincoln, Ill., '70——.

*RICHARD CHAPMAN DUNN; b., Augusta, Ga., Sep. 6, 1821; K.C., '47; U.T.S., '50-3; Ord. (Cong.), Mar. 19, '54; S.S., Dewitt & Jamesville, N.Y., '53-4; S.S., Peoria, Ill., '54; Pas., Toulon, Ill., '55-'67; S.S., Oneida, Ill., '67-8; Died, do., May 24, '68.

*EDWIN GOODELL; b., Westminster, Vt., July 19, 1824; D.C., '50; U.T.S., '50-3; Res. Lic., '53-4; Ord. (Cong.), June 12, '54; F.M., Smyrna, Asia, '54-5; Inv., Birmingham & Bloomfield, Mich., '56-'63; Died, Bloomfield, Mich., Sep. 29, '63.

GEORGE HENRY GOULD; b., Oakham, Mass., Feb. 20, 1827; A.C., '50; U.T.S, '50-1; And.T.S., '51-2; U.T.S., '52-3; Ord. (Cong.), Nov. 16, '62; S.S., Waukegan, Wis., '53; S.S., Kenosha, Wis., '54; Evang., '55-6; Trav. Europe, '57; Evang., '58-'62; S.S., Springfield, Mass., '62-4; Pas., Hartford, Ct., '64-'70; S.S., Worcester, Mass., '72-6; Prof. & Pas., A.C., Amherst, Mass., '76——. D.D., AC., '70.

TIMOTHY ALLYN HAZEN; b., West-Springfield, Mass., June 24, 1826; W.C., '49; E.W.T.S., '50-2; U.T.S., '52-3; Ord. (Cong.), Oct. 11, '54; Tea., Lenox, Mass., '53-4; Pas., Dalton, Mass., '54-9; S.S., Broadbrook, Ct., '59-'63; Pas., So. Egremont, Mass., '63-9; Pas., Housatonic, Mass., '69-'72; Pas., Goshen, Ct., '72——.

HENRY GRISWOLD JESUP; b., Westport, Ct., Jan. 23, 1826; Y.C., '47; U.T.S., '50-3; Ord. (Cong.), Ap. 26, '54; Pas., Stanwich, Ct., '54-'62; Inv., Amherst, Mass., '63——.

VERNETTE LE ROY LOCKWOOD; b., Rochester, N.Y., Dec. 12, 1825; K.C., '50; U.T.S., '50-3; Ord. (Cong.), Jan. .., '54; S.S., Galena, Ill., '53-4; Pas., Granville, Ill., '54-9; Pas. (Presb.), Rahway, N.J., '59-'64; W.C., Brooklyn, N.Y., '64-5; Pas., Durham, N.Y., '65-9; Pas., N. York Mills, N.Y., '69-'75; S.S., Hillsdale, Mich., '75——.

SAMUEL LOOMIS; b., Twinsburgh, Ohio, Feb. 8, 1829; W.R.C., '49; U.T.S., '50-3; Ord. (Presb.), ..., '57; Ag., A.T.S., Athens, Ga., '53-4; S.S., Grinnell, Io., '55-7; S.S., Roseville & New-Lexington, O., '57-8; Pas., Rensselaerville, N.Y., '59-'63; Pas., Vineland, N.J., '63-5; H.M., Chester, S.C., '66——.

*CHARLES FINNEY MARTIN; b., Galesburgh, Ill., ..., 1827; K.C., '46; Tea., Lisbon, Ill., '46–'50; U.T.S., '50–3; Ord. (Cong.), ..., '54; F.M., Copts, Cairo, Egypt, '54–8; Pas., Peru, Ill., '59 '63; D. Sec., A.T.S. (of Boston), Nashville, Tenn., '63–4; Died, do., Feb. 7, '64.

WARREN MAYO; b., Guilford, N.Y., Nov. 1, 1825; U.T.S., '50–3; Ord. (Presb.), Jan. 4, '54; S.S., Stamford, N.Y., '53–8; S.S., Minneola, Kan., '59; S.S., Ludlow, Mass., '60–2; Pas., Danby, N.Y., '62–6; Pas., Lodi, Wis., '67–'71; Pas., Baxter Springs, Kan., '72——.

JOHN McCAMPBELL; b., Dandridge, Tenn., Oct. 29, 1825; Mv.C., '49; U.T.S., '50–3; Ord. (Presb.), June 26, '53; S.S., Auburn, Miss., '53–7; S.S., Lexington, Miss., '57–'72; Ch., Conf. Army, '63–5; Pas., Monroe, La., '72–4; Pas., Grenada, Miss., '74——.

JAMES JOHN McMAHON; b., Tyrone, Ireland, Dec. 10, 1825; U.T.S., '50–3; Ord. (Presb.), Dec. 4, '53; Pas., Richmond, Va., '53–9; Pas., Marion, Va., '59–'64; W.C., N. Haverstraw, N.Y., '64——.

AARON BURR PEFFERS; b., New-York City, June 27, 1824; U.N.Y., '50; U.T.S., '50–3; Ord. (Cong.), May 28, '55; Pas., New-Fairfield, Ct., '55–8; S.S., Charlton Centre, N.Y., '58–9; Pas., Epsom, N.H., '60–5; Pas., N. Wrentham, Mass., '65–8; Pas., Schódack, N.Y., '69–'73; S.S., Dracut, Mass., '74——.

JOHN REID; b., Edinburgh, Scotland, Ap. 29, 1820; U.T.S., '50–3; Ord. (Presb.), Ap. 19, '54; Pas., Franklinville (L.I.), N.Y., '54–'60; S.S., New-Haven, N.Y., '61–6; Pas., Angelica, N.Y., '67–'74; S.S., Youngstown, N.Y., '74——.

JOSEPH EDWIN ROY; b., Martinsburgh, Ohio, Feb. 7, 1827; K.C., '48; U.T.S., '50–3; Ord. (Cong.), Oct. 15, '53; Pas., Brimfield, Ill., '53–5; Pas., Chicago, Ill., '55–'60; D. Sec., A.H.M.S., Chicago, Ill., '60——. D.D., K.C., '70.

ALFRED BROWN SWIFT; b., St. Albans, Vt., Sep. 3, 1827; U.Vt., '47; U.T.S., '49–'51, '52–3; Ord. (Presb.), Jan. 7, '55; Pas., Middle Granville, N.Y., '55'–'61; S.S. (Cong.), Enosburgh, Vt., '61——.

SIGISMUND UHLFELDER; b., Linkerstein, Bavaria, Oct. .., 1819; Ok.C., '48; U.T.S., '50–3; Ord. (Presb.), June 26, '53; S.S., Lower Liberty, O., '53–5; S.S., Marine, Ill., '56–7; S.S., Westfield, Wis., '57–9; S.S., Sherill's Mount, Io., '59–'62; Trade, N. York City, '63——.

THEODORE FRELINGHUYSEN WHITE; b., New-York City, July 11, 1830; U.N.Y., '49; U.T.S., '49–'50, '51–3; Ord. (Presb.), Jan. 4, '54; S.S., Greenville, N.Y., '53–6; Pas., Mendham, N.J., '56–'60; S.S., N. York City, '60–1; Pas., Delhi, N.Y., '62–5; Pas., Ithaca, N.Y., '65——. D.D., Mv.C., '71. 22.

JOSEPH R. ASH; b., Philadelphia, Pa., ..., 1827; Del.C., '49; U.T.S., '50–1.

JOSEPH AVERY BENT; b., Middlebury, Vt., Ap. 22, 1823; M.C., '45; Prin. Union Co., Ind., '45–7; Prin., Ac. Dep., Knox Coll., Galesburgh, Ill., '47–9; Tut., M.C., '49–'50; U.T.S., '50–1; And.T.S., '51–3; Ord. (Cong.), Nov.

1, '54; S.S., Stowe, Vt., '53–4; Pas., Cornwall, Vt., '54–6; S.S. & Tea., Hoyleton, Ill., '57–'66; Prof., Wh.C., Wheaton, Ill., '66–'71; Ag., Kan., do., '71——.

GEORGE A. CALDWELL; b., Newmarket, Tenn., ..., 1825; U.T.S., '50–1; Ord. (Presb.), ..., '53; S.S., Athens, Tenn., '53–'63; Ch., Conf. Army, '63–5; S.S., Bristol, Tenn., '65——.

CHARLES JEWETT COLLINS; b., Wilkesbarre, Pa., June 25, 1825; W.C., '45; U.T.S., '50; P.T.S., '51–4; Tea., Wilkesbarre, Pa., '55–6; Ord. (Presb.), Dec. 31, '56; Pas., Danville, Pa., '57–'65; Supt. P. Schools, Wilkesbarre, Pa., '65–'74; Prin., Coll. Prep. School, Princeton, N.J., '74——.

JUDSON HAWLEY HOPKINS; b., Astoria, N.Y., ..., 1830; R.C., '50; U.T.S., '50–2; P.T.S., '52–3; Ord. (Presb.), Dec. .., '60; S.S., Greenwich, Ct., '53–4; W.C., Ravenswood (L.I.), N.Y., '54–9; Pas., Newburgh, N.Y., '60–4; W.C., Ravenswood (L.I.), N.Y., '65–'70; S.M., do., '70–2; W.C., do., '72——.

*FRANCIS N. SHAW; b., Foxboro, Mass., ..., 1824; And.T.S., '50–1; U.T.S., '51; Died, ...

WILLIAM BEINHAUER SILBER; b., New-York City, Nov. 22, 1826; W.U., '50; U.T.S., '50–1; Prof., Coll. City of N.Y., '51–'70; Pres. Coll., Albion, Mich., '70–1; Ag., B. of Ed., Detroit, Mich., '71–3; Do., N. York City, '73——. Ph.D., N.Y.U., '68; M.D., Detroit Hom. Coll., '73; LL.D., Iowa Wes. Un., '74.

ALLEN TRAVER; b., Claverack, N.Y., Dec. 11, 1827; Pa.C., '51; U.T.S., '52–3; Ord. (Ev.Lu.), Sep. .., '54; S.S. (Presb.), La Fayette, N.Y., '54; S.S., Ludlowville, N.Y., '55; S.S., Belmont, N.Y., '56; Pas., Corfu, N.Y., '56–'67; Pas., Middle Granville, N.Y., '67–'71; Pas., Hebron, N.Y., '71–2; Pas., Wampsville, N.Y., '73——. 8.

1854.

ALBERT GRAHAM BEEBEE; b., Hartwick, N.Y., July 3, 1826; A.C., '50; U.T.S., '51–2; A.T.S., '52–3; U.T.S., '53–4; Ord. (Presb.), June 20, '54; F.M., Marash, Turkey, '54–9; Pas., Pleasant Mount & Unionville, Pa., '60–2; S.S., Hancock, N.Y., '62–3; Pas., Manitowoc, Wis., '64–5; S.S., Geneva, Ill., '65–7; W.C., Chicago, Ill., '68–9; W.C., Lombard, Ill., '69–'70; S.S., Spring Lake, Mich., '70–2; S.S., Milford, N.Y., '73–4; S.S., E. Worcester, N.Y., '74——.

WILLIAM EDWARD CALDWELL; b., Charlestown, Mass., June 6, 1825; U.T.S., '51–4; Ord. (Cong.), Feb. 10, '63; S.S., DeWitt, N.Y., '54–6; S.S., Wellfleet, Mass., '62–5; S.S., Lodi, Mich., '66–'71; S.S., Somerset, Mich., '71–4; S.S., Clio, Mich., '74——.

JAMES MONROE CARROLL; b., Arcadia, N.Y., Ap. 21, 1825; W.U., '51; U.T.S., '51–4; Tea., E. Greenwich, R.I., '54–7; Ord. (M.E.), Ap. 2, '59; Pas., Providence, R.I., '57–9; Pas., Westville, Ct., '59–'61; Pas., Bloomfield, Ct., '61–3; Pas., N. York City, '63–4; Pas., New-Canaan, Ct., '64–7; Pas., Bridgeport, Ct., '67–'70; Pas., Mt. Vernon, N.Y., '70–3; Pas., Mianus, N.Y., '73–6.

VARNUM DANIEL COLLINS; b., Brockport, N.Y., May 13, 1827; Wab.C., '50: U.T.S., '51-4; Ord. (Presb.), May 17, '55; F.M., Rio Janeiro, B., '55-6; S.S., Philadelphia, Pa., '56-7; Ag., A.B.S., S. America, '58-'60; S.S., Washington, D.C., '60-4; Agr. Ag., U.S.Gov., China, '64-5; W.C., London, Eng., '66——.

LUTHER HART CONE; b., Bristol, Ct., Feb. 19, 1824; Y.C., '47; U.T.S., '51-4; Ord. (Presb.), Ap. 5, '55; H.M., Indian Orchard, Mass., '55; S.S. & Pas. (Cong.), Chicopee, Mass., '56-'67; Pas., Springfield, Mass., '67——.

LA FAYETTE DUDLEY; b., Bath, N.Y., July 2, 1825; A.C., '51; U.T.S., '51-4; Ord. (Presb.), Feb. 8, '57; Tea., Davenport, Io., '54-5; Pas., Cedar Rapids, Io., '56-9; S.S., Atalissa, Io., '59-'61; Tea., Bath, N.Y., '62-4; Tea., Cornwall, Ct., '65——.

GEORGE E. EAGLETON; b., Murfreesboro, Tenn., Dec. 31, 1831; U.U., '51; U.T.S., '53-4; Ord. (Presb.), Ap. 8, '55; S.S., Macon & Cooksville, Miss., '55-6; S.S., Richland & Cornersville, Tenn., '56-7; S.S., Swan Creek & Petersburgh, Tenn., '57-'62; S.S., New-Market, Tenn., '62-5; S.S., Concord, N.C., '65-8; Pas., Mt. Holly, Ark., '68——.

WALTER FREAR; b., Poughkeepsie, N.Y., Aug. 16, 1828; Y.C., '51; U.T.S., '51-2; And.T.S., '52-3; U.T.S., '53-4; Res. Lic., N.H.T.S., '54-5; Ord. (Presb.), Oct. 17, '55; S.S., Iowa City, Cal., '55-6; S.S., Placerville, Cal., '57-'61; S.S. (Cong.), Grass Valley, Cal., '61-4; S.S., Santa Cruz, Cal., '65-'70; S.S., Honolulu, H.I., '70——.

THOMAS NELSON HASKELL; b., Mina, N.Y., Jan. 20, 1826; U.Mi., '51; U.T.S., '51-2; And.T.S., '52-3; U.T.S., '53-4; Ord. (Presb.), Feb. 7, '55; Pas., Washington, D.C., '54-8; Pas. (Cong.), E. Boston, Mass., '58-'62; Pas. (Presb.), E. Boston, Mass., '62-6; Prof., Univ. of Wisconsin, '67-9; Pas. (Cong.), Aurora, Ill., '69-'73; W.C., Denver, Col., '73——.

WILLIAM STEVENS KARR; b., Newark, N.J., Jan. 9, 1829; A.C., '51; U.T.S., '51-4; Ord. (Presb.), Sep. 26, '54; Pas., Brooklyn, N.Y., '54-'67; Pas. (Cong.), Chicopee, Mass., '67-8; Pas., Keene, N.H., '68-'72; Pas., Cambridge, Mass., '73-6; Prof., E.W.T.S., Hartford, Ct., '76——. D.D., A.C., '76.

MARTIN KELLOGG; b., Vernon, Ct., Mar. 15, 1828; Y.C., '50; U.T.S., '51-2; And.T.S., '52-3; U.T.S., '53-4; Res. Lic., N.H.T.S., '54-5; Ord. (Cong.), Oct. 2, '55; S.S., Shasta, Cal., '55-7; Pas., Grass Valley, Cal., '57-'60; Prof., Cal.C., Oakland, Cal., '60-9; Prof., Univ. of Cal., do., '69——.

ETHAN P. LARKIN; b., Westerly, R.I., ..., 1827; O.C., '52; U.T.S., '51-4; Tea., Milwaukee, Wis., .. —— ..; Trade, Peru, S. Am., .. ——.

*PATRICK J. LEO; b., ..., Ireland, ..., 1827; U.T.S., '51-4; Ord. (Ep.), ..., '58; Ag., A. & F.C.U., Boston, Mass., '54-7; Rec., Annsdown, Ireland, '58-'64; Died, do., Oct. .., '64.

HENRY AXTELL LOUNSBURY; b., Ovid, N.Y., Oct. 26, 1827; U.C., '49; Aub.T.S., '51-3; U.T.S., '53-4; Ord. (Cong.), Feb. 13, '56; Pas., Seabrook, N.H., '56-7; S.S., Beverly, Mass., '58-9; S.S., Wilton, Me., '60-2; S.S., Richmond, Me., '62–4 ; S.S., Barnstable (Hyannis), Mass., '66–9 ; W.C., Boston, Mass., '69–'70 ; S.S., Shirley Village, Mass., '70——.

WALDO WHITING LUDDEN ; b., Shelburne, Mass., ..., 1827 ; W.C., '51 ; U.T.S., '51–4 ; S.S., Magnolia, Io., '55–6 ; Tea. of Music, New-Haven, Ct., '57——.

JERRE LORENZO LYONS ; b., Montrose, Pa., Ap. 18, 1824 ; W.C., '51 ; U.T.S., '51–4 ; Ord. (Presb.), Nov. 9, '54 ; F.M., Beirut, Syria, '54–5 ; F.M., Tripoli, Syria, '55–'60 ; F.M., Sidon, Syria, '60–2 ; Inv., Montrose, Pa., '63–'71 ; Supt., A.B.S., Jacksonville, Fla., '72——.

WILLIAM T. MCELROY ; b., Lebanon, Ky., ..., 1830 ; Cr.C., '50 ; U.T.S., '51–4 ; Ord. (Presb.), ..., '54 ; S.S., McAfee, Ky., '54–7 ; W.C., Lebanon, Ky., '58–'60 ; Pas., Maysville, Ky., '60–2 ; S.S., Louisville, Ky., '62—— . . ; S.S., Perryville, Ky., . . ——.

WILLIAM EDWARD MERRIMAN ; b., Hinsdale, Mass., Oct. 20, 1825 ; W.C., '50 ; U.T.S., '51–4 ; Ord. (Cong.), Jan. 13, '57 ; S.S., S. Plainfield, Ct., '56–7 ; Pas., Batavia, Ill., '57–'60 ; S.S., Green Bay, Wis., '61–3 ; Prest., Rip.C., Ripon, Wis., '63——. D.D., W.C., '74.

JOHN WATKINS MOSELEY ; b., Fredericktown, Mo., Nov. 14, 1828 ; L.T.S., '51–3 ; U.T.S., '53–4 ; Ord. (Presb.), May . ., '54 ; H.M., Oneida Co., N.Y., '54 ; H.M., Deerfield, La., '55–6 ; H.M., Richland, La., '56–7 ; H.M., Deerfield, La., '57–'63 ; S.S., Shreveport, La., '63–5 ; Tea., ..., Va., '65–'72 ; S.S., Enon, Miss., '72–4 ; S.S., Garlandsville, Miss., '74——.

*FLOYD OVERTON ; b., Brookhaven (L.I.), N.Y., ..., 1823 ; A.C., '51 ; U.T.S., '51–4 ; Died, Elmwood, Ill., Aug. . ., '55.

SANFORD RICHARDSON ; b., Pekin, Ill., ..., 1825 ; K.C., '46 ; U.T.S., '51–4 ; Ord. (Presb.), June 25, '54 ; F.M., Erzeroom, Asia, '54–6 ; F.M., Arabkir, Asia, '56–'64 ; F.M., Angora, Asia, '64——.

OVA HOYT SEYMOUR ; b., Syracuse, N.Y., Sep. 14, 1826 ; U.C., '51 ; U.T.S., '51–4 ; Ord. (Presb.), June 13, '55 ; Pas., Deposit, N.Y., '54–7 ; Pas., Cortland, N.Y., '57–'63 ; Ch., U.S.Army, '63–5 ; W.C., Cortland, N.Y., '65 ; Pas., Hammondsport, N.Y., '65–9 ; Pas., Trumansburgh, N.Y., '69——.

THOMAS EDWARD SKINNER ; b., Harvey's Neck, N.C., Ap. 29, 1825 ; U.N.C., '47 ; U.T.S., '51–4 ; Ord. (Bap.), ..., '54 ; Pas., Petersburgh, Va., '54–5 ; Pas., Raleigh, N.C., '55–'67 ; Pas., Nashville, Tenn., '67–'70 ; Pas., Columbus, Ga., '70–2 ; Pas., Athens, Ga., '72–5 ; Pas., Macon, Ga., '75——. D.D., Furman Univ., Tenn., '66.

CHARLES CASEY STARBUCK ; b., Boston, Mass., Dec. 4, 1827 ; O.C., '49 ; O.T.S., '51–2 ; U.T.S., '52–4 ; Ord. (Cong.), Oct. 11, '55 ; F.M., Jamaica, W.I., '55–'61 ; Tea., N. York City, '62–6 ; F.M., Jamaica, W.I., '66–'71 ; Tea, Berea, Ky., '71–2 ; Pas., Wittenburgh, Io., '73–4 ; Pas., Keatskotoos, Neb., '74–6 ; S.S., Monroe, Neb., '76——.

*JOHN SHERIDAN ZELIE ; b., Franklin, N.Y., Oct. 27, 1824 ; A.C., '51 ; B.T.S., '51–3 ; U.T.S., '53–4 ; Ord. (Cong.), May 20, '55 ; S.S., Mokelumne Hill, Cal., '55–7 ; S.S., Santa Cruz, Cal., '57–'60 ; S.S., Redwood City, Cal., '61–3 ; S.S., Princeton, Mass., '64–6 ; Died, do., Aug. 21, '66. 25.

William Elliott Bassett; b., Derby, Ct., May 24, 1829; Y.C., '50; U.T.S., '51-2; N.H.T.S., '52-4; Res.Lic., do., '54-5; Ord. (Cong.), Oct. 14, '56; Pas., Central Village, Ct., '56-9; W.C., Andover, Mass., '60-1; S.S., N. Manchester, Ct., '61-3; S.S. & Pas., Warren, Ct., '63-'75; W.C., New-Haven, Ct., '75——.

James Bolton; b., Doe Run, Pa., Dec. 26, 1826; U.C., '51; U.T.S., '51-3; Ord. (R.D.), May 3, '56; Pas., Fordham, N.Y., '56-'65; Pas., Colt's Neck, N.J., '65——.

Theodore Bourne; b., Sing-Sing, N.Y., Mar. 2, 1822; U.T.S., '51-3; Sec., Af. Civ. Soc., N.Y.C., .. —— ..; Sec., do., London, Eng., .. —— ..; Gm. Ag., A.F.C.U., W.N.Y., .. —— ..; Ed. & Tea., N.Y.C., .. ——.

Chauncey Marvin Cady; b., Westport, N.Y., May 16, 1824; U.M., '51; U.T.S., '51-3; Ed. & Pub. of Music, N. York City, & Chicago, Ill., '53——

Henry Barton Chapin; b., Rochester, N.Y., Sep. 14, 1827; Y.C., '47; U.T.S., '51-2; P.T.S., '52-4; Ord. (Presb.), Oct. 29, '54; C.M., N. York City, '54-6; Pas., Steubenville, O., '56-8; Pas., Trenton, N.J., '58-'66; S.S. & Tea., N. York City, '67——; Ph.D., C.N.J., '68.

*James Johnston; b., Bordentown, N.J., ..., 1818; U.T.S., '51-3; Died, N. York City, Aug. 15, '53.

Jacob William Marcussohn; b., Odessa, Russia, July 11, 1826; W.C., '52; E.W.T.S., '52-3; U.T.S., '53-4; E.W.T.S., '54; Ord. (Cong.), Jan. 23, '55; F.M., Salonica, Turkey, '55-8; F.M., Constantinople, Turkey, '58-'62; S.S. (Presb.), Lockport, N.Y., '63-7; Pas., Lyndonville, N.Y., '67——.

Sidney Harper Marsh; b., U.T.S., Prince Edward Co., Va., Aug. 29, 1825; U.Vt., '46; U.T.S., '51-2; Ord. (Cong.), May .., '53; Prest., P.U., Forest Grove, Or., '54——. D.D., U.Vt., '62.

Alexander Vernon Murdoch; b., Glasgow, Scotland, Oct. 23, 1828; U.C., '45; U.T.S., '51-3; Ord. (Presb.), ..., '57; S.S., Madison, N.Y., '57-8; Ch., U.S.Army., '62-5; Lawyer, Elmira, N.Y., '65——. 9.

1855.

Charles Henry Barrett; b., ..., .., ..., 1821; Y.C., '52; U.T.S., '52-5; Sea Captain, '56-'62; W.C., N. York City, '62—— ..; W.C., Orange, N.J., .. ——.

Albert Booth; b., Springfield, Mass., Aug. 22, 1825; Y.C., '50; U.T.S., '52-3; E.W.T.S., '53-4; U.T.S., '54-5; Ord. (M.E.), Ap. 18, '59; S.S., Darien, Ct., '55-6; S.S., Westchester, N.Y., '57-8; Pas., Litchfield, Ct., '59-'60; Pas., Seymour, Ct., '61; Pas., Freeport & Bethel (L.I.), N.Y., '62-3; Pas., Rockville Centre (L.I.), N.Y., '64-5; Pas., Whitestone (L.I.), N.Y., '66-7; Pas., Woodbury, Ct., '68; Pas., Roxbury, Ct., '69-'70; Pas., New-Milford, Ct., '71-3; Pas., Bloomfield, Ct., '74-6.

Rabbi Joseph Wales Buckland; b., Deerfield, N.Y., Dec. 16, 1829; U.C., '50; U.T.S., '53-5; Ord. (Bap.), June 21, '55; Pas., N. York City, '55-6;

Pas., Sing Sing, N.Y., '57–'64 ; Pas., N. York City, '65–'71 ; Prof., Theo. Sem., Rochester, N.Y., '71——.

*EDWIN OTWAY BURNHAM ; b., Ghent, Ky., ..., 1824 ; H.C., '52 ; U.T.S., '52–5 ; Tea., Pennington, N.J., '55–6 ; Ord. (Cong.), ..., '58 ; S.S., Columbus, Io., '56–7 ; S.S., Wilton, Minn., '57—— .. ; S.S., Tivoli, Minn., .. ——.. ; Inv., California, '71–3 ; Died, Los Angeles, Cal., Aug. 1, '73.

WENTWORTH SANBORN BUTLER ; b., S. Deerfield, N.H., Sep. 30, 1826 ; D.C., '48 ; B.T.S., '52–3 ; U.T.S., '53–5 ; Librarian, Soc. Lib., N. York City, '55——.

EDWARD PAYSON CRANE ; b., Jefferson, N.Y., Mar. 6, 1832 ; U.N.Y., '51 ; U.T.S., '51–2, '53–5 ; Ord. (Presb.), Nov. 14, '55 ; Pas., Rockland Lake, N.Y., '55–7 ; S.S., St. Augustine, Fla., '57–9 ; S.S., Pilatka & Fernandina, Fla., '59–'65 ; Prof., Wt.U., Pittsburgh, Pa., '65——.

SAMUEL WORCESTER CRITTENDEN ; b., N. Adams, Mass., Feb. 22, 1824 ; U.T.S., '52–5 ; Ord. (Presb.), Ap. 29, '56 ; Pas., Carmel, N.Y., '56–7 ; Pas., Clifton (S.I.), N.Y., '58–9 ; Pas., Darby, Pa., '62–5 ; Ag., P.P.C., Phila., Pa., '65–'70 ; Sec., A. & F.C.U., N. York City, '71–2 ; Ag., Phila., Pa., '73——.

*IRA ODELL DE LONG ; b., Pleasant Valley, N.Y., Sep. 2, 1824 ; Aub.T.S., '52–4 ; U.T.S., '54–5 ; Res. Lic., '58–9 ; Ord. (Presb.), June 24, '63 ; S.S., Hornellsville, N.Y., '59–'63 ; S.S., Macedon, N.Y., '63–4 ; S.S., Honeoye Falls, N.Y., '64–8 ; Died, Macedon, N.Y., May 30, '68.

AMBROSE DUNN ; b., Erie, Pa., Jan. 18, 1828 ; A.C., '52 ; U.T.S., '52–5 ; Ord. (Presb.), June 23, '57 ; Pas., Fairview & Manchester, Pa., '57–'70 ; S.S., Greenwood, Ind., '70——.

*JAMES HARRISON DWIGHT ; b., Malta, n. Sicily, Oct. 9, 1830 ; Y.C., '52 ; U.T.S., '52–5 ; Res. Lic., '55–7 ; Ord. (Presb.), May 24, '57 ; Tea., Newark, N.J., '55–7 ; Pas., Cherry Valley, N.Y., '57–8 ; S.S. & Pas., Englewood, N.J., '59–'67 ; Ch., U.S. Army, '61–3 ; W.C., Englewood, N.J., '67–'72 ; Died, do., Dec. 2, '72.

JAMES CHIDESTER EGBERT ; b., New-York City, N.Y., Oct. 17, 1826 ; U.N.Y., '52 ; U.T.S., '52–5 ; Ord. (Presb.), June 13, '55 ; Pas., W. Hoboken, N.J., '55——.

ALBERT FITCH ; b., Boardman, O., Aug. 19, 1825 ; W.R.C., '52 ; U.T.S., '52–5 ; Ord. (Cong.), ..., '61 ; S.S., Greenport (L.I.), N.Y., '56–7 ; S.S., Orient (L.I.), N.Y., '58–'62 ; Ch., N. York City, '62–3 ; W.C., do., '63–7 ; Pas., W. Williamsfield, O., '67–'72 ; Pas., Elmwood, Ill., '72–3 ; Pas., Irvington, Neb., '73–5 ; Pas., Central City, Neb., '75——.

ALFRED LOOMIS HARRINGTON ; b., Quincy, Ill., ..., 1826 ; I.C., '49 ; U.T.S., '52–5; Ord. (Presb.), Ap. .., '55; S.S., Peru, Ill., '55–9; Agric., Tonica, Ill., '60——.

HENRY HARRIS JESSUP ; b., Montrose, Pa., Ap. 19, 1832 ; Y.C., '51 ; U.T.S., '52–5 ; Ord. (Presb.), Nov. 1, '55 ; F.M., Tripoli, Syria, '56–'60 ; F.M., Beirut, Syria, '60——. D.D., U.N.Y. & C.N.J., '65.

JOHN MCKEAN ; b., Magharascullion, Ireland, May 4, 1830 ; U.T.S., '52–5; Ord. (Presb.), Dec. 3, '56 ; Pas., Perry, Pa., '56–'60 ; S.S., Emlenton & Mt.

Vernon, Pa., '60-4 ; S.S., Perry, Pa., '65-6 ; S.S., Mill Creek & Mt. Pleasant, Pa., '67-8 ; S.S., Olathe, Kan., '68-'74 ; Pas., Little Valley, Pa., '74——.

EDWIN DYER NEWBERRY ; b., Augusta, N.Y., Mar. 11, 1827 ; Cl.U., '52 ; U.T.S.. '52-5 ; Ord. (Presb.), Ap. 14, '56 ; Pas., Philadelphia, Pa., '56-'62 ; Pas., Ionia, Mich., '62-4 ; Pas., Atco, N.J., '68-'72 ; Pas., Haddonfield, N.J., '72——.

GARDINER SPRING PLUMLEY ; b., Washington, D.C., Aug. 11, 1827 ; Y.C., '50 ; U.T.S., '52-5 ; Ord. (Presb.), Nov. 11, '55 ; Pas., N. York City, '55-7 ; Pas., Metuchen, N.J., '58-'75 ; Pas. (R.D.), N. York City, '75——.

TIMOTHY HOPKINS PORTER ; b., Waterbury, Ct., Feb. 16, 1826 ; Y.C., '48 ; Tea., Easton, Ct., '48 ; U.T.S., '52-5 ; Tea., Astoria (L.I.), N.Y., '55-'60 ; Prof., Peo.C., Havana, N.Y., '60-4 ; Banker, N. York City, '66——.

BELVILLE ROBERTS ; b., Warwick, Pa., Sep. 29, 1827 ; U.M., '52 ; U.T.S., '52-5 ; Ord. (Presb.), Ap. 20, '56 ; S.S., Hickman, Ky., '56-8 ; S.S., Stillwater, N.Y., '58-'60 ; Pas., Rochester, N.Y., '61-5 ; Pas., Freeport, Ill., '65-8 ; Inv., '69 ; S.S., Wheeling, Va., '70-1 ; Pas., Norristown, Pa., '71——.

JAMES PIERCE ROOT ; b., Tompkinsville, N.Y., Mar. 19, 1829 ; U.T.S., '52-5 ; Ord. (Cong.), Ap. 16, '56 ; H.M., College Point (L.I.), N.Y., '55-6 ; Sec., C.A.S., Brooklyn, N.Y., '57 ; Pas., N. Walton, N.Y., '57-'60 ; S.S., North Woodstock, Ct., '61 ; Pas., Providence (Elmwood,) R.I., '61-6 ; Pas., Perry Centre, N.Y., '66-'76 ; Pas., Pettaconset, Providence, R.I., '76——.

BELA NEWTON SEYMOUR ; b., East-Granville, Mass., Mar. 25, 1829 ; W.C., '52 ; U.T.S., '52-5 ; Ord. (Cong.), June 16, '55 ; S.S., Oroville, Cal., '56-8 ; S.S., Camptonville, Cal., '59-'65 ; Pas., Hayward's, Cal., '65-'72 ; Pas., Walpole, Mass., '72-3 ; Pas., New-Ipswich, Mass., '74——.

EDWARD STRATTON ; b., Philadelphia, Pa., Ap. 22, 1830 ; U.C., '52 ; U.T.S., '52-5 ; Ord. (Presb.), June 11, '56 ; Pas., Ashland, N.Y., '56-'60 ; Pas., Greenport (L.I.) N.Y., '60-'70 ; Pas., Port Jefferson (L.I.), N.Y., '70-1 ; Inv., Tom's River, N.J., '71-2 ; S.S., Fayetteville, N.Y., '72-3 ; Pas., Greenbush, N.Y., '73——.

DON CARLOS TAFT ; b., Swanzey, N.H., June 19, 1827 ; A.C., '52 ; U.T.S., '52-5 ; Ord. (Cong.), May 7, '55 ; Tea., Elmwood, Ill., '55-'62 ; Acting Prof., Pac. Univ., Forest Grove, Or., '63 ; Tea., Elmwood, Ill., '64-5 ; Tea., Metamora, Ill., '65-8 ; Tea., Minonk, Ill., '68-'71 ; Prof., Ill. Industrial Univ., Champaign, Ill., '71——.

TILLMAN CONKLING TROWBRIDGE ; b., Troy, Mich., Jan. 28, 1831 ; U.M., '52 ; U.T.S., '52-5 ; Ord. (Presb.), Nov. 15, '55 ; F.M., Constantinople, Turkey, '56-'74 ; United States, '74-6 ; F.M., Constantinople, Turkey, '76——.

ALLEN WRIGHT ; b., ..., Choc. Ter. ; ...., 1826 ; U.C., '52 ; U.T.S., '52-5 ; Ord. (Presb.), ..., '55 ; F.M., Armstrong Academy, Choc. Nation, Ind. Ter., '55-9 ; F.M., Boggy Depot, Choc. Nation, '59——. 25.

SAMUEL THOMAS ANDERSON ; b., Yatesville, Miss., ..., 1826 ; Cu.U., '52 ; U.T.S., '52-3 ; Ord. (C. Presb.), Aug. .., '54 ; Prof., Chapel Hill Coll., Texas, '54-8 ; Prof., U.C., Miss., '58-9 ; Prof., U.C., Ill., '59-'60 ; Prest., Mo. Fem. Col., '60-4 ; Pas., Waynesburgh, Pa., '64——.. ; Pas., Lebanon, O., ..——. D,D., Way.C., '64.

JOSEPH ROGERS ARMSTRONG ; b., Rock Hill, Mo., Ap. 9, 1827 ; Ma.C., '52 ; L.T.S., '52-3 ; U.T.S., '53-4 ; Ord. (Presb.), ..., '56 ; S.S., W. Ely, Mo., '56 ; Tea., Kirkwood, Mo., '59-'61 ; Tea. & S.S., Carrollton, Ill., '61-9 ; Tea. & S.S., Kirkwood, Mo., '69-'75 ; S.S., De Soto, Mo., '75——.

MARVIN BRIGGS ; b., North Castle, N.Y., Mar. 11, 1827 ; U.N.Y., '52 ; U.T.S., '52-3 ; Inv., '53-4 ; Tea., Fauquier Co., Va., '54-7 ; P.T.S., '58-'60 ; C.M., N. York City, '60-3 ; Ev., U.S. Army, '63-5 ; Trade, N. York City, '65——.

JOHN ALEXANDER BUCKNER ; b., Covington, Ky., ..., 1833 ; Cr.C., '52 ; P.T.S., '52-4 ; U.T.S., '55 ; Cotton Planter, Illawara, Carroll Parish, La., ..——.

WILLIAM NEAL CLEVELAND ; b., Clinton, N.Y., Ap. 7, 1832 ; H.C., '51 ; U.T.S., '52-4 ; Ord. (Presb.), ..., '56 ; Tea., Brooklyn, N.Y., '55-6 ; Tea., Holland Patent, N.Y., '56-8 ; S.S., Southampton (L.I.), N.Y., '59-'63 ; Tea., N. York City, '64-6 ; Tea., Brooklyn, N.Y., '67——.

NEWTON W. DARLINGTON ; b., West-Newton, O., May 17, 1826 ; Wab.C., '52 ; U.T.S., '52-3 ; Ord. (M.E.), Mar. 1, '63 ; Pas., Ludlow, Ky., '58-9 ; Pas., Maysville, Ky., '59-'60 ; Pas., Augusta, Ky., '61-2 ; Pas., Covington, Ky., '62-3 ; Pas., Newport, Ky., '63-5 ; Pas., Falmouth, Ky., '66-7 ; P.Eld., Maysville, Ky., '68-'71 ; P.Eld., Covington, Ky., '72-5 ; Pas., do., '76——.

DAVID MARGOT ; b., New-York City, ..., 1830 ; U.T.S., '52-4 ; Ord. (Ep.), ..., ..., N. York City, —— ; Rec., Rondout, N.Y., '64-5.

CORNELIUS WORTENDYKE LA FAYETTE MORROW ; b., Paterson, N.J., Aug. 16, 1824 ; W.U., '47 ; Tea., Newark, N.J., '49-'50 ; U.T.S., '52-3 ; Manuf., Paterson, N.J., '50-'69 ; Do., Brooklyn, N.Y., '69——.

CHARLES SEYMOUR ROBINSON ; b., Bennington, Vt., Mar. 31, 1829 ; W.C., '49 ; U.T.S., '52-3 ; P.T.S., '53-5 ; Ord. (Presb.), June 13, '55 ; Pas., Troy, N.Y., '55-'60 ; Pas., Brooklyn, N.Y., '60-8 ; Pas., Am. Chapel, Paris, France, '68-'70 ; Pas., N. York City, '70——. D.D., H.C., '66.

*EDWARD PARMELEE SMITH ; b., South-Britain, Ct., June 3, 1827 ; Y.C., '49 ; Tea., Mobile, Ala., '49-'52 ; N.H.T.S., '52-3 ; U.T.S., '53-4 ; And. T.S., '54-5 ; Ord. (Cong.), June 11, '56 ; Pas., Pepperell, Mass., '56-'62 ; Ag. & Field Sec., U.S.C.C., Philadelphia, Pa., '62-6 ; Field Sec., A.M.A., '66-'71 ; Indian Agent, Minnesota, '71-3 ; U.S. Com. of Ind. Affairs, Washington, D.C., '73-6 ; Prest., Howard Univ., do., '76 ; Died, Accra, W. Africa, June 15, '76.

HENRY MARTYN SWIFT ; b., Bennington, Vt., Mar. 22, 1832 ; W.C., '51 ; U.T.S., '52-4 ; Ord. (Cong.), ..., '60 ; S.S., Lamoille, Ill., '58-9 ; Ev., Middlebury, Vt., '59-'62 ; S.S. (Presb.), Milford, Mich., '62-'74 ; Ev., Detroit, Mich., '74-5 ; Ev., Fenton, Mich., '75——

RUSSELL DUDLEY VAN DEURSEN; b., Richmond, Va., Mar. 5, 1832; H.S.C., '52; U.T.S., '52-3; Civil Engineer, Ohio, '54-'60; Ord. (Presb.), Aug. 29, '61; S.S., Gallipolis, O., '61; Ch., U.S.Army, '61-2; S.S., Gallipolis, O., '62-7; Pas., Shelbyville, Ill., '67-'71; Pas., Paris, Ill., '71——.

WESLEY PRATT WRIGHT; b., Pompey, N.Y., Ap. 12, 1828; Vic.C., '46; U.T.S., 52-3; Concord Bib. In., '53-5; Ord. (M.), ..., '55; ...., Canada West, '55-'61; Prof., Wes. Fem. Coll., Toronto, Can., '61——. 13.

1856.

CHESTER SOLON ARMSTRONG; b., Parishville, N.Y., Sep. 4, 1826; U.M., '52; U.T.S., '53-6; Ord. (Presb.), Nov. 6, '56; Pas., Lansing, Mich., '56-'65; Ch., U.S.Army, '64-5; Pas., Lansing, Mich., '65-9; Pas., Alton, Ill., '69——. D.D., Hi.C., '76.

JAMES BLAIR BONAR; b., New-Abbey, Scotland, May 21, 1826; Wab.C., '53; U.T.S., '53-6; Ord. (Presb.), Mar. 18, '57; S.S., Peekskill, N.Y., '56-7; Pas., Montreal, C.E., '57-'69; Pas., (Cong.), New-Milford, Ct., '70——.

*ALONZO BROWN; b., Ossipee, N.H., May 25, 1826; D.C., '50; U.T.S., '53-6; Ord. (Presb.), Nov. 5, '56; Pas., Clifton (S.I.), N.Y., '56-7; Tea., N. York City, '58-'73; Died, do., Oct. .., '73.

ISRAEL BRUNDAGE; b., Greenfield, Pa., Aug. 24, 1828; A.C., '54; U.T.S., '53-6; Ord. (Presb.), Oct. 7, '56; S.S., Prompton & Waymart, Pa., '56-'64; S.S., Kirkwood, N.Y., '64-5; S.S., Conkling, N.Y., '66-7; S.S. (Cong.), Paxton, Ill., '67-'74; Pas. (Presb.), Rochelle, Ill., '74——.

*JACKSON GREEN COFFING; b., Redstone, Pa., Sep. 21, 1824; Ma.C., '53; U.T.S., '53-6; Res. Lic., '56-7; Ord. (Cong.), Nov. 9, '56; F.M., Aintab, W. Asia, '57-'61; F.M., Hadjin & Adana, W. Asia, '61-2; Killed by assassins, Alexandretta, W. Asia, Mar. 26, '62.

JOHN PAINE CUSHMAN; b., Troy, N.Y., Jan. 19, 1830; U.C., 51; U.T.S., '53-6; Ord. (Presb.), May 29, '60; Pas., Sand Lake, N.Y., '60-2; Pas. (Cong.), Brighton, Mass., '63-6; S.S., Granby, Mass., '67-'70; Pas., Royalston, Mass., '70-2; W.C., Troy, N.Y., '72——.

CHARLES HARDING; b., Whately, Mass., Nov. 21, 1827; Y.C., '53; U.T.S., '53-6; Ord. (Cong.), Aug. 1, '56; F.M., Bombay, India, '57-'62; F.M., Sholapur, India, '62——.

EDWIN LUCIUS HURD; b., Castile, N.Y., Dec. 22, 1824; K.C., '53; U.T.S., '53-6; Ord. (Pres.), Ap. 8, '57; S.S. & Pas., Augusta, Ill., '57-'69; Pas. Sandwich, Ill., '69-'72; Pas., Highland Park, Ill., '72-6. D.D., K.C., '72.

EVERETT BEMAN HURLBUT; b., Galesburgh, Ill., ..., 1830; K.C., '52; And.T.S., '53-4; U.T.S., '54-6; Res. Lic., And.T.S., '56-7; Ord. (Cong.), Nov. 1, '58; S.S., Fontanelle, Neb., '58-'63; S.S., Elkhorn City, Neb. Ter., '63-5; S.S., Irvington, Neb., '65-'70; W.C., Omaha, Neb., '71-4; S.S., Hayward, Cal., '75——.

MICHAEL D. KALOPOTHAKES; b., Athens, Greece, ..., 1826; U.A., '53; U.T.S., '53-6; Ord. (Presb.), Ap. 26, '57; Ed., Athens, Greece, '57——.

ALEXANDER McLEAN ; b., Glasgow, Scotland, Oct. 1, 1833 ; H.C., '53 ; U.T.S., '53–6 ; Ord. (Cong.), Jan. 21, '57 ; Pas., Fairfield, Ct., '57–'66 ; Pas. (Presb.), Buffalo, N.Y., '66–'74 ; Sec., A.B.S., N. York City, '74——. D.D., H.C., '74.

JAMES HARVEY PARSONS ; b., Franklin, N.Y., Ap. 21, 1826 ; W.C., '52 ; U.T.S., '53–6 ; Res. Lic., '56–7 ; Ord. (Presb.), ..., '60 : S.S., Rensselaerville, N.Y., '57–8 ; S.S., Coudersport, N.Y., '59–'62 ; Inv., '63–8 ; S.S., Otego, N.Y., '69–'70 ; Inv. & W.C., Franklin, N.Y., '71——.

HERMAN CAMP RIGGS ; b., Groton, N.Y., Oct. 2, 1832 ; U.N.Y., '52 ; U.T.S., '53–6 ; Res. Lic., '56–7 ; Ord. (Presb.), June 14, '57 ; S.S., St. Catharine's, C.W., '56–9 ; Pas., Potsdam, N.Y., '60–6 ; Pas. (Cong.), St. Albans, Vt., '67–'71 ; Pas., Rutherford Park, N.J., '72–6 ; Pas., Rochester, N.Y., '76——.

GEORGE LIVERMORE TUCKER ; b., Newbury, Vt., Sep. 19, 1827 ; Bel.C., '53 ; U.T.S., '53–6 ; Ord. (Cong.), Ap. 2, '57 ; S.S., Whippany, N.J., '56 ; S.S., N. York City, '56–7 ; S.S., Fox Lake, Wis., '57–'60 ; S.S., Trempeleau, Wis., '60–5 ; S.S. (Presb.), Brighton, Ill., '65–8 ; S.S., Quindaro, Ill., '69——.

HENRY MARTYN TUPPER ; b., Hardwick, Mass., June 10, 1830 ; Y.C., '50 ; U.T.S., '51–2, '54–6 ; Res. Lic., '56–7 ; Ord. (Cong.), Oct. 12, '59 ; Tea., Jacksonville, Ill., '58 ; Tea., Griggsville, Ill., '58–9 ; Pas., Waverly, Ill., '59–'71 ; Pas., Ontario, Ill., '72——.

CHARLES CLARK WALLACE ; b., New-York City, June 3, 1832 ; U.N.Y., '53 ; U.T.S., '53–6 ; Ord. (Presb.), June 4, '56 ; Pas., Tremont, N.Y., '56–'60 ; Pas., Perth Amboy, N.J., '60–4 ; Pas., Placerville, Cal., '64–8 ; Pas., Watertown, N.Y., '68–'70 ; Pas., Mahopac Falls, N.Y., '71——.

GEORGE HILLS WHITE ; b., Harrisburg, Pa., Dec. 29, 1830 ; Wab.C., '52 ; U.T.S., '53–6 ; Ord. (Presb.), Nov. 2, '56 ; F.M., Oorfa, W. Asia, '57–8 ; F.M., Marash, W. Asia, '58–'63 ; Inv., Chester, Vt., '64–5 ; S.S., Weathersfield, Vt., '66–7 ; S.S., Brookfield, Vt., '68 ; S.S., Sharon, Vt., '70–2 ; S.S., Chester, Io., '72——.

WILLIAM CLARKE WHITFORD ; b., West-Edmeston, N.Y., May 5, 1828 ; U.C., '53 ; U.T.S., '53–6 ; Ord. (7th D. Bap.), Ap. 13, '56 ; Pas., Milton, Wis., '56–9 ; Prin., Milton, Wis., '58–'67 ; Prest., Milton Coll., do., '67——.

MARINUS WILLETT ; b., New-York City, Oct. 10, 1826 ; W.C., '46 ; U.T.S., '53–6 ; Ord. (Cong.), May 19, '58 ; S.S., Port Chester, N.Y., '56–7 ; Pas., Black Rock, Ct., '58–'61 ; C.M. (Presb.), N.York City, '62–8 ; Ch. of Pub. Institutions, do., '68——.

19.

ROBERT COATES ALLISON ; b., Lamar, Pa., Feb. 2, 1823 ; A.C., '53 ; U.T.S., '53–4 ; Ord. (Presb.), June 3, '60 ; Prof., Ag.C., Pa., '59–'60 ; S.S., Tionesta, Pa., '60–3 ; S.S., La Fayette, N.Y., '64–6 ; W.C., Greensboro', Md., '66–9 ; Pas., Port Penn, Del., '69–'71 ; S.S., Scipio, N.Y., '71–6 ; S.S., Otisco, N.Y., '76——.

HENRY MARTYN BAIRD ; b., Philadelphia, Pa., Jan. 17, 1832 ; U.N.Y., '50 ; U.T.S., '53–5 ; P.T.S., '55–6 ; Tut., C.N.J., '55–9 ; Ord. (Presb.), Ap. 19, '66 ; Prof., U.N.Y., N. York City, '59——. Ph.D., C.N.J., '67.

ERASTUS NEWTON BATES; b., Chester, O., ..., 1828; W.C., '53; U.T.S., '53-4; Trade, Chester, O., .. —— ..; Law, .. ——.

*THEODORE HIRAM BENJAMIN; b., Bethel, Ct., ..., 1827; A.C., '52; And.T.S., '53-4; U.T.S., '54-5; Died, Bethel, Ct., Sep. 11, '55.

WILLIAM BURT DADA; b., Otisco, N.Y., Oct. 8, 1827; H.C., '52; Aub.T.S., '53-4; U.T.S., '54-5; Ord. (Presb.), July 1, '56; S.S., Skaneateles, N.Y., '56-8; S.S., Jackson, Mich., '59-'60; S.S., Minneapolis & Little Falls, Minn., '60; S.S. & Pas. (Cong.), Clear Water, Minn., '61-6; S.S., Lake City, Minn., '67-'71; S.S., E. Palmyra, N.Y., '73——.

FRANCIS FENELON FORD; b., East Haddam (Millington), Ct., ..., 1828; H.C., '51; U.T.S., '53-4; P.T.S., '54-6; Ord. (Presb.), Oct. 5, '57; S.S., Leroy, N.Y., '57-8; S.S., Danville, N.Y., '58-9; S.S., Newark, N.J., '63-4; Pas. (Cong.), Kalamazoo, Mich., '65-7; W.C., ..., Mich., '68-'70; Pas., Lewiston, Me., '71-2; Pas., Charlestown, Mass., '72-4; W.C., Madison, Wis., '75——.

EDWARD WARNER FRENCH; b., Barre, Vt., Aug. 23, 1829; W.C., '52; U.T.S., '53-4; Ord. (Presb.), Jan. 15, '57; S.S. & Pas., Bergen, Jersey City, N.J., '56——. D.D., W.C., '76.

JUSTUS CLEMENT FRENCH; b., Barre, Vt., May 3, 1832; W.C., '53; U.T.S., '53-5; Ord. (Cong.), Mar. 5, '57; Pas., Brooklyn, N.Y., '57-'70; Pas. (Presb.), do., '71——. D.D., W.C., '75.

JAMES RILEY HALE; b., Orwell, Vt., June 14, 1823; And.T.S., '53-4; U.T.S., '54-5; Ord. (Cong.), Ap. .., '58; S.S., De Kalb, N.Y., .. —— ..; S.S., Massena, N.Y., .. —— ..; Tea., York, Pa., ..——'61; Marine, U.S. Navy, '61-5; Trade, Charlestown, Mass., ..——..; Do., Portsmouth, N.H., ..——.

THOMAS HARRISON; b., Lisbon, Ill., ..., 1825; K.C., '53; U.T.S., '53-4.

*THEODORE HENRY HART; b., Harford, N.Y., Jan. 6, 1831; H.C., '52; U.T.S., '53-4; Trade, Canandaigua, N.Y., ..——..; Died, Philadelphia, Pa., Ap. 12, '61.

ISAAC SMITHSON HARTLEY; b., New-York City, Sep. 27, 1830; U.N.Y., '52; U.T.S., '53-4; And.T.S. '54-6; Res. Lic., '57-8; Ord. (R.D.), May 8, '64; Pas., N. York City, '64-9; Pas., Philadelphia, Pa., '70-1; Pas., Utica, N.Y., '71——. D.D., R.C., '73.

*MATTHEW WOOD HASKELL; b., Hardwick, Mass., July 7, 1827; A.C., '53; U.T.S., '53-4, '55-6; Died, Amherst, Mass., Nov. 25, '56.

CHARLES JENKINS HILL; b., Portland, Me., Feb. 2, 1830; W.C., '52; U.T.S., '53-4; And.T.S., '54-6; Ord. (Cong.), Jan. 28, '57; Pas., Nashua, N.H., '57-'64; S.S., Gloversville, N.Y., '65-8; Pas. (Presb.), Whitehall, N.Y., '68-'72; Pas. (Cong.), Derby (Ansonia), Ct., '72-5; Pas., Middletown, Ct., '75——.

*JOSEPH DANA HOWARD; b., Portland, Me., July 15, 1833; B.C., '52; U.T.S., '53-4; Law, Portland, Me., ..——..; Do., N. York City, ..——'72; Died, do., Jan. 15, '72.

CHARLES MCEWEN HYDE; b., New-York City, June, 8, 1832; W.C., '52; U.T.S., '53–4; Tea., Sheffield, Mass., '54–9; P.T.S., '59–'60; Ord. (Cong.), Aug. 19, '62; S.S., Goshen, Ct., '60–1; Pas., Brimfield, Mass., '62–'70; Pas., Haverhill, Mass., '70——. D.D., W.C., '72.

*HENRY MARTYN LILLY; b., Columbus, N.Y., Jan. 4, 1831; Bel.C., '53; U.T.S., '53–4; Studied Medicine, Ann Arbor, Mich., '56–9; Phys., Fond du Lac, Wis., '59–'70; Phys., U.S.Army, '61–5; Died, Fond du Lac, Wis., Nov. 28, '70. M.D., U.M., '59.

*JOHN WILLIAM MCMURRAN; b., Jeff. Co., Va., Ap. 20, 1830; U.C., '52; U.T. S., '54–5; Ord. (Presb.), Oct. .., '56; S.S., Fairfax C.H., Va., '55–6; S.S. & Pas., Pine View, Fauquier Co., Va., '56–'65; Pas., Morrisville, Va., '65–7; Died, do., Aug. 17, '67.

EDWARD CLARKSON MILES; b., Sharon, Ct., Oct. 2, 1831; U.N.Y., '49; U.T.S., '53–4; And.T.S., '54–6; Ord. (Cong.), June 28, '60; Pas., Stratham, N.H., '60–4; W.C., Exeter, N.H., '64–6; S.S., W. Falmouth, Me., '66–9; Assis. Sec., A.B.C.F.M., N. York City, '69——.

HAMILTON MORGAN; b., Aurora, N.Y., ..., 1823; U.T.S., '53–4.

CHARLES H. NORTON; b., ..., .., ..., 1822; U.Pa., '53; U.T.S., '53–4; Trade, N. York City, .. ——.

CHARLES RHODES POMEROY; b., Waybridge, Vt., June 15, 1830; W.U., '53; U.T.S., '53–4; Ord. (M.Ep.), ..., '68; Tea., Ft. Edward, N.Y., '54–5; Prin., Union Village, N.Y., '55–6; Prin., Cooperstown, N.Y., '56–7; Prin., Rochester, N.Y., '57–9; Prin., Lima, N.Y., '59–'60; Inv., '61–7; Pas., Batavia, N.Y., '68–9; Pas., Chariton, Io., '69–'70; Pas., Des Moines, Io., '70–1; Pas., Iowa City, Io., '72——.

HIRAM POTTER; b., Bath, N.Y., ..., 1831; H.C., '52; U.T.S., '53–4; Ed., Bath, N.Y., ..——..; Do., Milwaukee, Wis., ..——..; Coll. Customs, Pensacola, Fla., ..——.

HENRY AUGUSTUS SMITH; b., Palatine, N.Y., May 28, 1833; W.C., '53; U.T.S., '53–5; Ord. (Presb.), Oct. .., '58; Pas. E., Philadelphia, Pa., '58–'64; Pas., do. (Mantua), '64——.

WILLIAM CARTER WHITE; b., Owego, N.Y., Ap. 29, 1832; Wab.C., '52; U.T.S., '53–4; P.T.S., '54–6; Ord. (Presb.), July 24, '60; S.S., Cuba, N.Y., '60–8; Prof., Wab.C., Crawfordsville, Ind., '64——. 25.

1857.

JOSEPH ANDERSON; b., Nigg, Ross Co., Scotland, Dec. 16, 1836; N.Y.A., '54; U.T.S., '54–7; Res. Lic., '57–8; Ord. (Presb.), Nov. 8, '58; S.S. & Pas. (Cong.), Stamford, Ct., '59–'61; Pas., Norwalk, Ct., '61–4; S.S., Waterbury, Ct., '65——.

QUINCY BLAKELY; b., Pawlet, Vt., Sep. 17, 1824; U.Vt., '54; U.T.S., '54–7; Ord. (Cong.), Feb. 16, '59; S.S. & Pas., Rodman, N.Y., '58–'63; Pas., Campton, N.H., '64——.

THEODORE LUIN BYINGTON; b., Belvidere, N.J., ..., 1831; C.N.J., '49; U.T.S., '54-7; Res. Lic., '57-8; Ord. (Cong.), June 4, '58; F.M., Adrianople, Turkey, '58-'60; F.M. (Presb.), Eski Zagra, Turkey, '60——..; Pas., Newton, N.J., ..—— '74; F.M., Constantinople, Turkey, '74——.

EDWARD W. CHESTER; b., New-York City, July 12, 1828; U.T.S., '54-7; Ord. (Presb.), May 31, '57; S.S., Manhattanville, N.Y., '57-8; F.M., Tirupuvanum, India, '59-'61; F.M., Madras, India, '61-2; F.M., Madura, India, '62-3; F.M., Dindigul, India, '63——. M.D., .., ..

OLIVER ELLSWORTH COBB; b., New-York City, March 21, 1833; Y.C., '53; U.T.S., '54-7; Ord. (R.D.), Sep. 1, '57; Pas., Adriance (Hopewell), N.Y., '57-'72; Pas., Flushing, (L.I.), N.Y., '72——.

JAMES MILLIGAN DICKSON; b., Ryegate, Vt., Feb. 6, 1831; D.C., '53; Tea., Staten Island, N.Y., '53-4; Tea., Haverstraw, N.Y., '54; U.T.S., '54-7; Ord. (Presb.), Nov. 18, '57; Pas., Brooklyn, N.Y., '57-'63; Pas., Newark, N.J., '63-'70; Pas., Montgomery, N.Y., '70——.

WILLIAM BUCK DWIGHT; b., Constantinople, Turkey, May 22, 1833; Y.C., '54; U.T.S., '54-7; Res. Lic., N.H.T.S., '57-9; Prin., Englewood, N.J., '60-5; Prin., West-Point, N.Y., '67-'70; Ass. Prin. & Ed., New-Britain, Ct., '70——.

HENRY MARTYN HAZELTINE; b., Jamestown, N.Y., Aug. 28, 1831; W.C., '52; U.T.S., '54-7; Ord. (Cong.), Jan. 20, '60; Pas., Sherman, N.Y., '60-8; S.S., Perry, N.Y., '68-'70; S.S., Henrietta, N.Y., '70-2; Pas., North-Salem, N.Y., '72——.

*GEORGE DIAH ALONZO HEBARD; b., Brookfield, Vt., Sep. 6, 1831; D.C., '54; U.T.S., '54-7; Ord. (Presb.), Sep. .., '58; S.S., Clayville, N.Y., '57; S.S., Clinton, Io., '57-'61; S.S., Iowa City, '61-6; S.S. (Cong.), Iowa City, Io., '66-9; S.S., Oskaloosa, Io., '69-'70; Died, do., Dec. 14, '70.

CHARLES DOWNES HELMER; b., Canajoharie, N.Y., Nov. 18, 1827; Y.C., '52; Tea., D. & D.I., N. York City, '53-4; U.T.S., '54-7; Trav., Europe, '57-9; Ord. (Cong.), Sep. ..,'59; S.S., Hartford, Ct., '59-'60; Pas. (Presb.), Milwaukee, Wis., '60-5; Inv., N. York City, '65-6; Pas. (Cong.), Chicago, Ill., '66-'75; Pas., Brooklyn, N.Y., '76——. D.D., Bel.C., '75.

CHARLES HOOVER HOLLOWAY; b., Philadelphia, Pa., Aug. 16, 1831; A.C., '54; U.T.S., '54-7; Ord. (Presb.), Sep. 27, '57; S.S., Rensselaerville, N.Y., '57; Prof., Ash.C.I., '58; S.S., Ashland, N.Y., '59-'61; Pas., Shelter Isld., N.Y., '61-4; Tea., Randolph, N.Y., '64-5; Tea., Middletown, Del., '65-7; Tea., Cortland, N.Y., '68-'70; S.S., North-Salem, N.Y., '70-2; S.S., Tom's River, N.J., '72-3; Prof., Del.C., Newark, Del., '73——.

*CARLTON S. HORTON; b., New-York City, ..., 1832; W.C., '54; U.T.S., '54-7; Inv., Madeira Isld., '58-'64; Died, Buffalo, N.Y., Dec. 13, '64.

INGLIS LAURIE; b., Jacksonville, Ill., ..., 1825; I.C., '54; U.T.S., '54-7; Res. Lic., N.W.T.S., '57-8.

CHAUNCY LUCAS LOOMIS; b., Boonville, Mo., ..., 1819; W.R.C., '46; U.T.S., '56-7; Res. Lic., do., '57-9; Ord. (Cong.), ..., '59; F.M., Corisco, W. Af., '59——.

CHARLES HENRY PAYSON ; b., Leominster, Mass., Sep. 28, 1831 ; A.C., '52 ; U.T.S., '54-7 ; Ord. (Presb.), Nov. 25, '60 ; Ch. Miss., N. York City, '57——.

ROLLIN AUGUSTUS SAWYER ; b., Eaton, Can. East, July 13, 1830 ; W.R.C., '51 ; U.T.S., '54-7 ; Res. Lic., '57-8 ; Ord. (Presb.), Feb. 17, '58 ; Pas., Yonkers, N.Y., '58-'62 ; Pas., Newark, O., '62-9 ; Pas., Irvington, N.Y., '69——. D.D., W.R.C., '72.

JOSEPH FORD SUTTON ; b., Hardyston, N.J., ..., 1827 ; R.C., '52 ; U.T.S., '54-7 ; Ord. (Presb.), Dec. 8, '57 ; S.S., Hanover, N.J., '57-8 ; Pas., Parsipanny, N.J., '58-'61 ; Ch., U.S. Army, '62 ; Ag., U.S.C.C., '63-4 ; S.S., Howell, Mich., '64-5 ; Pas., Philadelphia, Pa., '65-'73 ; Ev. & Ed., do., '74——.

*LEWIS THOMPSON ; b., Volney, N.Y., Ap. 25, 1830 ; U.T.S., '54-7 ; Ord. (Presb.), June 9, '57 ; Pas., Whippany, N.J., '57-'69 ; Ed., Bricksburgh, N.J., '69-'71 ; Tea., Brooklyn, N.Y., '71-3 ; Died, do., Ap. 19, '73.

WILLIAM THOMSON ; b., Kilmarnock, Scotland, June 2, 1832 ; U.Pa., '54 ; U.T.S., '54-7 ; Ord. (Presb.), Ap. 27, '58 ; S.S., Blossburgh, Pa., '57-9 ; S.S., Tamaqua, Pa., '60-8 ; Pas., Duncannon, Pa., '68-'73 ; Pas., Stewartsville, N.J., '73——.

AVERY SKINNER WALKER ; b., Union Square, N.Y., Oct. 15, 1829 ; O.C., '54 ; U.T.S., '54-7 ; Ord. (Presb.), June 24, '57 ; S.S., Lodi, N.J., '57-'60 ; Pas. (Cong.), Rockville, Ct., '61-4 ; Pas., Dover, N.H., '64-8 ; Pas., Fair Haven, Mass., '68-'71 ; Pas., Gloversville, N.Y., '71——.

ERSKINE NORMAN WHITE ; b., New-York City, May 31, 1833 ; Y.C., '54 ; U.T.S., '54-7 ; Ord. (R.D.), June 9, '59 ; Pas., Richmond (S.I.), N.Y., '59-'62 ; Pas. (Presb.), New-Rochelle, N.Y., '62-8 ; Pas., Buffalo, N.Y., '68-'74 ; Pas., N. York City, '74——. D.D., U.N.Y., '74. 21.

WILLIAM ALVIN BARTLETT ; b., Binghamton, N.Y., Dec. 4, 1832 ; H.C., '52 ; U.T.S., '54-6 ; Ord. (Cong.), March 4, '58 ; Pas., Brooklyn, N.Y., '58-'68 ; Pas., Chicago, Ill., '68-'76 ; Pas. (Presb.), Indianapolis, Ind., '76——.

JOHN MILLOT ELLIS ; b., Jaffrey, N.H., March 27, 1831 ; O.C., '51 ; U.T.S., '55-6 ; O.T.S., '56-7 ; Ord. (Cong.), Oct. 17, '66 ; Prof., O.C., Oberlin, O., '58——.

ENOCH KRAIG EVANS ; b., Shawangunk, N.Y., May 27, 1821 ; A.C., '53 ; U.T.S., '53-4 ; Agric. & Tea., Jerseyville, Ill., '54——.

THEODORE ADOLPHUS GARDNER ; b., Pownal, Vt., Feb. 25, 1830 ; W.C., '53 ; U.T.S., '54-5 ; Ord. (R.D.), Ap. 16, '62 ; S.S., Manhattanville, N.Y., '55——.. ; S.S. & Pas., Buskirk's Bridge, N.Y., '61-6 ; S.S. (Cong.), Orient (L.I.), N.Y., '67-'71 ; S.S., Faribault, Minn., '73-4 ; S.S., Monroe, Wis., '75——.

*JOHN GIBSON ; b., Ryegate, Vt., June 1, 1830 ; U.C., '53 ; U.T.S., '54-5 ; Ord. (Presb.), ..., '60 ; S.S., Galena, Ill., '58-9 ; S.S., Wheatland, Io., '59 ; W.C., Washington, Io., '60-8 ; Died, Ryegate, Vt., March 8, '68.

CHARLES GORDON HAYES; b., Bennington Centre, Vt., ..., 1830; Y.C., '51; U.T.S., '54; Law, N. York City, '55——.

JOSEPH WELTON HUBBARD; b., Geneseo, N.Y., May 11, 1827; H.C., '50; U.T.S., '54–5; P.T.S., '55–7; Ord. (Presb.), Aug. 5, '57; Pas., Bridgeton, N.J., '57–'65; Pas., Cape Island, N.J., '65–7; S.S., Le Roy, N.Y., '67–'70; Pas., Dayton, N.J., '70–5; Prest. Northern Ill. Coll., '75——.

LYMAN HUGGINS JOHNSON; b., Marion, N.Y., Jan. 1, 1829; U.T.S., '54–6; Ord. (Cong.), Feb. .., '57; S.S., Elkhorn, Wis., '57–'60; S.S., Rockford, Ill., '60–1; S.S., Rockton, Ill., '61–3; S.S., Galena, Ill., '63–5; Inv., Ed. & Ev., '65——. Address, White House, O.

RUFUS OSGOOD MASON; b., E. Sullivan, N.H., Jan. 22, 1830; D.C., '54; U.T.S., '54–6; Tea., Cleveland, O., '56–7; M.D., Col. Phys. & Surg., N.Y., '59; Phys., N. York City, '59–'61; Ass. Surg., U.S.N., '61–5; Phys., N. York City, '65——.

JAMES QUICK; b., Royal Oak, Mich., Aug. 26, 1829; U.M., '54; U.T.S., '54–6; Ord. (Presb.), Ap. 12, '57; H.M., Illinois, '56–7; F.M., Panditeripo, Jaffna, Ceylon, India, '58–'68; W.C., Birmingham, Mich., '69–'71; S.S., Reading, Mich., '71–2; S.S., Blissfield, Mich., '72–4; S.S., Bryan, O., '74——.

DANIEL JAY SPRAGUE; b., Hampstead, Ct., March 11, 1831; A.C., '52; U.T.S., '54–5; Com. Agency, N. York City, '56——.

JAMES DUNLOP THOMAS; b., Washington, D.C., Dec. 13, 1833; Del.C., '54; U.T.S., '54–6; Ord. (Presb.), Ap. 19, '59; S.S., Lisbon, Md., '56–9; Pas., Makemie Chh., Accomac Co., Va., '59–'69; Pas., Wytheville, Va., '69——.

*JAMES UGLOW; b., New-York City, ..., 1827; U.N.Y., '47; U.T.S., '54–7; Phys., N. York City, '58–'64; Died, do., ..., '64.

BRADISH CALVIN WARD; b., St. Charles, Ill., ..., 1826; Jef.C., '52; U.T.S., '54–5; Ord. (Cong.), Ap. 8, '60; Tea., St. Charles, Ill., '57–9; S.S., Geneseo, Ill., '60–2; S.S., Waukegan, Ill., '63–4; Ch., U.S.Army, '64–5; W.C., N. York City, '65——..; S.S., Harwich, Mass., '73–5. 14.

1858.

WILLIAM WISNER ADAMS; b., Painesville, O., Aug. 15, 1831; W.C., '55; U.T.S., '55–8; Ord. (Cong.), Jan. 26, '60; S.S., Burlington, Io., '58–9; S.S., Como, Ill., '59–'60; S.S., Beloit, Wis., '61–3; Pas., Fall River, Mass., '64——. D.D., W.C., '73.

JOHN EZEKIEL BAKER; b., Schaghticoke, N.Y., Oct. 29, 1831; W.C., '53; U.T.S., '55–8; Ord. (Presb.), July 19, '59; Pas., Arkport & Burns, N.Y., '59–'62; S.S., Cuba, N.Y., '63–4; S.S., Mid. Granville, N.Y., '65–7; S.S., Honeoye Falls, N.Y., '68–9; S.S., Gates, N.Y., '70; Ch. of Pub. Institutions, Rochester, N.Y., '70——.

WILLIAM FREDERICK VINCENT BARTLETT; b., Portland, Me., Aug. 20, 1831; Y.C., '53; U.T.S., '55–8; Ord. (Presb.), Dec. .., '64; S.S., Natchez, Miss., '58–'64; S.S., N. Orleans, La., '64–5; S.S., Concord, N.H., '65–7; Trav.,

Europe, '67–'70; Prof., Oakland Coll., Miss., '70–4; Pas., Lexington, Ky., '75——. D.D., K.U., '76.

EDMUND WOODWARD BROWN; b., Burdett, N.Y., Nov. 3, 1831; Y.C., '55; U.T.S., '55–8; Ord. (Presb.), Jan. .., '61; S.S., S. Cornwall, Ct., '58; S.S., Alexandria, Va., '58–9; S.S., West-Dresden, N.Y., '59–'65; P.M., Whitesboro, N.Y., '65–6; S.S., Carthage, N.Y., '67–9; S.S., North-Bergen, N.Y., '70–2; S.S., Wellsville, N.Y., '72–4; S.S., Burdett, N.Y., '74——.

LA FAYETTE BUSHNELL; b., Henry Co., Mo., ..., 1825; U.T.S., '55–8; Not Ordained.

FRANCIS WILLIAM CASE; b., Whitewater, Wis., ..., 1828; Bel.C., '56; U.T.S., '55–8; Tea., N.Y.City, '58–9; Agric., Whitewater, Wis., '59——.

EDSON LYMAN CLARK; b., East-Hampton, Mass., Ap. 1, 1827; Y.C., '53; U.T.S., '56–8; Ord. (Cong.), Nov. 30, '59; S.S. & Pas., Dalton, Mass., '58–'66; S.S., North-Branford, Ct., '67——.

JOHN MATTHEWS CLYMER; b., Jefferson Co., Va., March 29, 1831; Del.C., '55; U.T.S., '55–8; Ord. (Presb.), Nov. 28, '58; S.S., Marion, Va., '58–9; Pas., Woodstock, Va., '59–'71; Pas., Keyser City, W. Va., '71——.

GEORGE ARBA DICKERMAN; b., Hamden, Ct., ..., 1830; Y.C., '55; U.T.S., '55–8; Res. Lic., N.H.T.S., '59–'60; S.S., Canaan, Ct., '60–1; W.C., Canaan, Ct., '61–4; W.C., ..., '64–8; S.S., St. Charles, Ill., '69–'71; W.C., Chicago, Ill., '71——.

LESTER MORSE DORMAN; b., Hamden, Ct., Nov. 5, 1829; Y.C., '54; U.T.S., '55–8; Ord. (Cong.), June 6, '60; S.S., Winsted, Ct., '59–'60; Pas., Manchester, Ct., '60–'70; Miss. & As. Rector (Ep.), N. York City, '71——.

DAVID FITCH; b., Boardman, O., ..., 1829; W.R.C., '55; U.T.S., '55–8; Res. Lic., '58–9; Tea., Flushing (L.I.), N.Y., '58–'61; Tea., Brooklyn (E.D.), N.Y., '62——.

JOSEPH KINGSBURY GREENE; b., Boston, Mass., ..., 1834; B.C., '55; U.T.S., '55–8; Ord. (Cong.), Nov. 10, '58; F.M., Nicomedia, Turkey, '59–'63; F.M., Broosa, Turkey, '63—— ..; F.M., Constantinople, Turkey, .. ——.

CHARLES THOMAS HALEY; b., New-York City, ..., 1833; C.N.J., '53; U.T.S., '55–8; Ord. (Presb.), Oct. 31, '60; Pas., Roseville, N.J., '60——. Address, Newark, N.J.

JOHN KELLOGG HARRIS; b., Ticonderoga, N.Y., Feb. 16, 1832; W.C., '52; U.T.S., '54–6, '57–8; Ord. (Presb.) May .., '59; S.S. & Pas., New-Monmouth, Va., '58–'61; Ch., Conf. Army, '62–5; S.S., Amherst, Va., '65–9; Tea. & S.S., Harrodsburgh, Ky., '69–'72; Ev. & S.S., Floyd C.H., Va., '72——.

JAMES SEYMOUR HOYT; b., New-Canaan, Ct., Ap. 18, 1830; Y.C., '51; U.T.S., '55–8; Ord. (Cong.), May 26, '58; Pas., Port Huron, Mich., '58–'76; Pas., Cambridgeport, Mass., '76——.

SAMUEL JESSUP; b., Florida, N.Y., May 23, 1833; C.N.J., '54; U.T.S., '55–8; Ord. (Presb.), May 3, '59; S.S., Berkshire, N.Y., '59; S.S., Amity, N.Y., '60; S.S. & Pas., Dansville, N.Y., '60–'72; Pas., Oneida, N.Y., '72——.

WILLIAM HENRY KNOUSE; b., New-York City, Oct. 15, 1829; U.N.Y., '51; U.T.S., '53-4, '55-8; Ord. (Cong.), May 4, '59; Pas., N. Greenwich, Ct., '59-'63; Pas., Cutchogue (L.I.), N.Y., '63-'70; Pas., Deep River, Ct., '70——.

GEORGE CLEMENT NOYES; b., Landaff, N.H., Aug. 4, 1833; I.C., '55; U.T.S., '55-8; Ord. (Presb.), Oct. 19, '59; Tea., Jacksonville, Ill., '58-9; S.S., La Porte, Ind., '59-'68; Pas., Evanston, Ill., '68——. D.D., N.W.U., '75.

SYLVESTER HILL OPDYKE; b., Everittstown, N.J., June 22, 1828; W.U., '53; U.T.S., '54-6, '57-8; Ord. (M.E.), Ap. 6, '62; S.S., Bloomfield, N.J., '58-'60; S.S., Clinton, N.J., '60-2; Pas., Flemington, N.J., '62-4; Pas., Rahway, N.J., '64-5; Pas., Elizabethport, N.J., '65-7; Pas., Tottenville (S.I.), N.Y., '67-9; Pas., Nyack, N.Y., '69-'71; Pas., Newark, N.J., '71-3; Pres. Elder, Newark, '73——.

WILLIAM LAERTES PAGE; b., Sangerfield, N.Y., Aug. 30, 1830; H.C., '54; U.T.S., '55-8; Ord. (Presb.), July 12, '59; S.S., Phelps, N.Y., '58-'62; S.S. (Cong.), Grand Rapids, Mich., '63; S.S. (Presb.), Wolcott, N.Y., '64——.

EDWARD PAYSON POWELL; b., Clinton, N.Y., ..., 1833; H.C., '53; U.T.S., '54-6, '57-8; Tut., H.C., '56-7; Ord. (Cong.), ..., '61; S.S., Clinton, N.Y., '58-'61; Pas., Adrian, Mich., '61-'71; Pas., St. Louis, Mo., '71-3.

ALEXANDER DAVID STOWELL; b., Rockville, Ill., ..., 1828; Y.C., '53; U.T.S., '55-8; Ord. (Cong.), Nov. 17, '58; Pas., Woodbridge, Ct., '58-'60; S.S., E. Granville, Mass., '60-3; S.S., Southampton, Mass., '63-5; S.S., Wilbraham, Mass., '65-7; W.C., do., '67-9; S.S., Muskegon, Mich.; '70-2; S.S., West-Groton, N.Y., '73——.

GEORGE MAIRS VAN DERLIP; b., Washington Co., N.Y., June .., 1835; U.N.Y., '51; U.T.S., '55-8; Trade, N. York City, '58-'71; Sec., S.S. Dep't, Bap. Pub. Soc., N. York City, '71——.

ROBERT HENRY WILLIAMSON; b., New-York City, ..., 1829; W.C., '53; Ep.T.S., '55-7; U.T.S., '57-8; S.S., Dodgeville, Wis., '58-9; S.S., Rockford, Ill., '64....; S.S., Wilkesbarre, Pa., ..——, '74. Deposed, '74. 24.

---

*ORLANDO NEWTON BENTON; b., Franklin, N.Y., Jan. 29, 1827; U.T.S., '55-6; Ord. (Presb.), Nov. 18, '57; S.S.M., Lynchburgh, Va., '56-7; S.S. & Pas., Apalachin, N.Y., '58-'61; Ch., U.S.Army, '61-2; Killed in battle, Newbern, N.C., Mar. 14, '62.

DANIEL N. BORDWELL; b., Lenox, N.Y., March 4, 1828; O.C., '52; Tut., O.C., '53-7; U.T.S., '55-6; O.T.S., '56-8; Ord. (Cong.), June 6, '59; S.S. & Pas., Le Claire, Io., '58-'60; S.S., Lansing, Io., '60-3; Ch., U.S.Army, '63-4; S.S., Charles City, Io., '64-8; S.S., Kalamazoo, Mich., '69-'72; S.S., Olivet, Mich., '73——.

HORATIO WOODWARD BROWN; b., Buffalo, N.Y., July 27, 1833; Y.C., '54; U.T.S., '55-6; Tut., Y.C., '56-9; Ord. (Cong.), Jan. 17, '59; S.S., Ripon, Wis., '59-'60; S.S., Burnett, N.Y., '61-3; Pas. (Presb.), Lyons, N.Y., '64-6; Pas., Brockport, N.Y., '67-'71; Pas., Williamsport, Pa., '72——.

Carroll Cutler; b., Windham, N.H., Jan. 31, 1829; Y.C., '54; U.T.S., '55–6; Tut., Y.C., '56–8; Europe, '58–9; Res. Lic., Y.C., '59–'60; Ord. (Presb.), Dec. 17, '73; Prof., W.R.C., Hudson, O., '60–'71; Prest., W.R.C., do., '71——. D.D., Ma.C., '72.

William Eastman Dickinson; b., North-Amherst, Mass., June 11, 1832; A.C., '55; U.T.S., '55–7; And.T.S., '57–8; Ord. (Cong.), Dec. 19, '60; S.S., E. Orleans, Mass., '60–2; S.S., Sprague, Ct., '63–5; S.S., Montville, Ct., '65–8; Pas., Canton, Mass., '68–'70; Pas., Walpole, N.H., '70–6; Pas., Chicopee, Mass., '76——.

Gideon Draper; b., Phelps, N.Y., June 22, 1828; D.C., '49; Studied Law, Ballston, N.Y., '50; Studied, Berlin, &c., Europe, '51–4; U.T.S., '56–7; Ord. (M.E.), May 12, '61; S.S., Salisbury, Ct., '57–9; S.S., Rhinebeck, N.Y., '59–'61; Pas., Sheffield, Mass., '61–3; Pas., White Plains, N.Y., '63–5; Prof., G.C., Lima, N.Y., '65–6; Pas., Garrison's, N.Y., '66–7; Pas., Tuckahoe, N.Y., '67–'70; Pas., Carmel, N.Y., '70–2; Superan., '72–5; Pas., Franklin, N.Y., '75——.

John G. Evans; b., Ann Arbor, Mich., ..., 1829; U.M., '54; U.T.S., '55–6.

Morris J. Franklin; b., ..., Prussia, ..., 1834; U.C., '55; U.T.S., '55–7; M.D., .., ..; C.M. of A.S.M.C. Jews, '57–'61; Surg., U.S.Army, '62–4; Phys. & Drug., N.York City, '65——.

Joshua Beers Hall; b., Madrid, N.Y., July 11, 1826; U.Vt., '53; U.T.S., '55–7; Aub.T.S., '57–8; Ord. (Presb.), Feb. 8, '59; Pas., Lysander, N.Y., '59–'64; Pas., Pittstown & Johnsonville, N.Y., '64–7; S.S., Lansingburgh, N.Y., '67–8; S.S., Elk Rapids, Mich., '70——.

James Garland Hamner; b., Baltimore, Md., Nov. 13, 1836; W.C., '55; U.T.S., '55–7; Ord. (Presb.), Nov. 1, '59; Pas., Milford, Del., '60–3; Pas., Phila., Pa., '64–9; Pas., Salisbury, Md., '69–'72; S.M., Baltimore, Md., '72–4; Pas., Waterville, N.Y., '74–5; Pas., Parkersburgh, W. Va., '75——.

Thomas Williamson Hooper; b., Hanover Co., Va., Nov. 2, 1832; H.S.C., '55; U.T.S., '55; U.T.S.Va., '56–7; Ord. (Presb.), Feb. .., '58; Pas., Pole Green & Salem Chh., Va., '58–'63; Pas., Liberty Chh., Va., & Ch. Conf. Army, '63–5; Pas., Christiansburgh, Va., '65–'70; Pas., Lynchburgh, Va., '70——.

Albert Barnes King; b., Rahway, N.J., ..., 1829; C.N.J., '55; U.T.S., '55–6; P.T.S., '57–8; Ord. (Presb.), ..., '61; S.S., N. York City, '58–'60; Pas., Red Bank, N.J., '61–2; S.S., Gilboa, N.Y., '62–3; Pas., Wyoming, Pa., '63–'72; S.S., Charlotte, N.Y., '72——.

Nathaniel McConaughy; b., Livermore, Pa., Oct. 11, 1825; W.R.C., '52; Tea, Winchester, Tenn., '53–5; U.T.S., '55–7; P.T.S., '57–8; Ord. (Presb.), June 12, '60; S.S. & Pas., Millville, N.J., '58–'66; S.S., Swedesboro, N.J., '66–8; S.S., Elwood, N.J., '68–'72; Engineer, Somerville, N.J., '72——.

Robert Lowry McMurran; b., Frederick Co., Va., May 7, 1835; U.C., '55; U.T.S., '55–7; Ord. (Presb.), Sep. .., '59; S.S., P. Edward C.H., Va., '59–'60; Pas., Shepherdstown, Va., '60–5; Pas., Culpepper, Va., '66–'70; Pas., Sykesville, Md., '70——.

GEORGE ALPHA MILLER; b., Andover, Ct., Mar. 3, 1831; W.C., '55; U.T.S., '55-7; E.W.T.S., '58-9; Ord. (Cong.), Nov. 29, '59; Pas., Burlington, Ct., '59 '64; S.S., Broadalbin, N.Y., '64-5; S.S., E. Pitcairn, N.Y., '65-7; S.S., Pt. Leyden, N.Y., '67-'73; W.C., Syracuse, N.Y., '73——.

CHARLES DEKAY NOTT; b., Norman Vale, N.Y., Sep. 12, 1833; U.C., '54; U.T.S., '55-6; N.B.T.S., '56-8; Ord. (R.D.), Oct. 25, '59; Pas., Mohawk, N.Y., '60-4; Pas. (Presb.), Manchester, N.J., '64-5; S.S. & Pas., Urbana, N.Y., '66-9; S.S., Kansas City, Mo., '70-1; Pas., St. Louis, Mo., '71-3; Pas., Davenport, Io., '73——. D.D., U.C., '74.

*HENRY ALBERTSON POST; b., Brooklyn, N.Y., Sep. 2, 1835; N.Y.A., '55; U.T.S., '55-6; P.T.S., '56-8; Ord. (Presb.), Jan. 10, '60; S.S., Warrensburgh, N.Y., '60-1; Died, do., Nov. 12, '61.

EDWIN WILBUR RICE; b., Kingsboro, N.Y., July 24, 1831; U.C., '54; U.T.S., '55-7; Ord. (Cong.), Sep. 5, '60; S.S.M., La Crosse, Wis., '59-'60; S.S.M., St. Louis, Mo., '60-1; S.S.M., La Crosse, Wis., '61-4; Gen. S.S.Ag., Milwaukee, Wis., '64-'71; As. Sec. & Ed., A.S.S.U., Philadelphia, Pa., '71——.

GEORGE P. RICHARDSON; b., Warren Co., Miss., Feb. 15, 1833; U.Mi., '55; U.T.S., '55-6; Inv., ——; Ord. (Presb.), ..., '57; S.S., Middleton, Miss., '57-8; Tea., Grenada, Miss., '61-9; Tea. & S.S., Garner Station & New-Hope, Miss., '70-4; Tea., Corsicana, Tex., '74——.

CHARLES MELLEN TYLER; b., Limington, Me., Jan. 8, 1831; Y.C., '55; U.T.S., '55-6; Ord. (Presb.), Feb. .., '57; Pas., Galesburgh, Ill., '57-9; Pas. (Cong.), Natick, Mass., '59-'66; Pas., Chicago, Ill., '67-'72; Pas., Ithaca, N.Y., '72——. 20.

1859.

*HENRY JACOB ACKER; b., Catskill, N.Y., ..., 1833; W.C., '56; U.T.S., '55-7, '58-9; Ord. (Cong.), June 23, '59; S.S., Greenport (L.I.), N.Y., '59-'60; Pas. (Presb.), Amity, N.Y., '61-5; Ch., U.S.Army, '63-5; D.Sec., A.T.S., New-Britain, Ct., '65-6; As. Sec., A.T.S., N. York City, '67-9; Pas., Pleasant Valley, N.Y., '69-'72; S.S., Brainerd, N.Y., '72-3; Died, Brainerd, N.Y., Jan. 1, '74.

GOODLOE BOWMAN BELL; b., Reading, Pa., June 14, 1832; Y.C., '52; U.T.S., '56-9; Ord. (Presb.), Oct. .., '59; S.S., Manhattanville, N.Y., '59; S.S., Hardiston, N.J., '59-'65; W.C., Elizabeth, N.J., '65-7; S.S., Ramapo, N.Y., '67-'70; Pas., N. York City, '71-4; Pas. (R.D.), Napanock, N.Y., '75——.

EDWIN CONE BISSELL; b., Schoharie, N.Y., March 2, 1832; A.C., '55; U.T.S., '56-9; Ord. (Cong.), Sep. 22, '59; Pas., Westhampton, Mass., '59-'64; Pas., San Francisco, Cal., '64-9; S.S., Honolulu, Oahu, '69-'70; Pas., Winchester, Mass., '71-3; Pas., Innsbruck, Austria, '74——. D.D., A.C., '74.

JESSE BRUSH; b., Huntington (L.I.), N.Y., June 11, 1830; U.N.Y., '54; U.T.S., '56-9; Ord. (Presb.), Oct. 17, '59; Pas., Susquehanna, Pa., '59-'61; S.S., Westhampton, Mass., '62-3; Ch., U.S.Army, '63-5; Pas. (Cong.), Vernon, Ct., '65-7; Pas., North-Cornwall, Ct., '67-'73; Pas., Berlin, Ct., '73-6; W.C., Brooklyn, N.Y., '76——.

WALTER HALSEY CLARK; b., Milton, N.Y., July 2, 1832; W.C., '54; Aub.T.S., '56–8; U.T.S., '58–9; Ord. (Presb.), June 30, '59; F.M., Gaboon, W. Af., '59–'61; F.M., Corisco Isld., W. Af., '61–9; S.S., Ponca, Neb., '70–2; S.S., Elk Valley, Neb., '72–4; S.S., Daily Branch, Neb., '74——.

EUGENE DOUGLASS; b., New-York City, ..., 1835; N.Y.A., '54; U.T.S., '56–9; Heid.U., Ger., '59–'62; U.S.Army, '62–5; W.C., Albany, N.Y., '65——.

*WILLIAM WILLARD EARLE; b., West-Troy, N.Y., Aug. 31, 1830; A.C., '56; U.T.S., '56–9; Ord. (Presb.), Jan. 29, '60; S.S., Canton, Miss., '59–'60; S.S., Sycamore, Ill., '60–1; Died, Worcester, Mass., Ap. 26, '61.

WILLIAM JACOB ERDMAN; b., Allentown, Pa., Ap. 28, 1834; H.C., '56; U.T.S., '56–9; Ord. (Presb.), Ap. .., '60; S.S., St. Catharines, C. W., '59–'60; S.S., St. Paul, Minn., '60–1; S.S., Fayetteville, N.Y., '61–7; Ch., U.S.Army, '64; Pas., Ann Arbor, Mich., '67–'71; S.S., Fort Wayne, Ind., '71–3; S.S., Chicago, Ill., '74——.

EDWARD PAYSON GOODWIN; b., Rome, N.Y., July 31, 1832; A.C., '56; U.T.S., '56–9; Ord. (Cong.), Nov. 10, '59; Pas., Burke, Vt., '59–'60; Pas., Columbus, O., '60–7; Pas., Chicago, Ill., '68——. D.D., W.R.C., '67, & A.C., '68.

CHARLES EDWIN GRIGGS; b., Pomfret, Ct., July 21, 1827; A.C., '56; U.T.S., '56–9; Not Ord.; S.S., South-Coventry, Ct., '59; S.S., Stafford, Ct., '61; S.S., Hampton, Ct., '62; S.S., Windham, Ct., '65; Scotland, '66; S.S., Eastford, Ct., '67; S.S., Hampton, Ct., '68 & '70; S.S., Willington, Ct., '71–2; S.S., Abington, Ct., '73; O.S., Chaplin, Ct., '73——.

HIRAM COLLINS HAYDN; b., Pompey, N.Y., Dec. 11, 1831; A.C., '56; U.T.S., '56–9; Ord. (Cong.), Jan. 16, '62; S.S., Montville, Ct., '59–'61; Pas., W. Meriden, Ct., '62–6; S.S., St. Johnsbury, Vt., '66; Pas., Painesville, O., '66–'71; S.S., St. Louis, Mo., '71–2; Pas. (Presb.), Cleveland, O., '72——. D.D., Woos.U., '75.

THEODORE JAMES HOLMES; b., Utica, N.Y., Ap. 26, 1833; Y.C., '53; U.T.S., '56–9; Ord. (Cong.), Nov. 22, '59; Pas., E. Hartford, Ct., '61–'72; Pas., Brooklyn, N.Y., '73–4; Pas., Baltimore, Md., '75——.

WILLIAM KENDRICK; b., Cynthiana, Ky., Sep. 1, 1824; U.T.S., '58–9; Ord. (Presb.), ..., '59; H.M., Kentucky, '59–'60; S.S., Montrose, Io., '60; S.S., Leon & Decatur, Io., '62–3; S.S., Sharon, Ill., '64–5; Ag., A.B.S., Iowa, '66–8; S.S., Moulton, Io., '68–'72; S.S., Gallatin, Mo., '73; S.S., Melvern & Rock Creek, Kan., '74——.

HENRY D. KIMBALL; b., ..., .., 1828; Y.C., '52; U.T.S., '52–3, '57–9; Ord. (Cong.), Mar. 19, '62; S.S., N. Woburn, Mass., '60–1; Pas., Sandwich, Mass., '62–3; S.S., N. York City, '63–4; Sec., C.U.A., N. York City, '64——

JOHN KIMBALL; b., Barton, Vt., Oct. 10, 1831; D.C., '56; U.T.S., '56–9; Ord. (Cong.), Oct. 1, '61; S.S., N. York City, '59–'60; S.S., Grass Valley, Cal., '61–2; S.S., San Francisco, Cal., '62–3; Ch., U.S.Army, '63–5; Supt. of Col. Schools, Washington, D.C., '65–9; Ag., A.M.A., Oakland, Cal., '69–'71;

S.S., San Francisco, Cal., '71–3 ; S.S., Chicago, Ill., '73–4 ; S.S., Santa Barbara, Cal., '74–5 ; C.M., San Francisco, Cal., '75——.

CHARLES EUGENE KNOX ; b., Knoxboro, N.Y., Dec. 27, 1833 ; H.C., '56 ; Aub.T.S., '56–7 ; U.T.S., '57–9 ; Tut., H.C., '59–'60 ; Ord. (Presb.), June 8, '64 ; Pas. E. (R.D.), Utica, N.Y., '60–2 ; S.S., Oswego, N.Y., '62–3 ; S.S., Morristown, N.J., '63–4 ; Pas. (Presb.), Bloomfield, N.J., '64–'73 ; Prest. Germ. Theo. School, do., '73——. D.D., C.N.J., '74.

JAMES TURNER LEFTWICH ; b., Liberty, Va., ..., 1835 ; C.N.J.. '56 ; U.T.S., '56–9 ; Ord. (Presb.), ..., '59 ; Pas., Alexandria, Va., '59–'61 ; S.S., Wytheville & Marion, Va., '62—— .. ; Pas., Atlanta, Ga., .., ——. D.D., W. & L.U., '74.

JOEL LINSLEY ; b., Cornwall, Vt., Nov. 27, 1827 ; A.C., '56 ; U.T.S., '56–9 ; Ord. (Cong.), Ap. 1, '60 ; S.S., Hillsboro, Ill., '60–1 ; S.S., Manlius, N.Y., '61–2 ; Agric., Millville, N.Y., '63——.

JAMES ANDREW LITTLE ; b., New-York City, July 20, 1837 ; N.Y.A., '54 ; U.T.S., '56–9 ; Ord. (Presb.), July 21, '61 ; S.S. Canastota, (R.D.), N.Y., '61–3 ; S.S. (Cong.), Paterson, N.J., '63–4 ; Pas. (Presb.), P. Amboy, N.J., '64–8 ; Pas., Hokendauqua, Pa., '68——.

THOMAS HOOKE MCCALLIE ; b., Washington, Tenn., Aug. 1, 1837 ; Bur.C., '56 ; U.T.S., '56–9 ; Ord. (Presb.), Sep. 29, '59 ; S.S., Bethesda & Lebanon Chhs., Miss., '59 ; S.S., Cleveland, Tenn., '60–2 ; S.S., Charleston, Tenn., '62–6 ; Pas., do., '66–'73 ; P.M., Knoxville, Tenn., '74——.

CHARLES GARDINER MCCULLY ; b., New-York City, Dec. 29, 1832 ; Y.C., '53 ; U.T.S., '56–9 ; Ord. (Cong.), July 17, '60 ; Pas., Milltown, St. Stephen, N.B., '60–6 ; Pas., Hallowell, Me., '66–'76 ; Pas., Calais, Me., '76——.

AUGUSTUS LEANDER MARDEN ; b., Easton, Mass., Nov. 9, 1830 ; D.C., '56 ; U.T.S., '56–9 ; Ord. (Cong.), May 30, '61 ; S.S., Cabot, Vt., '59–'60 ; S.S. & Pas., Piermont, N.H., '59——.

JAMES THOMAS MATTHEWS ; b., Charlestown, Mass., ..., 1830 ; Y.C., '54 ; U.T.S., '56–9 ; Ord. (Presb.), Nov. 28, '59 ; S.S., Port Jervis, N.Y., '59–'60 ; S.S., Kenosha, Wis., '60–4 ; W.C., Chicago, Ill., '64–5 ; Pas., do., '65–6 ; Ev., do., '67——.

ARTHUR MITCHELL ; b., Hudson, N.Y., Aug. 13, 1835 ; W.C., '53 ; Tut., L.F.C., Easton, Pa., '53–6 ; U.T.S., '56–9 ; Ord. (Presb.), May 9, '59 ; Pas., Richmond, Va., '59–'61 ; Pas., Morristown, N.J., '61–8 ; Pas., Chicago, Ill., '69——. D.D., W.C., '75.

GEORGE PIERSON, JR. ; b., Orange, N.J., Feb. 24, 1835 ; C.N.J., '53 ; U.T.S., '56–9 ; S.S., Waitsfield, Vt., '59–'60 ; Inv., Orange, N.J., '61——.

CHARLES HENRY RUSSELL ; b., Stratford, Ct., Oct. 23, 1827 ; U.T.S., '56–9 ; Ord. (Presb.), ..., '59 ; Pas., Williamsport, Md., '59–'61 ; U.S. Army, '62–4 ; Trade, Bridgeport, Ct., '64——.

WILLIAM AUGUSTUS SMITH ; b., Rutland, Vt., Sep. 1, 1834 ; Ma.C., '53 ; U.T.S., '56–9 ; Ord. (Cong.), May 14, '61 ; S.S., Coleraine, Mass., '59–'60 ; Pas., Rockland, Me., '61–3 ; Tut., Den.U., Granville, O., '63–5 ; S.S., Rushville, N.Y., '65; S.S., Hamilton, N.Y., '65–7; S.S., Ann Arbor, Mich., '68–'70; Pas., Morris, Ill., '71–3; S.S., Seneca Falls, N.Y., '73–5; S.S., Morrisville, N.Y., '75——.

ROBERT BAYARD SNOWDEN; b., New-York City, ..., 1833; W.C., '54; U.T.S., '54–5, '56–9; Res. Lic., '60–1; Ord. (Cong.), May 1, '61; S.S., Montville, Ct., '61–3; S.S., Ludlow, Vt., '64–5; Pas., Nevada City, Cal., '65–7; Pas., Redwood, Cal., '67–'70; Pas., Darien, Ct., '73–5; W.C. (Ep.), Brooklyn, N.Y., '75——.

CHARLES AUGUSTUS STODDARD; b., Boston, Mass., May 28, 1833; W.C., '54; U.T.S., '56–9; Ord. (Presb.), Sep. 18, '59; Pas., N. York City (Washington Heights), '59——. D.D., W.C., '71.

JAMES HENRY TAYLOR; b., Ballston Spa, N.Y., Jan. 3, 1829; B.C., '56; U.T.S., '56–9; Ord. (Presb.), Nov. 2, '59; Pas., New-Rochelle, N.Y., '59–'62; S.S. (Cong.), Eastport, Me., '62–3; Pas. (Presb.), Orange, N.J., '63–8; Pas., Lake Forest, Ill., '68–'75; Prof., L.F.U., do., '75–6; Pas., Rome, N.Y., '76——.

*CHARLES FINNEY WINSHIP; b., New-Hartford, N.Y., Ap. 21, 1826; K.C., '53; U.T.S., '57–9; Ord. (Cong.), Sep. 27, '59; F.M., Mendi Mission, W. Africa, '60–3; U. States, '63–5; Died, Princeton, Ill., July 1, '65.

JOHN MILTON WOLCOTT; b., West-Springfield, Mass., Nov. 20, 1838; Y.C., '54; U.T.S., '56–9; Ord. (Cong.), Feb. 20, '61; Pas., South-Britain, Ct., '61–5; Pas., Elizabethport, N.J., '65–8; S.S., New-Haven, Ct., '68–9; Pas., Cheshire, Ct., '69——.

SIMEON FOSTER WOODIN; b., Hillsdale, N.Y., May 11, 1833; W.C., '55; U.T.S., '56–9; Ord. (Presb.), June 19, '59; F.M., Foochow, China, '60–'70; U. States, '70–2; F.M., Foochow, China, '72——.

JAMES DUNHAM WYCKOFF; b., Ashland, O., Sep. 11, 1832; K.C., '56; U.T.S., '56–9; Ord. (Cong.), Oct. 25, '59; H.M., Rosefield & Lehigh, Ill., '59–'61; S.S., Maquon & Union Town, Ill., '61–4; S.S., Rosefield & Lehigh, Ill., '65; Ag. Chn. Com., Cairo, Ill., '65–6; S.S., Rosefield & Abingdon, Ill., '67–8; S.S., Altoona, Ill., '69–'76; S.S., Roseville, Ill., '76——. 34.

GOTTFRIED EDWARD ALEXANDER; b., New-York City, ..., 1833; L.T.S., '56–7; U.T.S., '57–8.

ROBERT ATKINSON; b., ..., Canada, Aug. 24, 1834; M.U., '56; M.T.S., '56–7; U.T.S., '57–8; Ord. (Bap.), Sep. 2, '58; Pas., Newark, N.J., '58–'68; Prest., University, Ottawa, Kan., '68——.

*THOMAS LYFORD AMBROSE; b., Ossipee, N.H., ..., 1829; B.C., '56; U.T.S., '56–7; And.T.S., '57–8; Ord. (Cong.), July 21, '58; F.M., Oroomiah, Persia, '58–'62; Ch., U.S.Army, '62–4; Died, of wounds, Ft. Monroe, Va., Aug. 19, '64.

*DANIEL HOYT BLAKE; b., Sutton, Vt., ..., 1829; K.C., '56; U.T.S., '56–8; Ord. (Cong.), June 9, '59; S.S., Mendota, Ill., '59–'60; S.S., Fond du

Lac, Wis., '60-1; Pas., Princeton, Ill., '62-4; Ag., A.M.A., Hilton Head, S.C., '64-5; S.S., Spencerport, N.Y., '65-7; Died, Stamford, Ct., Ap. 6, '69.

HENRY NITCHIE COBB; b., New-York City, Nov. 15, 1834; Y.C., '55; U.T.S., '56-7; Ord. (Presb.), May 16, '60; F.M., Oroomiah, Persia, '60-3; Inv., Tarrytown, N.Y., '63-5; Pas. (R.D.), Millbrook, N.Y., '66——.

JOHN PURSEL HAIRE; b., Elizabethtown, O., Ap. 25, 1831; W.C., '55; L.T.S., '56-7; And.T.S., '57-8; U.T.S., '58-9; Ord. (Presb.), Ap. .., '61; S.S., Elizabethtown, Berea & Cleves, O., '60-1; S.S., Aurora, Ind., '61-2; Prin., Pub. School, do., '62-3; Inv., Elizabethtown, O., '63-9; S.S., & Prin., Fox Lake, Wis., '70-3; Prof., R.C., Ripon, Wis., '73-5; Prin., Janesville, Wis., '75——.

WILLIAM ALLEN HALLOCK; b., Plainfield, Mass., Aug. 27, 1832; A.C., '55; N.H.T.S., '56-7; U.T.S., '57-8; E.W.T.S., '58-9; Ord. (Cong.), Oct. 24, '60; Pas., Gilead, Ct., '60-4; S.S., Kiantone, N.Y., '66-9; S.S., Jamestown, N.Y., '72-4; Pas., Bloomfield, Ct., '75——.

JESSE WINEGAR HOUGH; b., Groton, N.Y., Nov. 26, 1832; Y.C., '53; U.T.S., '56-8; Ord. (Presb.), Mar. 13, '59; Ch. Miss., N. York City, '58-'60; Pas. (Cong.), Williston, Vt., '60-5; Pas. (Presb.), Saginaw City, Mich., '65-7; Pas. (Cong.), Jackson, Mich., '67-'72; S.S., Santa Barbara, Cal., '72——.

HENRY LYNES HUBBELL; b., Wilton, Ct., ..., 1830; Y.C., '54; U.T.S., '56-7; And.T.S., '57-'9; Ord. (Cong.), Ap. 24, '61; Pas., Amherst, Mass., '61-5; W.C., do., '66-8; S.S., Ann Arbor, Mich., '69——.

HENRY G. McARTHUR; b., Porter, N.Y., March 25, 1834; K.C., '56; U.T.S., '56-8; C.T.S., '58-9; Ord. (Cong.), Aug. 10, '59; S.S., McGregor, Io., '59-'61; S.S., Oshkosh, Wis., '63-5; S.S., Griggsville, Ill., '66-'71; S.S., Geneseo, Ill., '72-4; W.C., Beloit, Wis., '74——.

ROBERT LEEPER McCORD; b., Bethel, Ill., Aug. 7, 1830; I.C., '56; U.T.S., '56-7; L.T.S., '57-9; Ord. (Cong.), Sep. 4, '61; S.S., New-Berlin, Ill., '60; Pas., Lincoln, Ill., '61-6; S.S., Toulon, Ill., '67——.

JOHN LAWRENCE MILLS; b., Norfolk, Ct., Sep. 18, 1832; Y.C., '55; U.T.S., '56-8; Tut., Y.C., '58-'61; S.S., Seymour, Ct., '62-4; Prof., Marietta Coll., O., '65——.

*DAVID OWEN; b., Beloit, Wis., ..., 1828; Bel.C., '56; U.T.S., '56; Died, N. York City, Nov. .., '56.

*THORNTON BIGELOW PENFIELD; b., Alden, N.Y., Oct. 2, 1834; O.C., '56; U.T.S., '56-8; Ord. (Cong.), Oct. .., '58; F.M., Brainerd, Jamaica, W.I., '58-'66; F.M., Madura, India, '66-'71; Died, do., Aug. 19, '71.

*GEORGE CHESTER ROBINSON; b., Hartwick, N.Y., Aug. 9, 1833; Y.C., '56; U.T.S., '56; Ord. (M.E.), ..., '57; Pas. Brooklyn, N.Y., '57-8; Pas., Cincinnati, O., '58-'62; Inv., Europe, '62; Died, Wellsboro, Pa., Sep. 21, '63.

HORACE PAYSON SMITH; b., Salem, Mass., ..., 1831; A.C., '54; U.T.S., '56-7; Ord. (Presb.), ..., ..; Tea., Huntsville, Ala., ..——..; Pas., Tuscumbia, Ala., ..——.

WILLIAM WOOD SQUIRE; b., Montreal, Can., ..., 1836; Q.C., '54; U.T.S., '56-7; Ord. (Wes.), ...; S.S., ..., C.E., '58——.

*AMHERST LORD THOMPSON; b., Peru, Mass., Ap. 16, 1834; A.C., '56; U.T.S., '56-7; And.T.S., '57-9; Ord. (Cong.), Feb. 2, '60; S.S. Ansonia, Ct., '59-'60; F.M., Oroomiah, Persia, '60; Died, Seir, Persia, Aug. 25, '60.

*JOHN WINN UNDERHILL; b., Ipswich, Mass., Ap. 21, 1829; A.C., '54; U.T.S., '56-7; And.T.S., '57-9; Ord. (Cong.), Oct. 5, '59; Pas., N. Amherst, Mass., '59-'62; Died, do., Oct. 17, '62.

WILLIAM HAYES WARD; b., Abingdon, Mass., June 25, 1835; A.C., '56; U.T.S., '56-7; Tut., Bel.C., '57-8; And.T.S., '58-9; Ord. (Cong.), Jan. 8, '60; S.S., & Pas., Oskaloosa, Kan., '59-'61; Tea., Easthampton, Mass., '61; Tea., Utica, N.Y., '62-5; Prof., R.C., Ripon, Wis., '65-7; Ed., N. York City, '68——. D.D., U.N.Y., & C.N.J., '73. 20.

1860.

EDWIN ALLEN; b., Barton, Vt., March 10, 1833; G.C., '57; L.T.S., '57-9; U.T.S., '59-'60; Ord. (Presb.), June 11, '62; S.S., Parma Centre, N.Y., '62-6; S.S., Edwardsburgh, Mich., '66-8; S.S., Stone Chh., N.Y., '68-'70; S.S., Bergen, N.Y., '70-2; S.S., Byron, N.Y., '73——.

*JOHN FRANCIS BAIRD; b., York, Pa., Aug. 24, 1835; U.T.S., '57-'60; S.S., Cedarville, N.J., '60-3; Died, do., Ap. .., '63.

ELIJAH CLARK BALDWIN; b., Milford, Ct., Dec. 4, 1832; U.T.S., '57-'60; Ord. (Cong.), Sep. 5, '60; Pas., Bethel, Ct., '60-5; Pas., Branford, Ct., '65——.

HENRY WATKINS BALLANTINE; b., Prince Edward Co., Va., Nov. 6, 1838; Ind.U., '56; U.T.S., '57-'60; Ord. (Presb.), Jan. 9, '61; S.S., Terre Haute, Ind., '61-2; F.M., Bombay, India, '63-5; S.S., Marietta, O., '65-9; Prof., Indiana Univ., '70-5; Pas., Bloomfield, N.J., '75——.

AUGUSTUS FIELD BEARD; b., Norwalk, Ct., May .., 1833; Y.C., '57; Aub.T.S., '57-8; U.T.S., '58-'60; Ord. (Cong.), May 24, '60; S.S., Cape Elizabeth, Me., '60-2; Pas., Bath, Me., '62-9; Pas., Syracuse, N.Y., '69——. D.D., S.U., '75.

FREDERIC MAYER BIRD; b., Philadelphia, Pa., June 28, 1838; U.Pa., '57; Hk.T.S., '57-9; U.T.S., '59-'60; Ord. (Lu.), Sep. .., '61; Pas., Rhinebeck, N.Y., '60-2; Ch., U.S.Army, '62-3; Pas., W. Philadelphia, Pa., '65-6; Pas., Valatie, N.Y., '66-9; Rec. (Ep.), Shamokin, Pa., '69-'70; Rec., Spotswood, N.J., '70-4; Rec., Indianapolis, Ind., '74-5; Rec., Hightstown, N.J., '75——.

HENRY MARTYN BRIDGMAN; b., Westhampton, Mass., Jan. 8, 1830; A.C., '57; E.W.T.S., '57-8; U.T.S., '58-'60; Ord. (Cong.), June 27, '60; F.M., Umzumbi, Zulu, S. Af., '60——.

LYSANDER TOWER BURBANK; b., Fitzwilliam, N.H., Nov. 24, 1828; W.C., '57; U.T.S., '57-'60; Ord. (Cong.), June 14, '60; F.M., Bitlis, Assyria, '30-9; S.S., Herndon, Va., '70——.

ELISÉE CHARLIER; b., Valdrōme, France, March 21, 1830; U.T.S., '57–'60; Ord. (Cong.), Oct. 19, '62; Ch., U.S. Army, '62–4; Tea., Philadelphia, Pa., '65—— ..; Prin., N. York City, .. ——.

ASAHEL LEWIS CLARK; b., Amherst, Mass., ..., 1832; A.C., '57; U.T.S., '57–'60; Ord. (Presb.), June 11, '61; Pas., Scranton (Hyde Park), Pa., '61–'71; Pas., Greenport (L.I.), N.Y., '71–'6; S.S., Elizabeth, N.J., '76.

ELISHA GREENE COBB; b., Canterbury, Ct., May 2, 1831; A.C., '57; U.T.S., '57–'60; Ord. (Presb.), June 20, '60; Pas., Peekskill, N.Y., '60–6; Pas., Florence, Mass., '66——.

ALFRED SOMERS COLLINS; b., New-York City, Sep. 1, 1838; U.N.Y., '57; U.T.S., '57–'60; Res. Lic., '60–1; Ord. (Presb.), Oct. 23, '61; S.S., Albany, N.Y., '63; S.S., Andover, N.J., '64; W.C., Brooklyn (E.D.), N.Y., '65——.

DAVID STUART DODGE; b., New-York City, Sep. 22, 1836; Y.C., '57; U.T.S., '57–'60; Ord. (Presb.), Oct. 16, '64; Trav., Europe, '62–3; W.C., N. York City, '64; Prof. E., Syr. C., Beirut, Syria, '64—— ..; C.M., N. York City, .. ——.

JOHN BERNARD FAIRBANK; b., Oakham, Mass., Sep. 6, 1831; I.C., '57; U.T.S., '57–'60; Ord. (Cong.), Oct. 24, '60; S.S., Fox Lake, Wis., '60–4; S.S., Fox Lake, Wis., '64–6; S.S., St. Joseph, Mich., '66–'70; S.S., Ft. Wayne, Ind., '70–5; Pas., Farmington, Ill., '75——.

JOHN MCLACHLAN FORBES; b., New-York City, March 8, 1837; N.Y.A., '54; U.T.S., '57–'60; Tea., N. York City, '60–2; Tea., Rahway, N.J., '62–4; Tea., N. York City, '64–'70; Prin., do., '70——.

LORENZO MARTEL GATES; b., Ann Arbor, Mich., ..., 1830; U.M., '57; U.T.S., '57–'60; Ord. (Presb.), Sep. 29, '60; Pas., Hillsdale, N.Y., '60–2; S.S., Lowell & Arlington, Wis., '62–3; Pas., Columbus, Wis., '63–4; S.S., Roscoe, Ill., '64–6; S.S., Lena, Ill., '66–8; S.S., Ottawa, Ill., '68–'75; S.S., Plato, Ill., '75——. Residence, Elgin, Ill.

GEORGE SEAMAN GRAY; b., New-York City, July 10, 1835; Y.C., '57; Aub.T.S., '57–9; U.T.S., '59–'60; S.S., Portland, Me., '60; S.S., Westbrook, Me., '60–2; S.S., Cincinnati, O., '62–3; Tea., Englewood, N.J., '63–6; Trade, Cincinnati, O., '66——.

JAMES ALPHEUS GRIFFES; b., Fleming, N.Y., May 4, 1832; U.M., '57; U.T.S., '57–'60; Ord. (Presb.), Nov. 21, '60; S.S., Salem, Mich., '59, & '60–1; S.S., Howell, Mich., '61–3; S.S., Salina, Saginaw, & Carrollton, Mich., '63–5; S.S., New-Market, Bethesda, Strawberry Plains, & Hopewell, Tenn., '65–9; P.M., Tenn., '69–'72; S.S., Beatrice, Neb., '72–3; S.S., Kearney Junction & Hastings, Neb., '73——.

NORMAN JONES; b., Washington, O., Nov. 28, 1832; D.C., '57; U.T.S., '57–'60; Ord. (Presb.), Ap. 13, '64; S.S., Yellow Springs, O., '61–4; Ch., U.S. Army, '65; H.M., Washington, O., '65–8; Pas., North-Fork & Union, O., '68–'72; Pas., Decatur, Ind., '72——.

JOHN HAMILTON MCMONAGLE; b., Chicago, Ill., ..., 1830; K.C., '57; U.T.S., '57–'60; Ord. (Cong.), Aug. 22, '60; S.S., Cooper, Me., '59–'60; Pas.,

E. Machias, Me., '60-1; S.S., Placerville, Cal., '61-3; Ch., U.S.Army, S.Francisco, Cal., '64—— ..; Pas., Manayunk, Pa., '71——.

IRVING MAGEE; b., Red Hook, N.Y., July 24, 1831; W.C., '57; U.T.S., '59-'60; Ord. (Lu.), Sep. 4, '60; Pas., Valatie, N.Y., '60-5; Pas., Baltimore, Md., '65-8; Pas., Chambersburgh, Pa., '68-9; Pas., Dayton, O., '69-'72; Pas., Albany, N.Y., '72——. D.D., Witt. C., '72.

JOHN ALLEN MAXWELL; b., New-York City, Dec. 29, 1833; U.N.Y., '57; U.T.S., '57-'60; Ord. (Presb.), Sep. 27, '60; Pas., S. Orange, N.J., '60-'71; Pas., Hazleton, Pa., '71-4; Pas., Bridgeton, N.J., '74——.

NELSON MILLARD; b., Delhi, N.Y., Oct. 2, 1834; U.C., '53; U.T.S., '59-'60; Trav., Europe, '60-1; Ord. (Presb.), May 13, '62; Pas., Montclair, N.J., '62-7; S.S., Chicago, Ill., '67-9; Pas., Peekskill, N.Y., '69-'71; Pas., Syracuse, N.Y., '71——. D.D., U.C., '74.

ALEXANDER DAVIS MOORE; b., Washington City, D.C., Jan. 21, 1836; Cn.C., '57; U.T.S., '57-'60; Ord. (Presb.), Oct. 21, '60; Pas., Dauphin, Pa., '60-8; Pas., Northumberland, Pa., '68-'76; Pas., Bethlehem, Pa., '76——.

GEORGE BENTON NEWCOMB; b., Allegheny, Pa., Nov. 24, 1835; W.C., '56; U.T.S., '58-'60; Ord. (Cong.), Oct. 15, '61; Pas., Bloomfield, Ct., '61-6; Pas., Wolcottville, Ct., '66-9; Pas., New-Haven, Ct., '69-'72; Pas., do., '72——.

EDMUND MORRIS PEASE; b., Granby, Mass., ..., 1829; A.C., '54; U.T.S.,'56-7; Tut., A.C.,'57-8; U.T.S.,'58-'60; M.D., ...; Physician, .. ——.

ARTHUR TAPPAN PIERSON; b., New-York City, March 6, 1837; H.C., '57; U.T.S., '57-'60; Ord. (Presb.), May 13, '60; S.S., W. Winsted, Ct., '60; Pas. (Cong.), Binghamton, N.Y.,'60-3; S.S., Norwalk, Ct., '63; Pas. (Presb.), Waterford, N.Y., '63-9; Pas., Detroit, Mich., '69——. D.D., K.C., '74.

JAMES AVERY SKINNER; b., Union Square, N.Y., Nov. 15, 1835; H.C., '57; U.T.S., '57-'60; Ord. (Presb.), Ap. 13, '61; Tut., H.C., '60-2; Ag., N. York City, '62-3; S.S., Santa Clara, Cal., '63-5; S.S., San Francisco, Cal., '65; S.S., Stockton, Cal., '65-8; S.S., Cleveland, O., '70-3; Pas., do., '73-5; D.Sup., P.B.P., Syracuse, N.Y., '75——.

DAVID HOUSTON TAYLOR; b., Hartford Co., Ct., Ap. 18, 1832; U.M., '57; U.T.S., '57-'60; Ord. (Presb.), Jan. 9, '60; S.S., Saginaw City, Mich., '59-'65; S.S., Ontonagon (L.S.), Mich., '65-7; S.S., Lapeer, Mich., '68-'73; S.S., Fenton, Mich., '73——.

JOHN SEYMOUR WHITMAN; b., Williamstown, Mass., Nov. 7, 1833; W.C., '54; U.T.S., '55-6; Aub.T.S., '57-8; U.T.S., '59-'60; Ord. (Cong.), Sep. 4, '61; S.S., Rochester, Minn., '61-2; S.S., Charlemont, Mass., '63-5; W.C., Williamstown, Mass., '65-6; Pas., Sprague, Ct., '66-9; W.C., Williamstown, Mass.; '69-'70; S.S., Lyndon, Vt., '71——.

HERMANN DIETRICH WRAGE; b., Flensburgh, Sleswick, Europe, May 1, 1831; U.N.Y., '57; U.T.S., '57-'60; Ord. (Presb.), June 10, '61; Ch., U.S.Army, '61-2; Tea., N. York City, '62-'72; S.S. (Lu.), .. ——. 31.

*David Beals; b., Charlemont, Mass., Jan. 28, 1829; A.C., '57; E.W.T.S., '57–8; U.T.S., '58–9; E.W.T.S., '59–'60; Ord. (Cong.), June 10, '63; S.S. & Pas., Hartland, Ct., '61–5; S.S., Southwick, Mass., '65–8; Died, do., Sep. 28, '68.

John Stottoff Beekman; b., Middlebush, N.J., Oct. 19, 1833; C.N.J., '57; U.T.S., '57–8; P.T.S., '58–'60; Ord. (Presb.), June 10, '63; S.S., Livingston, Ala., '60–1; Pas., Farmington, Ill., '63–6; Pas., French Grove, Ill., '66–'70; Inv. & W.C., '71–4; Pas., Amwell, N.J., '75——.

Philip Berry; b., Hackensack, N.J., Feb. 16, 1837; R.C., '57; U.T.S., '57–8; N.B.T.S., '58–'60; Ord. (R.D.), June 21, '60; Pas., Grand Rapids, Mich., '60–1; Pas., Scotia, N.Y., '61–3; F.M., Sidon, Syria, '63–5; Pas. & Tea., Athens, Pa., '65–'72; Pas., Sutton, Mass., '72–5; Pas., Belchertown, Mass., '75——.

Charles Goodrich Bisbee; b., Plainfield, Mass., Dec. 24, 1827; O.C., '57; O.T.S., '57–8; U.T.S., '58–9; O.T.S., '59–'60; Ord. (Cong.), Sep. 10, '61; S.S., Alpena, Mich., '60–5; Prin., Monroeville, O., '66; S.S., Fontenelle, Neb., '66–7; Prin., Neb. Univ., '68–9; Supt. Pub. Ins., '69–'74; S.S., Fontenelle, Neb., '74–5; S.S., Syracuse, Neb., '75——.

William Crawford; b., Barre, Vt., Jan. 3, 1835; A.C., '57; U.T.S., '57–8; And.T.S., '58–'60; Ord. (Cong.), May 2, '61; S.S., Clearwater, Minn., '60–2; S.S., Danvers, Mass., '62–3; S.S., Central City, Col. Ter., '63–8; Pas. (Presb.), Green Bay, Wis., '69——.

George Benson Dechant; b., Pottstown, Pa., June 27, 1827; U.T.S., '57–9; M.T.S., '59–'60; Ord. (Ger. Ref.), July .., '60; Pas., Fennersville, Pa., '60–'72; Pas. Catawissa, Pa., '72——.

*Alfred Nelson Denny; b., Bond Co., Ill., Dec. 7, 1830; I.C., '54; U.T.S., '57–9; Ord. (Presb.), Sep. 16, '60; S.S., Mason, Ill., '60–3; S.S., Nashville, Ill., '63–4; S.S., Moro, Ill., '64–8; Died, do., Sep. 29, '68.

Charles Brockway Dye; b., Broadalbin, N.Y., Nov. 7, 1828; Y.C., '57; U.T.S., '57–9; Res. Grad., N.H.T.S., '60–1; Ord. (Cong.), Oct. 26, '59; Pas., Torrington, Ct., '59–'60; Pas. (Presb.), Romulus, N.Y., '61–2; U.S.Navy, '63–4; S.S., West-Suffield, Ct., '64–5; S.S., N. Vineland, N.J., '66–8; S.S., New-Fairfield, Ct., '68–'71; O.S., Patterson, N.Y., '71——.

Alonzo Goodrich Fay; b., Cazenovia, N.Y., ..., 1833; U.T.S., '57–8; Law, N. York City, '59——.

Alexander Hutchins; b., Peekskill, N.Y., Jan. 22, 1835; W.C., '57; U.T.S., '57–8; M.D., Coll. Med., N.Y., '60; Physician, Brooklyn, N.Y., .. ——.

Mancius Holmes Hutton; b., New-York City, Oct. 13, 1837; U.N.Y., '57; U.T.S., '57–9; N.B.T.S., '59–'60; Res. Lic., U.T.S., '61–2; Ord. (R.D.), June 15, '64; Pas., Mt. Vernon, N.Y., '64——.

*Wenham Kidder; b., New-York City, ..., 1834; U.N.Y., '57; U.T.S., '57–9; Ord. (Bap.), ...; Died, Washington, O., Oct. 4, '72.

Peter McVicar; b., Le Sang, New-Brun., June 15, 1829; Bel.C., '56; U.T.S., '57–8; And.T.S., '58–'60; Ord. (Cong.), May 29, '61; Pas., Topeka,

Kan., '61–6; State Supt. of Pub. Ins., do., '66–'71; Prest., Washb. Coll., do., '71——. D.D., Bel.C., '71.

ELDRIDGE MIX; b., Atwater, O., Jan. 15, 1833; W.C., '54; U.T.S., '57–'60; Ord. (Presb.), Dec. 6, '60; S.S., N. York City, '60–1; Pas. (Cong.), Burlington, Vt., '62–7; Pas. (Presb.), Orange, N.J., '67——.

JAMES BAYLES PEARSON; b., New-York City, Sep. 26, 1829; W.U., '51; Tea., E. Hartford, Ct., '52; Tea., Flushing (L.I.), N.Y., '53–4; Prin., Fall River, Mass., '55–7; U.T.S., '58–9; Tea., N. York City, '59; Ord. (Cong.), Nov. 14, '60; Pas., Winsted, Ct., '60–2; S.S., Plymouth (Thomaston), Ct., '63–5; Life Insurance & Stocks, N. York City, '66——.

EDWARD ROBERTS; b., Remsen, N.Y., ..., 1830; U.C., '57; U.T.S., '57–8; Tea. of S. Music, N. York City, '59——.

*RANDOLPH SAILER; b., Woodbury, N.J., May 24, 1833; U.Pa., '57; U.T.S., '57–9; Ag., A.S.S.U., '59; Eyes failed; Trade, Philadelphia, Pa., '60–9; Died, do., Jan. 22, '69.

ERASTUS SEYMOUR; b., Palmyra, N.Y., Nov. 18, 1830; U.T.S., '57–'60; Ord. (Presb.), ..., '62; S.S. & Pas., Cochecton, N.Y., '60–3; Ch., Brooklyn, N.Y., '64–6; Ch. Miss., N. York City, '66——.

*ROBERT HALL WALTON; b., Hartford, Ct., ..., 1833; Del.C., '54; U.T.S., '57–8; Ord. (Presb.), ..., '60; S.S., Broadway, Va., .. —— ..; S.S., Cassville, Ga., .. ——'76; Died, do., Ap. 2, '76.

ALFRED TILESTON WATERMAN; b., Providence, R.I., Dec. 13, 1832; Y.C., '55; U.T.S., '57–8; P.T.S., '58–'60; Ord. (Cong.), Nov. 9, '64; Pas., Middletown (Westfield), Ct., '64–9; Pas., Kensington, Ct., '69–'74; S.S., Monroe, Ct., '75; S.S., Marshall, Mich., '76——.

NATHAN DANA WELLS; b., Northfield, N.H., June 17, 1831; Y.C., '57; U.T.S., '57–8; Law, N. York City, '60——.

CHARLES WETHERBY; b., Walpole, N.H., June 10, 1833; M.C., '56; U.T.S., '59; Ord. (Cong.), Sep. 1, '59; Pas., N. Cornwall, Ct., '59–'66; Pas., W. Winsted, Ct., '66–'71; Pas., Nashua, N.H., '71—— 22.

1861.

FREDERICK H. ADAMS; b., London, Eng., June 22, 1823; U.N.Y., '58; U.T.S., '58–'61; Ord. (Presb.), Ap. 25, '65; S.S., Constantia, N.Y., '61–4; S.S. Marquette (L.S.), Mich., '65–6; S.S., Saline, Mich., '67–9; S.S., Wilson, N.Y., '70–5; S.S., New-Hartford, Ct., '75——.

*WILLIAM SWAN ADAMSON; b., New-York City, ..., 1832; Aub.T.S., '58–9; U.T.S., '59–'61; Ord. (Cong.), Sep. 17, '61; S.S., Greene, N.Y., '61–2; S.S., Wolcotville, Ct., '63–6; S.S., Derby (Ansonia), Ct., '66–'70; Died, ...

WILLIAM ADDY; b., Montreal, Can., Aug. 11, 1836; U.C., '57; U.T.S., '58–'61; Ord. (Presb.), Oct. 23, '61; S.S., Windham, N.Y., '61–6; Pas., Franklin, N.Y., '66–'70; Pas., Marietta, O., '70——.

JAMES HERVEY BEALE; b., Tuscarora Valley, Pa., ..., 1834; Del.C., '58; U.T.S., '58–'61; Ord. (Presb.), Jan. 29, '62; Ch., U.S.Army, '63–4; S.S., Christiana, Del., '65–7; Pas., Philadelphia, Pa., '67——.

JAMES IVERSON BOSWELL; b., Philadelphia, Pa., Nov. 3, 1837; Di.C., '58; U.T.S., '58–'61; Ord. (M.E.), Ap. .., '65; S.S., Westfield, N.J., '61–3; S.S., Warren Co., N.J., '63–5; Pas., Somerville, N.J., '65–6; Pas., Elizabeth, N.J., '67–9; Pas., Newark, N.J., '70–2; Pas., Newton, N.J., '73–6.

ISAAC NELSON CALDWELL; b., New-Market, Tenn., ..., 1836; Mv.C., '58; U.T.S., '58–'61; E. Tenn., '61–4; ——, N.C., '65——.

SAMUEL CARLILE; b., Middletown Point, N.J., Aug. 7, 1833; U.N.Y., '55; U.T.S., '56–7; Studied Law, '57–9; U.T.S., '59–'61; Ord. (Presb.), May 20, '66; S.S. & W.C., N. York City, '61–5; S.S. & Pas., Brooklyn (E.D.), N.Y., '66–'70; W.C., do., '70–2; S.S. & Pas.E., Evansville, Ind., '72–5; W.C., N. York City, '76——.

LYMAN DWIGHT CHAPIN; b., Jewett, N.Y., Sep. 18, 1836; A.C., '58; U.T.S., '58–'61; Ord. (Presb.), July 6, '62; F.M., Tientsin, China, '63—— ..; F.M., Tung-Chow, China, ..——.

ROYAL WASHBURN CLARK; b., Amherst, Mass., ..., 1834; A.C. '58; U.T.S., '58–'61; Agric., Amherst, Mass., '62——.

JAMES WILLIAM COLEMAN; b., Amity, N.Y., June 8, 1833; C.N.J., '56; U.T.S., '58–'61; Ord. (Presb.), Mar. 6, '64; Pas., Darien, Ct., '64–'73; P.E., New-Haven, Ct., '73–4; Ev., N. York City, '74–5; Pas.E., Jacksonville, Fla., '75——.

SMITH CURTIS; b., Sherburne, N.Y., Dec. 21, 1834; U.C., '58; P.T.S., '58–9; U.T.S., '59–'61; Ord. (Cong.), Jan. 16, '62; S.S. & Tea., Fostoria, O., '62–5; Tea., Georgetown, Pa., '66 .. ——; Tea. & Ed., Beaver, Pa., .. ——'73; Clk., Ins. Dep. of Pa., ..., '73——.

ALBERT ERDMAN; b., Allentown, Pa., Oct. 28, 1838; H.C., '58; U.T.C., '58–'61; Ord. (Presb.), Sep. 29, '62; S.S., Deansville, N.Y., '61–2; Ch., U.S. Army, '62–3; Pas., Clinton, N.Y., '64–9; Pas., Morristown, N.J., '69——.

HENRY THORNTON FORD; b., Newark Valley, N.Y., May 12, 1832; W.C., '58; U.T.S., '58–'61; Ord. (Presb.), July 26, '66; S.S., Newark, N.J., '62–3; S.S., Rocky Hill, Ct., '63–6; Pas., Norristown, Pa., '66–'75; S.S., Adrian, Mich., '75——.

WILLIAM LUTHER GAYLORD; b., Woodstock, Ct., Oct. 14, 1831; E.W.T.S., '57–8; U.T.S., '58–9, '60–1; Ord. (Cong.), Sep. 14, '60; Pas., Fitz-william, N.H., '60–7; Pas., Nashua, N.H., '68–'70; Pas., W. Meriden, Ct., '70–5; Pas., Chicopee, Mass., '75——; A.M., D.C., '67.

*HENRY HASTINGS; b., Windham, Vt., Sep. 27, 1833; A.C., '58; U.T.S., '58–'61; Ord. (Cong.), June 11, '62; S.S., E. Machias, Me., '62–3; Died, Townsend, Vt., Jan. 19, '63.

ISAIAH BARDSLEY HOPWOOD; b., Bredbury, Cheshire, Eng., Nov. 6, 1831; U.N.Y., '59; Aub.T.S., '59–'60; U.T.S., '60–1; Ord. (Presb.), July 15, '61; Pas., Coventry, N.Y., '61–3; S.S., Oxford Furnace, N.J., '63–5; S.S.,

Parkville, (L.I.), N.Y., '66-7; Pas., Paterson, N.J., '67-'74; Pas., Newark, N.J., '74——.

SAMUEL JESSUP; b., Montrose, Pa., Dec. 21, 1834; U.T.S., '58-'61; Ord. (Presb.), Sep. 10, '61; Ch., U.S. Army, '61-3; F.M., Sidon, Syria, '63; F.M., Tripoli, Syria, '64-7; F.M., Sidon, Syria, '67——.

ALONZO PECK JOHNSON; b., Somers, Ct., May 18, 1832; U.T.S., '57-8, '59-'61; Ord. (Cong.), June 5, '62; S.S., Newark, N.J., '61-2; S.S., Charlemont, Mass., '62-3; H.M., U.S. Army, '63-4; S.S., Alton, N.H., '64-5; Pas., Waukesha, Wis., '65-6; S.S., (Presb.), Pontiac, Ill., '67-9; S.S., E. Saginaw, Mich., '69-'73; S.S., Elmore, O., '75——.

THEODORE KRUGER; b., Strasburg, France, ..., 1827; U.T.S., 1858-'61; Ord. (....), ...'62; Ch., U.S. Army, '62-5.

*JAMES McLAUGHLIN; b., Hudson, O., Oct. 25, 1829; I.C., '57; U.T.S., '58-'61; Ord. (Presb.), Oct. 8, '61; S.S. & Tea., Red Bluff, Cal., '61-7; W.C., Rio Vista, Cal., '67-8; S.S., Gilroy, Cal., '68-'70; Died, do., Aug. 17, '70.

FRANKLIN NOBLE; b., Washington, D.C., Aug. 25, 1837; W.C., '56; U.T.S., '58-'61; Ord. (Presb.), Ap. 30, '62; S.S. & Pas., Sandusky, O., '61-4; Pas. (Cong.), Torringford, Ct., '65-6; S.S., Brooklyn, N.Y., '66-'74; Pas. (Presb.), Hempstead (L.I.), N.Y., '74——.

MOSES PAYSON PARMELEE; b., Westford, Vt., May 4, 1834; U.Vt., '55; U.T.S., '58-'61; Ord. (Cong.), July 2, '61; Ch., U.S. Army, '61-2; F.M., Erzeroom, Asia, '63——.

SIDNEY PHŒNIX; b., Chicopee, Mass., Aug. 21, 1829; Y.C., '50; U.T.S., '58-'61; S.S., Roxbury & Richmond, Vt., '62; Agric., Rochester, N.Y., '63-5; Do., Vineland, N.J., '65-'73; Trade, Lake City, Minn., '73——.

GEORGE EDWARD POST; b., New-York City, Dec. 17, 1838; N.Y.A., '54; M.D., U.N.Y., '60; U.T.S., '58-'61; Ord. (Presb.), June 5, '61; Ch., U.S. Army, '61-3; F.M., Tripoli, Syria, '63-8; Prof., Beirut, Syria, '68——.

JOHN BUNYAN REEVE; b., Mattituck (L.I.), N.Y., Oct. 29, 1831; Cl.C., '58; U.T.S., '58-'61; Ord. (Presb.), June 5, '61; Pas., Philadelphia, Pa., '61-'71; Prof., Washington, D.C., '71-5; Pas., Philadelphia, Pa., '75——. D.D., L.U., '70.

ISAAC RILEY; b., New-York City, Feb. 2, 1835; Y.C., '58; U.T.S., '58-'61; Ord. (Presb.), Mar. 5, '62; S.S. & Pas., Middletown, Del., '61-4; Pas., Pottsville, Pa., '64-7; As. Pas., Newark, N.J., '67-8; Pas. (R.D.), N. York City, '68-'75; Pas. (Presb.), Buffalo, N.Y., '75——.

JAMES DOUGLAS ROBERTSON; b., Kelso, Scotland, May 1, 1833; U.T.S., '58-'61; Ord. (Presb.), Sep. 16, '62; S.S., Danbury, Ct., '61-5; S.S., Amenia, N.Y., '66-8; H.M., Bluffton, S.C., '69——.

EDSON ROGERS; b., Whitney's Point, N.Y., May 22, 1833; Y.C., '57; U.T.S., '58-'61; Ord. (Cong.), Oct. 21, '62; S.S., Cincinnatus, N.Y., '62——.

*LEVI PARSONS SABIN; b., Strongsville, O., Oct. 14, 1832; D.C., 1856; Tea., Freedom, O., '56; Do., Middlebury, O., '57; Do., Portsmouth, O., '57-8; U.T.S., '58-'61; Ord. (Presb.), Mar. 4, '63; S.S., New-London, Wis., '62-3;

Pas., Stockbridge, Wis., '63–4 ; U.S. Army, '64–5 ; S.S., College Hill, O., '65 ; Pas., Ellicottville, N.Y., '65–8 ; Pas., Central College, O., '68–'71 ; S.S., Chesaning, Mich., '71–2 ; S.S., Au Sable, Mich., '72–3 ; Died, Columbus, O., Nov. 10, '73.

Samuel Scoville ; b., West-Cornwall, Ct., Dec. 21, 1834 ; Y.C., '57 ; And.T.S., '57–9 ; U.T.S., '60–1 ; Ord. (Cong.), Sep. 17, '61 ; S.S. & Pas., Norwich, N.Y., '61——.

Charles Wheeler Sharp ; b., New-Haven, Ct., ..., 1832 ; Y.C., '59 ; U.T.S., '59–'61 ; Res. Lic., N.H.T.S., '61–2 ; Ord. (Cong.), June 28, '65 ; S.S., Hancock, N.Y., '64–5 ; Pas., Greene, N.Y., '65–7 ; ..——..

James Worthington Stark ; b., Colchester, Ct., March 4, 1833 ; U.M., '58 ; U.T.S., '58–'61 ; Ord. (Presb.), June 1, '62 ; S.S., Danville, Ill., '61–4 ; S.S., Jefferson, Wis., '64–5 ; S.S., Berlin, Wis., '65–6 ; S.S., Centralia, Ill., '66–'71 ; Pas., Bloomfield, Io., '71–3 ; Pas., Jerseyville, Ill., '73——.

George Burder Tolman ; b., Greensboro, Vt., July 24, 1832 ; U.Vt., '56 ; U.T.S., '56–8, '60–1 ; Ord. (Cong.), July 10, '62 ; Mem. of Leg., Greensboro, Vt., '61–2 ; Pas., Sheldon, Vt., '62–'71 ; S.S., Brookfield, Vt., '71——.

John Pillsbury Watson ; b., Gilford, N.H., Nov. 22, 1826 ; B.C., '56 ; B.T.S., '58–9 ; U.T.S., '59–'61 ; Ord. (Presb.), June 22, '62 ; Tea., Salisbury, Ct., '61–2 ; S.S., E. Putnam, Ct., '62–6 ; Tea., Hopewell, Pa., '66–7 ; S.S., Chanceford, Pa., '67–8 ; S.S., Leverett, Mass., '68–'71 ; S.S., Shutesbury, Mass., '71–3 ; Miss., E. Leverett, Mass., '71–4 ; S.S., Windsor, Ct., '75——. Address, Leverett, Mass.

Samuel Wyckoff ; b., Crawford Co., Pa., Dec. 11, 1829 ; Al.C., '58 ; U.T.S., '58–'61 ; Ord. (Presb.), Sep. 11, '61 ; S.S., Cherry Tree & Kerr's Hill, Pa., '61 ; S.S., Titusville, Pa., '62 ; Pas., Peoria, Ill., '63–5 ; Pas., Knoxville, Ill., '65–'70 ; Pas., Peru, Ind., '70–4 ; Pas., Portage, Wis., '74——. 35.

Joseph Perry Bixby ; b., Thompson, Ct., Jan. 28, 1833 ; W.C., '58 ; U.T.S., '58–'60 ; And.T.S., '60–1 ; Ord. (Cong.), Ap. 30, '62 ; S.S., Milford, Mass., '61–2 ; Pas. (Cong.), Boston, Mass., '62–4 ; Pas., (Presb.), do., '64–6 ; S.S. (Cong.), South Dedham (now Norwood), Mass., '66——.

Wolcott Calkins ; b., Corning, N.Y., June 10, 1831 ; Y.C., '56 ; U.T.S., '59–'60 ; Ord. (Cong.), Oct. 22, '62 ; As. Pas., Hartford, Ct., '62–4 ; Pas., (Presb.), Philadelphia, Pa., '64–7 ; Pas., Buffalo, N.Y., '67——.

*Samuel Abial Camp ; b., Charlotte, N.Y., Oct. 30, 1836 ; H.C., '58 ; U.T.S., '58–'60 ; Trav., Europe, '60–1 ; Died, ..., W. Va., ..., '62.

George Ryerson Carroll ; b., Oxford, Can. W., March 13, 1831 ; U.T.S., '58–'60 ; Ord. (Presb.), Dec. 16, '60 ; S.S., Maysville, Io., '60 ; Pas., Wyoming, Io., '61–8 ; Ch., U.S. Army, '64 ; P. & S. M., Io., '68–'75 ; S.S., St. Augustine, Fla., '75–6 ; O.S., Cedar Rapids, Io., '76——.

Isaac Clark ; b., Canterbury, Ct., June 30, 1833 ; Y.C., '56 ; U.T.S., '58–9 ; And.T.S., '59–'61 ; Ord. (Presb.), Nov. 12, '61 ; Pas., Elmira, N.Y., '61–8 ;

Pas. (Cong.), Aurora, Ill., '68–'72; Pas., Brooklyn, N.Y., '72–4; Pas. (Presb.), Rondout, N.Y., '74——.

MANUEL JACOB DRENNAN; b., Mansfield, O., ..., 1830; O.C. '57; U.T.S., '58–'60; Trav., Europe, '60–1; Ord. (Presb.), Oct. 26, '66; S.S., Windham, Ct., '62–3; Lit., N. York City, '63–6; Pas., Madison, Ind., '66–'71; Prof., Brooklyn, N.Y., '72–5; W.C., do., '75——.

HANFORD ABRAHAM EDSON; b., Scottsville, N.Y., March 14, 1837; W.C., '55; U.T.S., '58–'60; Trav., Europe, '60–1; Ord. (Presb.), Oct. 28, '62; Tea., Geneseo, N.Y., '61–2; S.S., Niagara Falls, N.Y., '62–4; Pas., Indianapolis, Ind., '64——. D.D., Han. C., '74.

ALFRED AUGUSTUS ELLSWORTH; b., Bath, Me., July 12, 1832; A.C., '58; U.T.S., '58–9; And.T.S., '59–'61; Ord. (Cong.), Sep. 4, '62; Pas., Milford, Mass., '62–5; S.S., Newbern, N.C., '65–7; Pas., Weymouth Landing, Mass., '67–'71; S.S., Waterloo, Io., '71——.

SAMUEL LANKTON GEROULD; b., East-Alstead, N.H., July 11, 1834; D.C., '58; U.T.S., '58–'60; Ord. (Cong.), Oct. 2, '61; Pas., Stoddard, N.H., '61–8; Ch., U.S. Army, '62–5; Pas., Goffstown, N.H., '69——.

ALVIN BANISTER GOODALE; b., Potsdam, N.Y., May 22, 1829; A.C., '58; U.T.S., '58–9; Studied Med., '59–'60; Ord. (Presb.), Feb. 5, '60; F.M., Marash, Asia, '61–5; S.S., Belle Plaine, Minn., '65–7; Prest., Parsons Coll., Cedar Rapids, Io., '67–9; Pas., Marshalltown, Io., '69–'73; Pas., Cedar Falls, Io., '73——. M.D., N.Y. Med. Coll., '60.

EDWARD PAYSON HAMMOND; b., Ellington, Ct., Sep. 1, 1831; W.C., '58; U.T.S., '58–9; Free Chh. Col., Edinburgh, '60–1; Ord. (Presb.), Jan. 2, '63; Ev., Vernon., Ct., '63——.

CHARLES HENRY HAYWOOD; b., Amsterdam, N.Y., ..., 1830; W.C., '51; U.T.S., '58; Tea., ...

GEORGE WILLIAM HOLLAND; b., Churchville, Va., July 16, 1838; Ro.C., '57; G.T.S., '58–9; U.T.S., '59–'60; G.T.S., '60–1; Ord. (Lu.), Dec. .., '64; S.S., Harrisonburgh, Va., '60–1; Conf. Army, '61–2; Prof., Roanoke Coll., '63–7; Pas., Harrisonburgh, Va., '67–'72; Pas., Pomaria, S.C., '73–4; Prof., Newberry Coll., Walhalla, S.C., '74——.

DANIEL KLOSS; b., Beavertown, Pa., Mar. 18, 1830; U.M., '58; G.T.S., '58–9; U.T.S., '59–'60; Ord. (Lu.), May 5, '61; S.S. & Pas., New-Berlin, Pa., '60–'71; Pas., Lykens, Pa., '71——.

FRANCIS LOBDELL; b., Danbury, Ct., Mar. 26, 1835; A.C., '58; U.T.S., '58–9; Ord., (Cong.), Nov. 3, '59; Pas., Warren, Ct., '59–'63; Pas., Bridgeport, Ct., '63–5; Rec. (Ep.), Cincinnati, O., '65–9; Rec., New-Haven, Ct., '69——.

CURTIS JERRE LYONS; b., Waimea, S. Islds., ..., 1833; W.C., '58; U.T.S., '58–'60.

THOMAS NICHOLS; b., Yonkers, N.Y., Feb. 5, 1838; C.N.J., '56; U.T.S., '58–'60; And.T.S., '60–1; Ord. (Presb.), Mar. 11, '63; Pas., Chester, N.Y., '63–'71; Pas. (R.D.), Queens (L.I.), N.Y., '71–5; Pas. (Presb.), New-Brunswick, N.J., '75——.

HENRY DAVENPORT NORTHROP; b., Poultney, N.Y., Mar. 10, 1836; A.C., '57; U.T.S., '58–9; Ord. (Cong.), Oct. 22, '60; Pas., Brooklyn, N.Y., '60–2; Pas., London, Eng., '63–'7; Pas. (Presb.), N. York City, '68–'74; Pas. (Cong.), Hartford, Ct., '74——.

FREDERICK WEBSTER OSBORN; b., ..., 1830; Y.C., '55; U.T.S., '58–'60; And.T.S., '60–1; S.S., Wolcottville, Ct., '62–3; Tea., N. York City, '63–4; S.S., Hartford, Ct., 64——.

SAMUEL LYMAN PINNEO; b., Newark, N.J., ..., 1835; Y.C., '56; U.T.S., '57–8, '59–'60; Trade, St. Louis, Mo.

GEORGE BURLEIGH SPALDING; b., Montpelier, Vt., Aug. 11, 1835; U.Vt., '56; U.T.S., '58–'60; And.T.S., '60–1; Ord. (Cong.), Oct. 5, '61; Pas., Vergennes, Vt., '61–4; Pas., Hartford, Ct., '64–9; Pas., Dover, N.H., '69——.

JOHN COLEMAN TAYLOR; b., Benton, N.Y., Feb. 28, 1833; U.C., '58; Aub.T.S., '58–9; U.T.S., '59–'60; And.T.S., '60–1; Ord. (Presb.), Feb. 12, '62; Pas., Sweden, N.Y., '62–5; S.S., Chattanooga, Tenn., '65; S.S., Corry, Pa., '65–7; S.S., St. Louis, Mo., '67; S.S. & Pas. (Cong.), Groton, N.Y., '67–'71; S.S., Milwaukee, Wis., '72–4; S.S. & Pas. (Presb.), Cuba, N.Y., '75——.

*JAMES EDWIN TOWER; b., Granby, Mass., June 10, 1834; A.C., '58; U.T.S., '58–'60; And.T.S., '60–1; S.S., N. Brookfield, Mass., '62; Died, Groton, Mass., Aug. 18, '62. 23.

1862.

WILLIAM AUGUSTUS ALRICH; b., Wilmington, Del., Ap. 23, 1836; Wn.C., '55; U.T.S., '59–'62; Ord. (Ep.), Mar. 4, '68; S.S., So. Washington, Vt., '61; Tea., ..., Md., '61–4; Ch., Conf. Army, '64–5; Rec., Fairfax C.H., Va., '67–9; Rec., Hanover Co., Va., '69–'74; Rec., Pittsylvania C.H., Va., '76——.

ALVIN BAKER; b., La Fayette, N.Y., Jan. 12, 1829; H. C., '59; U.T.S., '59–'62; Ord. (Presb.), Sep. 3, '62; S.S., Cornwall, N.Y., '62–4; S.S., Otisco, N.Y., '65–7; S.S., Lakeville, N.Y., '68–'70; S.S., Huron, O., '71–3; S.S., Green Springs, O., '73–5; S.S., Oakland, Cal., '76——.

MARTIN LUTHER BERGER; b., Mellenville, N.Y., Aug. 12, 1839; W.C., '59; U.T.S., '59–'62; Ord. (R.D.), June .., '63; Pas., E. Millstone, N.J., '63–5; Pas., Fishkill, N.Y., '65–8; Syracuse, N.Y., '68–'75; Pas. (Presb.), San Francisco, Cal., '76——.

WHITING CYRUS BIRCHARD; b., Cambridge, Pa., Jan. 21, 1835; Al.C., '58; U.T.S., '59–'62; Ord. (Presb.), Sep. 29, '62; S.S., Cherry Tree & Sunnville, Pa., '62–7; Pas., Rushville, Ill., '68–'72; S.S., Petroleum Centre, Pa., '72–4; Pas., Allegheny, Pa., '74——.

*LEWIS MEAD BIRGE; b., Vienna, O., Aug. 9, 1833; W.R.C., '57; U.T.S., '59–'62; Ord. (Presb.), Oct. 5, '62; Ch., U.S. Army, '62–5; Res. Grad., U.T.S., N. York City, '65; S.S., Charlestown, O., '65; W.C., Hudson, O., '66; Ag., Burlington, N.J., '66–8; C.M., Paterson, N.J., '69–'71; S.S., Grand Rapids, Mich., '71–3; Died, do., May 10, '73.

ZIBA NICHOLS BRADBURY; b., Sparta, N.J., Mar. 24, 1830; Y.C., '59; U.T.S., '59-'62; Ord. (Presb.), Jan. 14, '63; S.S., Howard, N.Y., '62-6; S.S., Pultney, N.Y., '67-'72; Pas., Howard, N.Y., '72——.

*WILLIAM THOMPSON CLAPP; b., Hudson, O., Ap. 12, 1838; W.R.C., '57; U.T.S., '59-'62; Ord. (Cong.), Dec. 16, '64; S.S., Edinburgh, O., '64-5; Died, do., Mar. 18, '65.

MALCOLM MCGREGOR DANA; b., Brooklyn, N.Y., June, 4, 1838; A.C., '59; U.T.S., '59-'62; Ord. (Presb.), Ap. 19, '63; S.S., Winsted, Ct., '62-4; Pas. (Cong.), Norwich, Ct., '64-'74; Pas., Norwich, Ct., '74——.

WILLIAM REED EASTMAN; b., New-York City, Oct. 19, 1835; Y.C., '54; U.T.S., '59-'62; Ord. (Presb.), Oct. 12, '62; Ch., U.S. Army, '62-4; S.S. (Cong.), Grantville, Mass., '64-5; S.S. & Pas., Southington (Plantsville), Ct., '65-'76; Pas., Suffield, Ct., '76——.

JOHN HARRINGTON EDWARDS; b., Acton, Mass., Sept. 22, 1834; Bel.C., '58; U.T.S., '59-'62; Ord. (Cong.), Feb. 4, '63; S.S. & Pas., W. Lebanon, N.H., '62-'71; Pas., Tidioute, Pa., '71-4; S.S., Switzerland, Pa., '75——.

*JOSIAH GOLD EVERTS; b., Havana, N.Y., Dec. 11, 1834; U.C., '60; U.T.S., '60-2; Died, Havana, N.Y., May 23, '63.

BENTLEY STEPHEN FOSTER; b., Montrose, Pa., Mar. 23, 1832; W.C., '57; U.T.S., '59-'62; Ord. (Presb.), July 12, '65; S.S., Franklin, Pa., '65-6; S.S., Archbald, Pa., '66-7; Pas., Dunmore, Pa., '67-'73; Pas., Andover, N.J., '74-5; S.S., Nunda, N.Y., '76——.

EDWARD PAYSON GARDNER; b., Buffalo, N.Y., Feb. 2, 1838; A.C., '58; U.T.S., '59-'62; Ord. (Presb.), Feb. 11, '64; S.S. & Pas., Cherry Valley, N.Y., '62-7; Pas., Hoboken, N.J., '67-'72; Pas., Cleveland, O., '72——.

JOHN QUINCY HALL; b., Norwalk, O., June 10, 1837; A.C., '59; U.T.S., '59-'62; Ord. (Presb.), Sep. 1, '63; S.S., Mt. Gilead & Ashley, O., '62-3; S.S. (Cong.), Darlington, Wis., 63-5; S.S. (Presb.), Taylor's Falls, Minn., & St. Croix Falls, Wis., '66-'71; Pas., Michigan City, Ind., '71——.

SAMUEL PIERSON HALSEY; b., Avon, N.Y., Aug. 11, 1834; U.T.S., '59-'62; Ord. (Presb.), July 8, '62; Pas., Rockaway, N.J., '62-5; Pas., Stamford, Ct., '65-7; Pas., Brooklyn, N.Y., '67——.

THOMAS WHITE HUGHES; b., St. Charles, Mo., ..., 1831; Mv.C., '59; U.T.S., '59-'62; C.M., N. York City, '62-'71; Ev. & Tea., Abington, Va., '72-4; Prin. & Pas., Taylorsville, Tenn., '75——.

ELNATHAN JUDSON; b., New-York City, ..., 1838; B.U., '59; U.T.S., '59-'62; Insane, Somerville, Mass., '64——.

CHARLES COTTON KIMBALL; b., Newport, N.H., May 20, 1834; Bel.C., '59; U.T.S., '59-62; Ord. (Presb.), Sep. 11, '63; S.S., New-Hartford, N.Y., '63-4; S.S., Leroy, N.Y., '64-7; Pas., Erie, Pa., '67——.

WILLIAM WALLACE KIRBY; b., Roslyn (L.I.), N.Y., June 12, 1830; U.C., '55; P.T.S., '59-'60; U.T.S., '60-2; S.S., Roslyn (L.I.), N.Y., '71-2; O.S., do., '62-'71, '72——.

DELAVAN LEVANT LEONARD; b., Lockport, N.Y., July 20, 1834; H.C., '59; U.T.S., '59-'62; Res. Lic., '62-3; Ord. (Cong.), June 8, '63; S.S., New-Britain, Ct., '63-4; S.S., Washington (New-Preston Hill), Ct., '64-6; S.S., Darlington, Wis., '66-'70; S.S., Normal, Ill., '70-4; S.S., Hannibal, Mo., '74-5; S.S., Northfield, Minn., '76——.

JOHN ELBERT LONG; b., Unity, O., Sep. 7, 1832; W.C., '59; U.T.S., '59-'62; Ord. (Presb.), Sep. 4, '64; S.S., Hublersburgh & Spring Mills, Pa., '62-9; S.S., Truxton, N.Y., '70-3; S.S., Preble, N.Y., '74——.

SAMUEL MURDOCK; b., Elizabeth, N.J., Ap. 2, 1828; W.C., '59; U.T.S., '59-'62; Ord. (Presb.), June 14, '65; Tea., Bloomfield, N.J., '62-3; S.S., Coshocton, N.Y., '63-4; S.S. & Pas., Cranford, N.J., '64-6; S.S., Trenton, Del., '67-'73; S.S. (Cong.), Guilford Centre, N.Y., '73-6; S.S. (Presb.), Vienna, W. Va., '76——.

ALFRED MARION PENLAND; b., Asheville, N.C., ..., 1833; Mv.C., '59; U.T.S., '59-'62; Ord. (Presb.), ..., '71; Tea., N. York City, '62-5; Tea., New-Brighton (S.I.), N.Y., '66-'71; S.S., Asheville, N.C., '72——.

JOHN THURSTON RHODES; b., Flatbush (L.I.), N.Y., ..., 1828; U.T.S., '59-'62; Tea., Flatbush (L.I.), N.Y., '62——.

ALBERT GLEASON RULIFFSON; b., Gilboa, N.Y., Ap. . ., 1833; U.T.S, '59-'62; Ord. (Presb.), Oct. 12, '62; C.M., N. York City, '62-4; S.M., Minneapolis, Minn., '64-'70; Sec., Chicago, Ill., '70-2; C.M., N. York City, '72——.

ROBERT CONDIT RUSSELL; b., Rossville, N.Y., Jan. 30, 1835; U.T.S., '59-'62; Ord. (Ep.), Feb. 8, '67; S.S., Bristol, Me., '62-4; Rec., North-Salem, N.Y., . .——.

AMOS FRANKLIN SHATTUCK; b., Hollis, N.H., July 9, 1832; A.C., '59; U.T.S., '59-'62; Ord. (Cong.), June 3, '68; S.S., Charlestown, N.H., '63-4; S.S., Surry, N.H., '64-6; S.S., Durham, Me., '67-8; S.S., Wooster, Vt., '70-1; W.C., Hollis, N.H., '72——.

CHARLES DANNELLY SHAW; b., Philadelphia, Pa., Dec. 17, 1834; U.T.S., '59-'62; Ord. (Presb.), Nov. 5, '62; Pas., Paterson, N.J., '62-7; Pas., Wilmington, Del., '67-'72; Pas., Springfield, Ill., '72-5; Pas., Paterson, N.J., '75——.

JAMES WOODWARD STRONG; b., Brownington, Vt., Sep. 29, 1833; Bel.C., '58; U.T.S., '59-'62; Ord. (Cong.), Sep. 28, '62; S.S., Brodhead, Wis., '62-4; S.S. & Pas., Faribault, Minn., '65-'70; Prest., Carleton Coll., Northfield, Minn., '70——. D.D., Bel.C., '71.

ELIAS FITCH TANNER; b., DeKalb, N.Y., Oct. 22, 1833; W.C., '58; U.T.S., '59-'62; Ord. (Presb.), Ap. . ., '64; S.S., Pardeeville, Wis., '62-4; S.S., Barton, Wis., '65-7; S.S., Grand Ledge, Mich., '67-9; S.S., La Salle, Mich., '70-3; S.S., California, Mich., '73——.

JAMES NELSON THRESHER; b., Stafford, Ct., ..., 1834; A.C., '59; U.T.S., '59-'62; Ord. (Bap.), ..., '63; S.S., St. Cloud, Minn., '63-4; S.S., Fair Haven, Minn., '64——. .; . ., Granville, O., . .——.

IRA CHARLES TYSON; b., Whitemarsh, Pa., March 3, 1830; U.T.S., '59-'62; Ord. (Presb.), Oct. 7, '62; Pas., Hughsonville, N.Y., '62-9; Pas., Bedford, N.H., '69——.

JAMES DUNCAN WILSON; b., Spring Mills, Pa., Ap. 3, 1836; A.C., '58; U.T.S., '59-'62; Ord. (Presb.), July 1, '63; S.S. & Pas., N. York City, '62——.

33.

JAMES MCKINNEY ALEXANDER; b., Wailuku, S. Islds., Jan. 29, 1835; W.C., '58; U.T.S., '59-'60; Ord. (Presb.), June 11, '65; S.S., San Leandro, Cal., '65-'70; S.S., Centreville, Cal., '70-2; F.M., Makaowas, S. Islds., '72——.

EUGENE HENRY AVERY; b., Sherburne, N.Y., May 15, 1837; Bel.C., '58; U.T.S., '59-'61; Ord. (Cong.), Ap. 22, '63; S.S., Roscoe, Ill., '63-4; Pas., (Presb.), Warren, Ill., '64-'70; Pas., Sioux City, Io., '70——.

*DANIEL BOWE; b., Agawam, Mass., Jan. 13, 1833; Y.C., '59; U.T.S., '59-'60; And.T.S., '60-2; U.S.Ag., Port Royal, S.C., '62; Died, N. York City, Oct. 30, '62.

JOHN PETER BRISCOE; b., Bristol, Tenn., ..., 1834; Mv.C., '59; U.T.S., '59-'61; Ord. (Presb.), ..., '62; S.S., Blountville, Tenn., '62——.

GEORGE WHITEHILL CHAMBERLAIN; b., ..., ..., 1839; Del.C., '57; U.T.S., '59-'61; Ord. (Presb.) ...., '65; Bib. Col., Rio Janeiro, S.A., '62-5; F.M., do., '66——.

GEORGE HENRY COFFEY; b., Mullingar, Ireland, Aug. 15, 1835; Y.C., '59; U.T.S., '59-'60; Ord. (Cong.), Jan. 22, '62; S.S., Morrisania, N.Y., '60-1; S.S., Saugerties, N.Y., '61-4; Pas., Jackson, Mich., '65-8; Law, N. York City, '69——.

RUFUS CHOATE CROCKER; b., Maroa, Ill., ..., 1834; K.C., '57; U.T.S., '59-'61; U.S.Army, '61-4; Trade, Decatur, Ill., '65——.

*SYLVANUS SANBORN DEARBORN; b., Northfield, N.H., Sep. 15, 1830; D.C., '55; Tea., Acton, N.H., '55; Tea., Princeton, Ill., '56-7; Law., ..., Ill., '57-8; Agric., ..., N.H., '58-9; U.T.S., '59-'60; Ep.T.S, '62-4; Ord. (Ep.), Dec. 18, '64; Rec., Clermont, N.Y., '65; Europe, '66; Died, N. York City, Jan. 8, '67.

HENRY SWIFT DE FOREST; b., S. Edmeston, N.Y., March 17, 1833; Y.C., '57; N.H.T.S., '59-'60; U.T.S., '60-1; Tut., Y.C., '61-3; Ord. (Cong.), Aug. 2, '63; Ch., U.S.Army, '63-5; S.S., Des Moines, Io., '66-'70; Pas., Council Bluffs, Io., '71——.

DANIEL BLISS DUDLEY; b., Lebanon, N.H., Dec. 25, 1833; D.C., '56; Tea., La Grange, Ga., & Abbeville, Ala., '56-9; U.T.S., '59-'60; Studied Law, Albany, N.Y., '60-2; Law., N. York City, '64——.

HORACE FRANKLIN DUDLEY; b., Hanover, N.H., Jan. 31, 1832; D.C., '59; U.T.S., '59-'60; Aub.T.S., '60-2; Ord. (Cong.), Sep. 6, '65; S.S., S. Trenton, N.Y., '62-5; S.S., Paris, N.Y., '65-7; S.S., Morrisville, N.Y., '67-'73; Pas., Warsaw, N.Y., '73——.

Daniel Henry Evans; b., Ripley, O., Ap. 16, 1838; M.U., '59; Al.T.S., '59-'60; U.T.S., '60-1; And.T.S., '61-2; Ord. (Presb.), Ap. 16, '63; S.S., Blissfield & Palmyra, Mich., '62-5; Pas., Grand Haven, Mich., '65-9; S.S., Pittsburgh, Pa., '69; Pas., Youngstown, O., '70——.

Charles Hall Everest; b., New-Lebanon, N.Y., Feb. 14, 1837; W.C., '59; U.T.S., '59-'61; Ord. (Cong.), Dec. 30, '61; Pas., Owego, N.Y., '61-5; Pas., Brooklyn, N.Y., '65——.

Flavius Lyle Ewing; b., Farmington, Tenn., Aug. 3, 1838; Mv.C., '59; U.T.S., '59-'61; Ord. (Presb.), Ap. .., '62; S.S., Lynnville & Petersburgh, Tenn., '62-3; S.S., Bethberei & Richland, Tenn., '63-5; S.S., Pulaski, Tenn., '66-9; Trav., Europe and the East, '70; S.S., Huntsville, Ala., '71; S.S., Talladega, Ala., '71-2; Pas., do., '72——.

Rufus Barnard Guild; b., West-Halifax, Vt., July 25, 1831; K.C., '58; U.T.S., '59-'60, '61; Prin., Galesburgh, Ill., '60-2; C.T.S., '62-4; Ord. (Cong.), Nov. 4, '64; Pas., Galva, Ill., '64——.

John Thomas Gulick; b., Honolulu, Oahu, ..., 1832; W.C., '59; U.T.S., '59-'62; Ord. (Cong.), Aug. 22, '64; F.M., Kalgan, N. China, '64——.

Henry Hopkins; b., Williamstown, Mass., Nov. 30, 1837; W.C., '58; U.T.S., '59-'61; Ord. (Cong.), Sep. 23, '61; Ch., U.S.Army, '61-4; W.C., Williamstown, Mass., '64-5; Pas., Westfield, Mass., '66——.

James Wakeman Hubbell; b., Wilton, Ct., March 29, 1835; Y.C., '57; U.T.S., '59-'60; And.T.S., '61-3; Ord. (Cong.), Sep. 21, '64; S.S., Plainville, Ct., '63-4; Pas., Milford, Ct., '64-9; Pas., New-Haven, Ct., '69——.

Joseph Walker Marsh; b., Burlington, Vt., Mar. .., 1836; U.Vt., '57; U.T.S., '59-'60; Prof., Pac.U., Forest Grove, Or., '67——.

Victor Miller; b., Clear Spring, Md., Oct. 24, 1834; Pa.C., '58; G.T.S., '59-'60; U.T.S., '60-1; G.T.S., '61-2; Ord. (Lu.), Oct. .., '62; Pas., New-Wilmington, Pa., '62-5; Pas., Fayetteville, Pa., '65——; Tea., Washington Co., Md., ..——..; Prin., Mechanicstown, Md., ..——.

William Enos Boise Moore; b., Agawam, Mass., Ap. 22, 1831; A.C., '58; U.T.S., '59-'60; And.T.S., '60-2; Ord. (Cong.), Oct. 4, '65; S.S., Tolland, Mass., '62; S.S., Barnstable (Centreville), Mass., '62-3; S.S., Montgomery, Mass., '63-4; S.S., Huntington, Mass., '65-7; S.S. & Pas., Bolton, Ct., '67——.

Marcus North Preston; b., Gowanda, N.Y., July 1, 1835; W.C., '59; U.T.S., '59-'60; Aub.T.S., '60-2; Ord. (Presb.), Oct. 2, '62; Pas., Skaneateles, N.Y., '62——.

*Justin Gamaliel Riley; b., Rochester, N.Y., June 14, 1834; W.C., '59; U.T.S., '59-'61; Tea., Brooklyn, N.Y., '62——..; Agric., Washingtonville, N.Y., ..——, '73; Died, do., March 5, '73.

Leicester Jotham Sawyer; b., ..., ..., ..., .., 1837; K.C., '59; U.T.S., '59-'61; N.H.T.S., '62; U.S.Army, '62-3; Ord. (Cong.), Jan. 24, '64; Pas., Sheboygan, Wis., '64-5; S.S., Mantorville, Minn., '65-8; S.S., Burlingame, Kan., '68-'75.

MOODY ADONIRAM STEVENS; b., Bedford, N.H., Feb. 7, 1828; U.T.S., '59-'61; Ord. (Cong.), Dec. 9, '62; Ch., U.S.Army, '61; S.S., Plympton, Mass., '62-4; S.S., Bellows Falls, Vt., '64-7; S.S., Ashburnham, Mass., '67-9; Pas., Cohasset, Mass., '70——.

WILLIAM JACKSON STOUTENBURGH; b., Macedonia, Pa., Sep. 20, 1833; Aub.T.S., '59-'60; U.T.S., '60-1; Ord. (Presb.), Sep. 17, '61; Pas., N. York City, '61-4; Pas. (Cong.), Allen's Grove, Wis., '64-6; S.S. (Presb.), Manitowoc, Wis., '66-8; S.S., Tecumseh, Mich., '68-'74; S.S., Birmingham, Mich., '74——.

EDWARD GERRISH THURBER; b., Monroe, Mich., May 28, 1836; U.M., '57; U.T.S., '59-'61; And.T.S., '61-2; Ord. (Cong.), Oct. 29, '62; S.S. & Pas., Walpole, Mass., '62-'70; Pas. (Presb.), Syracuse, N.Y., '70——.

JOSEPH HOPKINS TWICHELL; b., Southington, Ct., May 27, 1833; Y.C., '59-'61; And.T.S., '64-5; Ord. (Cong.), Jan. 30, '63; Ch., U.S.Army, '61-4; Pas., Hartford, Ct., '65——.

WILLIAM JAMES WRIGHT; b., Weybridge, Vt., ..., 1831; U.C., '57; U.T.S., '59-'60; P.T.S., '60-2; Ord. (Presb.), June 20, '63; Ch., U.S.Army, '63-5; Pas., Ringoes, N.J., '66-8; Pas., Pomeroy, O., '68-'71; Tea., Philadelphia, Pa., '71-4; S.S., Wellsburgh, W. Va., '74-5; Prof., Chambersburgh, Pa., '76; Ph.D., U.C., '76. 29.

1863.

CHARLES TREAT BERRY; b., Dover, N.J., March 18, 1838; C.N.J., '60; U.T.S., '60-3; Ord. (Presb.), Mar. 17, '63; S.S., Newark, N.J., '63; Pas., Valatie, N.Y., '63-9; Pas., Caldwell, N.J., '69——.

ALBERT CASTLE BISHOP; b., Warrensburgh, N.Y., Sep. 12, 1840; U.N.Y., '60; U.T.S., '60-3; Ord. (Presb.), May 15, '64; S.S. Warrensburgh, N.Y., '63-5; Pas., Sand Lake, N.Y., '65-'75; Pas., West-Troy, N.Y., '75——.

GEORGE MILLS BOYNTON; b., Brooklyn, N.Y., May 13, 1837; Y.C., '58; U.T.S., '60-3; Ord. (Presb.), Oct. 28, '63; Pas., Riverdale, N.Y., '63-7; Pas. (Cong.), Guilford, Ct., '68-'72; Pas., Newark, N.J., '72——.

FREDERICK ADOLPHUS MILLER BROWN; b., New-York City, Sep. 27, 1835; U.C., '60; U.T.S., '60-3; Ord. (Presb.), May 15, '64; S.S. & Pas., Parsippany, N.J., '63-6; Pas., Delhi, N.Y., '66——.

GEORGE FARNSWORTH CHAPIN; b., Newport, N.H., May 26, 1836; A.C., '60; U.T.S., '60-3; Res. Lic., '63-4; Ord. (Presb.), June .., '66; Tea., N.Y., '63-5; S.S. & Pas., Lawrence, Kan., '65-8; S.S., Irving, Kan., '69-'72; S.S., Brimfield, Mass., '72-3; S.S., Alstead & Langdon, N.H., '73——.

WILLIAM HENDEE CLARK; b., Hudson, O., Ap. 11, 1837; W.R.C., '59; U.T.S., '60-3; Ord. (Presb.), Jan. 6, '64; Pas., Spencertown, N.Y., '64-5; Ch. Miss., N. York City, '65-'72; Pas., Paterson, N.J., '72——.

HENRY JOSIAH CRANE; b., Middletown, N.Y., June 27, 1836; U.N.Y., '60; U.T.S., '60-3; Ord. (Presb.), Sep. 7, '63; S.S., Wysox, Pa., '63-'70; Pas., Hunter, N.Y., '71-5; S.S., Gibson, Pa., '75——.

Bishop Falkner; b., ..., England, Ap. 4, 1834; U.T.S., '60–3; Ord. (Cong.), Jan. 25, '65; S.S. & Pas., Brooklyn, N.Y., '63——.

James Byron Finch; b., Southampton, Mass., Dec. 29, 1832; A.C., '62; U.T.S., '60–3; Ord. (Presb.), June 5, '63; S.S., Orient (L.I.), N.Y., '63–5; S.S., Nebraska City, Neb., '65–7; Pas., Hempstead (L.I.), N.Y., '67–'75; W.C., Orient (L.I.), N.Y., '75——.

Henry Martyn Grant; b., Oroomiah, Persia, June 3, 1836; Aub.T.S., '60–2; U.T.S., '62–3; Ord. (Cong.), Nov. 17, '63; Pas., N. Canaan, Ct., '63–6; S.S., Webster Grove, Mo., '66–9; S.S., Smyrna, N.Y., '70–4; W.C., Sterling, N.J., '75——.

Ellsworth Jerome Hill; b., Leroy, N.Y., Dec. 1, 1833; U.T.S., '60–3; Ord. (Presb.), Ap. 26, '64; S.S., Thornton Station, Ill., '64–6; S.S., Will, Ill., '67–8; Inv., Preston, Minn., '69; Do., Kankakee, Ill., '70; Tea., do., '71–4; Tea., Englewood, Ill., '75——.

Joel Jackson Hough; b., Groton, N.Y., Ap. 3, 1835; Y.C., '59; U.T.S., '61–3; Ord. (Presb.), Ap. 20, '64; S.S., Cannonsville, N.Y., '63–7; Pas., Franklin, N.Y., '67–'73; Pas. (Cong.), Danbury, Ct., '73——.

John McVey; b., Glasgow, Scotland, Feb. 22, 1837; U.N.Y., '60; U.T.S., '60–3; Ord. (Presb.), Dec. 17, '63; S.S., N. York City, '63–4; Pas., New-Lebanon, N.Y., '64–'72; Pas., Dayton, O., '72–4; Pas., Binghamton, Pa., '75——.

*William Wisner Martin; b., Rahway, N.J., Dec. 18, 1837; Y.C. '60; U.T.S., '60–1; And.T.S., '61–2; U.T.S., '62–3; Ord. (Presb.), June 18, '63; S.S., Sonora, Cal., '63–4; S.S., San Francisco, Cal., '64; Pas., San José, Cal., '65; Died, Brooklyn, N.Y., Oct. 16, '65.

John Henry Meacham; b., Springville, Pa., Nov. 16, 1823; U.C., '52; Tea., Hanover C.H., Va., '52–3; Alex.T.S., '53–4; Ag., A.S.S.U., Va., '54; U.T.S., Va., '55–7; Col., A.T.S., & Ag., N.C. & Va., '57–'61; U.T.S., '61–3; Del., U.S.C.C., '63–4; C.M., N. York City, '64–6; Agric. & Colporteur, Springville, N.Y., '67——.

*Edwin Elisha Merriam; b., Mason, N.H., Aug. 3, 1836; A.C., '58; U.T.S., '60–3; Ord. (Presb.), Aug. 3, '64; Pas., Salem, Pa., '64–5; Died, do., Feb. 17, '65.

Almon Baxter Merwin; b., Brooklyn, N.Y., June 25, 1835; Y.C., '57; U.T.S., '57, '59–'60; P.T.S., '60–1; U.T.S., '62–3; Tut., D. & D.I., N. York City, '63–5; Miss. Supt., A.S.S.Union, N. Iowa, '65–6; Tea., Newark, N.J., '66–'74; Prof., do., '74——.

William Dwight Morton; b., Brooklyn, N.Y., June 8, 1837; U.C., '57; U.T.S., '60–3; Ord. (Cong.), June 29, '64; Pas., Huntington, Ct., '64–9; S.S., Chester, Ct., '69——.

*Alexander Nesbitt; b., New-York City, Jan. 14, 1842; N.Y.A., '60; U.T.S., '60–3; Ord. (Presb.), Sep. 17, '63; Pas., Tremont, N.Y., '63–'75; Died, do., Jan. 7, '75.

Abram Jay Quick; b., South-Branch, N.J., March 11, 1832; W.C., '60; U.T.S., '60–3; Ord. (Cong.), Mar. 7, '64; S.S., Richmond, Mass., '63–4; Pas.,

Seymour, Ct., '65–7; S.S. (Presb.), Cannonsville, N.Y., '67–'70; S.S., Lenox & Wampsville, N.Y., '70–2; S.S., Amboy, N.Y., '72–5; Pas., Rochester, N.H., '75——.

Adoniram Judson Rich; b., Cooper, Me., Dec. 6, 1834; N.T.I., '60–2; U.T.S., '63; Ord. (Cong.), Mar. 30, '64; Pas., Dorchester, Mass., '63–7; Pas., Westminster, Mass., '67–'70; Pas. (Unit.), Brookfield, Mass., '70——.

Leonard Eldro Richards; b., Wayne Co., O., Aug. 7, 1831; O.W.U., '59; U.T.S., '60–3; Ord. (Presb.), Sep. 15, '63; S.S., Moresville & S. Gilboa, N.Y., '63–4; S.S., Stamford, N.Y., '64——.

*Robert Hugh Richardson; b., Liberty, Va., Mar. 13, 1834; U.T.S., '60–3; C.M., N. York City, '63; Died, do., Oct. 6, '63.

Ezra Davis Shaw; b., McLean, N.Y., Aug. 10, 1831; Ma.C., '60; U.T.S., '60–3; Ord. (Presb.), Aug. 10, '64; S.S., Wilkesville, O., '63–4; S.S., Middleport, O., '64–5; S.S., Jackson, O., '65–6; Tea., Barlow, O., '66–7; S.S., Shiloh, Gilead, & Franklin, Ind., '67–9; S.S. (Cong.), Summer Hill, N.Y., '69–'72; Pas. (Presb.), Victory, N.Y., '72–5; Tea., Moravia, N.Y., '75——.

*John Paine Torrey; b., Burlington, Vt., Jan. 21, 1838; U.Vt., '58; U.T.S., '60–3; Died, Beverly, Mass., July 22, '63.

John Walker; b., Exeter, Me., ..., 1833; A.C., '58; U.T.S., '59–'60, '61–3; S.S., Cooper, Me., '62; Tea., ..., N.H., '63——.

William White Williams; b., Tuscaloosa, Ala., Jan. 2, 1838; W.C., '59; U.T.S., '59–'60, '61–3; Ord. (Presb.), May 14, '65; Temp. Ag., Phila., Pa., '63——. 27.

Jonathan Waverly Bachman; b., Kingsport, Tenn., Oct. 9, 1837; U.T.S., '60–1; Conf. Army, '62–4; Ord. (Presb.), Sep. .., '64; Ch., Conf. Army, '64–5; S.S., Rogersville & New-Providence, Tenn., '65–'73; Pas., Chattanooga, Tenn., '73——.

Nathan Bachman; b., Kingsport, Tenn., Dec. 13, 1832; E. & H.C., '57; U.T.S., '60–1; Ord. (Presb.), ..., '63; S.S., Kingsport, Tenn., '63–7; S.S., Knoxville, Tenn., '67——.

Moses Bradford Boardman; b., Francestown, N.H., May 25, 1833; A.C., '60; U.T.S., '60–2; And.T.S., '62–3; Ord. (Cong.), Oct. 1, '63; Pas., Lynnfield Centre, Mass., '63–'70; Pas., Brimfield, Mass., '70–3; W.C. & Inv., Harwinton, Ct., '73——.

Harry Brodhead; b., White Lake, N.Y., July 2, 1837; Y.C., '59; U.T.S., '60–1; LL.B., C.C., '64; Law, N. York City, '64——.

Samuel Dunham; b., Southington, Ct., Feb. 8, 1835; Y.C., '60; U.T.S., '60–2; And.T.S., '62–3; Ord. (Cong.), Oct. 4, '64; S.S. & Pas., W. Brookfield, Mass., '63–'70; S.S., Norwalk, Ct., '70–2; Pas., Binghamton, N.Y., '73–6; Pas., Brockport, N.Y., '76——.

*Charles Easton; b., Wellsville, N.Y., July 3, 1833; Y.C., '59; Tea., Memphis, Tenn., '59–'60; U.T.S., '60–1; Inv., Black River Falls, Wis., '61–2; Do., Wellsville, N.Y., '62–3; Died, do., Ap. 5, '63.

DAVID ROWE EDDY; b., Palmyra, N.Y., Ap. 13, 1835; U.C., '60; U.T.S., '60–1; Ord. (Presb.), ... , '61; S.S., Wenona, Ill., '61–2; S.S. & Pas., Belvidere, Ill., '62–'72; S.S., Flint, Mich., '73–5; S.S., Brockport, N.Y., '75——.

*WILLIAM AUGUSTUS HASELTON; b., Bellows' Falls, Vt., July 27, 1834; D.C., '58; U.T.S., '60–1; And.T.S., '61–3; Tea., ——'64; Died, Swissvale, Pa., Aug. 13, '64.

HENRY FRANCIS HYDE; b., Killingly, Ct., Dec. 22, 1834; A.C., '59; U.T.S., '60–1; E.W.T.S., '61–3; Ord. (Cong.), June 1, '64; Pas., W. Woodstock, Ct., '64–7; Pas., Pomfret, Ct., '67–'72; Pas., Rockville, Ct., '72——.

GEORGE LACON LEYBURN; b., Mâne, Greece, May 21, 1839; W.C.Va., '59; U.T.S., '60–1; Ord. (Presb.), Oct. . . , '67; S.S., Liberty, Va., '62–5; U.T.S., Va., '66–7; Pas., Winchester, Va., '67–'75; F.M., Athens, Greece, '75——.

DAVID MCALLISTER; b., New-York City, Aug. 25, 1835; U.C., '60; Al.T.S., '60–1; U.T.S., '61–2; Ord. (Presb.), Dec. 16, '63; Ed., N. York City, '62–3; Pas., Walton, N.Y., '63–'71; Sec. Nat. Ref. Ass., N. York City, '71–5, and, do., Philadelphia, Pa., '75——.

WILLIAM C. MACY; b., Hudson, N.Y., Nov. 10, 1832; U.C., '60; U.T.S., '60–1; Tea., W. Bloomfield, N.Y., '61; Tut., U.C., '63; Adj. Prof., U.C., Schenectady, N.Y., '65–6; Tea., N. York City, '67——.

ISRAEL GRIFFITHS MATTHEWS; b., Howard Co., Md., Dec. 31, 1838; U.T.S., '60–1; Ord. (M. Prot.), ... , . . ; . . , Lynchburg, Va., . .——.

*LUCIUS LATHROP MERRICK; b., Monson, Mass., June 8, 1829; A.C., '60; E.W.T.S., '60–1; U.T.S., '61–2; U.S.Army, '62–4; Died of wounds, Bermuda Hundred, Va., Oct. 7, '64.

SAMUEL MILLER; b., Augusta, N.Y., Nov. 1, 1829; H.C., '60; U.T.S., '60–1; Aub.T.S., '61–3; Ord. (Cong.), Jan. 13, '64; S.S., Eaton, N.Y., '63–7; S.S., Sherburne, N.Y., '67–4; S.S., Deansville, N.Y., '75——.

REECE MARSHALL NEWPORT; b., Sharpsburgh, Pa., May 29, 1838; Ma.C., '60; U.T.S., '60–1; U.S.Army, '61–6; Trade, Brainerd, Minn., '66——.

THEODORE STRONG POND; b., New-York City, Sep. 13, 1838; H.C., '60; U.T.S., '60–1; And.T.S., '61–3; Tea., N. York City, '63–4; Trav., Europe, '65–6; Ord. (Cong.), Aug. 29, '67; S.S., William's Bridge, N.Y., '66; Pas., Middlefield, Ct., '67–9; F.M., Mardin, E. Turkey, '69–'73; W.C., Brooklyn, N.Y., '74——.

EDWARD AUGUSTUS RAND; b., Portsmouth, N.H., Ap. 5, 1837; B.C., '57; U.T.S., '61–2; U.S.Army, '62–4; Ord. (Cong.), Mar. 2, '65; S.S. & Pas., Amesbury Mills, Mass., '64–7; Pas., S. Boston, Mass., '67——.

WILLIAM WILBERFORCE ROSE; b., Honesdale, Pa., July 17, 1837; Bl.C., '59; U.T.S., '60–2; Ord. (Cong.), Dec. 24, '62; S.S., Chesterfield, Mass., '62–6; S.S., Pittsfield, Ill., '67–'74; S.S., Rockford, Ill., '75——.

MILTON LEONARD SEVERANCE; b., Middlebury, Vt., Oct. 14, 1830; M.C., '59; U.T.S., '60–2; And.T.S., '62–3; Ord. (Cong.), Feb. 17, '64; S.S. & Pas., Boscawen, N.H., '63–8; Pas., Orwell, Vt., '69——.

Edward Clarence Smith; b., Palatine, N.Y., May 13, 1835; U.T.S., '60-2; Tea. & Prin., Phila., Pa., '62——.

Judson Smith; b., Middlefield, Mass., June 28, 1837; A.C., '59; O.T.S., '60-2; U.T.S., '62-3; O.T.S., '63; Tut., O.C., Oberlin, O., '64; Tea., Williston, Mass., '66; Ord. (Cong.), Oct. 16, '66; Prof., O.C., Oberlin, O., '66-70; Prof., O.T.S., do., '70——.

Edmund Root Stiles; b., Clarksfield, O., July 12, 1834; O.C., '59; O.T.S., '60-2; U.T.S., '62-3; O.T.S., '63; Ord. (Cong.), Feb. 2, '64; S.S., Brighton, O., '63-4; S.S., Lowell, Mich., '65-6; S.S. & Pas., Manchester, Io., '67——. 23.

1864.

Edwin Norton Andrews; b., New-Britain, Ct., Sep. 1, 1832; A.C., '61; U.T.S., '61-4; Ord. (Cong.), Jan. 5, '64; Ch., U.S.Army, Memphis, Tenn., '64-5; W.C., New-Britain, Ct., '65; Pas., Canaan, Ct., '65-7; Pas., Kansas City, Mo., '67-9; Ev. & S.S., Crystal Lake, Ill., '69-'75; Pas., St. Charles, Ill., '75——.

Charles Waldron Buckley; b., Unadilla, N.Y., Feb. 18, 1835; Bel.C., '60; U.T.S., '61-4; Ord. (Presb.), Dec. 17, '63; Ch., U.S.Army, Montgomery, Ala., '64; Ag., Freedmen's Bureau, Montgomery, Ala., '65-6; W.C., do., . . ——.

Lester Hall Elliot; b., Corydon, N.H., Aug. 1, 1835; U.Vt., '61; U.T.S., '61-4; Ord. (Cong.), May 2, '66; S.S., Colchester, Vt., '64-5; S.S. & Pas., Winooski, Vt., '65-'72; S.S., Bradford, Vt., '73——.

David Ruddach Frazer; b., Baltimore, Md., July 10, 1837; C.N.J., '61; U.T.S., '61-4; Ord. (Presb.), Mar. 8, '65; Pas., Clifton (S.I.), N.Y., '65-7; Pas., Hudson, N.Y., '67-'72; Pas., Buffalo, N.Y., '72——.

*Walter Harris Giles; b., Rockport, Mass., Oct. 26, 1837; A.C., '61; P.T.S., '61-2; U.T.S., '62-4; Ord. (Cong.), Aug. 26, '64; F.M., Cesarea, W.Turkey, '65-7; Died, Constantinople, Turkey, May 21, '67.

George Hermon Griffin; b., New-York City, May 13, 1839; Y.C., '60; U.T.S., '61-4; Ord. (Cong.), June 22, '65; Pas., Milford, Ct., '65——.

Andrew Jackson Hetrick; b., Hetricks, Pa., July 5, 1837; C.N.J., '60; U.T.S., '61-4; Ord. (Cong.), Sep. 14, '65; S.S. & Pas., Westport, Ct., '64-'72; S.S., Preston, Ct., '72-5; W.C., do., '75——.

John Cephas Houghton; b., Harvard, Mass., Dec. 26, 1836; A.C., '61; B.T.S., '61-2; P.T.S., '62-3; U.T.S., '63-4; Inv. & W.C., Still River, Mass., '64-6; Agric., N. York City, '66——.

Martin Parkinson Jones; b., Philadelphia, Pa., July 29, 1832; U.Pa., '61; U.T.S., '61-4; Ord. (Presb.), ..., '65; S.S., Paoli, Pa., '64-5; Pas., Chester City, Pa., '65-8; W.C., Philadelphia, Pa., '69-'71; S.S., Concordia, Kan., '72-4; W.C., Grand Rapids, Mich., '75——.

Oliver Addison Kingsbury; b., New-York City, Aug. 20, 1839; Y.C., '60; U.T.S., '61-4; Ord. (Presb.), Dec. 11, '66; S.S. (Cong.), Mid. Haddam, Ct., '65-6; Pas. (Presb.), Joliet, Ill., '66-9; Pas., Wappinger's Falls, N.Y., '70-3; Ed., A.T.S., N. York City, '73-6; S.S., Corona (L.I.), N.Y., '74——.

THOMAS MARSHALL ; b., East-Weare, N.H., Ap. 4, 1831 ; D.C., '57 ; Tea., Wilson Sem., N.C., '57-'60 ; U.T.S., '61-4 ; Ord. (Presb.), Dec. 18, '64 ; S.S. & Pas., Mankato, Minn., '64-9 ; Pas., St. Louis, Mo., '70——.

GEORGE FRANKLIN MERRIAM ; b., Mason, N.H., Oct. 20, 1836 ; A.C., '61 ; P.T.S., '61-2 ; U.T.S., '62-4 ; Ord. (Cong.), March 9, '65 ; S.S. & Pas., Greenville, N.H., '64——.

WILLIAM WHITING NEWELL, JR.; b., Boston, Mass., Aug. 23, 1839 ; U.N.Y., '61; U.T.S., '61-4 ; Ord. (Presb.), Sep. 25, '64 ; S.S., Cooperstown, N.Y., '64-5 ; Pas., Wappinger's Falls, N.Y., '65-8 ; Pas., Monroe, Mich. '69-'71 ; Pas., N. York City, '71-4 ; Pas., Newburyport, Mass., '74——.

EDWARD PHILLIPS PAYSON ; b., Lyme, Ct., March 15, 1840; Y.C., '61; U.T.S., '61-4; Ord. (Presb.), Feb. 22, '64 ; Ch., U.S. Army, '64-5 ; S.S., Mott Haven & Manhattanville, N.Y., '65-6 ; S.S., N. York City, '66-7 ; Pas. (Cong.), Kent, Ct., '67-'70; Pas. (Presb.), N. York City, '70-5 ; Pas. (Cong.), Derby (Ansonia), Ct., '76——.

NATHAN MANNING SHERWOOD ; b., Fishkill, N.Y., Feb. 17, 1839 ; N.B.T.S., '61-2 ; U.T.S., '62-4 ; Ord. (Presb.), May 10, '65 ; Pas., Paterson, N.Y., '65-8 ; S.S. (R.D.), Cold Spring, N.Y., '68-9 ; Pas. (Presb.), Elmira, N.Y., '69-'75 ; S.S., Washingtonville, N.Y., '75——.

JOHN PHILIP STEIN ; b., Annville, Pa., June 11, 1836 ; F.M.C., '61 ; M.T.S., '61-3 ; U.T.S., '63-4 ; Ord. (G.R.), July 25, '64 ; Pas., Schuylkill Haven, Pa., '64-'71 ; Pas., Pottsville, Pa., '71——.

HENRY AUGUSTUS PEARSON TORREY ; b., Beverly, Mass., Jan. 8, 1837 ; U.Vt., '58 ; U.T.S., '61-4 ; Ord. (Cong.), May 3, '65 ; Pas., Vergennes, Vt., '65-8 ; Prof., U.Vt., Burlington, Vt., '68——.

HORACE ROBBINS WILLIAMS ; b., Farmington, Ct., Feb. 20, 1835 ; A.C., '60 ; U.T.S., '61-4 ; Ord. (Cong.), May 5, '64 ; S.S., Almont, Mich., '64——.

CHARLES ENT WILSON ; b., Holmdel, N.J., March 30, 1841 ; M.U., '61 ; U.T.S., '61-4 ; Ord. (Bap.), ... ; S.S., Seville, N.J., '64——.. ; S.S., Cape Island, N.J., ..——.

CHRISTIAN WISNER ; b., Hopfau, Würtemberg, Ger., Nov. 10, 1836; U.T.S., '61-4 ; Ord. (Presb.), Ap. 9, '64 ; Pas., Bloomfield & Orange, N.J., '64-8 ; S.S., Garden City, Lake Crystal & Madelia, Minn., '68-'71 ; S.S., New-Ulm, Home & Eden, Minn., '71-3 ; S.S., Chicago, Ill., '73-6.

FRANK PORTER WOODBURY ; b., Beverly, Mass., March 18, 1839; W.C., '60 ; U.T.S., '61-2 ; And.T.S., '62-3 ; U.T.S., '63-4 ; Ord. (Cong.), Jan. 13, '64 ; S.S. & Prof., Ol.C., Olivet, Mich., '64-6 ; Pas., Meriden, N.H., '66-7 ; S.S., Flint, Mich., '67-'70 ; S.S., Rockford, Ill., '70——. 21.

JOHN HENRY BECKER ; b., Saratoga Co., N.Y., Dec. 25, 1836 ; U.C., '61 ; U.T.S., '61-2 ; Inv., Cohoes, N.Y., '62——.. ; Do., Elgin, Ill., ..——.

CHARLES AUGUSTUS BRIGGS ; b., New-York City, Jan. 15, 1841 ; U.T.S., '61-3 ; Trade, N. York City, '63-6 ; Univ., Berlin, Prussia, '66-9 ; Ord.

(Presb.), June 30, '70; Pas., Roselle, N.J., '70–4; Prof., U.T.S., N. York City, '74——. D.D., C.N.J., '75.

SAMUEL RUSSELL BUTLER; b., Northampton, Mass., July 21, 1837; W.C., '58; U.T.S., '62–4; Ord. (Cong.), ..., '66; Miss., Labrador, '66–9; S.S., Hutchinson, Minn., '69–'70; S.S., Washington, Me., '70–1; Miss., Labrador, '72——.

JAY CLIZBE; b., Amsterdam, N.Y., June 16, 1836; U.C., '61; U.T.S., '61–2; And.T.S., '62–4; Ord. (Cong.), Ap. 5, '65; Pas., Amherst, Mass., '65–7; S.S., East-Minneapolis, Minn., '67–8; S.S., Marshall, Mich., '70–1; S.S. & Pas., Newark Valley, N.Y., '72——.

LEMUEL JACOB DEAL; b., Philadelphia, Pa., Feb. 24, 1842; U.Pa., '60; U.T.S., '61–3; M.D., U.Pa., '64; Ass't Surgeon, U.S. Army, N. Orleans, La., ...; Physician, St. Louis, Mo., . .——.

DANIEL DENISON; b., Hampton, Ct., Sep. 4, 1838; Y.C., '60; U.T.S., '61–2; And.T.S., '62–4; Ag., U.S.C.C., '64–5; Ord. (Cong.), Dec. 30, '73; Pas., Middle Haddam, Ct., '73——.

CHAUNCEY GOODRICH; b., Hinsdale, Mass., June 4, 1836; W.C., '61; U.T.S., '61–2; And.T.S., '62–4; Ord. (Cong.), Sep. 21, '64; F.M., Peking, China, '64——.

JAMES HASWELL HARWOOD; b., Bennington, Vt., Sep. 9, 1837; W.C., '60; U.T.S., '61–2; Tea., '62–3; Ord. (Cong.), Jan. 28, '63; S.S., Crystal Lake & Ridgefield, Ill., '63; Pas., Chicago, Ill., '64–7; Pas., Springfield, Mo., '68–'73; Fin. Ag, Drury Coll., Mo., '73——.

SAMUEL COX HAY; b., Newark, N.J., Oct. 1, 1836; U.T.S., '61–3; Ord. (Presb.), Dec. 8, '63; S.S., Peotone, Ill., '64–5; S.S., Delhi, N.Y., '66–7; S.S., Peotone, Ill., '67——. .; S.S., Woodstock, Ill., . .——'74; W.C., Perth Amboy, N.J., '74–5; S.S. (Cong.), Crystal Lake, Ill., '75——.

ROBERT GROSVENOR HUTCHINS; b., West-Killingly, Ct., Ap. 25, 1838; W.C., '61; U.T.S., '61–2; And.T.S., '62–4; Ord. (Cong.), June 13, '66; S.S., Fitchburgh, Mass., '64–6; Pas., E. Brooklyn, N.Y., '66——.

JOSIAH EDWARDS KITTREDGE; b., Montclair, N.J., Oct. 12, 1836; Y.C., '60; U.T.S., '61; And.T.S., '62–4; Europe & the East, '66–8; Ord. (Cong.), March 10, '69; Pas., Glastonbury, Ct., '69–'73; W.C., do., '73–5; . . . ., Florence, Italy, '75——.

NATHANIEL MIGHILL; b., Rowley, Mass., Aug. 25, 1839; A.C., '60; U.T.S., '61–2; And.T.S., '62–4; Tut., A.C., '64; Ord. (Cong.), Sep. 29, '64; Pas., E. Cambridge, Mass., '64–7; Pas., Brattleboro, Vt., '67–'75; Pas., Worcester, Mass., '75——.

HENRY FRANKLIN CLOUGH NICHOLS; b., Kingston, N.H., Feb. 9, 1833; W.C., '59; U.T.S., '61–2; Tea., Canton, N.Y., '63–4; S.S., Norfolk & Raynorville, N.Y., '65–6; Trade, New-Lisbon, Wis., '67——.

THOMAS HUNTINGTON PEASE; b., Albany, N.Y., Dec. 3, 1837; U.Vt., '57; U.T.S., '61–3; Tea., Westchester, Pa., & Fairfield, Ct., '63; Tea., Sand Lake, N.Y., & Stockbridge, Mass., '63–4; Law Student, Detroit, Mich., '64–6; Journalist, do., '66–8; Do., N. York City, '68——.

Aaron Peck; b., Orange, N.J., June 7, 1836; C.N.J., '57; U.T.S., '61-4; Ord. (Presb.), Ap. .., '66; D. Sec., A.S.S.U. & H.M., Cleveland, O., '64-7; Pas., Perth Amboy, N.J., '69——.

Charles Herbert Richards; b., Meriden, N.H., March 18, 1839; Y.C., '60; U.T.S., '61-2, '63-4; And.T.S., '64-5; Ord. (Cong.), July 16, '66; S.S., Duxbury, Vt., '64; S.S., Kokomo, Ind., '66-7; Pas., Madison, Wis., '67——.

Joseph Thomas Robert, Jr.; b., Robertville, S.C., Aug. 7, 1835; U.T.S., '62-3; Literary Work, Chicago, Ill., ..——.

Sylvester Franklin Schoonmaker; b., Albany, N.Y., Nov. 5, 1836; Y.C., '61; U.T.S., '61-2; Ord. (Cong.), ..., '62; Ch., U.S. Army, '62——

William Thayer Smith; b., New-York City, March 30, 1839; Y.C., '60; P.T.S., '61-2; U.T.S., '62-3; Inv., Hanover, N.H., '64——.

William Henry Thorne; b., ..., England, Feb. 12, 1838; U.T.S., '61-3; Ord. (Presb.), June 7, '64; Pas., Allentown, Pa., '64-5; Pas., Darby, Pa., '66-8; Apostatized, '68.

Erskine Uhl; b., Poughkeepsie, N.Y., Ap. 12, 1841; U.N.Y., '60; U.T.S., '61-3; Tea., Poughkeepsie, N.Y., '63-'71; Sec., Y.M.C.A., do., '72-5; Ass't Sec. Internat. Ex. Com. of Y.M.C.A., do., '75——. 21.

1865.

William Henry Beard; b., Norton, Mass., Ap. 1, 1836; U.T.S., '62-5; Ord. (Cong.), Nov. 19, '67; S.S., Freedom, Me., '66-9; S.S., Harwich, Mass., '69-'70; S.S., Wilton, Me., '72; S.S., South-Killingly, Ct., '73——.

Alpheus Whitney Billings; b., Franklin Co., Mass., Ap. 29, 1836; W.C., '61; U.T.S., '62-5; Ag., A.T.S., Lansing, Mich., '65; Do., Illinois, ..——.

Zerah Franklin Blakely; b., Madison, Ind., May 31, 1838; Wab.C., '62; U.T.S., '62-5; Res. Lic., L.T.S., Cincinnati, O., '65-6; Ord. (Presb.), ..., '66; S.S., Savannah, Mo., '66; S.S., Solomon City, Kan., '66-7; W.C., Salina, Kan., '67-'70.

Elijah Levings Burnett; b., De Kalb, N.Y., Dec. 30, 1839; U.Vt., '62; U.T.S., '62-5; Ord. (Presb.), Jan. 31, '67; S.S., Coleraine, Mass., '65-6; Pas., Philadelphia (Mantua), Pa., '66-7; Pas., Rock Island, Ill., '68-'70; Europe, '70-1; Pas., Florida, N.Y., '71-5; Pas., Washington, Ind., '75——.

John Jay Crane; b., Schaghticoke Point, N.Y., Aug. 21, 1841; U.N.Y., '61; U.T.S., '62-5; Ord. (Presb.), June 25, '67; Pas., Rose Valley, N.Y., '67-9; Pas., Stanhope, N.J., '70——.

Joseph Danielson; b., West-Killingly, Ct., Ap. 20, 1835; W.C., '61; U.T.S., '61-2, '63-5; Ord. (Cong.), Aug. 9, '65; Pas., Westbrook (Saccarappa), Me., '65-9; Pas., Saugerties, N.Y., '69——.

JAMES WILSON DAVIS; b., Montpelier, Vt., Oct. 2, 1837; U.Vt., '62; U.T.S., '62–5; Tea., Shrewsbury, N.J., '65–'71; Tea., N. York City (Harlem), '71——.

BENJAMIN ANGIER DEAN; b., Shrewsbury, Mass., Nov. 4, 1838; A.C., '62; P.T.S., '62–4; U.T.S., '64–5; Res. Lic., And.T.S., '65–6; Ord. (Cong.), July 20, '66; S.S., Monticello, Minn., '67–9; S.S., Garnavillo, Io., '69–'72; S.S., Sibley, Io., '72——.

DANIEL WORDEN FOX; b., Brooklyn, N.Y., Nov. 5, 1838; A.C., '62; U.T.S., '62–5; Ord. (Cong.), Aug. 15, '65; Pas., Newtown, Ct., '65–7; Pas., South-Royalston, Vt., '68–'70; Pas. (Presb.), Flanders, N.J., '70——.

ELLIOT CHAPIN HALL; b., Jamestown, N.Y., Ap. 29, 1838; Y.C., '62; N.H.T.S., '62–4; U.T.S., '64–5; Ord. (Cong.), June 13, '66; S.S., Farmington, Pa., '65–7; S.S., Otto, N.Y., '67–9; S.S., Kiantone, N.Y.,'69——.

JAMES BARTLETT HAMMOND; b., Boston, Mass., Ap. 23, 1839; U.Vt., '61; U.T.S., '61–3, '63–5; Lit., Berlin, Europe, '65——..; Tea., N. York City, ..——.

WILLIAM ALBERT JAMES; b., Pomfret, Ct., March 4, 1833; W.C., '62; U.T.S., '62–5; Ord. (Cong.), ..., '67; Pas., Chelsea, Vt., '67–'70; S.S., N. Woodstock, Ct., '71–5; Pas., Marysville, O., '75——.

RUSSELL MELZO KEYES; b., Conneaut, O., Dec. 22, 1837; Bel.C., '61; U.T.S., '62–5; Ord. (Cong.), Aug. 5, '65; S.S., Conneaut, O., '65——.

DAVID LITCHARD KIEHLE; b., Dansville, N.Y., Feb. 7, 1837; H.C., '61; U.T.S., '62–5; Ord. (Presb.), May 8, '65; S.S., Preston, Minn., '65–'75; Prin., State Normal School, St. Cloud, Minn., '75——.

NATHANIEL SCHUYLER MOORE; b., Brooklyn, N.Y., Feb. 18, 1839; Y.C., '61; And.T.S., '62–3; U.T.S., '63–5; Ord. (Presb.), Nov. 11, '68; S.S., Port Penn, Del., '68; S.S., Westford, N.Y., '68; S.S. (Cong.), Gilmanton Iron Works, N.H., '70–4; S.S., Norway, Me., '74–5; S.S., Westport, Mass.,'75——.

MASON NOBLE, JR.; b., New-York City, Sep. 12, 1842; W.C., '62; U.T.S., '62–5; Res. Lic., And.T.S., '65–6; Ord. (Cong.), Dec. 29, '69; S.S., Canaan, Ct., '66–8; S.S. & Pas., Sheffield, Mass., '69——.

CYRUS MURDOCK PERRY; b., Holden, Mass., Oct. 5, 1839; A.C., '62; U.T.S., '62–5; Ord. (Cong.), Mar. 28, '65; Ch., U.S. Army, '65; S.S., North-Gage, N.Y., '66–8; Pas., Jordan, N.Y., '68–'72; S.S., Southwick, Mass., '73——.

JAMES ALEXANDER ROBERT; b., Robertville, S.C., Oct. 9, 1838; N.T.I., '62–4; U.T.S.,'64–5; Law Student, Berlin, Prussia, & Athens, Greece, '66——..; Prof., Vassar Coll., Poughkeepsie, N.Y., '67–9; Prof., Burlington Univ., Iowa, '69——..; Lawyer, Nebraska City, Neb., ..——..; Prest., Cooper Ins., Dayton, O., ..——. A.M., Y.C., '67.

SILAS RICHARDS SELDEN; b., New-York City, Dec. 26, 1822; Y.C., '45; U.T.S., '62–5; Trade, N. York City, '65——..; Cashier, Pacific Bank, N. York City ..——.

RICHARD VAN WYCKE SNOW; b., Troy, N.Y., Oct. 16, 1841; M.U., '63; M.T.S., '63–4; U.T.S., '65; Ord. (Bap.), ..., ..

AUSTIN PARSONS STOCKWELL; b., Hadley, Mass., Dec. 2, 1837; A.C., '62; U.T.S., '62-5; Ord. (Presb.), May 14, '65; Pas., Pleasant Plains, N.Y., '65-9; Ass't Pas. (R.D.), Millbrook, N.Y., '69-'72; Pas., Gravesend (L.I.), N.Y., '72——.

THOMAS GAIRDNER THURSTON; b., Honolulu, Oahu, May 9, 1836; Y.C., '62; U.T.S., '62-5; Ord. (Presb.), Oct. 21, '66; Pas., Wailuku, S. Islds., '66-8; S.S. (Cong.), Grass Valley, Cal., '68-'71; S.S., Hayward's, Cal., '71-5; S.S., Taylorsville, N.C., '76——. 22.

SAMUEL TAYLOR CLARKE; b., Canterbury, Ct., June 16, 1843; H.C, '62; U.T.S., '62-4; Ord. (Presb.), ..., '65; Pas., Detroit, Mich., '65-9; Pas., Owego, N.Y., '69-'75; Pas., Elmira, N.Y., '75——.

EDWARD BENTON COE; b., Milford, Ct., June 11, 1842; Y.C., '62; U.T.S., '62-3; Prof., Y.C., New-Haven, Ct., '63——.

JAMES OTIS DENNISTON; b., New-York City, Dec. 14, 1835; Y.C., '56; U.T.S., '61-2; U.S.Army, '63-5; Ord. (R.D.), May .., '67; S.S., Tioronda, N.Y., '67-8; Pas. (Presb.), Matawan, N.J., '69-'70; Pas., Erie, Pa., '71-2; S.S., Kingston, N.Y., '73-6; S.S., Washingtonville, N.Y., '76——.

FRANCIS JOEL FAIRBANKS; b., Ashburnham, Mass., Sep. 8, 1835; A.C., '62; P.T.S., '62-3; U.T.S., '63-4; Ord. (Cong.), Aug. 31, '64; Pas., E. Westminster, Vt., '64-'72; S.S., Ayer, Mass., '72-4; S.S., Paxton, Mass., '74——.

SAMUEL AUGUSTUS KOCH FRANCIS; b., Amity, Pa., Ap. 14, 1837; P.C., '62; U.T.S., '62-4; G.T.S., '64-5; Ord. (Lu.), Sep. 5, '64; Pas., Philadelphia, Pa., '64-6; Pas., Petersburgh, Pa., '66-7; Pas., Philadelphia, Pa., '67——.

JOHN ABBOTT FRENCH; b., Nashua, N.H., Mar. 28, 1840; W.C., '42; U.T.S., '62-4; Travel, '64.

EDWARD SELAH FRISBEE; b., Delhi, N.Y., Feb. 2, 1837; A.C., '60; U.T.S., '62-3; Tea., Northampton, Mass., '63——

*SILAS HARVEY MELLIS; b., Brooklyn, N.Y., May 6, 1834; U.T.S., '62-4; And.T.S., '64-5; Ord. (Cong.), Jan. 17, '66; S.S., Empire City, Col., '65-6; Died, Central City, Col., May 25, '66.

*LANSFORD STUART PAGE; b., Sangerfield, N.Y., Feb. 21, 1837; H.C., '62; U.T.S., '62-3; Died, Avon, N.Y., July .., '63.

EBEN BURT PARSONS; b., Pittsfield, Mass., Mar. 3, 1835; W.C., '59; U.T.S., '62-4; Aub.T.S., '64-5; Ord. (Presb.), Ap. 11, '65; Ch., U.S.Army, '65; S.S., Turin, N.Y., '65-7; S.S., Sauquoit, N.Y., '67-8; Pas., Baldwinsville, N.Y., '68——.

JAMES ANDREWS SCHULTZ; b., Fairview Village, Pa., Oct. 13, 1836; F. & M.C., '62; U.T.S., '62-3; M.T.S., '63-4; U.T.S., '64; Inv., Fairview Vil., Pa., '64——.

*CHARLES HERBERT STANLEY; b., Beverly, Mass., May 24, 1838; D.C., '59; Tea., Pembroke, N.H., '59-'60; Tea., Gilmanton, N.H., '61-2; U.T.S., '62-4; Died, Beverly, Mass., June 8, '64.

*Henry Beman Underwood; b., Irvington, N.J., Dec. 25, 1839; W.C., '62; U.T.S., '62–3; And.T.S., '63–5; Ord. (Cong.), Jan. 19, '66; S.S., Ringwood, Ill., '65–7; S.S., E. Long Meadow, Mass., '67–8; S.S., Marlborough, N.H., '69; S.S., Baxter Springs, Kan., '69–'70; S.S., Hillsboro Bridge, N.H., '71–3; S.S., Algona, Io., '73–5; Died, do., Sep. 2, '75.

*Gulick Van Aken; b., New-York City, Ap. 22, 1840; P.T.S., '62–3; U.T.S., '63–4; Ord. (Presb.), Oct. 16, '64; Pas., Philadelphia, Pa., '64–7; Pas. (R.D.), Freehold, N.J., '67–'71; Pas., E. Kingston, N.Y., '71–2; Died, Montclair, N.J., Oct. 20, '72.

Charles Henry Somers Williams; b., Poughkeepsie, N.Y., Oct. 7, 1836; U.C., '56; U.T.S., '63–4; Ord. (Cong.), Jan. 16, '68; Pas., Concord, Mass., '68–'70; Law, Boston, Mass., '71; Do., N. York City, '72——.

*Charles Coe Wright; b., Hudson, O., Jan. 30, 1840; W.R.C., '61; U.T.S., '62–3; Died, N. York City, Feb. .., '63. 16.

1866.

Charles Hume Baldwin; b., Windsor, Mass., Mar. 11, 1838; W.C., '63; U.T.S., '63–6; Ord. (Presb.), Ap. 30, '67; Pas., Peekskill, N.Y., '67–9; Pas., Johnstown, N.Y., '69–'72; Pas., Cleveland, O., '72–4; W.C., Westfield, Mass., '74–5; Pas. (Cong.), Medford, Mass., '75——.

Charles Winterfield Baldwin; b., Bunker Hill, Md., Mar. 23, 1840; Y.C., '61; N.H.T.S., '64–5; U.T.S., '65–6; Ord. (M.E.), Mar. 6, '70; S.S., Severn, Md., '68–'70; Pas., Ryland, Md., '70–2; Pas., Westminster, Md., '72–3; Pas., Hereford, Md., '73–4; Pas., Baltimore, Md., '74——.

Horace Publius Virgilius Bogue; b., Clinton, N.Y., Dec. 18, 1842; H.C., '63; U.T.S., '63–6; Ord. (Presb.), July 25, '66; Tut., H.C., Clinton, N.Y., '66–7; S.S., Potsdam, N.Y., '67–9; Pas. (Cong.), Vergennes, Vt., '69–'72; S.S. (Presb.), East-Avon, N.Y., '74——.

Ernest F. Borchers; b., Berlin, Prussia, Aug. 23, 1839; U.T.S., '63–6; Ord. (Cong.), Jan. 14, '69; S.S., Mechanic Falls, Me., '66–7; S.S., Oxford, Me., '67–8; S.S. & Pas., North-Bridgton, Me., '68–'71; S.S., Lake View, N.J., '71–2; S.S., North-Yarmouth, Me., '73——.

Henry Cooper; b., Allegheny Co., Pa., Feb. 24, 1837; U.R., '63; L.T.S., '63–4; U.T.S., '64–6; Ord. (Presb.), May 11, '66; S.S., Blue Earth City, Minn., '66–7; S.S., Rochester, Ind., '68; S.S., Mt. Pleasant, Ind., '69; Pas., McConnelsville, O., '70–2; Pas., Neshannock Falls, Pa., '72——.

Thomas Crowther; b., Bridlington, Yorkshire, Eng., July 7, 1840; N.Y.A., '58; P.T.S., '63–4; U.T.S., '64–6; Ord. (Cong.), Aug. 6, '67; S.S. & Pas., Southfield, Mass., '67–'70; S.S., Mill River, '71–2; Pas., Pittsfield, Mass., '72–5; ...., Brooklyn, N.Y., '75——.

Stephen Winchester Dana; b., Canaan, N.Y., Nov. 17, 1840; W.C., '61; U.T.S., '63–6; Ord. (Presb.), Ap. 11, '67; Pas., Belvidere, Pa., '67–8; Pas., West-Philadelphia, Pa., '68——.

EDGAR VAN HAMIN DANNER; b., Logan, O., Sep. 15, 1842; Bel.C., '60; U.T.S., '63-6; Ord. (Cong.), Jan. 3, '67; Pas., Cuyahoga Falls, O., '67——.

WILLIAM ARNOTT DUNNING; b., Middletown, N.Y., Mar. 24, 1841; W.C., '63; U.T.S., '63-6; Ord. (Presb.), Sep. 12, '66; Pas., Conklin, N.Y., '66-8; Pas., Williamsport, Pa., '68-9; Pas., Franklin, N.Y., '69——.

DAVID WILLIAMS EVANS; b., Caermarthen, South-Wales, Sep. 21, 1839; Bel.C., '62; U.T.S., '63-6; Ord. (Presb.), Ap. 25, '66; S.S., Galena, Ill,, '66; S.S., Sauk Centre, Minn., '67-8; S.S., Sparland, Ill., '69-'70; Pas., Mineral Point, Wis., '71-4; S.S., Chippewa Falls, Wis., '75; Pas., Urbana, Ill., '76——.

*JOSEPH HASKELL FELTCH; b., ..., .., May 20, 1837; W.C., '63; U.T.S., '63-6; Ord. (Cong.), June 29, '67; Pas., Cummington, Mass., '67-'70; Died, do., Jan. 19, '70.

JOSEPH FITCH GAYLORD; b., Norfolk, Ct., Nov. 4, 1836; Y.C., '63; U.T.S., '63-6; Ord. (Cong.), Nov. 7, '67; S.S., Torringford, Ct., '67-9; Pas., Worthington, Mass., '69-'73; S.S., Manistee, Mich., '73——.

RICHARD HENRY GIDMAN; b., Stamford, Eng., Sep. 14, 1840; W.U., '63; Tea., Manchester, Ct., '63-4; U.T.S., '64-6; Ord. (Cong.), Aug. 27, '67; Pas., Bangor, N.Y., '67-9; Pas., Lisle, N.Y., '69-'71; S.S., Morris, Ct., '72-5; Pas., North-Madison, Ct., '76——.

*DAVID GRAHAM GRIEVE; b., Linwood, n. Glasgow, Scotland, Sep. 14, 1837; U.T.S., '64-6; Ord. (Presb.), May 11, '66; H.M., Brownsville, Tex., '66; Died, do., Dec. 3, '66.

ALANSON CURRIER HERRICK; b., Hebron, Me., May 17, 1834; Wtv.C., '57; U.T.S., '63-6; Ord. (Bap.), ..., ..; ...., Canton, Me., ..——.

HAMILTON BISHOP HOLMES; b., Brooklyn, N.Y., Aug. 31, 1841; U.N.Y., '63; U.T.S., '63-6; Ord. (Presb.), ..., ..; S.S., East-Hartford, Ct., '66-7; Pas., Kingston, N.Y., '70-1; ...., Philadelphia, Pa., '72——..; ...., Brooklyn, N.Y., ..——.

*ANSEL LAMSON; b., Pittsburgh, Pa., July 29, 1834; Har.C., '58; U.T.S., '63-6; Tea., Brooklyn, N.Y., '66-8; Died, N. York City, Ap. 12, '68.

WILLIAM APPLETON LAWRENCE; b., Pepperell, Mass., Oct. 26, 1834; A.C., '61; P.T.S., '61-2; U.S.C. Comm., '62-4; U.T.S., '64-6; Ord. (Cong.), July 6, '66; Sec., C. Aid Soc., Brooklyn, N.Y., '66-'73; Trade, N. York City, '73——.

PHILO FRENCH LEAVENS; b., Berkshire, Vt., Nov. 19, 1838; U.Vt., '61; U.T.S., '63-6; Ord. (Presb.), Jan. 17, '68; S.S. & Pas., Passaic, N.J., '67——.

ROCKWOOD McQUESTEN; b., Plymouth, N.H., Sep. 29, 1839; C.C., '63; U.T.S., '63-6; Ord. (Presb.), May 11, '66; S.S., Le Sueur, Minn., '66-'71; Pas., Winona, Minn., '71——.

DANIEL STROBEL MARTIN; b., New-York City, June 30, 1842; U.N.Y., '63; U.T.S., '63-6; Prof., Rutgers' Fem. Coll., N. York City, '67——.

JAMES GILBERT MASON; b., Jonesboro, Tenn., Oct. 30, 1841; W.C., '63; U.T.S., '63-6; Ord. (Presb.), July 1, '66; Pas., Woodhaven (L.I.), N.Y., '66-7; Pas., Jonesboro', Tenn., '67-'72; Pas., Washington, D.C., '72-5; W.C., do., '75-6; S.S., Sedalia, Mo., '76——.

SAMUEL SWAIN MITCHELL; b., Hudson, N.Y., Sep. 8, 1840; W.C., '63; U.T.S., '64-7; Ord. (Presb.), Oct. 3, '66; F.M., Abeih, Syria, '66-8; S.S., Jefferson, Wis., '69-'70; Inv. & W.C., Chicago, Ill., '70——.

DAVID STARRETT MORGAN; b., Johnson, Vt., Jan. 24, 1835; U.T.S., '61-2; And.T.S., '64-5; U.T.S., '65-6; Ord. (Cong.), June 26, '67; Pas., Worthington, Mass., '67-9; S.S., Montello, Wis., '69-'72; Pas., La Porte City, Io., '72——.

ANDREW JACKSON PARK; b., South-Ryegate, Vt., July 22, 1834; U.N.Y., '63; U.T.S., '63-6; Ord. (Presb.), Ap. 22, '66; Miss., Brownsville, Tex., '66-8; Miss., Northern Mexico, '68-'72; Pas. (R.D.), Jersey City, N.J., '73——.

THOMAS CLARK STEELE; b., Pittsburgh, Pa., May 5, 1838; Y.C., '63; W.T.S., '63-4; U.T.S., '64-6; Ord. (Presb.), June 20, '71; S.S. & Pas., White Plains, N.Y., '71-3; Tea., New-Rochelle, N.Y., '74——.

LEWIS OLSON THOMPSON; b., ..., Norway, Mar. 13, 1839; Bel.C., '63; U.T.S., '63-6; Ord. (Presb.), Jan. 28, '69; Prof., N.W.U., Watertown, Wis., '66-8; S.S., Belle Plaine, Minn., '68-9; Prest., N.W.U., Watertown, Wis., '69-'72; Ag., Indianapolis, Ind., '72-3; S.S., Cottage Grove, Wis., '73-5; Pas., Peoria, Ill., '76——.

CHARLES VAN NORDEN; b., New-York City, Oct. 10, 1843; H.C., '63; U.T.S., '63-6; Ord. (Cong.), Dec. 19, '66; Pas., New-Orleans, La., '66-8; Pas., Beverly, Mass., '68-'73; Pas., St. Albans, Vt., '73——.

THERON LINSLEY WALDO; b., Prattsburgh, N.Y., Dec. 2, 1839; H.C., '63; U.T.S., '63-6; Ord. (Presb.), Ap. 15, '68; S.S., Carrollton, Mich., '66-7; S.S., Midland City, Mich., '67-8; S.S., St. Charles, Mich., '68-9; S.S., Big Rapids, Mich., '69-'70; S.S., Manchester, Mich., '71-3; S.S., Pulteney, N.Y., '73-6; S.S., Painted Post, N.Y., '76——.

CHARLES CHAPLIN WATSON; b., Gilford, N.H., Sep. 25, 1835; B.C., '63; U.T.S., '63-6; Ord. (Cong.), July 11, '67; Pas., Dover, N.H., '67-'71; Pas., Hinsdale, N.H., '71——.

EDWARD PHINEAS WELLS; b., Salisbury, Ct., Mar. 4, 1834; W.C., '64; U.T.S., '64-6; Ord. (Presb.), Ap. 15, '66; S.S. (Cong.), East-Machias, Me., '66-7; S.S., Williamstown, Mass., '67-8; Pas. (Presb.), Denver, Col., '68-'75; Pas., Chicago, Ill., '75——.

JOHN WRIGHT; b., Wilmington, Del., Nov. 20, 1836; U.C., '63; P.T.S., '63-5; U.T.S., '65-6; Ord. (Ep.), June 20, '67; Ass't Min. & Ch. Min., Philadelphia, Pa., '66-9; Rec., Bay City, Mich., '69-'74; Rec., Boston, Mass., '74——.

32.

EDWIN AUGUSTUS ADAMS; b., Franklin, Mass., Oct. 21, 1837; A.C., '61; U.T.S., '64-5; And.T.S., '65-8; Ord. (Cong.), Sep. 3, '68; Pas., North-Manchester, Ct., '68-'72; F.M., Prague, Bohemia, '73——.

CHARLES WOOLSEY COIT; b., New-Rochelle, N.Y., Dec. 14, 1840; Y.C., '62; U.T.S., '63-5; Tea., N. York City, '65; Agric., Grand Rapids, Mich., '66——.

SIMEON HACKLEY; b., Plainfield, N.Y., Mar. 6, 1833; H.C., '53; U.T.S., '63-4; Tea. of Chinese, San Francisco, Cal., ..——.

CHAUNCEY LEWIS HAMLEN; b., Cleveland, O., Nov. 2, 1840; W.R.C., '63; U.T.S., '63-4; And.T.S., '64-6; Ord. (Cong.), July 2, '67; S.S., Louisiana, Mo., '66-8; S.S., Brooklyn, O., '68-'71; S.S., Aurora, O., '72——.

SAMUEL AUGUSTUS HAYT, JR.; b., Fishkill, N.Y., June 13, 1841; C.N.J., '63; P.T.S., '63-4; U.T.S., '64-5; Ord. (R.D.), Oct. .., '67; Ev., Albany, N.Y., '67-8; Pas. (Presb.), Belvidere, N.J., '68-'70; Pas., Ballston Spa, N.Y., '70——.

WEBSTER HAZLEWOOD; b., Roxbury, Mass., Dec. 10, 1839; W.C., '63; U.T.S., '63-6; Ord. (Cong.), May 5, '69; S.S., Northbridge, Mass., '66-8; S.S., Slatersville, R.I., '68-'71; S.S., Stoneham, Mass., '72-4; S.S., Everett, Mass., '75-6.

*FREDERIC HOSFORD; b., Brooklyn, N.Y., Nov. 18, 1841; U.N.Y., '62; P.T.S., '63-5; U.T.S., '65-6; Died, N. York City, Feb. 7, '66.

*EMMONS JOHNSON HUGHITT; b., Genoa, N.Y., July 28, '1840; A.C., '63; P.T.S., '63-4; U.T.S., '64; Died, N. York City, Oct. 28, '64.

BERNARD PAINE; b., East-Randolph, Mass., Sep. 21, 1834; D.C., '63; U.T.S., '63-4; And.T.S., '64-6; Ord. (Cong.), June 6, '67; Pas., New-Bedford, Mass., '67-'71; Pas., Foxborough, Mass., '71——.

DAVID BRAINERD PERRY; b., Worcester, Mass., Mar. 7, 1839; Y.C., '63; P.T.S., '63-4; U.T.S., '64-5; N.H.T.S., '65-7; Ord. (Cong.), July 11, '72; Tut., Y.C., '65-7, '70-1; S.S., Aurora, Sutton, & Howard, Neb., '72; Tea., Crete, Neb., '72-3; Prof., Doane Coll., do., '73——.

WILLIAM HAMILTON PHIPPS; b., Paxton, Mass., July 3, 1841; A.C., '62; U.T.S., '63-4; And.T.S., '64-6; Ord. (Cong.), Aug. 29, '66; S.S., Empire City, Col., '66-9; S.S., North-Beverly, Mass., '69-'70; S.S., Southboro, Mass., '70-1; S.S., East-Woodstock, Ct., '71-3; S.S., Poquannock, Ct., '73——.

HENRY LUDLOW TELLER; b., York Town, N.Y., Aug. 23, 1838; U.T.S., '62-3, '64-5; Ord. (Cong.), May 15, '66; Pas., North-Stamford, Ct., '66-8; Pas. (Presb.), Plainfield, N.J., '68-'70; Pas., Amsterdam, N.Y., '70——.

CHARLES NELSON WILDER; b., Gardner, Mass., Aug. 10, 1837; U.Vt., '63; U.T.S., '63-5; Pas., Essex, N.Y., '66——. 13.

1867.

Alpheus Newell Andrus; b., Poughkeepsie, N.Y., July 17, 1843; W.C., '64; U.T.S., '64–7; Res. Lic., do., '67–8; Ord. (Presb.), Feb. 23, '68; F.M., Mardin, E. Turkey, '68——.

William Henry Belden; b., Newark, N.J., Aug. 3, 1841; Y.C., '63; U.T.S., '63–5, '66–7; Res. Lic., do., '67–8; Ord. (Presb.), May 2, '72; Journalist, N. York City, '67–'72; Pas., Branchville, N.J., '72——.

Lewis Bond, Jr.; b., Plainfield, N.J., Oct. 18, 1839; C.N.J., '64; U.T.S., '64–7; Res. Lic., do., '67–8; Ord. (Presb.), ..., '68; F.M., Eski Zaghra, Turkey, '68——.

Henry Matthias Booth; b., New-York City, Oct. 3, 1843; W.C., '64; U.T.S., '64–7; Ord. (Presb.), Sep. 19, '67; Pas., Englewood, N.J., '67——.

Cristopher Rush Brown; b., New-York City, Feb. 20, 1840; U.T.S., '64–7; Ord. (Presb.), May 21, '68; S.S., New-Haven, Ct., '68; S.S., Troy, N.Y., '69–'70; S.S., Melrose, N.Y., '71; Pas., Newtown (L.I.), N.Y., '74——.

Edward Harvey Curtis; b., Madison, Ind., May 4, 1843; K.C., '63; U.T.S., '64–7; Ord. (Presb.), April .., '68; S.S., Lacon, Ill., '67–'71; S.S., Geneseo, Ill., '71–3; S.S., Waukegan, Ill., '73——.

William Alonzo Cutler; b., Alton, Ill., Nov. 27, 1845; I.C., '64; N.W.T.S., '64–5; U.T.S., '65–7; Ord. (Cong.), June 10, '68; S.S., Bridgewater, Vt., '67; S.S., Oak Grove, Wis., '68; S.S., Holly, Mich., '69; S.S., Little Falls, Minn., '70–4; S.S., Dallas City, Minn., '75——.

Julius LeMoyne Danner; b., Logan, O., Sep. 15, 1842; Bel.C., '63; U.T.S., '64–7; Ord. (Cong.), Sep. 11, '67; Pas., Fort Lee, N.J., '67–'70; Pas. (R.D.), N. York City, '70–3; Pas. (Presb.), East-Orange, N.J., '73——.

Edward Herrick Griffin; b., Williamstown, Mass., Nov. 18, 1843; W.C., '62; P.T.S., '63–5; U.T.S., '66–7; Ord. (Cong.), Feb. 6, '68; Pas., Burlington, Vt., '68–'72; Prof., W.C., Williamstown, Mass., '72——.

John Pease Harsen; b., New-York City, May 16, 1844; N.Y.A., '64; U.T.S., '64–7; Ord. (Presb.), Feb. 13, '68; S.S., Martinsburgh, N.Y., '67–'70; Pas., Pleasanton, Kan., '70–2; Pas., Wichita, Kan., '72——.

William Hutton; b., ..., Ireland, Ap. 16, 1838; H.C., '64; U.T.S., '64–7; Ord. (Presb.), Oct. 27, '67; Pas., Philadelphia, Pa., '67——.

Herman Dutilh Jenkins; b., Columbus, O., Jan. 14, 1842; H.C., '64; Aub.T.S., '64–5; U.T.S., '65–7; Ord. (Presb.), Sep. 21, '68; Pas., Joliet, Ill., '68–'73; Pas., Freeport, Ill., '73——.

Charles Augustus Kingsbury; b., Newton, Mass., Nov. 16, 1839; W.C., '64; U.T.S., '64–7; Ord. (Cong.), Nov. 14, '72; Pas., Marion, Mass., '72–6.

Joseph Joachim Lampe; b., Ratjendorf Propelei, Holstein, Germany, May 26, 1837; K.C., '64; U.T.S., '64–7; Ord. (Presb.), Oct. 27, '67; Ch.Miss., N. York City, '67——.

William Edwin Locke; b., New-Ipswich, N.H., Aug. 14, 1837; A.C., '64; U.T.S., '64–7; Res. Lic., do., '67–8; Ord. (Cong.), ..., '68; F.M., Samokov, Western Turkey, '68——.

Richard Cary Morse; b., Hudson, N.Y., Sep. 19, 1841; Y.C., '62; U.T.S., '65–6; P.T.S., '66–7; U.T.S., '67; Ord. (Presb.), Dec. 21, '68; Ed., N. York City, '67–'71; Sec., Ex. Com., Y.M.C.A. of U.S., do., '73——.

Isaac Platt Powell; b., Clinton, N.Y., May 7, 1838; H.C., '60; U.T.S., '65–7; Ord. (Cong.), Oct. 28, '68; Pas., North-Canaan, Ct., '69–'74; W.C., Clinton, N. Y., '74——.

William Henry Reid; b., Johnstown, N.Y., June 5, 1839; U.C., '64; P.T.S., '64–5; U.T.S., '65–7; Ord. (Ep.), Dec. 6, '67; Ass't Min., Brooklyn, N.Y., '67; Rec., do., '69–'74; Rec. (Ref. Ep.), do., '74——.

Frank Russell; b., Marion, N.Y., May 19, 1840; Ad.C., '64; U.T.S., '64–7; Ord. (Cong.), May 15, '67; Pas., Philadelphia, Pa., '67–8; Pas., Brooklyn, N.Y., '68–'74; Pas., Kalamazoo, Mich., '74——.

George William Sheldon; b., Summerville, S.C., Jan. 28, 1843; C.N.J., '63; U.T.S., '63–5; P.T.S., '66; U.T.S., '67; Ord. (Presb.), May 5, '70; Instructor, U.T.S., '67–'73; Lit. Work, Europe & N. York City, '73——.

Henry Hamlin Stebbins; b., New-York City, June 3, 1839; Y.C., '62; Tea., N. York City, '62–5; U.T.S., '64–6; P.T.S., '66–7; U.T.S., '67; Ord. (Presb.), Oct. 8, '67; Pas., Riverdale, N.Y., '67–'73; Pas., Oswego, N.Y., '74——.

Leander Allen Tallmadge; b., Parsippany, N.J., Oct. 31, 1832; Y.C., '55; U.T.S., '59–'61, '66–7; Tea., Deckertown, N.J., '62–6; Tea., Elizabeth, N.J., '67——. .; Tea., Jersey City, N.J., . .——. .; Tea., Elizabeth, N.J., . .——.

William Henry Teel; b., Clinton, N.Y., Nov. 30, 1843; H.C., '63; U.T.S., '64–7; Ord. (Cong.), Oct. 28, '68; S.S., South-Canaan, Ct., '68–9; W.C., Newark (Woodside), N.J., '69–'71; S.S., Gloucester (Lanesville), Mass., '71——.

Elbert S. Todd; b., Adrian, Mich., Feb. 8, 1844; Ad. C., '64; G.B.I., '64–6; U.T.S., '66–7; Ord. (M.E.), Ap. 10, '67; Pas., Martinez, Cal., '69–'70; Pas., San Francisco, Cal., '70–2; Pas., San José, Cal., '72–5; Pas., San Francisco, Cal., '75——.

Charles Chapin Tracy; b., East-Smithfield, Pa., Oct. 31, 1838; W.C., '64; U.T.S., '64–7; Ord. (Presb.), July 7, '67; F.M., Marsovan, Turkey, Asia, '68——.

Earl Johnson Ward; b., Duxbury, Vt., Oct. 9, 1836; U.Vt., '64; U.T.S., '64–7; Ord. (Cong.), March 11, '68; S.S. & Pas., Grafton, Vt., '67——.

Albert Orville Wright; b., Rome, N.Y., June 23, 1842; Bel.C., '64; U.T.S., '64–7; Ord. (Cong.), Nov. 20, '67; Pas., Waterloo, Wis., '67–'70; Pas., New-Lisbon, Wis., '71–5; Prin. & S.S., Fox Lake, Wis., '75——.

EDWARD BINGHAM WRIGHT; b., Hudson, O., May 11, 1838; W.R.C., '59; U.T.S., '61–2; U.S. Army, '62–5; U.T.S., '65–7; Ord. (Presb.), Sep. 28, '67; S.S. & Pas., Stillwater, Minn., '67–'72; Pas., Austin, Texas, '72——. D.D., W.R.C., '76. 28.

EPHRAIM ELIPHALET PEARSON ABBOT; b., Concord, N.H., Sep. 20, 1841; D.C., '63; U.T.S., '64–6; And.T.S., '66–7; Ord. (Cong.), May 6, '68; Pas., Meriden, N.H., '68–'73; Pas., Newport, N.H., '74——.

CECIL FRANKLIN PATCH BANCROFT; b., New-Ipswich, N.H., Nov. 25, 1837; D.C., '60; Tea., Mt. Vernon, N.H., '60–4; U.T.S., '64–5; And.T.S., '56–7; Ord. (Cong.), May 1, '67; Prof., Chattanooga, Tenn., '67–'71; Stud., Halle, Germany, '72; Prin., Andover, Mass., '73——. Ph.D., U. State of N.Y., '74.

CORNELIUS RYCKMAN BLAUVELT; b., New-York City, May 6, 1843; U.N.Y., '64; P.T.S., '64–6; U.T.S., '66–7; Ord. (R.D.), May 6, '68; Pas., E. New-York, '68–'74; Pas., Newark, N.J., '74——.

SAMUEL INGERSOLL BRIANT; b., Beverly, Mass., July 28, 1839; U.Vt., '63; U.T.S., '64–6; And.T.S., '66–7; Ord. (Cong.), Ap. 22, '68; Pas., Sharon, Mass., '68–'74; Pas., Hartford, Vt., '75——.

WILBUR FISK BRUSH; b., New-York City, Dec. 6, 1839; U.T.S., '64–7; Ord. (M.E.), Ap. 10, '70; S.S., North-Canaan, Ct., '66; S.S., Charlotteville, N.Y., '67; S.S., Franklin, N.Y., '68; Pas., Coxsackie, N.Y., '70–2; Pas., Ellenville, N.Y., '73–4; Pas., Fishkill Village, N.Y., '75——.

GEORGE PHELPS BYINGTON; b., Hinesburgh, Vt., Aug. 17, 1838; U.Vt., '63; U.T.S., '64–6; And.T.S., '66–7; Ord. (Cong.), Mar. 11, '68; Pas., Benson, Vt., '68–9; Pas., Westford, Vt., '69——.

WALTER CONDICT; b., Morristown, N.J., Mar. 21, 1841; W.C., '62; U.T.S., '64–6; P.T.S., '66–7; Ord. (Presb.), Sep. 3, '68; Pas., Newark, N.J., '68–'72; Pas., Little Falls, N.Y., '73–5; S.S., Jamestown, N.Y., '75——.

JAMES ALEXANDER DALY; b., Munstereven, Ireland, Ap. 11, 1838; Cal.C., '64; U.T.S., '64–6; And.T.S., '66–7; Ord. (Cong.), Mar. 17, '68; S.S., Streaton, Cal., '68–'70; S.S., Williamsport, Pa., '70–2; S.S., Painesville, O., '72——.

JOHN GAYLORD DAVENPORT; b., Wilton, Ct., Nov. 24, 1840; W.C., '63; U.T.S., '64–5; Tut., W.C., '65–7; Ord. (Cong.), July 1, '68; Pas., Bridgeport, Ct., '68——.

MICHAEL ANGELO DOUGHERTY; b., Brooklyn, N.Y., May 15, 1839; N.Y.A., '64; U.T.S., '64–6; And.T.S., '66–7; Ord. (Bap.), ..., ..; Pas., Great Falls, N.H., '69–'70; ...., Andover, Mass., '70–1; ...., Newton Centre, Mass., '71——.

LEWIS GREGORY; b., Wilton, Ct., June 17, 1842; Y.C., '64; U.T.S., '64–5; And.T.S., '66–8; Ord. (Cong.), Oct. 15, '68; Pas., West-Amesbury, Mass., '62–'75; S.S., Lincoln, Neb., '75——.

JOSEPH LANMAN; b., Norwich, Ct., Ap. 9, 1840; Y.C., '64; U.T.S., '64–6; And.T.S., '66–7; Ord. (Presb.), June 2, '68; Pas., Windham, N.H., '68–'72; Pas., Lynn, Mass., '72–3; Pas. (Cong.), Westhampton, Mass., '74——.

ALONZO MARTIN MAY; b., Allegany Co., N. Y., Mar. 20, 1838; Bel.C., '64; U.T.S., '64–7; Ord. (Ep.), ..., .., '71; Miss., Waukon, Io., '67–'71; Rec., do., '71——.

GEORGE SYLVESTER MORRIS; b., Norwich, Vt., Nov. 15, 1840; D.C., '61; Tea., Royalton, Vt., '61–2; U.S. Army, '62–3; Tut., D.C., '63–4; U.T.S., '64–6; Stud., Berlin, Prussia, '66——..; Prof., U.M., Ann Arbor, Mich., '70——.

CHARLES MYRON PALMER; b., Orford, N.H., Jan. 16, 1837; D.C., '62; Tea., Brimfield, Mass., '62–4; U.T.S., '64–5; And.T.S., '65–7; Ord. (Cong.), Dec. 8, '68; S.S. & Pas., Harrisville, N.H., '67–'71; S.S., Cornish, N.H., '71–3; Pas., Meriden, N.H., '73——.

JOHN WESLEY PETERS; b., Lancaster, O., Oct. 4, 1842; O.W.U., '64; U.T.S., '64–6; Ev.T.S., '66–7; Ord. (M.E.), Aug. 28, '70; S.S., Columbia & Pendleton, O., '67–8; S.S. & Pas., Cincinnati, O., '68–'71; Pas., Spring Grove, O., '71–2; Pas., Winton Place, O., '72; Pas., Zanesville, O., '73–6. D.D., G.B.I., '68.

EDWIN RUTHVEN SULLIVAN; b., Zanesville, O., Feb. 11, 1844; Del.C., '64; U.T.S., '64–6; Ord. (M.E.), ..——..; S.S., Alexandria, O., '67–8; .., ..., ——.

HENRY MARTYN TENNEY; b., Hanover, N. H., May 16, 1841; A.C., '64; U.T.S., '64–5; And.T.S., '65–7; Ord. (Cong.), Oct. 31, '68; Pas., Dorchester Village, Mass., '68–'70; Pas., Winona, Minn., '70–5; Pas., Steubenville, O., '75——.

*DE WITT HURD THOMAS; b., Metuchen, N.J., Oct. 20, 1841; W.C., '64; U.T.S., '64; Died, N. York City, Dec. 1, '64.

MONSON ALVA WILLCOX; b., Bainbridge (now Afton), N.Y., Aug. 12, 1841; M.U., '62; N.T.I., '64–5; U.T.I., '65–6; Ord. (Bap.), Ap. 25, '67; Pas., Burlington, Vt., '67——.

MOSELEY HOOKER WILLIAMS; b., Terryville, Ct., Dec. 23, 1839; Y.C., '64; U.T.S., '64–6; And.T.S., '66–7; Ord. (Cong.), Mar. 26, '68; S.S. & Pas., Philadelphia, Pa., '67–9; S.S., Brooklyn, N.Y., '69–'70; Pas., Portland, Me., '70–3; S.S., Philadelphia, Pa., '74——.

*KENELM WINSLOW; b., Geneva, N.Y., June 15, 1843; U.T.S., '64–5; Europe, '66——..; Died, ..., '69. 22.

1868.

HENRY AUSTIN BEEMAN; b., Dresden, O., Aug. 15, 1838; Ma.C., '65; L.T.S., '65–7; U.T.S., '67–8; Ord. (Presb.), Nov. 11, '68; S.S. & Pas., Roseville, Uniontown, Unity & New-Lexington, O., '66–'71; S.S., Oakfield, O., '71–3; S.S., Roseville, Uniontown, Unity & New-Lexington, O., '73——.

ALLEN PAGE BISSELL; b., Au Sable Forks, N.Y., Sep. 15, 1835; U.Vt., '58; U.T.S., '65–8; Ord. (Presb.), Oct. 18, '68; Pas., Blue Earth City, Minn., '68–'71; Pas., Menominee, Wis., '71–2; Instr. & Prof., Bl.U., Carlinville, Ill., 72——.

CHARLES PINCKNEY BLANCHARD; b., Richmond, Ind., Mar. 13, 1843; Y.C., '65; U.T.S., '65–8; Ord. (Presb.), Oct. 4, '68; S.S., Garnett, Kan., '68–9; S.S. (Cong.), West-Brookfield, Mass., '69–'70; W.C. & Inv., do., '71——.

JOSIAH JOHNSON BROWN; b., Newark, N.J., Aug. 29, 1839; R.C., '60; N.B.T.S., '65–6; U.T.S., '66–8; Ord. (Presb.), Oct. .., '68; H.M., Clinton, Mo., '68–9; S.S., Independence, Kan., '69–'70; S.S., Milton, O., '71–2; W.C., Toledo, O., '72——.

THOMAS JEFFERSON BROWN; b., Philadelphia, Pa., July 23, 1840; Y.C., '65; U.T.S., '65–8; Ord. (Presb.), June 9, '68; Pas., Philadelphia, Pa., '68–'71; Pas., Utica, N.Y., '71——.

JOSEPH STANLEY CHAPMAN; b., Irasburgh, Vt., Jan. 18, 1838; D.C., '65; U.T.S., '65; L.T.S., '66–7; U.T.S., '67–8; Ord. (Presb.), Jan. 28, '69; S.S., Le Roy, Minn., '69–'70; ...., ——.

TOLIVER FRANKLIN CASKEY; b., Darke Co., O., Aug. 29, 1838; Y.C., '65; U.T.S., '65–8; Ord. (Ep.), ..., '70; Miss., & As. Min. & Rec., N. York City, '68–'71; S.S., New-Haven, Ct., '72–'3; Rec., Williamsport, Pa., '73——.

ALLEN CLARK; b., Whitehall, N.Y., Oct. 12, 1841; W.U., '65; U.T.S., '65–8; Ord. (Cong.), May 2, '68; Pas., Seymour, Ct., '68–9; Pas., Wilton, Io., '69–'70; Ed., Davenport, Io., '71–2; .., Whitehall, N.Y., '73–4; S.S., Bridgeport, Ct., '74——.

HOWARD CORNELL; b., Wilton, N.Y., Sep. 10, 1840; U.C., '65; Aub.T.S., '65–6; U.T.S., '66–8; Ord. (Presb.), Mar. 17, '74; S.S., Wading River (L.I.), N.Y., '70; S.S. & Pas., Constantia, N.Y., '71——.

JOHN PUSHEE DEMERIT; b., Montpelier, Vt., May 21, 1836; U.Vt., '61; U.T.S., '65–8; Ord. (Cong.), May 31, '70; S.S., Albany, Vt., '68–'71; S.S., Pawlet, Vt., '71–3; W.C., South-Meriden, Ct., '73——.

OSCAR HENRY ELMER; b., Unionville, N.Y., Aug. 27, 1844; H.C., '65; U.T.S., '65–8; Ord. (Presb.), Jan. 28, '69; S.S., Sauk Centre, Minn., '68–'71; S.S., Moorhead, Minn., '71——.

THEODORE YALE GARDNER; b., Cleveland, O., Dec. 23, 1840; W.R.C., '64; U.T.S., '65–'8; Ord. (Presb.), Oct. 2, '68; S.S. & Pas., Fort Scott, Kan., '68–'71; S.S. & Pas., Lawrence, Kan., '71–4; S.S., Streetsboro, O., '74–6; Pas., Hudson, O., '76——.

WILLIS GAYLORD CLARK; b., Utica, N.Y., Aug. 12, 1840; U.R., '65; R.T.S., '65–7; U.T.S., '67–8; Ord. (Presb.), Oct. 6, '68; Pas., Union Corners, N.Y., '68–'70; S.S., Ossian, N.Y., '70–1; S.S., Arkport & Burns, N.Y., '71–2; S.S., Franklinville, N.Y., '72–3; O.S., Rochester, N.Y., '73–4; S.S., Gates, N.Y., '74–5; O.S., Rochester, N.Y., '75——.

JOSEPH MILTON GREENE; b., Setauket (L.I.), N.Y., Aug. 11, 1842; C.N.J., '65; P.T.S., '65–6; U.T.S., '67–8; Ord. (Presb.), May 12, '68; Pas., Brooklyn, N.Y., '68–'72; Pas., West-Brighton (S.I.), N.Y., '72——.

JOHN VALENTINE GRISWOLD; b., Gibraltar, Mich., Ap. 13, 1837; U.C., '65; U.T.S., '65–8; Ord. (Presb.), June 16, '68; Pas., Washingtonville, N.Y., '68–'71; S.S., Brooklyn, N.Y., '71–2; Pas., Port Jefferson (L.I), N.Y., '72——.

CYRUS HAMLIN; b., Boston, Mass., Dec. 24, 1843; U.T.S., '66–8; Ord. (Cong.), Oct. 29, '68; Pas., Bellows Falls, Vt., '68–'74; S.S., Brooklyn, N.Y., '74——.

THEODORUS BAILEY HASCALL; b., Malone, N.Y., July 9, 1841; W.C., '65; U.T.S., '65–8; Ord. (Presb.), ..., '69; P.M., Plattsburgh, N.Y., '68–9; S.S. & C.M., Brooklyn, N.Y., '69–'71; S.S., Winnebago City, Minn., '71–2; Pas., Cassopolis, Mich, '72–3; S.S. (Cong.), Romeo, Mich., '73–4; .., San José, Cal., '75——..; .., ——, S. Islds., ..——.

*DAVID HOPKINS; b., Tartua-Kelly, Ireland, Mar. 4, 1839; U.N.Y., '65; U.T.S., '65–8; Ord. (Presb.), Jan. 9, '69; S.S. & Pas., New-Rochelle, N.Y., '68–9; Died, Tartua-Kelly, Ireland, Nov. 1, '69.

THEODORE FRELINGHUYSEN JESSUP; b., Florida, N.Y., Oct. 10, 1841; Har.C., '64; U.T.S., '65–8; Ord. (Presb.), Oct. 4, 68; S.S., Kansas City, Mo., '68; Pas., Garnett, Kan., '69–'70; Tea., Troy, N.Y., '71–3; Pas., Au Sable Grove, Ill., '73——. Address, Kendall, Ill.

CYRUS AUGUSTUS JOHNSON; b., Middletown, Ct., May 11, 1839; W.U., '65; U.T.S., '65–8; Ord. (Bap.), July .., '68; Pas., Cohoes, N.Y., '68–9; Trav., Europe, '69–'70; Pas., Whitehall, N.Y., '71–3; Pas., Greenwich, N.Y., '73——.

JOHN KERSHAW; b., ..., May 14, 1842; U.T.S., '65–8; Ord. (Ep.), ..., ..; .., Camden, S.C., .. ——.

JAMES LEWIS; b., Hamden, N.Y., May 23, 1836; A.C., '61; U.S. Army, '61–5; U.T.S., '65–8; Ord. (Presb.), July 14, '69; S.S. & Pas., Humboldt, Kan., '68–'74; Pas., Howell, Mich., '74——.

ALBERT JOSIAH LYMAN; b., Williston, Vt., Dec. 24, 1845; N.W.T.S., '65–6; U.T.S., '66–8; Ord. (Cong.), Sep. 7, '70; S.S. & Pas., Milford, Ct., '69–'73; Pas., Brooklyn, N.Y., '74——.

*GEORGE WASHINGTON MARTIN; b., Philadelphia, Pa., Aug. 17, 1839; H.C., '65; U.T.S., '65–8; Ord. (Cong.), June 25, '68; Pas., Saugerties, N.Y., '68–9; Pas. (Presb.), Schaghticoke, N.Y., '69–'71; Inv. & W.C., Denver, Col., '71–2; Died, do., June 2, '72.

CHARLES HENRY MCCREERY; b., Mt. Morris, N.Y., Feb. 23, 1838; U.M., '60; U.T.S., '61–2; U. S. Army, '62–5; Ass't Com., Freed. Bureau, Columbia, S.C., '65; U.T.S., '66–8; Ord. (Presb.), Oct. 4, '68; S.S. & Pas., Chetopa, Kan., '68——.

SAMUEL VALENTINE MCDUFFEE; b., Keene, Vt., Jan. 9, 1835; B.T.S., '65–7; U.T.S., '67–8; Ord. (Cong.), May 12, '69; S.S., Wayne, Io., '68–9; S.S.,

Acworth, N.H, '69–'70; S.S., Barton, Vt., '70–3; W.C., Fisherville, N.H., '73–5; S.S., Ludlow Centre, Mass., '75——.

BENJAMIN FRANKLIN McNEIL; b., Genoa, N.Y., Ap. 4, 1827; U.T.S., '66–8; Ord. (Presb.), Oct. .., '68; S.S., Wathena, Ill., '68; S.S., Beatrice, Neb., '68–'71; S.S., Fairbury & Alexander, Neb., '71–2; S.S., Union Grove, Ill., '73–4; Ed., Newark, N.J., '76——.

BENJAMIN FRANKLIN MILLER; b., Holly, N.H., Feb. 21, 1839; H.C., '62; U.T.S., '65–8; Ord. (Ep.), ..., '69; Rec., Millbrook, N.Y., '69——.

GEORGE PLEASANTS NOBLE; b., New-York City, Jan. 4, 1845; W.C., '65; U.T.S., '65–8; Ord. (Presb.), July 26, '68; S.S. (R.D.), Brooklyn, N.Y., '68–9; Pas. (Presb.), Weehawken, N.J., '69–'71; Pas., Malden, N.Y., '71——.

*THOMAS PATON; b., ..., Scotland, Oct. 26, 1837; U.T.S., '65–8; Inv., '68–9; Died, N. York City, Ap. 19, '69.

BERNHARD PICK; b., Kempen, Posen, Prussia, Dec. 19, 1842; U.T.S., '65–8; Ord. (Presb.), Ap. 8, '68; Pas., N. York City, .. —— '74; Pas., Rochester, N.Y., '74——.

EDWARD NOYES POMEROY; b., North-Yarmouth, Me., Ap. 6, 1836; U.T.S., '65–8; Ord. (Cong.), Nov. 11, '68; S.S., Riga, N.Y., '68–9; S.S., Bergen, N.Y., '69–'73; Pas., West-Springfield, Mass., '73——.

RICHARD HUBBARD RUST; b., Ellington, Ct., Sep. 5, 1842; W.U., '65; Tea., Cincinnati, O., '65; U.T.S., '66–8; Ord. (M.E.), Ap. .., '68; Pas., Brooklyn, N.Y., '68–9; Trav., Europe, '70; Pas., Sag Harbor (L.I.), N.Y., '71–2; Pas., New-Britain, Ct., '73–6.

SAMUEL AUGUSTUS STODDARD; b., Coventry, N.Y., Ap. 20, 1835; A.C., '62; U.S. Army, '62–5; U.T.S., '65–8; Ord. (Presb.), Oct. .., '68; S.S., Holton, Kan., '68–'70; S.S. & Pas., Independence, Kan., '70–4; S.S., Fort Gibson, Ind. Ter., '74——.

JAMES PATTERSON STRATTON; b., Philadelphia, Pa., Ap. 24, 1839; H.C., '65; U.T.S., '65–8; Ord. (Presb.), May .., '68; Pas., Malden, N.Y., '68–'70; Pas., Mexico, N.Y., '70——.

JOHN WILLIAM TEAL; b., Rhinebeck, N.Y., Ap. 14, 1839; Y.C., '64; U.T.S., '65–8; Ord. (Presb.), Sep. 17, '68; Pas. Cornwall-on-Hudson, N.Y., '68——.

JOHN THOMSON; b., Maryston, Scotland, Ap. 15, 1838; U.M., '65; U.T.S., '65–8; Ord. (Cong.), Sep. 22, '69; S.S., Swampscott, Mass., '68–'70; Pas., South-Abington, Mass., '71——.

*WATSON WILLARD TORREY; b., Groton, Mass., Mar. 24, 1842; W.C., '65; U.T.S., '65–8; Ord. (Cong.), Ap. 30, '68; Pas., Sherman, Ct., '68–9; Pas., Iowa Falls, Io., '69; Died, Groton, Mass., Oct. 4, '69.

GEORGE UNANGST WENNER; b., Bethlehem, Pa., May 17, 1844; Y.C., '65; U.T.S., '65–8; Ord. (Lu.), Oct. 19, '68; Pas., N. York City, 69——.

WILLIAM WESTERFIELD, Jr.; b., New-York City, Aug. 21, 1844; N.Y.A., '64; U.T.S., '65–8; Ord. (Cong.), Oct. 10, '71; Pas., Morrisania, N.Y., '71–6; W.C., N. York City, '76——.

EMERSON GEORGE WICKS; b., Charlton, N.Y., Jan. 22, 1845; U.C., '65; U.T.S., '65–8; Ord. (Cong.), Oct. 2, '72; S.S., Glencoe, Minn., '72–4; S.S., Wabash, Minn., '74–5.

WILLIAM HENRY WOLCOTT; b., Shoreham, Vt., Mar. 2, 1843; M.C., '64; U.T.S., '65–8; Ord. (Cong.), May 11, '70; S.S., Wadham's Mills, N.Y., '70–3; S.S., Dudley, Mass., '73——.

WALTER EUGENE COLBURN WRIGHT; b., Whitehall, N.Y., Oct. 26, 1843; O.C., '65; U.T.S., '65–8; Ord. (Cong.), Oct. 1, '68; Pas., Philadelphia, Pa., '68–'74; Ch., Munich, Germany, '74–5; Pas., Danvers, Mass., '75——. 43.

SALMON MERRITT ALLEN; b., Rochester, N.Y., Jan. 7, 1842; Bel. C., '65; U.T.S., '65–6; Law., Allen's Grove., Wis., '67—..; Law, Lawrence, Kan., ..——.

RUSSELL NEVINS BELLOWS; b., New-York City, Ap. 12, 1842; Har.C., '65; U.T.S., '65–6; Ord. (Unit.), Nov. 24, '72; S.S., Walpole, N.H., '68–9; S.S., N. York City, '69–'70; Ed., do., '71–4; S.S., Washington, D.C., '74–5.

LEONARD ABRAM BRADLEY; b., ..., Mar. 14, 1833; Y.C., '55; U.T.S., '65–6; Law, N. York City, '66——.

ALBERT WARREN CLARK; b., Georgia, Vt., June 27, 1842; U.Vt., '65; U.T.S., '65–6; Ord. (Cong.), Nov. 19, '68; Pas., Gilead, Ct., '68–'72; F.M., Gratz, Styria, Austria, '72——.

MARTIN LUTHER D'OOGÉ; b., Zonnemaire, Netherlands, July 17, 1839; U.M., '62; U.T.S., '65–6; Prof., U.M., Ann Arbor, Mich., '67——. Ph.D., U. Leipzig.

GEORGE DICKMAN GRAY; b., New-York City, Feb. 14, 1844; A.C., '65; U.T.S., '65–6; Clerk, San Francisco, Cal., ..——.

THOMAS LAFON GULICK; b., Kauai, Hawaiian Islds., Ap. 10, 1839; W.C., '65; U.T.S., '65–7; And.T.S., '67–8; Ord. (Cong.), May 15, '70; C.M., N. York City, '68–9; S.S. (Presb.), Montreal, Can., '70; F.M., Santander, Spain, .. ——.

*NEHEMIAH PIERCE; b., Londonderry, Vt., Nov. 5, 1837; U.Vt., '65; U.T.S., '65–6; Ord. (Bap.), ..., '67; Pas., Bellows Falls, Vt., '67–'71; Pas., Springfield, Ill., '71–3; Died, do., Mar. 25, '73.

ISRAEL CORIELL PIERSON; b., Westfield, N.J., Aug. 22, 1843; U.N.Y., '65; U.T.S., '65–6; Tea., Plainfield, N.J., '66——.

FREDERICK BOLTON SAVAGE; b., Hayward, Minn., Ap. 30, 1844; W.C., '65; U.T.S., '65–7; Ord. (Presb.), ..., '72; S.S., Lanesboro, Minn., '72–3; S.S. & Pas., Cooperstown, N.Y., '73–5; W.C., Hayward, Minn., '75——.

MARTIN KELLOGG SCHERMERHORN; b., Albany, N.Y., Mar. 20, 1843; W.C., '65; U.T.S., '65–7; Ord. (Presb.), July 19, '67; Pas., Amenia, N.Y., '67–'70; Pas. (Unit.), Boston, Mass., '70–4; Pas., Buffalo, N.Y., '74——.

LEWIS SHERMAN; b., West-Rupert, Vt., Nov. 25, 1843; U.C., '65; U.T.S., '65–6.

LYMAN MUNSON SHOREY; b., Industry, Me., Oct. 29, 1836; W.C., '65; U.T.S., '65–6; Trade, N. York City, '66——.

MORTIMER SMITH; b., Chatham Four Corners, N.Y., July 7, 1842; U.C., '65; U.T.S., '65–7; Ord. (Cong.), ..., '68; S.S., Canfield, O., '70–1; S.S., Wilton, Io., '72–4; ...., O., ..——.

ROBERT JOHN SOMERVILLE; b., ..., Ireland, Feb. 14, 1838; U.Edinb., '60; U.T.S., '65–6; Returned to Ireland.

EVERITT BURBRIDGE THOMSON; b., Crawfordsville, Ind., Dec. 6, 1843; Wab.C., '64; L.T.S., '65–7; U.T.S., '67–8; Ord. (Presb.), Feb. 25, '69; S.S., Peru & Wabash., Ind., '68–'70; Pas., Piqua, O., '70——.

FRANK THOMPSON; b., New-York City, Dec. 14, 1835; W.C., '65; U.T.S., '65–6; Ord. (Cong.), Nov. 12, '68; F.M., ..., Sandw. Islds., '68–'75; Pas., Windham, Ct., '75——.

GEORGE LEWIS WESTGATE; b., Fall River, Mass., Ap. 12, 1844; W.U., '65; U.T.S., '65–7; Ord. (M.E.), Mar. 20, '70; S.S., Phenix, R.I., '67–'70; Pas., Bristol, R.I., '70–1; Pas., Providence, R.I., '71–4; Pas., Brooklyn, N.Y., '74——.

*THEODORE WILDER; b., Chester, O., Dec. 29, 1837; O.C., '65; O.T.S., '65; U.T.S., '66–7; O.T.S., '67–8; Prof., Rip.C., Ripon, Wis., ..——'71; Died, do., Mar. 8, '71.

EDWARD MOORE WILLIAMS; b., Chicago, Ill., Nov. 15, 1841; Y.C., '64; U.T.S., '65–6; And.T.S., '66–7; C.T.S., '67–8; Ord. (Cong.), Feb. 25, '69; S.S., Austin, Minn., '69–'70; Pas., Faribault, Minn., '70–3; Pas., Minneapolis, Minn., '75——. 20.

1869.

JOHN MATHER ALLIS; b., Troy, N.Y., Dec. 15, 1839; C.N.J., '66; U.T.S., '66–9; Ord. (Presb.), ..., '69; S.S., Albany, N.Y., '69–'71; Pas., Lansing, Mich., '71–4; S.S., Anaheim & Orange, Cal., '74–6; Pas., San Francisco, Cal., '76——.

JOHN STRAUN BAYNE; b., Lacon, Ill., Jan. 18, 1842; W.C., '65; U.T.S., '66–9; Ord. (Cong.), May 18, '69; Pas., Stanwich, Ct., '69–'72; S.S., Greenwich, Ct., '73–5; S.S., Portland, Ct., '75——.

*HENRY BELKNAP; b., East-Barnard, Vt., May 29, 1840; U.Vt., '66; U.T.S., '66–9; Died, ..., '70.

ROBERT CAIRD BELL; b., Dumfrieshire, Scotland, Mar. 7, 1841; U.N.Y., '66; N.H.T.S., '66–7; U.T.S., '67–9; Ord. (Cong.), Nov. 3, '69; Pas., Bethel, Ct., '69–'72; Pas., Orange, Mass., '72–5; Pas., Darien, Ct., '75——.

*GEORGE BRAYTON; b., Western, N.Y., Jan. 8, 1844; A.C., '66; U.T.S., '66–7; P.T.S., '67–8; U.T.S., '68–9; Ord. (Presb.), June 29, '69; Pas., Norwood, N.J., '69–'72; Pas., Newark, N.J., '72–3; Died, Utica, N.Y., June 9, '73.

HENRY PARK COLLIN; b., Benton, N.Y., July 26, 1843; Y.C., '65; U.T.S., '66-9; Ord. (Cong.), Nov. 25, '69; S.S., Seymour, Ct., '69-'70; Trav. & Study, Europe, '71-2; S.S. (Presb.), Oxford, N.Y., '73——.

PEREZ DICKINSON COWAN; b., Knoxville, Tenn., Dec. 26, 1843; A.C., '66; U.T.S., '66-7; P.T.S., '67-8; U.T.S., '68-9; Ord. (Presb.), Ap. 8, '69; S.S., Rogersville & New-Market, Tenn., '69-'72; Prest., Fem. Coll., Rogersville, Tenn., '71-2; S.S., Jonesborough, Tenn., '72——.

TIMOTHY GRENVILLE DARLING; b., Nassau, N.P., Bahamas, Oct. 5, 1842; W.C., '64; P.T.S., '66-8; U.T.S., '68-9; Ord. (Presb.), June 18, '73; Ass't Min., Baltimore, Md., '70-3; Pas., Schenectady, N.Y., '73——.

AMOS HAMMOND DEAN; b., Bethlehem, N.Y., June 16, 1843; H.C., '64; U.T.S., '65-7, '68-9; Ord. (Presb.), May 16, '69; Pas., Albany, N.Y., '69-'73; Pas., Joliet, Ill., '73——.

MYRON SAMUEL DUDLEY; b., Peru, Vt., Feb. 20, 1837; W.C., '63; And.T.S., '66-7; U.T.S., '67-9; Ord. (Cong.), Sep. 28, '71; S.S., Otego, N.Y., '69-'70; S.S., Peacham, Vt., '71-4; Pas., Cromwell, Ct., '74——.

GEORGE LYSANDER EDWARDS; b., Middletown, Ct., Feb. 25, 1839; W.U., '63; Tea., Stamford, Ct., '63-4; Tea., N. York City, '64; U.T.S., '66-9; Ord. (Cong.), ..., '69; Pas., Jamesport, N.Y., '69-'71; S.S., Katonah, N.Y., '71-2; Pas., Baiting Hollow (L.I.), N.Y., '72-4; W.C., do., '74——.

JAMES ALEXANDER FERGUSON; b., Oswegatchie, N.Y., May 12, 1843; H.C., '65; P.T.S., '66-7; U.T.S., '67-9; Ord. (Presb.), May 18, '69; Pas., Hanover, N.J., '69——.

HOMER TAYLOR FULLER; b., Lempster, N.H., Nov. 15, 1838; D.C., '64; Tea., Fredonia, N.Y., '64-6; And.T.S., '66-7; U.T.S., '68-9; Ord. (Cong.), Jan. 19, '70; S.S., Peshtigo, Wis., '69-'71; Prin., St. Johnsbury, Vt., '71——.

SULLIVAN FRENCH GALE; b., Plainfield, Vt., Feb. 11, 1842; U.Vt., '64; U.T.S., '66-9; Ord. (Cong.), June 23, '69; Pas., New-Marlboro, Mass., '69-'76; Pas. E., Brandon, Vt., '76——.

FREDERICK VAN DERVEER GARRETSON; b., New-Brunswick, N.J., Dec. 10, 1839; Y.C., '66; N.H.T.S., '66-7; U.T.S., '67-9; Ord. (Presb.), Oct. 23, '71; Ass't Pas., Ellsworth, Me., '73-6; W.C., Bangor, Me., '76——.

WILLIAM GIDDINGS; b., Great Barrington, Mass., June 26, 1839; W.C., '65; U.T.S., '66-9; Ord. (Cong.), May 1, '71; S.S., Shelby & Whitehall, Mich., '70; S.S., Saunders Co., Neb., '70-3; W.C., Nahoo, Neb., '73——.

GEORGE AUGUSTUS GRAVES; b., Salisbury, Vt., Mar. 15, 1840; W.U., '65; Tea., Jonesville, N.Y., '65-6; Tea., Carmel, N.Y., '66-7; U.T.S., '67-9; Ord. (M.E.), Ap. 9, '71; S.S., Parkville, N.Y., '69-'71; Europe, '71; Pas., Norwalk, Ct., '72; Pas., Bridgehampton (L.I.), N.Y., '73-4; Pas., Litchfield, Ct., '75——.

EUGENE RUSSELL HENDRIX; b., Fayette, Mo., May 17, 1847; W.U., '67; U.T.S., '67-9; Ord. (M.E.), Sep. 11, '70; S.S., Leavenworth, Kan., '69-'70; Pas., Macon, Mo., '70-2; Pas., St. Joseph, Mo., '72-5.

MERRILL NATHANIEL HUTCHINSON; b., Dalton, N.H., Feb. 2, 1835; U.T.S., '66-9; Ord. (Presb.), Dec. 12, '69; S.S., Irvington, N.Y., '69-'70; C.M.,

N. York City, '70-1; Pas., Dunellen, N.J., '71-2; F.M., Mexico City, Mex., '72——.

SYLVANUS GEDNEY KEYSER; b., New-York City, Oct. 21, 1845; U.N.Y., '66; U.T.S., '66-9; Ord. (M.E.), Ap. 6, '76; S.S., Hillside, N.Y., '69-'72; S.S., Modena, N.Y., '72-4; S.S. & Pas., Sugar Loaf, N.Y., '74——.

HOWARD KINGSBURY; b., New-York City, Feb. 3, 1842; Y.C., '63; Tut, Irvington, N.Y., '63-5; do., Berlin & Dresden, Ger., '66-7; U.T.S., '67-9; Ord. (Presb.), June 20, '69; S.S., Carlisle, Pa., '69; S.S., Rome, N.Y., '70; Pas., Newark, O., '71——.

WILLIAM CARLOS MARTYN; b., New-York City, Dec. 15, 1841; U.T.S., '67-9; Ord. (Cong.), June 25, '69; Pas., St. Louis, Mo., '69-'71; Pas., Portsmouth, N.H., '71-6; Pas. (R.D.), N. York City, '76——.

GEORGE EGBERT NORTHRUP; b., Stanford, N.Y., Sep. 30, 1829; G.B.I., '66-7; U.T.S., '67-9; Ord. (Wes.), ..., ..; S.S., N. York City, '69-'71; S.S. & Pas., Rockland Lake (Waldberg), N.Y., '71-5; S.S., Cochecton & Damascus, N.Y., '75——.

ALFONSO ROSOLTHE OLNEY; b., Speedsville, N.Y., Nov. 20, 1842; U.C., '67; U.T.S., '67-9; Ord. (Presb.), Sep. 26, '69; S.S., Waterloo, Io., '69-'70; S.S., Janesville, Io., '70-4; S.S., Addison, N.Y., '75——.

NINIAN BEALL REMICK; b., Williamsport, Md., Feb. 14, 1844; C.N.J., '66; P.T.S., '66-8; U.T.S., '68-9; Ord. (Presb.), Oct. 30, '69; Pas., Troy, N.Y., '69——.

EDWARD RIGGS; b., Constantinople, Turkey, June 30, 1844; C.N.J., '65; U.T.S., '67-9; Ord. (Presb.), June 13, '69; F.M., Sivas, Turkey, Asia, '69——.

JAMES ROBERTSON; b., Belgrave, Ont., Ap. 24, 1839; U.C.T., '66; P.T.S., '66-8; U.T.S., '68-9; Ord. (Presb.), Nov. 18, '69; Pas., Winnipeg, Can., '69——.

HENRY TURBELL ROSE; b., Centreville, N.Y., May 1, 1843; Bel.C., '66; U.T.S., '66-9; Ord. (Cong.), May 30, '70; S.S., Lombard, Ill., '70-2; Pas. (Presb.), Grand Haven, Mich., '72-5; Pas. (Cong.), Milwaukee, Wis., '75——.

STEALY BATES ROSSITER; b., Berne, N.Y., May 22, 1842; U.C., '65; U.T.S., '65-6, '67-9; Ord. (Presb.), Ap. .., '69; Pas. (Cong.), Elizabethport, N.J., '69-'73; Pas. (Presb.), N. York City, '73——.

ALEXANDER SHAW; b., Aberdeen, Scotland, May 19, 1839; U.T.S., '66-9; Ord. (R.D.), June 28, '69; Miss., West-End, N.J., '69-'70; Miss., Jersey City, N.J., '70-2; Miss., Brooklyn, N.Y., '72——.

ISAAC SWIFT; b., Geneva, N.Y., Nov. 24, 1845; U.T.S., '66-9; Ord. (Presb.), Sep. 14, '70; S.S. & Pas., Midland City, Mich., '69-'72; S.S., Oakfield, N.Y., '72——.

LUCIUS ROMAIN SWINNEY; b., Hopewell, N.J., Dec. 23, 1837; U.T.S., '66-9; Ord. (7th D. Bap.), Oct. 11, '69; Pas, Alfred, N.Y., '69; Prof., Alf.U., do., '71——.

CYRUS BAXTER WHITCOMB; b., Otisco, N.Y., July 2, 1839; H.T.S., '66-7; U.T.S., '67-9; Res. Lic., do., '69-'70; Ord. (Cong.), Oct. 14, '74; S.S., Somers, N.Y., '69-'70; S.S., Bethany, Ct., '71-2; S.S., Derby, Ct., '72-3 S.S., Chester, Mass., '74-5; S.S. & Pas., Shelburne Falls, Mass., '76——.

*HENRY OTIS WHITNEY; b., Williston, Vt., Dec. 26, 1840; Y.C., '66; N.H.T.S., '66-7; U.T.S., '67-9; Ord. (Cong.), July 20, '69; S.S., Elko, Nev., '69-'70; Died, do., Mar. 1, '70.

THOMAS RUDOLPH WILLIAMS; b., Darien, N.Y., Mar. 15, 1826; Alf.U., '53; ....; Ord. (7th D. Bap.), June 30, '61; Pas., Westerly, R.I., '61-3; Prof., Alf.U., '63-6; U.T.S., '66-9; Pas., Plainfield, N.J., '66-'71; Prof., Alf.U., Alfred, N.Y., '71——. D.D., Milton C., '74.

MARTIN LUTHER WILLISTON; b., Attleboro, Mass., Mar. 20, 1843; A.C., '64; And.T.S., '66-8; U.T.S., '68-9; Ord. (Cong.), Mar. 3, '70; S.S. & Pas., Flushing (L.I.), N.Y., '69-'72; Pas., Galesburgh, Ill., '72——.

GEORGE WARREN WOOD, JR.; b., Bebek, Turkey, Jan. 1, 1844; H.C., '65; U.T.S., '66-9; Ord. (Presb.), Ap. 11, '72; S.S., Au Sable, Mich., '69-'72; S.S., Charlevoix, Mich., '72. 37.

JOHN AMOS BEDIENT; b., Smithville, N.Y., Aug. 21, 1839; O.C., '66; O.T.S., '66-7; U.T.S., '67-8; Tea., Oberlin, O., '68-9; Ord. (Cong.), Nov. 29, '69; S.S., Litchfield, O., '68; Pas., Montgomery, Ala., '69-'70; Pas., Greenwood, Mo., '71——.

JOHN COYLE; b., Paterson, N.J., June 6, 1838; U.T.S., '66-8; Ord. (M.E.), ..., '71; S.S., ..., Staten Island, N.Y., '70-2; Pas., Englewood, N.J., '72-3; Pas., Newark, N.J., '73-5; Pas., San Francisco, Cal., '75——.

CHARLES GRANDISON FAIRCHILD; b., Birmingham, Mich., Sep. 10, 1843; O.C., '66; U.T.S., '66-7; O.T.S., '67-9; Prof., State Norm. Sch., Trenton, N.J., '69-'71; Prof., Ber.C., Berea, K., '71——.

THEODORE WELD GULICK; b., Honolulu, Sandw. Islds., ...; U.T.S., '66-7.

EDWARD YOUNG HINCKS; b., Bucksport, Me., Aug. 13, 1844; Y.C., '66; U.T.S., '66-7; And. T.S., '68-70; Ord. (Cong.), Oct. 18, '70; Pas., Portland, Me., '70——.

ROBERT HOSKINS; b., Bennington, Vt., May 7, 1843; W.C., '66; U.T.S., '66-7; Ord. (M.E.), Jan. .., '67; F.M., Bijnour, India, '68-9; F.M., Budaon, India, '70-5; United States, '76——.

THEODORE WHITEFIELD HUNT; b., Metuchen, N.J., Feb. 19, 1844; C.N.J., '65; U.T.S., '66-8; P.T.S., '68-9; Tut., C.N.J., '68-'71; Study, Europe, '71; Assis't Prof., C.N.J., Princeton, N.J., '71——.

OTTO MEERWEIN; b., ..., Prussia, Jan. 19, 1840; U.B., '62; U.T.S., '67-8; Ord. (Lu.), ..., '70; ...., Philadelphia, Pa., '70——.

MARK LANE MILFORD; b., Attica, Ind., Jan. 12, 1844; Wab.C., '64; L.T.S., '66-7; U.T.S., '67-8; Ord. (Presb.), ..., ..; S.S., Logan, O.,'70-1; Pas., Seymour, Ind.,'72-4; Pas., Delta, O., '74-6; W.C., Attica, Ind., '76——.

DUNCAN CHAMBERS MILNER; b., Mt. Pleasant, O., Mar. 10, 1841; W. & J. C., '66; U.T.S., '66-8; Ord. (Presb.), Oct. 4, '68; S.S., Osceola, Mo., '68-'71; S.S., Kansas City, Mo., '71-5; Pas., Ottawa, Kan., '75——.

*WILLIAM FORMAN MORRIS; b., Vinton Falls, N.J., Dec. 10, 1843; W.U., '67; U.T.S., '67-8; Dr.T.S., '68-9; Ord. (M.E.), dea., ..., '69; S.S., Bricksburgh, N.J., '69-'70; Died, Vinton Falls, N.J., June 23, '70.

*JOHN OGLE, JR.; b., Stapleton (S.I.), N.Y., Mar. 1, 1840; U.N.Y., '66; U.T.S., '66-9; Died, Stapleton (S.I.), N.Y., Ap. 17, '69.

RICHARD SIGISMUND ROSENTHAL; b., ..., Prussia, Mar. 27, 1844; U.T.S., '66-8; Ord. (Presb.), Ap. 29, '68; Pas., Orange, N.J., '68-'71; Trade, New-York City, '72——.

HORACE SYLVESTER SHAPLEIGH; b., Lebanon, Me., Mar. 11, 1844; And.T.S., '66-8; U.T.S., '68-9; Ord. (Cong.), Dec. 8, '69; Pas., South-Egremont, Mass., '69-'71; Inv., '72-5; S.S., Essex Junction, Vt., '75; Inv., Atlantic City, N.J., '76——.

HENRY ALBERT STIMSON; b., New-York City, Sep. 28, 1842; Y.C., '65; U.T.S., '66-7; And.T.S., '67-9; Ord. (Cong.), May 25, '70; S.S. & Pas., Minneapolis, Minn., '69——.

*SAMUEL DENTON WILLIAMS; b., Mineola (L.I.), N.Y., June 23, 1844; U.N.Y., '66; U.T.S., '66-8; Died, Mineola (L.I.), N.Y., Oct. 5, '68.

JOHN NESBIT WILSON; b., Salem, O., Oct. 22, 1841; W.R.C., '66; W.T.S., '66-8; U.T.S., '68-9; W.T.S., '69; Ord. (Presb.), Ap. 25, '69; S.S., Blairstown, Io., '69-'71; S.S., Anemosa, Io., '71-4; Ag., Hopkinton, Io., '74-5; Pas., Newton, Io., '75——. 17.

1870.

JOHN ALONZO ADAMS; b., Ashland, O., May 21, 1842; K.C., '67; U.T.C., '67-'70; S.S., (Cong.), Marshfield, Mo., '70-3; Prof. & Acting Prest., Straight U., New-Orleans, La., '73——.

GEORGE STUART BAKER; b., Medford, Mass., July 29, 1838; U.T.S., '67-'70; Ord. (Ep.), Dec. 18, '70; As.Min., Rochester, N.Y., '70—..; Rec., Batavia, N. Y., ..——.

*WILLIAM WALLACE BECKWITH; b., Watertown, N.Y., Aug. 13, 1830; U.T.S., '66-8, '69-'70; Died, Utica, N.Y., June .., '70.

EDWARD GIBBS BICKFORD; b., Honeoye Falls, N.Y., July 27, 1844; Gen.C., '67; Aub.T.S., '67-9; U.T.S., '69-'70; Ord. (Presb.), Mar. 5, '72; S.S. & Pas., Chaumont, N.Y., '71-4; Miss. Prof., Marash, Turkey, Asia, '74——.

JOHN HALLECK BROWN; b., Stroudsburgh, Pa., May 17, 1843; U.T.S., '67-'70; Ord. (Presb.), Sep. 27, '70; S.S., Worcester, N.Y., '70-2; S.S., Preble, N.Y., '72-4; S.S., Canisteo, N.Y., '74——.

William Fisk Brown; b., Beloit, Wis., March 18, 1845; Bel.C., 66; U.T.S., '68-70; Ord. (Presb.), ..., '71; S.S., Black River Falls, Wis., '71-3; Pas., Maywood, Ill., '74-6; S.S., Beaver Dam, Wis., '76——.

Edward Read Burkhalter; b., New-York City, Aug. 21, 1844; C.N.J., '62; U.T.S., '67-'70; Ord. (Presb.), Oct. 26, '70; Pas., New-Rochelle, N.Y., '70-6; Pas., Cedar Rapids, Iowa, '76——.

David James Burrell; b., Mt. Pleasant, Pa., Aug. 1, 1844; Y.C., '67; N.W.T.S., '67-8; U.T.S., '68-'70; Ord. (Presb.), Ap. 9, '72; Ev. & Pas., Chicago, Ill., '71-6; Pas., Dubuque, Iowa, '76——.

Arthur Crosby; b., New-Brunswick, N.J., Ap. 10, 1847; R.C., '68; U.T.S., '68-'70; Ord. (Presb.), Oct. 24, '70; Ch. Miss., N. York City, '70-2; Pas. (Cong.), Kent, Ct., '72-3; Pas. (Presb.), Brooklyn, N.Y., '73——.

Samuel Ives Curtiss, Jr.; b., Union, Ct., Feb. 5, 1844; A.C.,'67; U.T.S., '67-'70; Ord. (Presb.), June 8, '74; Ch. Miss., N. York City, '70-2; Study, Buda, Germany, '72-3; S.S., Leipzig, Germany, '73——.

Walter Wells Curtis; b., Unionville, S.C., Oct. 1, 1845; Bel.C., '66; U.T.S., '67-'70; Ord. (Cong.), Mar. 20, '72; S.S., Huntly, Ill., '71-3; S.S., North-Walton, N.Y., '74——.

Peter Zaccheus Easton; b., ..., May 30, 1846; N.Y.A., '65; U.T.S., '67-'70; Ord. (Presb.), Ap. 28, '72; S.S., Comac (L.I.), N. Y., '70-1; F.M., Tabreez, Persia, '72——.

Edward William Fisher; b., Cincinnati, O., Ap. 5, 1836; U.T.S., '67-'70; Res. Lic., do., '70-1; Ord. (Presb.), Ap. 9, '74; S.S., Pleasant Plains, N.Y., '70-1; Ev., Fort Lee, N.J., '71-2; Ev., North New-York, '72-3; S.S., Oswegatchie, N.Y., '73-5; S.S. (Cong.), Parishville, N.Y., '75——.

Daniel Neal Grummon; b., Newark, N.J., Feb. 20, 1844; C.N.J., '65; U.T.S., '67-'70; Ord. (Presb.), Nov. 11, '73; S.S., Otego, N.Y., '71; Pas., Bainbridge, N.Y., '73——.

Russell Thaddeus Hall; b., Richmond, Va., Oct. 6, 1844; O.C., '65; U.T S., '67-'70; Ord. (Cong.), Sep. 8, '70; Pas., Pittsford, Vt., '70——.

Nicholas C. Helfrich; b., Crawford Co., O., Jan. 9, 1837; Ib.C., '63; Tea., ..., '63-9; U.T.S., '69-'70; Ord. (Presb.), Nov. 3, '70; Pas., New-Concord & Norwich, O., '70-4; S.S., McConnellsville, O., '74-5; Pas., Newton Falls, O., '75——.

Martin Foster Hollister; b., Danby, N.Y., Oct. 6, 1837; H.C., '67; U.T.S., '67-'70; Ord. (Presb.), June 3, '70; Pas., Newark, N.J., '70——.

James Foster Knowles; b., Riverhead (L.I.), N.Y., Aug. 31, 1837; U.C., '68; U.T.S., '68-'70; Ord. (Presb.), Nov. 1, '70; S.S., Grand Ledge, Mich., '70-1; S.S., South-Bend, Ind., '71-3; S.S., East-Nassau, N.Y., '73-4; S.S., Corvallis, Or., '75——.

Lewis Lampman; b., Coxsackie, N.Y., Feb. 5, 1843; Y.C., '66; U.T.S., '66-8, '69-'70; Ord. (Presb.), ..., '70; Pas., Jamaica (L.I.), N.Y., '70——.

GEORGE AUGUSTUS LOCKWOOD; b., Clinton, Mich., Dec. 28, 1843; Y.C., '66; U.T.S., '67–'70; Ord. (Cong.), Nov. 26, '70; S.S., Oxford, Me., '70——.

PAYSON WILLISTON LYMAN; b., East-Hampton, Mass., Feb. 28, 1842; A.C., '67; U.T.S., '67–'70; Ord. (Cong.), May 10, '71; Pas., Belchertown, Mass., '71——.

ALBERT McCALLA; b., Bloomington, Ind., Dec. 1, 1846; Mon.C., '66; N.W.T.S., '67–9; U.T.S., '69–'70; Ord. (Presb.), June 30, '70; S.S., Libertyville, Ill., '69; Pas., Emporia, Kan., '70–5; Prof., Parsons Coll., Fairfield, Io., '75——.

HENRY ZWINGLE McLAIN; b., Ripley, O., Nov. 16, 1846; Wab.C., '67; U.T.S., '67–'70; S.S. (Presb.), Pasta, Kan., '70–3; Tut. & As. Prof., Wab.C., Crawfordsville, Ind., '73——.

JAMES MARSHALL; b., Glasgow, Scotland, Ap. 13, 1842; N.Y.A., '63; U.T.S., '63–4; '67–'70; Res. Lic. do., '70–1; Ord. (Cong.), Dec. 10, '71; S.S., Brooklyn, N.Y., '71–3; Pas., Acworth, N.H., '74——.

JAMES HARRISON METEER; b., Sharpsburgh, Ky., Nov. 16, 1833; Wab.C., '67; U.T.S., '67–'70; Ord. (Presb.), Aug. 7, '70; Ch. Miss., N. York City, '70–2; S.S., Parsons, Kan., '72–4; S.S., Brazil, Ind., '74——.

ALFRED EDWARDS MYERS; b., New-York City, Dec. 29, 1844; W.C., '66; N.B.T.S., '66–7; P.T.S., '68–9; U.T.S., '69–'70; Ord. (R.D.), May .., '70; Ch. Miss., Brooklyn, N.Y., '70–1; Europe, '71–2; Pas., Bronxville, N.Y., '73——.

LUTHER ALLEN OSTRANDER; b., Franklinville, N.Y., July 14, 1843; H.C., '65; Aub.T.S., '68–9; U.T.S., '69–'70; Ord. (Presb.), Nov. .., '71; Pas., Dubuque, Io., '71–6; S.S., Owego, N.Y., '76——.

ELIZUR HULL PRATT; b., Durham, N.Y., Aug. 10, 1842; W.C., '67; Aub.T.S., '67–9; U.T.S., '69–'70; Ord. (Presb.), May .., '71; S.S., Cape Vincent, N.Y., '71——.

JOSEPH HOWARD REID; b., Bruce, Mich., Dec. 21, 1842; U.M., '67; U.T.S., '67–'70; Ord. (Presb.), Nov. 6, '70; Pas., Manhattan, Kan., '70–5; S.S., Vassar, Mich., '75——.

HENRY HOUGHTON RICE; b., Middlebury, Vt., Jan. 26, 1847; W.R.C., '67; U.T.S., '67–'70; Ord. (Presb.), Oct. 6, '70; S.S., Parma, O., '69; Pas., Norwalk, O., '70–4; Pas., Sacramento, Cal., '75——.

ALEXANDER BROWN RIGGS; b., Portsmouth, O., June 21, 1842; Jeff.C., '63; Law, Nashville, Tenn., & Pittsburgh, Pa., '63–7; Aub.T.S., '67–9; U.T.S., '69–'70; Ord. (R.D.), Dec. 1, '70; S.S. & Pas., Fort Plain, N.Y., '70——.

JAMES RODGERS; b., Hammond, N.Y., Oct. 9, 1840; H.C., '65; P.T.S., '67–9; U.T.S., '69–'70; Ord. (Presb.), Ap. .., '71; S.S., Hammond, N.Y., '71–3; S.S., Wilmar, Minn., '73–5; S.S., Farmington, Ct., '75——.

CHARLES SIMPSON; b., Ithaca, N.Y., Jan. 26, 1840; H.C., '66; U.T.S., '67–'70; Ord. (Presb.), May .., '70; S.S., Addison, N.Y., '70–2; S.S., Pike, N.Y., '73–5; S.S., Lansing, Mich., '75——.

ARTHUR HENDERSON SMITH; b., Vernon, Ct., July 18, 1845; Bel.C., '67; And.T.S., '67–9; U.T.S., '69–'70; Ord. (Cong.), May 29, '72; S.S., Ann Arbor, Mich., '70–1; F.M., Tientsin, China, '72——.

JOHN JAY STRONG; b., Warrensville, O., Sep. 1, 1838; O.C., 66; O.T.S., '66–7; U.T.S., '67–8, '69–'70; Ord. (Cong.), Oct. 23, '70; Pas., Talladega, Ala., '70–3; Tea., Leech Lake, Minn., '73–4; Miss., A.S.S.U., Talladega, Ala., '74——.

CASSIUS MARCELLUS TERRY; b., Clymer, N.Y., July 21, 1845; A.C., '67; U.T.S., '67–'70; Ord. (Cong.), Nov. 3, '71; S.S. & Pas., New-Bedford, Mass., '70–2; S.S. & Pas., St. Paul, Minn., '72——.

RICHARD RICHARDSON WILLIAMS; b., New-York City, Sep. 19, 1843; U.T.S., '68–'70; Ord. (Cong.), ..., ..; S.S., Cincinnati, O., '70–1; S.S., Minersville, Pa., '71——.

ALFRED VICTOR WITTMEYER; b., Alsace, France, Jan. 11, 1847; U.T.S., '67–'70; Study, Paris, France, '70–1; Prof., do., '71–4; Study & Tea., do., '74——. 38.

JOHN HENRY BARROWS; b., Medina, Mich., July 11, 1847; Ol.C., '67; N.H.T.S., '67–8; U.T.S., '68–9; Ord. (Cong.), Ap. 29, '75; S.S., Springfield, Ill., '72–5; Pas., Lawrence, Mass., '75——.

WALTER MANNING BARROWS; b., Franklin, Mich., Ap. 12, 1846; Ol.C., '67; N.H.T.S., '67–8; U.T.S., '68–9; Ord. (Cong.), Nov. 1, '71; S.S., Arvonia, Kan., '69–'70; S.S., North-Topeka, Kan., '70–1; S.S., Marshall, Mich., '71–3; S.S., Salt Lake, Ut.Ter., '73——.

ROBERT CARL BEER; b., Gebhardshain, Rhine-Prussia, May 8, 1842; U.Bonn, '65; U.T.S., '68–9; Ord. (Lu.), Oct. 25, '69; S.S., Thomsonville, N.Y., '69–'70; Pas., Tea., & Ed., Baltimore, Md., '70——. Ph.D., U.Bonn.

GILBERT LIVINGSTON BISHOP; b., New-York City, May 1, 1845; Y.C., '66; U.T.S., '67–9; Ord. (Ep.), ..., ..; S.S. & Rec., Philadelphia (Hestonville), Pa., '70——.

JOHN BROWN; b., Kyles-of-Bute, Scotland, Ap. 8, 1843; U.G., '64; U.T.S., '67–9; Ord. (Presb.), Oct. 10, '69; S.S., San Francisco, Cal., '70–1; S.S., Elko, Nev., '71–2; Pas., Vienna & Lewensville, Va., '73–5; Pas., Washington, D.C., '76——.

LYMAN DARROW CALKINS; b., Brooklyn, N.Y., Jan. 13, 1845; W.C., '67; U.T.S., '67–8; P.T.S., '68–'70; Ord. (Cong.), Nov. 21, '71; S.S. & Pas. (Presb.), Muncy, Pa., '71–3; Pas. (Cong.), West-Springfield, Mass., '73——.

ROSELLE THEODORE CROSS; b., Richville, N.Y., Aug. 21, 1844; O.C., '67; U.T.S., '67–8; O.T.S., '68–9; Ord. (Cong.), Nov. 4, '69; Prin., Oberlin, O., '69–'73; S.S., Hamilton, N.Y., '74–6; Pas. E., Colorado Springs, Col., '76——.

IRA SEYMOUR DODD; b., Bloomfield, N.J., Mar. 2, 1842; Y.C., '67; P.T.S., '67–8; U.T.S., '68–9; P.T.S., '69–'70; Ord. (Presb.), May 11, '70; S.S. & Pas., Garnett, Kan., '70–2; Pas., Winnebago City, Minn., '72——.

WILLIAM PHINEAS FISHER; b., Galt, Ont., Nov. 17, 1843; A.C., '66; U.T.S., '67-9; Study, Germany, '69-'71; Ord. (Cong.), Feb. 2, '73; Pas. E., Norwood, N.J., '72-3; S.S., Rocky Hill, Ct., '74——.

WILLIAM COUTANT FOWLER; b., Newburgh, N.Y., Aug. 19, 1839; U.T.S., '67-8; Ord. (R.D.), ..., ..; Pas., Stuyvesant Falls, N.Y., '74——.

ALBERT HORATIO GALLATIN; b., New-York City, Mar. 7, 1839; U.N.Y., '59; U.T.S., '67-8; Prof., Cooper Union, N. York City, .. ——.

*WILLIAM HENRY GATES; b., Oberlin, O., June 2, 1845; O.C., '67; U.T.S., '67-8; S.S., Philadelphia, N.Y., '68; Died, New-London, O., Oct. 18, '68.

CHARLES CLARKE HARRAH; b., Hopedale, O., Jan. 6, 1841; U.T.S., '67-9; C.T.S., '69-'70; Ord. (Cong.), Aug. 3, '70; S.S., Monroe, Io., '70-1; S.S. & Pas., Brookfield, Mo., '71-5; Pas., Monroe, Io., '76——.

GEORGE WILSON LEMERT; b., Dresden, O., Sep. 30, 1839; Ma.C., '63; U.T.S., '67-8; Trade, Dresden, O., '68——.

EDMUND HURLBURD POST; b., Logansport, Ind., Aug. 6, 1845; Wab.C., '66; U.T.S.. '67-8; L.T.S., '68-'70; Ord. (Presb.), Ap. 14, '70; S.S., Lake Prairie, Ind., '70-3; S.S., Santa Clara, Cal., '73-5; S.S., Danville, Ind., '75——.

ISAAC RAPER PRIOR; b., Delaware, O., July 22, 1840; Ad.C., '64; U.T.S., '67-'70; Ord. (Cong.), May 19, '72; S.S., Rehoboth, Mass., '73——.

DOUGLAS PERKINS PUTNAM; b., Jersey, O., Feb. 8, 1844; Wab.C. '67; U.T.S., '67-8; L.T.S., '68-'70; Ord. (Presb.), Sep. 15, '70; Pas., Portsmouth, O., '70-1; Pas., Monroe, Mich., '71——.

HENRY SPELLMEYER; b., Bronx Village, N.Y., Nov. 25, 1847; U.N.Y., '66; U.T.S., '67-9; Ord. (M.E.), Mar. .., '73; S.S., Stapleton (S.I.), N.Y., '70-2; S.S. & Pas., Bloomfield, N.J., '72-5; Pas., Newark, N.J., '75——.

JAMES EDWARD TODD; b., Clarksfield, O., Feb. 11, 1846; O.C., '67; U.T.S., '67-9; O.T.S., '69-'70; S.S., Amherst, O., '69-'70; Prof., Tabor Coll., Iowa, '71——.

MORRIS ASHHURST TYNG; b., Philadelphia, Pa., Dec. 29, 1841; W.C., '61; U.T.S., '67-9; Ord. (Ep.), Mar. 18, '70; As. Min., N. York City, '68-'70; Prof., Theo. Sem., Gambier, O., '70-3; Ch.Miss. & O.S., N. York City, '74——.

EDWARD ABBOTT VAN DYCK; b., Abeih, Syria, Mar. 31, 1846; U.T.S., '67-9; Interpreter, Am. Consulate, Beirût, Syria.

ALBERT ALLEN WRIGHT; b., Oberlin, O., Ap. 27, 1846; O.C., '65; U.T.S., '67-8; O.T.S., '68-'70; S. of Mines, C.C., N. York City, '71; Prof., Ber. C., Berea, Ky., '71-4; Prof., O.C., Oberlin, O., '74——.

CASSIUS EUGENE WRIGHT; b., Morgan, O., Dec. 11, 1844; O.C., '67; U.T.S., '67-8; O.T.S., '68-'70; Ord. (Cong.), Feb. 3, '71; S.S. & Pas., Norwalk, O., '69-'75; Pas., Austin, Minn., '75——. 23.

1871.

GUSTAVUS ALBERTUS ALEXY; b., Rosenau, Austria, May 21, 1833; U.Milan, .. ; U.T.S., '68–'71; Res. Lic., do., '71–2; Ord. (Presb.), June 16, '72; F.M., Barcelona, Spain, '72–4; C.M., N. York City, '74——.

WALTER HOWARD AYERS; b., Canterbury, N.H., Ap. 26, 1845; D.C., '68; U.T.S., '68–'71; Ord. (Cong.), July 16, '72; S.S., Bethel, Me., '71; S.S., Winooski, Vt., '72; S.S., Castleton, Vt., '73–4; Pas., Lebanon, N.H., '74–5; W.C., do., '75——.

HENRY CHASE BRADBURY; b., Williamsport, Pa., Aug. 15, 1844; A.C., '66; U.T.S., '68–'71; Ord. (Presb.), ..., '72; Ch. Miss., N. York City, '70–1; S.S., Lindsey & Minneapolis, Kan., '71——.

JAMES DE HART BRUEN; b., New-Windsor, N.Y., Dec. 17, 1849; U.T.S., '68–'71; Ord. (Presb.), May 11, '71; Tea., N. York City, ..., .. ; Pas., Summit, N.J., '71——. A.M., W.C., '71.

WILLIAM BRACKETT CARY; b., Cherry Valley, N.Y., Aug. 8, 1841; U.T.S., '68–'71; Ord. (Presb.), Sep. .., '71; Pas., Solomon City, Kan., '71——.

THEODORE FRELINGHUYSEN CHAMBERS; b., Raritan, N.J., May 19, 1849; C.C.N.Y., '68; U.T.S., '68–'71; Ord. (R.D.), Oct. 23, '72; Tea., N. York City, '71–2; Pas., Oakland, N.J., '72–6; Pas. (Presb.), Deckertown (Wantage), N.J., '76——.

EDWARD PRYOR CLARK; b., Mercer, Pa., Aug. 10, 1847; Al.C., '67; U.T.S., '68–'71; Ord. (Presb.), Aug. 3, '71; S.S., Port Austin, Mich., '71——.

WILLIAM JAMES CUMMING; b., New-York City, July 22, 1847; C.C., N.Y., '67; U.T.S., '68–'71; Tea., Norwalk, Ct., '72–3; Tea., N. York City, '74–5; Ord. (Presb.), Aug. 8, '76; Pas., Yorktown, N.Y., '76——.

SILAS AUGUSTUS DAVENPORT; b., Brooklyn, N.Y., June 27, 1846; Y.C., '68; P.T.S., '68–'70; U.T.S., '70–1; Ord. (Presb.), Ap. .., '71; Med.Miss., Ningpo, China, '74–5; Pas., Port Carbon, Pa., '75——. M.D., Coll. P. & S., N.Y.C., '73.

JOHN OGDEN GORDON; b., Pittsburgh, Pa., March 10, 1850; W. & U., '66; Aub.T.S., '68–'70; U.T.S., '70–1; Ord. (Presb.), March 26, '72; S.S. & Pas., Rensselaerville, N.Y., '71——

GRANVILLE STANLEY HALL; b., Ashfield, Mass., Feb. 1, 1845; W.C., '67; U.T.S., '67–8, '70–1; Study, Germany, '69–'70; Prof., Ant.C., Yellow Springs, O., '72——.

HENRY HARRISON HAMILTON; b., Chester, Mass., Feb. 1, 1842; A.C., '68; U.T.S., '68–'71; Ord. (Cong.), Sep. 1, '72; Pas., Westford, Mass., '72——.

TEUNIS SLINGERLAND HAMLIN; b., Glenville, N.Y., May 31, 1847; U.C., '67; U.T.S., '69–'71; Ord. (Presb.), Sep. 28, '71; Pas., Troy (Woodside), N.Y., '71——.

OSCAR JOSHUA HARDIN; b., Newton, N.J., Sep. 30, 1845; L.F.C., '68; U.T.S., '68–'71; Ord. (Presb.), Oct. 10, '71; F.M., Tripoli, Syria, '71——.

AARON STEWART HARTMAN; b., Gettysburgh, Pa., Dec. 19, 1845; Get.C., '68; U.T.S., '69–'71; Ord. (Lu.), Oct. .., '71; Pas., Ghent, N. Y., '71–3; Pas., Brooklyn, N. Y., '73–5; Pas., Chambersburgh, Pa., '75——.

WILLIAM JOHN HOAR; b., Greenwood, Pa., Feb. 11, 1845; C.N.J., '67; P.T.S., '68–'70; U.T.S., '70–1; Ord. (Presb.), Feb. 14, '72; S.S., Wilmar & Diamond Lake, Minn., '71–2; Pas., Lancaster, Pa., '73–4; Pas., Bearstown (Cedar Grove), Pa., '75——.

JOHN HENRY HOUSE; b., Painesville, O., May 29, 1845; W.R.C., '68; U.T.S., '68–'71; Ord. (Cong.), Sep. 22, '71; S.S., Garretsville, O., '71–2; F.M., Eski Zagra, Turkey, Europe, '73——.

FRANK ALONZO JOHNSON; b., Boston, Mass., Ap. 26, 1845; H.C., '68; U.T.S., '68–'71; Ord. (Cong.), Oct. 3, '71; Pas., Lodi, N.J., '71–5; Pas., Chester, N.J., '75——.

EDWIN RUFUS LEWIS; b., Madison, Ind., Ap. 2, 1839; A.C., '61; U.S. Army, '61–4; Physician, Amherst, Mass., '65–8; U.T.S., '68–'70; Ord. (Presb.), Nov. 7, '70; F.M. & Prof., Beirut, Syria, '70——. M.D., Har.C., '67.

PATRICK DANIEL MCELROY; b., ..., Mar. 17, 1843; U., Salamanca, Sp., '69; U.T.S., '70–1;....

MATTHEW GRANT MANN; b., Würtemberg, Germany, Feb. 1, 1842; U.N.Y., '69; U.T.S., '63–4, '67–8, '69–'71; Ord. (Presb.), Ap. 17, '73; S.S. & Miss., Eugene City, Or., '72–5; S.S., Astoria, Or., '75——.

CHARLES NOBLE; b., New-York City, Dec. 3, 1847; W.C., '66; U.T.S., '68–'71; Ord. (Cong.), Dec. 17, '73; Pas., Franklin, N.Y., '73——.

ISAAC NEWTON OTIS; b., Prairieville, Mich., Ap. 1, 1845; U.M., '67; U.T.S., '68–'71; Ord. (Presb.), June 3, '71; S.S., Paw Paw, Mich., '71–2; S.S. & Pas., Stillwater, Minn., '72——.

WILLARD PARSONS; b., Franklin, N.Y., Sep. 8, 1842; U.T.S., '68–'71; Ord. (Cong.), May 12, '72; Ch. Miss., Brooklyn, N.Y., ..——..; S.S. (Presb.), Sherman, Pa., ..——.

GEORGE SHIPMAN PAYSON; b., Harpersfield, N.Y., Sep. 11, 1845; Y.C., '66; U.T.S., '68–'71; Ord. (Presb.), June 8, '74; S.S. & Pas., N. York City (Inwood), '74——.

LEWIS ALEXANDER PLATTS; b., Chapman's Creek, O., Feb. 21, 1840; Alf.Un., '66; U.T.S., '68–'71; Ord. (7th D. Bap.), July 25, '66; S.S. & Pas., Nile, N.Y., '66–8; Pas., New-Market, N.J., '68——.

*GEORGE NIVER SNYDER; b., Honesdale, Pa., March 27, 1844; H.C., '68; U.T.S., '68–'71; Ord. (R.D.), June .., '71; S.S., Elmsford, N.Y., '71–2; S.S., White Plains, N.Y., '72; Died, do., Nov. 2, '72.

WILLIAM HENRY SNYDER; b., Lewisburgh, Pa., Jan. 16, 1842; U.C., '68; U.T.S., '68–'71; Res. Lic., do., '71–2; Ord. (Presb.), Nov. 17, '73; S.S. (Cong.), Chicago, Ill., '72–3; S.S. & Pas., Abilene, Kan., '73——.

JOSIAH WELCH; b., Holiday's Cove, W.Va., Sep. 2, 1842; W. & J.C., '68; P.T.S., '68–'70; U.T.S., '70–1; Ord. (Presb.), Sep. 4, '71; S.S. & Pas., Salt Lake City, U.T., '71——.

CHRISTIAN WILLARD WINNIE; b., Shandaken, N.Y., Feb. 5, 1838; U.T.S., '68-'71; Ord. (Presb.), Oct. 13, '71; S.S., St. James, Minn., '71-4; S.S., Absecon, N.J., '74——.

FRANK ALPHONSO WOOD; b., Meriden, N.H., Feb. 10, 1845; U.N.Y., '67; U.T.S., '68-'71; Ord. (Presb.), Oct. 24, '71; F.M., Sidon, Zahleh, & Abeih, Syria, '71——.

JOHN HOPKINS WORCESTER, JR.; b., St. Johnsbury, Vt., Ap. 2, 1845; U.Vt., '65; U.T.S., '67-9, '70-1; Europe, '69-'70; Ord. (Presb.), Jan. 10, '72; Pas., South-Orange, N.J., '72——. 32.

LEVI FRANCIS BICKFORD; b., Hartford, Ind., Jan. 9, 1840; O.C., '68; O.T.S., '68-'70; U.T.S., '70-1; Ord. (Cong.), Jan. 16, '72; S.S., Allegan, Mich., '71-3; S.S., St. John's, Mich., '73-4; S.S., Lamoille, Ill., '74——.

JUSTUS NEWTON BROWN; b., ..., May 23, 1844; O.C., '67; O.T.S., '68-9; U.T.S., '69-'70; O.T.S., '70-1; Ord. (Cong.), ..., '71; Ed., Oberlin, O., '71-3; S.S., Talladega, Ala., '74——.

CHARLES A. BURDICK; b., Mystic, Ct., Dec. 29, 1829; Alf.U., ...; U.T.S., '69-'70; . . . .

ALMON WHITNEY BURR; b., Strongsville, O., Jan. 18, 1845; O.C., '68; U.T.S., '68-9; O.T.S., '69-'70; Tut., O.C., '70-4; And.T.S., '74-5; Ord. (Cong.), July 27, '75; Prin., Hallowell, Me., '75——.

NELSON FARR COBLEIGH; b., Littleton, N.H., Oct. 12, 1844; A.C., '68; U.T.S., '68-'70; Ord. (Cong.), Aug. 16, '71; S.S. & Pas., Marshfield, Vt., '70——.

CHARLES TERRY COLLINS; b., Hartford, Ct., Oct. 14, 1845; Y.C., '67; U.T.S., '68-9; And.T.S., '69-'71; Ord. (Presb.), Dec. 21, '71; Ch.Miss., N. York City, '71-4; Pas. (Cong.), Cleveland, O., '74——.

CHARLES CARLYLE DARWIN; b., Paris, Tenn., Jan. 27, 1848; O.C., '68; U.T.S., '68-9; O.T.S., '69-'70; Tut., Howard Univ., Washington, D.C., '72——. .; Ass't Librarian, Cong., do., . .——.

GEORGE FREDERICK FLICHTNER; b., Union, Me., May 11, 1847; A.C., '67; U.T.S., '68-9; Ord. (Ep.), Jan. 12, '72; Rec., Newark, N.J., '70——.

JOHN GAIUS FRASER; b., Ferrisburgh, Vt., Oct. 6, 1846; O.C., '67; U.T.S., '68-9; O.T.S., '69-'71; Ord. (Cong.), Oct. 11, '71; Pas., East-Toledo, O., '71——.

HERMAN AUGUSTUS FRENCH; b., Granville, Ill., July 3, 1845; O.C., '68; U.T.S., '68-9; O.T.S., '69-'71; Ord. (Cong.), May . ., '73; S.S. & Pas., Milford, Neb., '72——.

SAMUEL SMITH GILSON; b., New-Derry, Pa., Oct. 28, 1843; W.&J.C., '66; Tea., Elder's Ridge, Pa., '66-7; W.T.S., '68-'70; U.T.S., '70-1; Ord.

(Presb.), Oct. 14, '72; S.S., Garrison's, N.Y., '71; Prof., Warren Coll., Ky., '71-2; S.S. & Pas., Bowling Green, Ky., '72-4; Pas., Uniontown, Pa., '74——.

Alfred Van Cleve Johnson; b., New-York City, June 10, 1847; U.N.Y., '67; U.T.S., '69-'70; N.H.T.S., '70-1; Ord. (Presb.), Nov. 6, '73; Pas., Chatham, N.J., '73——.

John H. Kopf; b., ..., Oct. 22, 1846; U.T.S., '68-'71; ...., S.S., Madrid, N.Y., '74——.

John Love, Jr.; b., New-York City, May 5, 1847; U.R., '68; U.T.S., '68-'70; Ord. (Bap.), Aug. 5, '70; Pas., N. York City, '70-2; Pas., Albany, N.Y., '72-5; Pas., Chelsea, Mass., '75——.

Clifton Gregory Marshall; b., Pittsburgh, Pa., May 1, 1844; W.R.C., '67; U.T.S., '67-8.

*Benjamin Christopher Robertson; b., Harpeth Hall, Tenn., June 5, 1846; A.C., '68; U.T.S., '68-'70; Died, Tallahassee, Fla., Dec. 7, '71.

Charles Henry Rowley; b., Moriah, N.Y., May 7, 1842; M.C., '68; U.T.S., '68-9; And.T.S., '69-'71; S.S., Sheldon, Vt., '72-4; S.S., Potsdam, N.Y., '75——.

Frederick Adolphus Schauffler; b., Constantinople, Turkey, Nov. 7, 1845; W.C., '67; U.T.S., '68-9; And.T.S., '69-'71; Ord. (Cong.), Sep. 13, '71; S.S., Brookfield, Mass., '71-2; Ch.Miss., N. York City, '73——.

Joseph Franklin Shoards; b., New-York City, Jan 1, 1845; M.U., '68; U.T.S., '69-'70; Sec., N. York City, '71——.

Moses Bross Thomas; b., Barryville, N.Y., June 18, 1845; W.C., '67; And.T.S., '67-8; U.T.S., '68-9; Study, Williamstown, Mass., '69-'71; Ord. (Presb.), May 9, '72; Pas., Islip (L.I.), N.Y., '72——.

Franklin Parker Wood; b., Enfield, N.H., Nov. 22, 1844; D.C., '68; U.T.S., '68-'70; And.T.S., '70-1; Ord. (Cong.), July 24, '71; S.S. & Pas., Acton, Mass., '71——.

Henry Collins Woodruff; b., ..., .., Feb. 16, 1845; Y.C., '68; U.T.S., '68-9; And.T.S., '69-'71. 22.

1872.

Charles Baldrey Austin; b., Philadelphia, Pa., Jan. 20, 1848; H.C., '68; U.T.S., '69-'72; Ord. (Presb.), Nov. 14, '72; Pas., Cohocton, N.Y., '72——.

Turner Smith Bailey; b., Bloomingville, O., Ap. 19, 1841; Io.U., '69; N.W.T.S., '69-'71; U.T.S., '71-2; Ord. (Presb.), Ap. 24, '72; S.S. & Pas., Farley, Io., '71——.

Francis Marion Baker; b., Richmond, Va., Nov. 10, 1839; L.U., '69; U.T.S., '69-'72; Ord. (Ep.), Sep. 28, '72; Rec., Richmond, Va., '72——.

WILLIAM GAY BALLANTINE; b., Washington, D.C., Dec. 7, 1848; Mar.C., '68; U.T.S., '69-'72; Prof., Rip.C., Ripon, Wis., '74——.

MARCELLUS BOWEN; b., Marion, O., Ap. 6, 1846; Y.C., '66; U.T.S., '68-9,'70-2; Ord. (Presb.), Oct. 24, '72; Pas., Springfield, N.J., '72-4; F.M., Manissa, n. Smyrna, Turkey, Asia, '74——.

HENRY LEVAN BUNSTEIN; b., Easton, Pa., Aug. 18, 1844; L.F.C., '64; U.T.S., '70-2; Ord. (Presb.), Feb. 25, '73; Pas., Philadelphia, Pa., '73——.

WILLIAM INVERARITY CHALMERS; b., New-York City, Oct. 14, 1850; C.C.N.Y., '69; U.T.S., '69-'72; Ord. (Cong.), Oct. 22, '72; S.S. & Pas., Riverhead (L.I), N.Y., '72——.

CHALMERS DURAND CHAPMAN; b., ..., .., Ap. 14, 1845; U.N.Y., '66; U.T.S., '71-2; Ord. (Presb.), ..., '73; Pas., Mt. Olive, N.J., '73-5;

COLBERT MOUSSEAUX DES ISLETS; b., Dayton, Pa., Dec. 25, 1845; C.N.J., '69; P.T.S., '69-'71; U.T.S., '71-2; Ord. (Presb.), May 22, '72; Pas., Hamlinton, Pa., '72-4; S.S., Leon, Io., '74——.

JAMES FRANKLIN DONALDSON; b., New-York City, Ap. 22, 1844; C.C.N.Y., '67; U.T.S., '69-'72; Ord. (Presb.), Oct. 18, '75; S.S. (Cong.), East-Arlington, Vt., '72-3; S.S. (Presb.), Chazy, N.Y., '73-4; S.S., Eckford (P. O., Marshall), Mich., '74——.

SAMUEL VAN SANTVOORD FISHER; b., Schenectady, N.Y., Ap. 27, 1845; O.C., '68; U.T.S., '69-'72; Ord. (Cong.), Dec. 3, '74; S.S., Menasha, Wis., '74——.

LEWIS RAY FOOTE; b., South New-Berlin, N.Y., Mar. 29, 1844; H.C., '69; U.T.S., '69-'72; Ord. (Presb.), May 21, '72; Ch. Miss., N. York City, '72-3; Pas., Brooklyn, N.Y., '73——.

CLARENCE GEDDES; b., Lewisburgh, Pa., Nov. 2, 1841; U.T.S., '69-'72; Ord. (Presb.), July 16, '73; S.S. & Pas., Tenafly, N.J., '72——.

EDWARD HUGH HARVEY; b., Cazenovia, N.Y., Feb. 11, 1845; Kal.C., '69; N.W.T.S., '69-'71; U.T.S., '71-2; Ord. (Presb.), Ap. 30, '72; Pas., West-Summit, N.J., '72-4; S.S. & Pas., Albion, Mich., '74——.

MATTHEW CANTINE JULIEN; b., New-York City, Feb. 21, 1849; C.C.N.Y., '69; U.T.S., '69-'72; Ord. (Cong.), Dec. 11, '72; Pas., New-Bedford, Mass., '72——.

WILLIAM GOSSER MARTS; b., Oakland Cross-Roads, Pa., May 9, 1841; K.C., '69; N.H.T.S., '69-'70; U.T.S., '70-2; Ord. (Cong.), Oct. 22, '72; S.S., Mt. Pleasant, Io., '72-3; S.S., Chillicothe, Mo., '73; S.S., South-Amherst, Mass., '73-4; Miss., Raleigh, N.C., '74-5; Miss., Talladega, Ala., '76——.

GEORGE RAYMOND MILTON; b., Pawlett, Eng., May 4, 1840; O.C., '69; U.T.S., '69-'72; Ord. (Cong.), Jan. 18, '76; S.S., Jonesville, Mich., '73-4; S.S., St. Cloud, Minn., '75——.

GEORGE BALDWIN NEWELL; b., Montgomery, N.Y., Ap. 12, 1847; U.N.Y., '69; U.T.S., '69-'72; S.S., Atlantic City, N.J., '72-3; Law, N. York City, '74——.

Charles Stedman Newhall; b., Boston, Mass., Oct. 4, 1843; A.C., '69; U.T.S., '69–'72; Ord. (Cong.), Dec. 11, '72; Pas., Oriskany Falls, N.Y., '72–4; S.S. (Presb.), Oceanic, N.J., '74——.

Eugene Castle Olney; b., Weedsport, N.Y., Feb. 14, 1844; Hi.C., '67; Prin., Manchester, Mich., '67–9; U.T.S., '69–'72; Ord. (Presb.), Sep. 25, '72; S.S., Quincy, Mich, '72–4; S.S. (Cong.), Grand Rapids, Mich., '74–6; S.S., Traverse City, Mich., '76——.

Samuel Parry, Jr.; b., Lambertville, N.J., Mar. 29, 1845; Y.C., '68; P.T.S., '69–'71; U.T.S., '71–2; Ord. (Presb.), Ap. 30, '73; Pas., Pluckamin, N.J., '73——.

John Redpath; b., Burnside, Scotland, June 17, 1842; U.T.S., '69–'72; Ord. (Presb.), Sep. 25, '72; S.S., Clam Lake, Mich., '72–5; Ev., Petoskey, Mich., '75——.

William Russell Scarritt; b., St. Louis, Mo., July 14, 1846; A.C., '69; U.T.S., '69–'72; ..——..; Res. Lic., W.T.S., '75–6.

Adelbert Jay Schlager; b., Jewett, N.Y., June 28, 1846; H.C., '69; U.T.S., '69–'72; Ord. (Presb.), Nov. 20, '72; Pas., Pleasant Mount, Pa., '72–5; S.S., Scranton, Pa., '75——.

Thomas Lawrence Sexton; b., Poland, O., Mar. 29, 1839; W.F.J.C., '69; N.W.T.S., '69–'71; U.T.S., '71–2; Ord. (Presb.), May 9, '72; Pas., Troy, N.Y., '72–5; S.S., New-London, Io., '75——.

David Lyle Smart; b., Brooklyn, N.Y., May 9, 1841; B.T.S., '69–'71; U.T.S., '71–2;

Lewis French Stearns; b., Newburyport, Mass., Mar. 10, 1847; C.N.J., '67; P.T.S., '68–'70; U.T.S., '71–2; Ord. (Presb.), Oct. 14, '73; Pas., Norwood, N.J., '73–5; Pas., Albion, Mich., '76——.

Rodney Lawrence Tabor; b., Quincy, Mass., Sep. 21, 1845; W.C., '69; U.T.S., '69–'72; Ord. (Cong.), July 3, '72; S.S. & Pas., West-Hartland, Ct., '72–4; S.S. & Pas. (Presb.), Alameda, Cal., '74——.

Josiah Tetley; b., Bolton, Eng., Dec. 5, 1839; U.T.S., '69–'72; Ord. (M.E.), Ap. 25, '74; S.S., Callicoon, N.Y., '73–4; S.S., Shavertown, N.Y., '74——.

James Marshall Thompson; b., Carlisle, Ind., Aug. 29, 1845; Han.C., '69; U.T.S., '69–'72; Ord. (Presb.), May 23, '72; Ch. Miss., N. York City, '72–3; S.S. & Pas., Philadelphia (Mantua), Pa., '74——.

Edward Payson Whallon; b., Putnamville, Ind., Mar. 30, 1849; Han.C., '68; N.W.T.S., '69–'71; U.T.S., '71–2; Ord. (Presb.), Ap. 25, '71; S.S., Kasson & Dodge Centre, Minn., '70–1; Pas., Liberty, Ind., '72——.

Joseph Henry Whitehead; b., New-York City, Oct. 18, 1847; W.C., '69; U.T.S., '69–'72; Ord. (R.D.), July 23, '72; Pas., Pompton Plains, N.J., '72——.

Oscar Ubestro Whitford; b., Plainfield, N.Y., May 12, 1837; Alf.U., '63; Alf.T.S., '69–'70; U.T.S., '70–2; Ord. (7th D. Bap.), Sep. 22, '72; S.S & Pas., Farina, Ill., '72——.

33.

Charles Newton Fitch; b., Geneva, O., Jan. 25, 1846; O.C., '69; U.T.S., '69–'70; N.H.T.S., '70–2; Ord. (Cong.), May 12, '74; Pas. N. Cornwall, Ct., '74——.

John Boyd Johnston; b., Hillsboro, O., Ap. 4, 1848; Mi.U., '68; L.T.S., '69–'70; U.T.S., '70–1; Ord. (Presb.), Dec. 30, '73; S.S., Hillsboro, O., '72–3; Pas., McArthur, O., '73–4; W.C., Hillsboro, O., '75–6; W.C., Edgewood, Ill., '76——.

*Chester Winthrop Jones; b., Galva, Ill., Mar. 17, 1845; K.C., '69; U.T.S., '69–'71; Died, Galva, Ill., May 4, '72.

Charles Ami Lador; b., St. Croix, Switz., June 17, 1842; U.T.S., '69–'71; Tea. & Prof., East Hampton, Mass., '71——.

Thomas Chalmers Murray; b., Elizabeth, N.J., Feb. 18, 1850; W.C., '69; U.T.S., '69–'71; P.T.S., '71–2; Halle, Ger., '72–3; Göttingen, Ger., '73–5; As.Prof., J.H.U., Baltimore, Md., '76——.

Charles Benjamin Ogilvie; b., Muscatine, Io., Jan. 14, 1845; C.N.J., '67; N.W.T.S., '69–'71; U.T.S., '71–2; N.W.T.S., '72; Law, Muscatine, Io., '73——.

Samuel N. Oviatt; b., Milford, Ct., Sep. 17, ...; U.T.S., '69–'70.

Howard Royce Parmelee; b., Twinsburgh, O., Mar. 18, 1846; W.R.C., '69; L.T.S., '69–'70; U.T.S., '70–1; L.T.S., '71–2; Ord. (Presb.), Ap. 10, '73; S.S., Hampden & McArthur, O., '72–3; S.S. (Cong.), Mesopotamia, O., '73——.

Henry Alanson Starks; b., Troy, N.Y., Aug. 6, 1846; W.U., '69; U.T.S., '69–'71; Bos.T.S., '71–2; Ord (M.E.), ..., '75; S.S., Schaghticoke, N.Y., '72–3; Pas., Hart's Falls, N.Y., '73–5; S.S., Gloversville, N.Y., '75——.

Henry Randall Waite; b., Utica, N.Y., Dec. 16, 1846; H.C., '68; U.T.S., '69–'70; Ord. (Cong.), ...,..; Rome, Italy, '73–4; .. N. York City, '75——.

David Winters; b., Co. Monaghan, Ireland, Jan. 4, 1842; K.C., Ont., '68; P.T.S., '69–'71; U.T.S., '71–2; Ord. (Presb.), Ap. 30, '72; Pas., Paterson, N.J., '72–4; Pas., Philadelphia, Pa., '74——.

Robert McEwen Woods; b., Enfield, Mass., Jan. 24, 1847; A.C., '69; U.T.S., '69–'70; And.T.S., '70–1; Tea., Amherst, Mass., '71–3; Tea., Enfield, Mass., '73——.

Claiborne Addison Young; b., Boone Co., Ind., May 29, 1845; Wab.C., '69; U.T.S., '69–'70; .., Maple Springs, Tex., .. ——. 13.

1873.

Francis Herbert Bagley; b., Boston, Mass., Jan. 16, 1840; H.C., '70; U.T.S., '70–3; Ord. (Presb.), May 20, '73; Pas. (R.D.), Greenburgh, N.Y., '73–5; O.S., New-Brighton (S.I), N.Y., '75–6; O.S., River Vale, N. J., '76——.

ISAAC BAIRD; b., Onslow, N. Scotia, Aug. 22, 1841; P.T.S., '70–1; U.T.S., '71–3; Ord. (Presb.), Mar. 3, '73; F.M., Odanah, Wis., '73——.

JOHN ALBERT BALDWIN; b., Detroit, Mich., June 27, 1847; U.M., '70; U.T.S., '70–3; Ord. (Cong.), Oct. 14, '75; Pas., New-Baltimore, Mich., 75——.

WILLIAM MELANCTHON BARTHOLOMEW; b., Valparaiso, Ind., Ap. 7, 1845; C.N.J., '70; U.T.S., '70–3; U. Leipzig, Ger., '73–4; S.S., Arlington Heights, Ill., '75——.

FRANK TAPPAN BAYLEY; b., Boston, Mass., Aug. 19, 1846; U.T.S., '69–'70, '71–3; Ord. (Cong.), Sep. 3, '73; Pas., Canandaigua, N.Y., '73——.

ALBERT BUSHNELL; b., Salisbury, Ct., Sep. 30, 1847; U.T.S., '70–3; Ord. (Cong.), ..., '73; Pas., Chicago, Ill., '73——.

ARCHIBALD ALEXANDER CONEY; b., Princetown, N.Y., July 4, 1844; U.T.S., '70–3; Inv., West-Milton, N.Y., '73——.

CHARLES HERBERT DANIELS; b., Lyme, N.H., July 6, 1847; A.C., '70; U.T.S., '70–3; Ord. (Cong.), Nov. 20, '73; Pas., Montaigne, Mass., '73——.

HENRY ADOLPHUS DAVENPORT; b., North-Stamford, Ct., Mar. 26, 1845; A.C., '70; U.T.S., '69–'70, '71–3; Ord. (Cong.), June 18, '73; Ch.Miss., N. York City, '73——.

BROWN HOPKINS EMERSON; b., Valley of Chester Co., Pa., Aug. 30, 1843; U.T.S., '70–3; Ord. (Presb.), Sep. 30, '73; S.S., Ridgebury, N.Y., '73–5; S.S., Litchfield, N.H., '75——.

AMZI BABBITT EMMONS; b., Chester, N.J., Nov. 9, 1846; A.C., '69; U.T.S., 69–'71, '72–3; Ord (Cong.), Oct. 28, '73; S.S., Stratton, Vt., '73–4; S.S., Jamaica, Vt., '74——.

WILLIAM LUTHER FINDLEY; b., New-Wilmington, Pa., Aug. 23, 1846; Westm.C., '65; P.T.S., '70–2; U.T.S., '72–3. Address, N. York City.

DONALD FLETCHER; b., Coburg, Ont., Sep. 29, 1849; K.C., Ont., '70; N.W.T.S., '70–2; U.T.S., '72–3; Ord. (Presb.), July 22, '73; Pas., N. York City (North), '73–5; Pas., Northville, Mich., '75–6; S.S., Chicago, Ill., '76——.

WILLIAM HOWARD FORD; b., Lebanon, N.Y., Sep. 12, 1848; U.T.S., '70–3; Ord. (Presb.), ..., '74; Pas. (R.D.), Fort Miller, N.Y., '75——.

JOSEPH MILLS GELSTON; b., Rushville, N.Y., June 27, 1848; U.M., '69; U.T.S., '70–3; Ord. (Presb.), Oct. 21, '73; Pas., Plymouth, Mich., '73–5; Pas., Pontiac, Mich., '75——.

JOHN GILLIS; b., Orwell, Prince Edward Island, Mar. 20, 1839; N.W.T.S., '70–1; U.T.S., '71–3; Ord. (Presb.), Ap. 28, '73; F.M., Wewoka, Ind.T., '73——.

*ROBERT BEALS HALL; b., Ashfield, Mass., Dec. 30, 1845; W.C., '70; U.T.S., '71–3; Ord. (Cong.), Nov. 13, '73; Pas., Wolfeborough, N.H., '73–5; Pas., Cambridgeport, Mass., '75–6; Died, do., Nov. 2, '76.

EDGAR AUGUSTUS HAMILTON; b., Hamilton's Settlement, Wis., Mar. 8, 1841; O.C., '70; U.T.S., '70-3; Ord. (Presb.), Oct. 28, '73; Pas., Deckertown, N.J., '73——.

JAMES HART HOADLEY; b., Collinsville, N.Y., Feb. 28, 1847; H.C., '70; U.T.S., '70-3; Ord. (Presb.), Mar. 13, '73; Ch. Miss., N. York City, '73——.

SAMUEL WHITTLESEY HOWLAND; b., Jaffna, Ceylon, Mar. 4, 1848; A.C., '70; U.T.S.,'70-3; Ord. (Cong.), May 7, '73; F.M., Manepy, Ceylon,'73——.

MYRON WINSLOW HUNT; b., Madras, India, Dec. 5, 1846; A.C., '70; U.T.S., '70-3; Ord. (Cong.), June 26, '73; F.M., Pautingfoo, China, '73——.

SAMUEL MACAULEY JACKSON; b., New-York City, June 19, 1851; C.C. N.Y., '70; P.T.S., '70-1; U.T.S., '71-3; Europe, '73-5. Address, N. York City.

THOMAS DARLINGTON JESTER; b., Dilworthtown, Pa., Nov. 17, 1842; H.C., '70; U.T.S., '70-3; Ord. (Presb.), Jan. 15, '74; S.S. & Pas., Middletown, & Glen Riddle, Pa., '76——.

CALEB E. JONES; b., Danville, Ky., Mar. 21, 1844; Cr.C., '71; D.T.S., '70-2; U.T.S., '72-3; Ord. (Presb.), ..., '73; S.S., Belleville & Scotch Plains, Kan., '73——.

KENNETH FRANK JUNOR; b., St. Mary's, Ont., Aug. 31, 1846; U.C.T., '70; K.C., Ont., '70-2; U.T.S., '72-3; Ord. (Presb.), ..., '73; Pas., Hamilton, Bermuda, '73——.

JAMES KIRKLAND; b., Richland, Mich., July 30, 1844; Cor.U., '69; U.T.S., '70-3.

APPLETON PARK LYON; b., Springfield, Pa., June 12, 1840; A.C., '70; U.T.S., '70-3; Tea., N. York City, '73——.

EUGENE RUSSELL MILLS; b., Lyme, N.H., June 19, 1841; Wab.C.,'70; L.T.S., '70-1; U.T.S., '71-3; Ord. (Presb.), Nov. 6, '43; Pas., Lyons, Io., '73——.

WILLIAM PLESTED; b., Chatham, Ont., Dec. 16, 1842; N.W.U., '70; U.T.S., '70-3; Ch.Miss., N. York City, '73——.

JAMES PERRY SCHELL; b., Iowa City, Io., Jan. 29, 1845; Io.U., '70; N.W.T.S., '70-1; U.T.S., '71-3; Ord. (Presb.), Ap. 16, '73; S.S., Alta City, Mich., '73-4; S.S., Woodburn, Io., '74-5; S.S., Iowa City, Io., '75——.

HOMER SHEELEY; b., Millersburgh, O., Jan. 11, 1841; Mi.U., '70; D.T.S., '70-2; U.T.S., '72-3; Ord. (Presb.), June 10, '74; Pas., Perryville, Loudonville, & Clear Fork, O., '74-5.

LAURENS TILTON SHULER; b., Amsterdam, N.Y., Sep. 2, 1849; U.T.S., '69-'71, '72-3; Ord. (Presb.), Oct. 28, '73; Pas., Wantage, N.J., '73-6; W.C., Schenectady, N.Y., '76; S.S., West Town, N. Y., '76——.

ANGUS SINCLAIR; b, Quebec, Canada, May 28, 1842; U.C.T., '70; K.C., Ont., '70-2; U.T.S., '72-3; Tea., Canada, '73-5; Tea., Windsor, Ont., '76——.

WILLIAM HENRY SWIFT ; b., Geneva, N.Y., Feb. 2, 1848 ; A.C., '70 ; U.T.S., '70-3 ; Ord. (Presb.), May 7, '74 ; Pas., Wilkesbarre, Pa., '74——.

JOHN WESLEY TALBOT ; b., Pleasant Hill, Mo., Oct. 8, 1841 ; Han.C., '70 ; D.T.S., '70-2 ; U.T.S., '72-3 ; S.S. (Presb.), Wadesburgh, Mo., '73-5 ; Agric., Pleasant Hill, Mo., '75-6 ; S.S., Dawn and Coloma, Mo., '76——.

ISAAC BUCKLEW TEMBROOK ; b., Newark, N.J., Mar. 18, 1836 ; Lin.U., '70 ; U.T.S., '70-3 ; Ord. (Presb.), Nov. 12, '73.

WILLIAM DAVY THOMAS ; b., Carmarthen, Wales, Jan. 5, 1843 ; C.N.J., '70 ; P.T.S., '70-1 ; U.T.S., '71-3 ; Ord. (Presb.), Ap. 30, '76 ; S.S. & Pas., Leavenworth, Kan., '75——.

ADONIRUM JUDSON TITSWORTH ; b., Shiloh, N.J., Oct. 23, 1845 ; A.C., '70 : U.T.S., '70-3 ; Ord. (Cong.), June 3, '73 ; Pas., Westfield, Mass., '73——.

MATTHEW WADE ; b., Ross, O., Oct. 18, 1848 ; Mi.U., '70 ; U.T.S., '70-3 ; Ord. (Presb.), ..., . . ; S.S., Perry, Kan., '74-5 ; S.S., Holton, Kan., '75——.

CHARLES AUGUSTUS WOOD ; b., Chicago, Ill., Aug. 13, 1835 ; U.Va., '54 ; N.W.T.S., '70-2 ; U.T.S., '72-3 ; Ord. (Presb.), July 9, '73 ; Ev., Silver City, N. Mex., '73-5 ; S.S., Vienna, Rolling Prairie, & Lone Tree, Kan., '75——.

40.

NELSON AYRES ; b., Sing Sing, N.Y., Mar. 20, 1848 ; K.C., '70 ; U.T.S., '70-1 ; Na.T.S., '71-3 ; Ord. (Ep.), June 1, '73 ; S.S., Bryan, Tex., '73 ; Rec., Corpus Christi, Tex., '74——.

CHARLES KEELER CANFIELD ; b., Stevensville, Pa., Mar. 16, 1843 ; L.F.C., '70 ; U.T.S., '70-2 ; Ord. (Presb.), Nov. . ., '72 ; S.S. & Pas., Bowman's Creek, Pa., '72——.

CHARLES BATEMAN GILLETTE ; b., Perrinton, N.Y., Mar. 25, 1845 ; U.C., '70 ; U.T.S., '70-2 ; Aub.T.S., '72-3 ; Ord. (Presb.), Oct. 22, '73 ; Pas., Emporium, Pa., '73-5 ; S.S., Milwaukee, Wis., '75 ; S.S., Campbelltown, N.Y., '75——.

JACOB WINANS HADDEN ; b., Rahway, N.J., May 16, 1844 ; Bel.C., '70 ; U.T.S., '70-1 ; Address, Elizabeth, N.J.

CHARLES JOSHUA KETCHAM JONES ; b., Franklin, N.J., July 13, 1845 ; R.C., '70 ; U.T.S., '70-2 ; Ord. (Cong.), Ap. 2, '73 ; S.S. & Pas., Orient (L.I.), N.Y., '72-4 ; S.S., Brooklyn, N.Y., '74-5 ; S.S., Nantucket, Mass., '75——.

CHARLES HARVEY LITTLE ; b., Madison, Ind., Sep. 20, 1848 ; Wab.C., '70 ; U.T.S., '70-1 ; L.T.S., '71-3 ; Ord. (Presb.), Ap. 7, '74 ; S.S., Lawrenceburgh, Ind., '73-5 ; Pas., College Hill, O., '75——.

BENJAMIN FRANKLIN NEWTON ; b., Swanton, Vt., Oct. 20, 1841 ; Hi.C., '70 ; U.T.S., '70-3 ; Ord. (Ep.), June 14, '73 ; Rec., Ipswich, Mass., '73——.

GEORGE STERLING ; b., New-Milford, Ct., July 27, 1842 ; A.C., '70 ; U.T.S., '70-2 ; And.T.S., '72-3 ; Ord. (Cong.), ..., '74 ; S.S., Wayland, Mich., '74——.

THOMAS DANLY SUPLEE; b., West-Philadelphia, Pa., Ap. 17, 1846; C.N.J., '70; U.T.S., '70-1; P.T.S., '71-3; .., Philadelphia, Pa., '73-5.

ALBERT FRANCIS TENNEY; b., South-Braintree, Mass., July 24, 1847; A.C., '69; U.T.S., '70-2; Tea., Sing Sing, N.Y., '73——. 10.

1874.

CHARLES ELMER ALLISON; b., Florida, N.Y., July 21, 1847; H.C., '70; U.T.S., '71-4; Ch. Miss., Yonkers, N.Y., '74——.

ABRAHAM J. BEEKMAN; b., New-York City, Oct. 21, 1838; U.T.S., '70-2, '73-4; Ord. (R.D.), ..., '74; S.S., Norris, Ill., '74-5.

JAMES PAUL BRYANT; b., Poughkeepsie, N.Y., Mar. 25, 1839; U.C., '70; U.T.S., '70-2, '73-4.

THEODORE FRELINGHUYSEN BURNHAM; b., Deckertown, N.J., Aug. 31, 1845; U.N.Y., '71; U.T.S., '71-4; Ord. (Presb.), May 28, '74; Pas., Freeport (L.I.), N.Y., '74——.

CHARLES DODD CRANE; b., West-Bloomfield, N.J., Feb. 12, 1849; C.N.J., '69; U.T.S., '71-4; Ord. (Cong.), June 11, '74; S.S., Clinton & Benton, Me., '73; Pas., Clinton, Me., '74-5; S.S., Waterville, Me., '75——.

ELBERT WILMOT CUMINGS; b., Palmyra, N.Y., Nov. 8, 1847; H.C., '71; U.T.S., '71-4; S.S., Fairville, N.Y., '75——.

ALLEN FORD DE CAMP; b., Charlottesburgh, N.J., Feb. 9, 1848; W.C., '71; Aub.T.S., '71-3; U.T.S., '73-4; Ord. Presb.), Dec. .., '74; S.S. & Pas., Shawano, Wis., '73——.

ELIJAH WINCHESTER DONALD; b., Andover, Mass., July 31, 1848; A.C., '69; P.E.D.S., '71; U.T.S., '72-4; Ord. (Ep.), Oct. 17, '75; Ass't Min. & Rec., N. York City, '74——.

JAMES TOOKER FORD; b., Groton, Mass., Aug. 3, 1848; W.C., '71; Aub.T.S., '71-2; U.T.S., '72-4; Ord. (Presb.), June 6, '76; S.S., Packwaukie & Oxford, Wis., '74——.

JOHN KENNEDY FOWLER; b., Covington, N.Y., Sep. 22, 1848; U.R., '70; U.T.S., '70-1, '72-4; Ord. (Presb.), Nov. 10, '74; Pas., Caledonia, N.Y., '74——.

JAMES ABRAHAM GERHARD; b., Host, Pa., Sep. 7, 1849; F. & M.C., '71; U.T.S., '71-4; S.S. (Presb.), North-Platte, Neb., '76——.

FISHER GUTELIUS; b., Mifflinburgh, Pa., July 17, 1845; L.F.C., '71; U.T.S., '71-4; Ord. (Presb.), July .., '74; Pas., Moscow, N.Y., '74——.

MATTHIAS LORING HAINES; b., Aurora, Ind., May 4, 1850; Wab.C., '71; U.T.S., '71-4; Ord. (R.D.), May 27, '74; Pas., Astoria (L.I.), N.Y., '74——.

JOHN PHILETUS HALE; b., Milwaukee, Wis., Aug. 23, 1850; Bel.C., '71; U.T.S., '71-4; Ord. (Presb.), Oct. 13, '74; S.S. & Pas., Jersey City (Claremont), N.J., '74——.

Edward Cleeves Hood; b., Lawrenceville, Pa., Ap. 21, 1848; C.N.J., '68; U.T.S., '71-4; Ord. (Presb.), May 5, '74; Ev., Passaic, N.J., '74-5; S.S., Hingham, Mass., '75——.

Francis Bickford Hornbrooke; b., Wheeling, W. Va., May 7, 1849; O.U., '70; Har.D.S., '71-3; U.T.S., '73-4; Ord. (Cong.), Aug. 27, '74; Pas., East-Hampton, Ct., '74; Pas. (Unit.), Weston, Mass., '76——.

Henry Thomas Hunter; b., New-York City, Dec. 12, 1833; U.N.Y., '52; U.T.S., '52-4; Tea., N. York City, '58-'60; Prin., Stockbridge, Mass., '62-4; Do., Bath, Me., '67-8; U.T.S., '70-1, 73-4; Ord. (Presb.), Dec. 5, '76; S.S., Williston, Vt., '74; S.S., Hartland, Vt., '75; Pas., N. York City, '76——.

Amos Augustus Kiehle; b., Dansville, N.Y., Mar. 22, 1847; H.C., '71; U.T.S., '71-4; Ord. (Presb.), Oct. 21, '74; Pas., Minneapolis, Minn., '74——.

Charles Leaman; b., Leaman Place, Pa., Sep. 3, 1845; C.N.J., '71; U.T.S., '71-4; Ord. (Presb.), June 17, '74; F.M, Shanghai, China, '74——.

Edward Payson Linnell; b., Granville, O., Ap. 18, 1846; H.C., '71; U.T.S., '71-4; Ord. (Presb.), Oct. 8, '74; Pas., German Valley, N.J., '74——.

William Augustus Lynch; b., Baltimore, Md., Mar. 30, 1850; Lin.U., '71; U.T.S., '71-4; Ord. (Presb.), May 5, '74; Pas., Elizabeth, N.J., '74-6; Pas., Troy, N.Y., '76——.

William Chalmers Macbeth; b., Cumberland, Md., Dec. 25, 1852; U.T.S., '71-4: Residenc, Morgantown, W.Va., '74——.

William Freeman Matthews; b., Bethel, Vt., Oct. 31, 1849; U.M., '70; U.T.S., '71-4; Ord. (Presb.), Dec. 20, '74; Ch.Miss., N. York City, '74——.

Duncan Livingston McKechnie; b., Cheltenham, Ont., May 31, 1842; U.C.T., '71; K.C., Ont., '71-2; U.T.S., '72-4; Ord. (Presb.), Sep. 28, '75; Pas., Bothwell, Ont., '75——.

John Calvin Miller; b., Apple Creek, O., Sep. 12, 1844; Woos.U., '71; U.T.S., '71-4; Ord. (Presb.), June 30, '74; Pas., Garrett, & S.S., Sugar Valley & Reader, Kan., '74——.

Oliver Cromwell Morse; b., Hudson, N.Y., Sep. 18, 1847; Y.C., '68; U.T.S., '68-9; P.T.S., '69-'70, '72-3; U.T.S., '73-4; O.S., N. York City, '74——.

Norman Ferdinand Nickerson; b., South-East, N.Y., Nov. 26, 1836; U.T.S., '71-4; Ord. (Presb.), Oct. 7, '75; Pas., Evans' Mills (Le Ray), Pa., '75——.

William D. Perry; b., Hunter, N.Y., Nov. 1, 1844; A.C., '70; U.T.S., '70-2, '73-4; Ord. (R.D.), ..., '74; Pas., E. St. John's, Laurel Hill, N.Y., '74-5; W.C., Hudson, N.Y., '75——.

Mellen David Stone; b., Chester, Vt., June 7, 1848; D.C., '70; U.T.S., '70-1; H.T.S., '71-2; U.T.S., '73-4; S.S., Windham, Vt., '74-5; Inv. & W.C., do., '75——.

Charles Robert Stroh; b., ..., .., Jan. 7, 1850; U.T.S., '71-4.

DAVID JEWETT WALLER, JR. ; b., Bloomsburgh, Pa., June 17, 1846; L.F.C., '70; P.T.S., '71-2; U.T.S., '72-4; Ord. (Presb.), ..., .., '74; Pas., Philadelphia, Pa., '74-6; Ev., Bloomsburgh, Pa., '76——.

JOHN LESTER WELLS ; b., Pomeroy, O., Jan. 13, 1846; Ma.C., '71; U.T.S., '71-4; Ord. (Presb.), Sep. 15, '74; Ch. Miss., Newark, N.J., '74——.

ROBERT HENRY WILKINSON ; b., New-York City, Mar. 23, 1844 ; U.T.S., '70-1, '72-4; Ord. (Cong.), Aug. 25, '74; Pas., North-Stamford, Ct., '74-5 ; S.S. (Presb,), Plymouth, Mich., '76——. 33.

THOMAS McCULLOCK CHRYSTIE; b., Colchester, N. Scotia, Mar. 14, 1848; Dal.C., '68; U.T.S., '71-3; Ord. (Presb.), Oct. 30, '73; F.M., Trinidad, W. Ind., '74——.

*LUTHER BARTON ; b., ..., .., Feb. 9, 1850 ; R.C., '70 ; U.T.S., '71-4; Tea., N. York City, '74-6; Died, Delaware Water Gap, Pa., Aug. 11, '76——.

JOHN HOLLEY CLARK ; b., Lyons, N.Y., Feb. 21, 1850; U.C., '70; U.T.S., '71-2 ; Residence, Lyons, N. Y., '73——.

GIDEON STEBBINS WHITE CRAWFORD ; b., Knoxville, Tenn., Aug. 20, 1849; Mv.C., '71; U.T.S., '71-3; L.T.S., '73-4; Ord. (Presb.), Ap. 15, '75; Prof., Mv.C., Maryville, Tenn., '75——.

MEIGS VELPEAU CROUSE ; b., Dayton, Ind., Aug. 8, 1851; Wab.C., '71; U.T.S., '71-2; L.T.S., '72-3; Ord. (Presb.), Nov. 2, '75; Pas., Franklin, O., '75——.

HENRY MARTYN GOODELL ; b., Ann Arbor, Mich., Oct. 20, 1846 ; U.M., '71; C.T.S., '71-2; U.T.S., '72-3; C.T.S., '73-4; S.S., Kankakee, Ill., .., ——.

CHARLES LEMON HALL ; b., Winchester, Eng., Sep. 18, 1847; C.C.N.Y., '66; U.T.S., '71-2; And.T.S., '72-3 ; Ord. (Cong.), Feb. 22, '76 ; H.M., Springfield, D.T., '74-6 ; F.M., do., '76——.

JOSHUA ASBURY HILL ; b., Washington, D.C., Nov. 29, 1846 ; Lin.U., '71 ; U.T.S., '71-3.

JOSEPH HAMPTON LEONARD; b., Chicago, Ill., Ap. 13, 1847 ; U.T.S., '71-2.

RALPH WARDLAW LILLIE ; b., New-York City, May 8, 1841 ; U.T.S., '71-3.

GEORGE MICHAEL ; b., Shawnee, Pa., Mar. 15, 1843 ; Pa.C., '71 ; U.T.S., '71-2 ; N.H.T.S., '72-4; Ord. (Cong.), July 8, '74; S.S., Stanton, Mich., '74-5; S.S., Milton Mills, N.H., '75-6; Pas., Freeport, Me., '76——.

WATSON BIRCHARD MILLARD; b., Dexter, Mich., Sep. 13, 1848 ; U.M., '71; C.T.S., '71-2; U.T.S., '72-3; C.T.S., '73-4; Ord. (Cong.), June 18, '74; Pas., St. Louis, Mo., '74-5 ; S.S., Memphis, Tenn., '75——.

SPENCER SUMMERFIELD ROCHE; b., Philadelphia, Pa., Jan. 22, 1849; C.C., '70; U.T.S., '71-3; Ep.T.S., '73-4; Ord. (Ep.), May 31,, '74; S.S., Brooklyn, N.Y., '74——.

THOMAS SMALLWOOD SAMSON; b., Washington, D.C., Oct. 26, 1845; Cn.C., '71; U.T.S., '71-3; N.T.I., '74-5; Ord. (Bap.), ..., '75; .., Newton, Mass., '75——.

WALTER SCOTT; b., Sing-Sing, N.Y., Nov. 29, 1846; U.C., '68; U.T.S., '72-3; Tea., Sing Sing, N.Y., '73-6; Ord. (Bap.), Nov. 9, '76.

WALTER QUINCY SCOTT; b., Dayton, O., Dec. 19, 1845; L.F.C., '69; U.T.S., '72-3; Ord. (Presb.), Feb. 15, '74; Pas., Philadelphia, Pa., '74——.

EDWARD DUNN VANCE; b., Fairview, Pa., Sep. 3, 1846; W.R.C., '71; U.T.S., '71-3; L.T.S., '73-4; Ord. (Presb.), Dec. 16, '74; Pas., Kinsman, O., '74——. 17.

1875.

FRANKLIN PEASE BERRY; b., Dover, N.J., Feb. 26, 1846; C.N.J., '72; U.T.S., '72-5; Inv., Experiment Mills, Pa., '75-6; Do., Dover, N.J., '76——.

JAMES GRAY BOLTON; b., Co. Derry, Ireland, Mar. 17, 1847; U.T.S., '72-5; Ord. (Presb.), June 28, '75; Ch. Miss., Philadelphia, Pa., '75——.

WALTER AUGUSTUS BROOKS; b., Leroy, N.Y., Aug. 2, 1849; U.M., '72; U.T.S., '72-5; Ord. (Presb.), Oct. 14, '75; Pas., Trenton, N.J., '75——.

DAVID HENSHEY CAMPBELL; b., Davidsburgh, Pa., July 28, 1846; L.F.C., '72; U.T.S., '72-5; Ord. (Presb.), June 17, '75; Pas., Ansonville (Fruit Hill), Pa., '75——.

CHARLES NEAL CATE; b., Reading, Mass., Jan. 24, 1849; U.T.S., '72-5; Ord. (Cong.), Aug. 18, '75; S.S., North & East Woodstock, Ct., '75——.

WASHINGTON CHOATE; b., Essex, Mass., Jan. 17, 1846; A.C., '70; U.T.S., '73-5; Ord. (Cong.), Sep. 29, '75; Pas., Manchester, N.H., '75——.

JOHN COWAN; b., Parkesburgh, Pa., Mar. 26, 1848; L.F.C., '71; U.T.S., '72-5; Ord. (Presb.), May 25, '75; S.S., Essex & Williston, Vt., '75——.

ALLEN GALCHE DANIELS; b., Urbana, O., Aug. 9, 1850; U.W., '72; U.T.S., '72-5; Ord. (Presb.), Ap. 14, '75; Tea., Santa Fé, N. Mex., '75; Pas., Humboldt, Kan., '76——.

JOHN HUSS EASTMAN; b., Sandy Hill, N.Y., Aug. 23, 1849; A.C., '69; U.T.S., '72-5; Ord. (Presb.), July 8, '75; Pas., Katonah, N.Y., '75——.

DANIEL ARUNAH FERGUSON; b., Auburn, N.Y., July 10, 1850; H.C., '71; U.T.S., '72-5; Ord. (Presb.), Feb. 24, '76; S.S. & Pas., Hammond, N.Y., '75——.

WILLISON BOWERS FRENCH; b., Delaware, O., Mar. 17, 1850; Ken.C., '72; U.T.S., '72-5; Ord. (Ep.), Dea., June 23, '75; S.S., Wooster, O., '75——.

WILLIAM FRIZZELL; b., Georgetown, Ont., Ap. 30, 1844; K.C., Ont., '71; Do., Theo. Dep., '72–3; U.T.S., '73–5; Res. Lic., do., '75–6; C.M., N. York City, '75–6; Europe, '76——.

EDWIN FINNEY FULTON; b., Philadelphia, Pa., May 16, 1846; U.Pa., '72; U.T.S., '72–5; Ord. (Presb.), Oct. 12, '75; Pas., Gap, Pa., '75——.

JOHN SCOON GARDNER; b., Harlingen, N.J., Nov. 1, 1850; C.N.J., '71; U.T.S., '72–5; Ord. (R. D.), Aug. 23, '76; S.S., Morris Plains, N.J., '75–6; Pas., Middleburgh, N.Y., '76——.

GEORGE REM GARRETSON; b., Jersey City, N.J., May 21, 1850; R.C., '70; N.B.T.S., '70–1; U.T.S., '71–3; Europe, '73–4; U.T.S., '74–5; Ord. (R. D.), Dec. 1, '75; Pas., Long Island City & Laurel Hill (L.I.), N.Y., '75——.

JOSEPH FRANKLIN GIBBS; b., Blanford, Mass., Jan. 7, 1845; O.T.S., '72–4; U.T.S., '74–5; Ord. (Cong.), Dec. 16, '75; O.S., Griffin's Mills, N.Y., '75–6; S.S., East Hamburgh, N.Y., '76——.

JAMES ISAAC GOOD; b., York, Pa., Dec. 31, 1850; L.F.C., '72; U.T.S., '72–5; Ord. (G.R.), June 16, '75; Pas., York, Pa., '75——.

JOHN C. GOURLEY; b., Murraysville, Pa., Mar. 14, 1849; W.&.J.C., '72; W.T.S., '72–4; U.T.S., '74–5; O.S., Murraysville, Pa., '75–6; Pas. E., Cameron & Lathrop, Mo., '76——.

HENRY CHAPIN GRANGER; b., Great Barrington, Mass., Dec. 21, 1847; U.M., '71; U.T.S., '72–5; S.S. (Cong.), Mill River, Mass., '75–6.

JAMES WINTHROP HAGEMAN; b., Nyack, N.Y., Mar. 18, 1852; C.N.J., '72; U.T.S., '72–5; Ord. (Presb.), May 13, '75; S.S., Wausau, Wis., '75——.

LYMAN EDWIN HANNA; b., Lodi, O., July 5, 1847; W.R.C., '72; Aub.T.S., '72–3; U.T.S., '73–5; Ord. (Presb.), Sep. 20, '75; S.S., Clayton & Dover, Mich., '75——.

ARTHUR JOHNSON; b., Newark, N.J., July 22, 1848; C.N.J., '72; P.T.S., '72–3; U.T.S., '73–5; S.S. (Presb.), Nanticoke, Wanamie, & Shickshinny, Pa., '75——.

CALVIN KEYSER; b., Bellaire, O., Jan. 30, 1846; A.C., '71; U.T.S., '71–3, '74–5; Ord. (Cong.), Dec. 28, '75; Pas., Fall River, Mass., '75——.

ACHILLES LYSANDER LODER; b., South-Whitehall, Pa., Mar. 10, 1848; C.N J., '72; P.T.S., '72–3; U.T.S., '73–5; H.M., Queensville, Ont., '75; S.S., Prescott, Wis., '75; S.S., Milwaukee, Wis., '76——.

BRAINERD TAYLOR MCCLELLAND; b., Oberlin, O., Feb. 11, 1845; O.C., '69; O.T.S., '72–4; U.T.S., '74–5; Ord. (Presb.), Ap. 9, '75; S.S., Brownwood, Tex., '75——.

CLINTON DONALD MCDONALD; b., Glasgow, Scotland, June 17, 1842; K.C., Ont., '72–4; U.T.S., '74–5; Ord. (Presb.), Nov. 23, '75; Pas., Point Edward, Ont., '75——.

STEWART MEANS; b., Steubenville, O., Aug. 4, 1852; U.T.S., '72–5; Cam.T.S., '75–6; Ord. (Ep.), Dea., June 24, '75.

WALTER SCOTT PETERSON; b., Canoga, N.Y., Dec. 20, 1848; H.C., '72; U.T.S., '72–5; Ord. (Presb.), Sep. 22, '75; S.S., Brandts, Pa., '75——.

ISAAC MCKENDREE PITTENGER; b., Mansfield, O., Nov. 14, 1843; Bald.U., '72; U.T.S., '72–5; Ord (Presb.), June 9, '75; Pas., Breckville, O., '75——.

CHARLES BENJAMIN RAMSDELL; b, New-York City, June 12, 1843; Y.C., '72; P.T.S., '72–3; U.T.S., '73–5; Ord. (Presb.), Dec. 13, '75; Pas., Washington, D.C., '75——.

WILLIAM OTIS RUSTON; b., New-York City, Dec. 6, 1852; C.C.N.Y., '72; U.T.S., '72–5; Ord. (Presb.), Oct. 5, '75; Pas., Fair Mount, N.J., '75——.

GEORGE NICOL SMITH; b., Seneca, N.Y., July 29, 1848; Hob.C., '72; U.T.S., '72–3; Edinburgh, Scotland, '73–4; U.T.S., '74–5; Ord. (Presb.), May 12, '76; S.S., Cañon City & Rosita, Col., '75——.

DANIEL STAVER; b., Dayton, O., Jan. 30, 1845; H.T.S., '71–2; U.T.S., '72–5; Ord. (Cong.), Feb. 19, 75; F.M., Cesarea, Syria, '75——.

CHARLES CUMMINGS STEARNS; b., West-Hartford, Ct., Dec. 10, 1850; Y.C., '72; U.T.S., '72–5; Ord. (Cong.), Sep. 20, '75; F.M., Smyrna, Turkey, Asia, '75——.

ALEXANDER C. STEWART; b., Sand Hill, Ont., Nov. 24, 1846; K.C., Ont., '72–3; U.T.S., '73–5; Ord. (Presb.), Oct. 13, '75; Pas., North-Gower, Ont., '75——.

HOWARD ARUNAH TALBOT; b., Claridon, O., Jan. 26, 1848; Y.C., '72; U.T.S., '72–5; Ord. (Presb.), May 4, '75; Ch., Miss., N. York City, '75——.

RODERICK TERRY; b., Brooklyn, N.Y., Ap. 1, 1849; Y.C., '70; U.T.S., '74–5; Ord. (Presb.), Nov. 9, '75; Pas., Peekskill, N.Y., '75——.

HENRY HOMER WASHBURN; b., Boston, Mass., Feb. 22, 1839; U.T.S., '72–5; Ord. (Ref.Ep.), Feb. 9, '76; Rec., Baltimore, Md., '75——.

CHARLES THEODORE WEITZEL; b., Buchan, Würtemberg, Ger., May 12, 1847; Y.C., '69; U.T.S., '74–5; Ord. (Cong.), Ap. 18, '76; S.S. & Pas., Norwich Town, Ct., '75——.

JAMES DELONG WILLIAMSON; b., Cleveland, O., Mar. 12, 1849; W.R.C., '70; And.T.S., '72–4; U.T.S., '74–5; Ord. (Presb.), Oct. 26, '75; S.S., & Pas., Norwalk, O., '75——.

DANIEL MORRIS WOOLLEY; b., Long Branch, N.J., Aug. 1, 1850; U.T.S., '71–4, '74–5; S.S. (Presb.), Cairo, N.Y., '75——. 41.

ALBERT FRANKLIN ABBOTT; b., Hillsborough, N.H., Dec. 15, 1847; M.C., '72; N.H.T.S., '72–3; U.T.S., '73–4.

THEODORE ELIJAH BURTON; b., Grinnell, Io., Dec. 20, 1850; O.C., '72; U.T.S., '72–3.

Albert Bigelow Carner; b., New-York City, Jan. 12, 1847; C.N.J., '68; U.T.S., '71-2, '73-4.

*John Conger Freeman; b., Haverstraw, N.Y., Mar. 1, 1851; U.N.Y., '72; P.T.S., '72-3; U.T.S., '73-4; Died, Haverstraw, N.Y., Jan. 11, '75.

Charles Cuthbert Hall; b., New-York City, Sep. 3, 1852; W.C., '72; U.T.S, '72-3; Ord. (Presb.), Dec. 2, '75; Pas., Newburgh, N.Y., '75——.

Thomas James Hamilton; b., Bristol, Pa., Sep. 1, 1849; U.T.S., '70-1, '73-4.

John Andrew Hanna; b., Rising Sun, Ind., Feb. 19, 1848; H.T.S., '71-3; U.T S., '74-5; Ord. (Cong.), Oct. 15, '75; S.S., Thompson, Ct., '75——.

Robert H. Kline; b., Pleasant Gap, Pa., Sep. 5, 1844; Pa.C., '71; U.T.S., '71-2, '73-4; Ph.T.S., '74-5; Ord. (Ep.), ..., '75; Rec., Pioche, Nev., '75——.

Hugh Maguire; b., Sligo, Ireland, Ap. 26, 1846; Ken.C., '71; U.T.S., '71-2, '73-4; Ord. (Presb.), Dec. 8, '74; H.M., Aylwin, Can., '74——.

Louis Henry Mitchell; b., Baltimore, Md., Feb. 8, 1846; U.W., '72; U.T.S., '72-3; Ord. (Presb.), Oct. .., '74; S.S., Cedarville & Rock River, Ill., '75——.

William Stratton Pryse; b., Palmyra, O., Ap. 26, 1849; Wab.C., '71; U.T.S., '72-3; L.T.S., '73-5; Ord. (Presb.), Oct. 21, '75; S.S., Belle Plaine & Jordan, Minn., '75——.

Luther Albert Swope; b., Hanover, Pa., Dec. 3, 1842; Muhl.C., '68; U.T.S., '72-3.

William Henry Tallmadge; b., Trumansburgh, N.Y., June 13, 1845; Cor.U., '71; Aub.T.S., '72-3; U.T.S., '73-4; S.F.T.S., '74-5; S.S., Woodbridge & Galt, Cal., '75——.

William Howell Thomas; b., Swansea, S. Wales, June 27, 1849; U.T.S., '71-2, '73-4.

Charles Austin Tibbals; b., Brooklyn, N.Y., Dec. 11, 1850; Y.C., '72; U.T.S., '72-4; Ord. (M.E.), ..., '75; S.S., Norwalk, Ct., '75——.

Joseph Harrison Wright; b., Mullagreenan, Ireland, July 19, 1849; U.C., '72; U.T.S., '72-4; Nbg. T.S., '74-5; Ord. (Presb.), May 26, '75; S.S., Davenport, N.Y., '75——. 16.

1876.

Enoch Benson; b., Bridgeton, N.J., Sep. 30, 1849; L.F.C., '73; U.T.S., '73-6; Ord. (Presb.), Nov. 1, '76; S.S., North-Bend & Maple Creek, Neb., '76——.

Sidney James Brownson; b., St. Lawrence Co., N.Y., Jan. 8, 1845; L.T.S., '73-5; U.T.S., '75-6; Ord. (Presb.), ..., '76; S.S., Scipio & Oak Grove, Ind., '76——.

Arthur Newell Bruen; b., Rockaway, N.J., Oct. 29, 1850; C.N.J., '72; P.T.S., '73-4; U.T.S., '74-6; S.S. (Presb.), Jasper, N.Y., '76——.

Edward Bryan; b., Port Chester, N.Y., Nov. 18, 1851; L.F.C., '71; W.T.S., '72-5; U.T.S., '75-6; Ord. (Presb.), Dec. 5, '76; Pas., St. Petersburgh, Pa., '76——.

Charles Edward Burns; b., Duncannon, Pa., Aug. 13, 1846; L.F.C., '73; U.T.S., '74-6; Ord.(Presb.), Nov. 13, '76; Pas. Beemerville, N.J., '76——.

George Larkin Clark; b., Tewksbury, Mass., Aug. 16, 1849; A.C., '72; N.H.T.S., '73-5; U.T.S., '75-6; F.M., ..., ——.

William Wynkoop Cook; b., Richbow, Pa., Nov. 21, 1843; R.C., '73; U.T.S., '73-6; Ch. Miss., Philadelphia, Pa., '76——.

Joseph Westby Earnshaw; b., Ravenfield, Yorkshire, Eng., Jan. 9, 1846; U.T.S., '73-6; Ch. Miss., N. York City, '76; Ord. (Presb.), Aug. 2, '76; Pas., Greenport (L.I.), N.Y., '76——.

George Alfred Ford; b., Aleppo, Syria, May 30, 1831; W.C., '72; U.T.S., '73-6; Ord. (Presb.), Nov. 13, '76; S.S., Ramapo, N.Y., '76——.

Henry Wisewell Gelston; b., Rushville, N.Y., Mar. 18, 1850; U.M., '73; U.T.S., '73-6; Ord. (Presb.), Oct. .., '76; Pas., Northville, Mich., '76——.

John Milton Hart; b., West-Cornwall, Ct., June 5, 1845; Y.C., '67; N.H.T.S., '73-5; U.T.S., '75-6.

Giles Parmelee Hawley; b., Potsdam, N.Y., July 13, 1848; U.C., '71; U.T.S., '74-6; Ord. (Presb.), Oct. 15, '76; Pas., Saratoga, N.Y., '76——.

James Wilson Hillman; b., Ulster Co., N.Y., Mar. 4, 1853; U.N.Y., '73; U.T.S., '73-6; Ord. (Presb.), Nov. 3, '76; Pas., Morris Plains, N.J., '76——.

James Howard Hoyt; b., Saratoga, N.Y., July 13, 1847; U.C., '73; U.T.S., '73-6; S.S. (R.D.), Greenburgh, N.Y., '76——.

John Hutchings; b., Portsmouth, Eng., June 20, 1848; U.W., '73; W.T.S., '73-5; U.T.S., '75-6; Ord. (R.D.), Nov. 28, '76; Pas., Bronxville, N.Y., '76——.

Henry Martyn Kellogg; b., New-Boston, N.H., Ap. 2, 1851; D.C., '73; P.T.S., '73-5; U.T.S., '75-6; S.S. (Cong.), North-Hadley, Mass., '76——.

John Thomas Lloyd; b., Melin-y-Wig, North-Wales, Aug. 15, 1850; U.T.S., '74-6; Ord. (Presb.), May 12, '76; Pas., Brooklyn (Green Point), N.Y., '76——.

Raymond De Witt Mallary; b., Fulton, N.Y., Sep. 28, 1851; A.C., '72; U.T.S., '73-6; Ord. (Cong.), Oct. 12, '76; Pas., Williamsport, Pa., '76——.

Eugene Lusette Mapes; b., Florida, N.Y., Jan. 17, 1847; U.C., '73; U.T.S., '73-6; Tea., N. York City, '76——.

Samuel McBride; b., Tandragee, Ireland, Nov. 5, 1847; U.T.S., '73-6; Ch. Miss., Newark, N.J., '76——.

Thomas McNinch; b., Turbotville, Pa., Aug. 6, 1843; L.F.C., '73; P.T.S., '73-5; U.T.S., '75-6; S.S. (Presb.), Wallace, Pa., '76——.

Henry Goodell Miller; b., Hartford, Ct., Aug. 11, 1848; U.T.S., '73-6; S.S. (Presb.), Minneapolis, , Kan., '76——.

Granville Webster Nims; b., Roxbury, N.H., July 17, 1848; A.C., '73; U.T.S., '73-6; S.S., ..., Ct., '76——.

HENRY ALANSON POWELL; b., Chatham, N.Y., Sep. 13, 1851; U.C., '73; U.T.S., '73-6; Ord. (R.D.), June 29, '76; Pas., Bushwick (L.I.), N.Y., '76——.

GEORGE JERMAIN RICHARDS; b., Hector, N.Y., Sep. 11, 1849; W.R.C., '72; P.T.S., '73-5; U.T.S., '75-6; Ord. (Presb.), Oct. 10, '76; S.S., Richland Centre, Wis., '76——.

HENRY MARTYN SANDERS; b., New-York City, Nov. 20, 1849; Y.C., '72; U.T.S., '73-6; Ord. (Bap.), Sep. 28, '76; Pas., Yonkers, N.Y., '76——.

DAVID SCHLEY SCHAFF; b., Mercersburgh, Pa., Oct. 17, 1852; Y.C., '73; U.T.S., '73-6; Pas. E., Baltimore, Md., '76; Oc.S., N. York City, '76——.

GEORGE HENRY SMITH; b., Sutton, St. Edmunds, Eng., Ap. 16, 1849; N.W.U., '74; U.T.S., '74-6; Ord. (M.E.), Ap. 9, '76; Pas., N. York City (Harlem), '76——.

FREDERICK JOUTE STANLEY; b., Nashville, Tenn., Dec. 27, 1848; Wab.C., '73; U.T.S., '73-6; Ord. (Presb.), ..., '76; Pas., Bloomington, Minn., '76——.

DAVID FAY STEWART; b., York, N.Y., July 16, 1848; U.R., '72; U.T.S., '72-4, '75-6; S.S., Caledonia, N.Y., '76——.

CHARLES SYMINGTON; b., Baltimore, Md., Oct. 17, 1848; W.T.S., '73-5; U.T.S., '75-6. Residence, N. York City.

SAMUEL LAWRENCE WARD; b., Oneida Lake, N.Y., Feb. 2, 1850; Wab.C., '73; P.T.S., '73-4; U.T.S., '74-6; Ord. (Presb.), ..., '76; F.M., Tabriz, Persia, '76——.

WILLIAM FORCE WHITAKER; b., Southold (L.I.), N.Y., May 6, 1853; U.Pa., '73; U.T.S., '73-6; Ord. (Presb.), Nov. 1, '76; S.S., Bridgehampton (L.I.), N.Y., '76——.

EDGAR LA MAR WILLIAMS; b., Bucyrus, O., Nov. 7, 1848; N.W.T.S., '73-5; U.T.S., '75-6; Ord. (Presb.), June 7, '76; Pas., Indianapolis, Ind., '76——.

ANASTATIUS DIAMANTES ZARAPHONITHES; b., Andros, Gr. Archipelago, Europe, Ap. .., 1844; Wh.C., '73; U.T.S., '73-6. Residence, N. York City. 35.

NEWTON DEXTER; b., Albany, N.Y., Mar. 3, 1850; U.C., '73; U.T.S., '73; N.H.T.S., '74-6.

DANIEL CASWELL MCINTYRE; b., Duart, Ont., May 31, 1845; Alb.C., '72; P.T.S., '73-4; U.T.S., '74-5; Free Coll., Edinburgh, Scotland, '75-6.

SAMUEL MCLANAHAN; b., Greencastle, Pa., Feb. 12, 1853; C.N.J., '73; U.T.S., '73-5; P.T.S., '75-6; Res.Lic., U.T.S., '76; S.S., Waynesboro', Pa., '76——.

EDWARD ANSON PADDOCK; b., Baraboo, Wis., Mar. 29, 1843; O.C., '72; U.T.S., '73-5; O.T.S, '75-6; Ord. (Presb.), ..., '76; Pas., South-Haven, Mich., '76——. 4.

SUMMARY.

Class.	Graduates.	Others.	Deceased.	Class.	Graduates.	Others.	Deceased.
1837	1			1857	21	14	5
1838	6	3	3	1858	24	20	2
1839	21	11	17	1859	34	20	10
1840	12	16	11	1860	31	22	6
1841	20	21	15	1861	35	23	6
1842	24	32	16	1862	33	29	6
1843	24	19	11	1863	27	23	8
1844	20	16	11	1864	21	21	1
1845	26	25	12	1865	22	16	6
1846	24	16	11	1866	32	13	5
1847	35	15	19	1867	28	22	2
1848	29	9	8	1868	43	20	6
1849	25	22	12	1869	37	17	6
1850	30	15	6	1870	38	23	2
1851	19	16	12	1871	32	22	2
1852	22	18	12	1872	33	13	1
1853	22	8	5	1873	40	10	1
1854	25	9	4	1874	33	17	1
1855	25	13	4	1875	41	18	1
1856	19	25	8	1876	35	4	

Whole number of Graduates..................................1069
Whole number of other Students.............................. 678
Complete number of Students.................... 1747
Reported as Deceased.. 274
Supposed to be Living,.......................................1473
Number of Foreign Missionaries.............................. 104

THE ASSOCIATED ALUMNI.

THE Society of "The Associated Alumni of the Union Theological Seminary of the City of New-York" was organized May 11, 1842. It is composed of "all who have been members of the Institution and are in the ministry, and are not Alumni of other Institutions."

OFFICERS.

REV. FREDERICK GORHAM CLARK, D.D., *President.*
REV. CHARLES AUGUSTUS BRIGGS, D.D., *Secretary.*

EXECUTIVE COMMITTEE.

Rev. Thomas S. Hastings, D.D.,
Rev. Erskine N. White, D.D.,
Rev. Elijah D. Murphy, D.D.,
Rev. Charles H. Payson,
Rev. Albert Erdman,
Rev. James D. Wilson,
Rev. J. Edson Rockwell, D.D.,
Rev. Charles D. Helmer, D.D.,
Rev. George H. Griffin,
Rev. George M. Boynton,
Rev. Wilson Phraner,
Rev. Henry M. Booth.

CLASS SECRETARIES.

1837. Rev. A. Bordman Lambert, D.D............. Rupert, Vt.
1838. Rev. Burtis C. Megie, D.D.................. Pleasant Grove, N. J.
1839. Rev. Daniel E. Megie....................... Boonton, N. J.
1840. Rev. Charles P. Bush, D.D.................. New-York City.
1841. Rev. J. Edson Rockwell, D.D................ Stapleton (S. I)., N.Y.
1842. Rev. Edward Hopper, D.D.................. New-York City.
1843. Rev. Samuel H. Hall, D.D................. New-York City.
1844. Rev. George F. Wiswell, D.D............... Philadelphia, Pa.
1845. Rev. F. Gorham Clark, D.D.................. New-York City.
1846. Rev. Amasa S. Freeman...................... Haverstraw, N. Y.
1847. Rev. Robert Aikman, D.D.................... Madison, N. J.
1848. Rev. Cornelius Earle......................... Catasauqua, Pa.
1849. Rev. William Aikman, D.D.................. Detroit, Mich.
1850. Rev. Wilson Phraner.......................... Sing Sing, N. Y.
1851. Rev. Thomas S. Hastings, D.D.............. New-York City.
1852. Rev. Charles W. Baird, D.D................ Rye, N. Y.

1853. Rev. Carson W. Adams.....................N.Y.City (West-Farms), N.Y
1854. Rev. Martin Kellogg........................Oakland, Cal.
1855. Rev. Gardiner S. Plumley...................New-York City.
1856. Rev. Alexander McLean, D.D................New-York City.
1857. Rev. Erskine N. White, D.D.................New-York City.
1858. Rev. George C. Noyes, D.D..................Evanston, Ill.
1859. Rev. Charles A. Stoddard, D.D..............New-York City.
1860. Rev. James A. Skinner......................Syracuse, N. Y.
1861. Rev. Isaiah B. Hopwood.....................Newark, N. J.
1862. Rev. James D. Wilson.......................New-York City.
1863. Rev. George M. Boynton.....................Newark, N. J.
1864. Rev. George H. Griffin.....................Milford, Ct.
1865. Rev. Samuel T. Clarke......................Elmira, N. Y.
1866. Rev. Rockwood McQuesten...................Winona, Minn.
1867. Rev. Henry M. Booth.........................Englewood, N. J.
1868. Rev. George U. Wenner......................New-York City.
1869. Rev. Stealy B. Rossiter.....................New-York City.
1870. Rev. Edward R. Burkhalter..................Cedar Rapids, Io.
1871. Rev. James D. Bruen........................Summit, N. J.
1872. Rev. Henry L. Bunstein.....................Philadelphia, Pa.
1873. Rev. James H. Hoadley......................New-York City.
1874. Rev. John L. Wells..........................Newark, N. J.
1875. Rev. John H. Eastman.......................Katonah, N. Y.
1876. Rev. John T. Lloyd.........................B'klyn (Green Point), N. Y.

When not chosen by their respective classes, these Secretaries have been appointed, *pro tempore*, by the Executive Committee.

ANNUAL MEETING.

The Annual Meeting of the Society is held on the Tuesday next preceding the second Monday of May, in the Chapel of the Seminary, No. 9 University Place, New-York City, in connection with the Anniversary of the Institution. The exercises consist of a business meeting, Class Reports from the Secretaries, and papers on various appropriate topics; together with an oration in the evening of the same day.

It is very desirable that each Class make a full Annual Report of its Statistics; also that they hold a special Reunion on the fifth, tenth, fifteenth, and twentieth anniversaries of their graduation, and at the end of every five years thereafter.

It is expected, in accordance with a standing rule to that effect, that the Alumni will promptly report to their Class Secretary any change in their residence or occupation.

NOTES AND EXPLANATIONS.

In the preparation of this Catalogue, the utmost fullness and accuracy of information have been sought. It has been obtained, when practicable, directly from the persons concerned. In a majority of cases, it has been necessary to procure it from other sources, involving an expenditure of much time and labor in consulting the Records of Ecclesiastical Bodies, the Reports of Missionary Societies, the Triennial Catalogues of Literary Institutions, extended files of weekly, monthly, and quarterly Periodicals, and the personal recollections of fellow-students. In some cases, only meagre and imperfect information could be obtained; in others, none at all. An approximation only to entire fullness and perfect accuracy could, therefore, be secured. It is earnestly requested that all omissions and mistakes be communicated to the Compiler, Rev. Edwin F. Hatfield, D.D., or the Class Secretary, for the next General Catalogue.

The following order has been observed :

1. The Name, in full, when it could be ascertained.
2. The Place and Date of Birth.
3. The Place and Time of Graduation, if any.
4. The Place and Time of Theological Study.
5. The Date and Denomination of Ordination, if any.
6. The Character, Place, and Time of Occupation, subsequent to the Theological Course.
7. The Source and Time of Honorary Degrees.

Under each year the names of the Students are arranged, alphabetically, in two lists ; the first includes all who finished their Theological Course here, and received a Diploma from this Seminary ; the second, separated from the former by a (——◆——) dash, all other Students who have, at any time during the three years, been regularly connected with the Class.

The Dead are, as usual, distinguished by an (*) asterisk. A (——.) dash with a period indicates present residence ; without a period, the last known residence. The Geographical Abbreviations are such as are in common use, and will readily be understood. The same is true of the Months of the year, and Academic Titles. Below will be found a Schedule of the other

ABBREVIATIONS.

1. LITERARY AND THEOLOGICAL INSTITUTIONS.

A.C.	Amherst College, Mass.
Ad.C.	Adrian College, Mich.
Ag.C.	Agricultural College.
Al.C.	Allegheny College, Pa.
Alb.C.	Albert College.
Alex.T.S.	Alexandria Theo. Sem., Va.
Alf.U.	Alfred University, N.Y.
And.T.S.	Andover Theo. Sem., Mass.
Ash.C.I.	Ashland Coll. Inst., N.Y.
Aub.T.S.	Auburn Theo. Sem., N.Y.
B.C.	Bowdoin College, Me.
B.T.S.	Bangor Theo. Sem., Me.
B.U.	Brown University, R. I.
Bal.U.	Baldwin University, Ohio.
Bel.C.	Beloit College, Wis.
Belf.C.	Belfast College, Ireland.
Ber.C.	Berea College, Ky.
Bib.Ins.	Biblical Institute.
Bl.U.	Blackburn University, Ill.
Bos.T.S.	Boston Theo. Sem., Mass.
Bt.C.	Burritt College, Tenn.
C.C.	Columbia College, N.Y.
C.C.N.Y.	Coll. of the City of N. York.
C.N.J.	College of N. Jersey.
C.T.S.	Chicago Theo. Sem., Ill.
Cal.C.	College of California.
Cam.T.S.	Cambridge Theo. Sem., Mass.
Cl.U.	Cleveland University, O.
Cn.C.	Columbian College, D. C.
Col.C.	Columbia College, N.Y.
Col.T.S.	Columbia Theo. Sem., S. C.
Coll.P.&S.	Coll. of Physicians and Surg.

Corn.U.	Cornell University, N.Y.	N.T.I.	Newton Theo. Insti., Mass.
Cr.C.	Centre College, Ky.	N.Y.A.	New-York Free Acad., N. Y.
Cu.U.	Cumberland Univ., Tenn.	N.Y.M'd. Coll.	New-York Medical College.
Cumb.C.	Cumberland College, Ky.		
D.C.	Dartmouth College, N.H.	N.U.	Nashville University, Tenn.
D.T.S.	Danville Theo. Sem., Ky.	N.W.T.S.	North-West'n Theo. Sem., Ill.
D. & D.I.	Deaf and Dumb Institute.	N.W.U.	North-Western University, Ill.
Dal.C.	Dalhousie College, N.S.	Ok.C.	Oakland College, Miss.
Del.C.	Delaware College, Del.	O.C.	Oberlin College, O.
Den.U.	Denison University, O.	O.T.S.	Oberlin Theo. Sem., O.
Di.C.	Dickinson College, Pa.	O.U.	Ohio University, Ohio.
Dr.T.S.	Drew Theo. Sem., N.J.	O.W.U.	Ohio Wesleyan Univ., O.
E. & H.C.	Emory & Henry College, Va.	Ol.C.	Olivet College, Mich.
E.W.T.S.	East-Windsor Theo. Sem., Ct.	O.I.	Oneida Institute, N. Y.
Ep.T.S.	Gen. Epis. Theo. Sem., N.Y.	P.U.	Pacific University, Oregon.
Ev.T.S.	Evanston Theo. Sem., Ill.	P.C.	People's College, N. Y.
F. & M.C.	Franklin & Marshall Col., Pa.	P.T.S.	Princeton Theo. Sem., N. J.
G.C.	Genesee College, N.Y.	P.E.D.S.	Prot. Epis. Div. School.
G.B.I.	Garret Biblical Institute, Ill.	Pa.C.	Pennsylvania College, Pa.
G.T.S.	Gettysburgh Theo. Sem., Pa.	Q.C.	Quebec College, C.E.
Gil.T.S.	Gilmanton Theo. Sem., N. H.	Rip.C.	Ripon College, Wis.
H.C.	Hamilton College, N. Y.	Ro.C.	Roanoke College, Va.
H.S.C.	Hampden Sydney College, Va.	R.T.S.	Rochester Theo. Sem., N. Y.
Han.C.	Hanover College, Ind.	R.C.	Rutgers College, N. J.
H.T.S.	Hartford Theo. Sem., Ct.	S.F.T.S.	S. Francisco Theo. Sem., Cal.
Hk.S.	Hartwick Seminary, N. Y.	S.U.	Syracuse University, N. Y.
Har.C.	Harvard College, Mass.	Syr.C.	Syrian College, Asia.
Heid.U.	Heidelberg University, Ger.	T.T.S.	Troy Theo. Sem., N. Y.
High.U.	Highland University, Kan.	U.C.	Union College, N. Y.
Hi.C.	Hillsdale College, Mich.	U.T.S.	Union Theo. Seminary, N. Y.
Hob.C.	Hobart College, N. Y.	U.T.S.Va.	Union Theo. Seminary, Va.
Ib.C.	Iberia College, Ohio.	U.U.	Union University, Tenn.
I.C.	Illinois College, Ill.	U.Ala.	University of Alabama.
I.A.U.	Indiana Asbury Univ., Ind.	U.A.	University of Athens, Greece.
Ind.U.	Indiana University, Ind.	U.B.	Univ. of Berlin, Prussia.
Ing.U.	Ingham University, N. Y.	U.Bonn.	University of Bonn, Ger.
Io.U.	Iowa University, Iowa.	U.C.T.	Univ'ty Col., Toronto, Ont.
I.W.U.	Iowa Wesleyan Univ., Iowa.	U.Chic.	Univ. of Chicago, Ill.
Ja.C.	Jackson College, Tenn.	U.E.T.	Univ. of East-Tennessee.
J.C.	Jefferson College, Pa.	U.G.	Univ. of Glasgow, Scotland.
J.H.U.	Johns Hopkins Univ., Md.	U.M.	Univ. of Michigan.
Kal.C.	Kalamazoo College, Mich.	U.Mi.	Univ. of Mississippi.
K.U.	Kentucky University, Ky.	U.N.C.	Univ. of North-Carolina.
Ken.C.	Kenyon College, Ohio.	U.N.Y.	Univ. of the City of N. York.
Kg.C.	King College, Tenn.	U.Pa.	Univ. of Pennsylvania.
K.C.	Knox College, Ill.	U. R.	Univ. of Rochester, N. Y.
K.C., Ont.	Knox College, Ont.	U.T.	Univ. of Toronto, Ont.
L.F.C.	La Fayette College, Pa.	U. Va.	University of Virginia.
L.F.U.	Lake Forest University.	U.Vt.	University of Vermont.
L.T.S.	Lane Theo. Sem., O.	U.W.	University of Wisconsin.
L.U.	Lewisburgh University, Pa.	Vic.C.	Victoria College, C.W.
M.T.S.	Madison Theo. Sem., N.Y.	Wab.C.	Wabash College, Ind.
M.U.	Madison University, N. Y.	Wn.C.	Washington College, Pa.
Ma.C.	Marietta College, O.	W.&J.C.	Wash. & Jefferson Coll., Pa.
Mv.C.	Maryville College, Tenn.	W. & L.U.	Washington & Lee Univ., Va.
Mi.U.	Miami University, Ohio.	W.C.Va.	Washington College, Va.
M.C.	Middlebury College, Vt.	Way.C.	Waynesburgh College, Pa.
Mi.C.	Mississippi College, Miss.	W.U.	Wesleyan University, Ct.
Na.T.S.	Nashotah Theo. Sem., Wis.	Westm.C.	Westminster College, Pa.
N.B.T.S.	N.Brunswick Theo.Sem., N.J.	W.R.C.	Western Reserve College, O.
Nbg.T.S.	Newburgh Theo. Sem., N. Y.	Wt.U.	Western University, Pa.
N.H.T.S.	New-Haven Theo. Sem., Ct.	W.T.S.	Western Theo. Sem., Pa.

Wh.C Wheaton College , Ill.
Witt.C. Wittenberg College, Ohio.
W.C. Williams College, Mass.
Woos.U. Wooster University, Ohio.
Y.C. Yale College, Ct.

2. BENEVOLENT INSTITUTIONS.

A.B.C.F.M. Am.Board,Com.For.Missions.
A.B.S. American Bible Society.
A.E.S. American Education Society.
A.& F.C.U. Amer. & For. Chris. Union.
A.H.M.S. American Home Miss. Society.
A.M.A. Am. Missionary Association.
A.P.S. American Protestant Society.
A.S.F.S. Am. Seamen's Friend Soc.
A.S.M.C.J. Am. Soc. for Melior. the Con. of the Jews.
A.S.S.U. Amer. Sunday-School Union.
A.T.S. American Tract Society.
A.T.S.of B. Am. Tract Soc. of Boston.
C.A.S. Children's Aid Society.
C.U.A. Christian Union Association.
Coll. & TheoSoc. Collegiate & Theological Soc.
Nat. Ref. Ass. National Reform Association.
P.B.Pub. Presb. Board of Publication.
P.C.H.M. Presb. Com., Home Missions.
Presb. Ed. Com. Presbyterian Education Com.
Presb. His. Soc. Presbyterian Historical Soc.
P.P.C. Presbyterian Publicat'n Com.
U.S.C.C. United States Christian Com.

3. MISCELLANEOUS.

Ac. Dep. Academic Department.
Adj. Prof. Adjunct Professor.
Ag. Agent.
Agric. Agriculture.
As. Com. Assistant Commissioner.
As. Min. Assistant Minister.
As. Pas. Associate Pastor.
As. Prof. Assistant Professor.
As. Surg. Assistant Surgeon.
As. Sec. Assistant Secretary.
Bap. Baptist.
Ch. Miss. Chapel Missionary.
Ch. Chaplain.
C.M. City Missionary.
C.Pas. Colleague Pastor.
Col. Colporteur.
Col. T.S. Colporteur of Tract Society.
Cong. Congregational.
Cor. Sec. Corresponding Secretary.
D.Sec. District Secretary.
D.Supt. District Superintendent.
Ed. Editor.
Ep. Episcopal.
Ev. Evangelist.
F.M. Foreign Missionary.
Gen.Ass. General Assembly.
G.R. German Reformed.
Ger.Tea. German Teacher.
H.M. Home Missionary.
Ind.Meth. Independent Methodist.
Inv. Invalid.
Lit. Literary Pursuits.
Lu. Lutheran.
Manuf. Manufacturer.
M. of Leg. Member of Legislature.
Mer. Merchant.
M.E. Methodist Episcopal.
Miss. Missionary.
Miss.Supt. Missionary Superintendent.
Mod. Moderator.
O.S.orOc.S. Occasional Supply.
Ord. Ordained.
Pas. Pastor.
Pas.E. Pastor Elect.
Phil.Dep. Philosophical Department.
Phys. Physician.
P.Elder. Presiding Elder.
P.M. Presbyterial Missionary.
Presb. Presbyterian.
Prest. President.
Prin. Principal.
Prof. Professor.
Prot.Miss. Protestant Missionary.
R.R.Sup. Rail Road Superintendent.
Rec. Rector.
R.D. Reformed Dutch.
Ref.Ep. Reformed Episcopal.
Res.Grad. Resident Graduate.
Res.Lic. Resident Licentiate.
R.C. Roman Catholic.
Sea. Ch. Seamen's Chaplain.
Sec. Secretary.
Soc.Lib. Society Library.
S.S. Stated Supply.
S.S.Dep. Sunday-School Department.
S.S.Ag. Sunday-School Agent.
S.S.M. Sunday-School Missionary.
Superan. Superannuated.
Supt. Superintendent.
S.M. Synodical Missionary.
Tea. Teacher.
Temp.Ag. Temperance Agent.
Tem.Sup. Temporary Supply.
Trav. Traveling.
Tut. Tutor.
Unit. Unitarian.
U.S.Ag. United States Agent.
U.S.Com. U. States Commissioner.
Wes. Wesleyan.
W.B.Ed.Soc. Western Bap.Education Soc.
W.C. Without Charge.

ADDITIONS AND CORRECTIONS.

[Mostly from information received too late for insertion in the proper place.]

CLASS.

1839. JAMES S. EVANS.—*Insert*, "b., Bristol, Bucks Co., Pa., Sep. 25, 1817."

1839. BENJAMIN G. RILEY.—*Add*, "'76; W.C., do., '76——."

1842. ERASTUS C. SPOONER.—*Read*, "M.C., '39," restoring C.

1848. RUFUS KING.—*Insert* (after "N.Y."), "Ap. 13."

1848. EDWARD B. WALSWORTH.—*Insert* (after "Cleveland, O."), "Sep. 29, 1819."

1849. MARSHALL KENSHAW.—*Insert* (after "Mass., '63"), "-'76; Tea., Newtonville, Mass., '76——.

1851. SANFORD W. ROE.—*Insert* (after "N.Y., '70"), "-6; Pas., Lebanon, N.J., '76——.

1853. GEORGE H. GOULD.—*Erase*, "Prof. & Pas., A.C., Amherst, Mass., '76——."

1858. DAVID FITCH.—*Read*, "1828," instead of "1829."

1858. EDWARD P. POWELL.—*Add*, "Pas. (Unit.), Chicago, Ill., '74——."

1859. WALTER H. CLARK.—*Add*, "P.O. Address, Ponca, Neb."

1859. JAMES T. MATTHEWS.—*Read*, "b., Boston, Mass., Mar. 14, 1830."

1860. ASAHEL L. CLARK.—*Insert* (after "Mass."), "July 25."

1862. RUFUS C. CROCKER.—*Read*, "b., Londonderry, N.H., Aug. 16, 1834."

INDEX.

Abbot, Ephraim E. P., 1867
Abbott, Albert F., 1875
Abbott, Jacob J., 1845
Abraham, Andrew, 1848
Acker, Henry J., 1859
Adams, Carson W., 1853
Adams, Charles L., 1850
Adams, Edwin A., 1866
Adams, Frederick H., 1861
Adams, James A., 1870
Adams, William W., D.D., 1858
Adamson, William S., 1861
Addy, William, 1861
Aiken, James, 1842
Aikman, Robert, D.D., 1847
Aikman, William, D.D., 1849
Alexander, G. Edward, 1859
Alexander, James McK., 1862
Alexy, Gustav, 1871
Allen, Edwin, 1860
Allen, John B., 1843
Allen, Samuel H., 1844
Allen, Solomon M., 1868
Aller, Nathan S., 1847
Allis, John M., 1869
Allison, Charles E., 1874
Allison, Robert C., 1856
Alrich, William A., 1862
Ambrose, Thomas L., 1859
Anderson, Joseph, 1857
Anderson, Robert C., 1847
Anderson, Samuel T., D.D.,1855
Andrews, Edwin N., 1864
Andrus, Alpheus N., 1867
Angier, Luther H., 1839
Angier, Marshall B., 1847
Armsby, Lauren, 1845
Armstrong,Chester S.,D.D.1856,
Armstrong, J. Rogers, 1855
Arnold, Austin, 1851
Arthur, Thomas S., 1845
Ash, Joseph R., 1853
Atkinson, Charles M., D.D.,1848
Atkinson, Robert, 1841
Atkinson, Robert, 1859
Atterbury, John G, D.D., 1846
Austin, Charles B., 1872
Avery, Eugene H., 1862
Ayers, Walter H., 1871
Ayres, Nelson, 1873

Babb, Clement E., D.D., 1849
Babcock, Joseph H., 1845
Bacheler, Francis E M., 1850
Bachman, Jonathan W., 1863
Bachman, Nathan, 1863
Bagley, Frank H., 1873
Bagnall, William R., 1843
Bailey, John W., D.D., 1852
Bailey, Samuel W., 1845
Bailey, Turner S., 1872
Baird, Charles W., D.D., 1852
Baird, Henry M., Ph.D., 1856
Baird, Isaac, 1873
Baird, John F., 1860
Baker, Alvin, 1862
Baker, Francis M., 1872
Baker, George S., 1870
Baker, John E., 1858
Baldwin, Charles H., 1866
Baldwin, Charles W., 1866
Baldwin, Elijah C., 1860
Baldwin, John A., 1873
Ballantine, Henry W., 1860
Ballantine, William G., 1872
Ball, Jasper N., 1852
Bancroft, Cecil F. P., 1867
Barker, William P., 1851
Barnes, Erastus S., 1841
Barrett, Charles H., 1855
Barrett, Myron, 1851
Barrows, George W., 1844
Barrows, John H., 1870
Barrows, Simon, 1845
Barrows, Walter M., 1870
Barrows, William, D.D., 1836
Barstow, Ephraim T., 1844
Bartholomew, William M., 1873
Bartlett, David E., 1840
Bartlett, Edward G., 1849
Bartlett, Joseph, 1843
Bartlett, P. Mason, D.D., 1853
Bartlett, William A., 1857
Bartlett, Wm. F. V., D.D., 1858
Barton, Luther, 1874
Bassett, William E., 1854
Bates, Erastus N., 1856
Bayley, Frank T., 1873
Bayne, John S., 1869
Beale, J. Hervey, 1861
Beals, David, 1860
Beard, Augustus F., D.D., 1860
Beard, William H., 1865
Beardsley, Bronson B., 1849
Becker, J. Henry, 1864
Beckwith, William W., 1870
Bedient, John Amos, 1869
Beebe, Abijah P., 1842
Beebee, Albert G., 1854
Beekman, Abraham J., 1874
Beekman, John S., 1860
Beeman, Henry A., 1868
Beer, Robert C., Ph.D., 1870
Belden, Henry, 1838
Belden, William, 1839
Belden, William H., 1867
Belknap, Henry, 1869
Bell, Goodloe B., 1859
Bell, Robert C., 1869
Bellows, Russell N., 1868
Benjamin, Theodore H., 1856
Benson, Enoch, 1876
Bent, Joseph A., 1853
Benton, John E., 1850
Benton, Orlando N., 1858
Berger, Martin L., 1862
Berry, Charles T., 1863
Berry, Franklin P., 1875
Berry, Philip, 1860
Best, Jacob, 1848
Bickford, Edward G., 1870
Bickford, Levi F., 1871
Billings, Alpheus W., 1865
Birchard, Whiting C., 1862
Bird, Frederick M., 1860
Birge, Lewis M., 1862
Bisbee, Charles G., 1860
Bishop, Albert C., 1863
Bishop, Gilbert L., 1870
Bissell, Allen P., 1868
Bissell, Edwin C., D.D., 1859
Bixby, Joseph P., 1861
Blake, Daniel H., 1859
Blake, Horace T., 1843
Blakely, Jacob E., 1851
Blakely, Quincy, 1857
Blakely, Zerah F., 1865
Blanchard, Charles P., 1868
Blauvelt, Cornelius R., 1867
Boardman, Moses B., 1863
Bogue, Horace P. V., 1866
Boing, Elias L., 1853
Bokum, Hermann, 1841
Bolton, James, 1854
Bolton, James G., 1875
Bonar, James B., 1856
Bond, Daniel, 1851
Bond, Lewis, Jr., 1867
Bond, William B., 1839
Bonney, Elijah H., 1844
Booth, Albert, 1855
Booth, Henry M., 1867
Borchers, Ernest F., 1866
Bordwell, Daniel N., 1858
Boswell, James I., 1861
Bourne, Theodore, 1854
Bowe, Daniel, 1862
Bowen, George, 1847
Bowen, Marcellus, 1872
Boyd, Erasmus J., 1840
Boynton, George M., 1863
Brace, Charles L., 1850
Bradbury, Henry C., 1871
Bradbury, Ziba N., 1862
Bradley, Leonard A., 1868
Bradshaw, John, 1850
Bragg, Jessie K., 1841
Brantly, Edwin T., 1846
Brayton, George, 1869
Brayton, Isaac H., 1849
Breed, William P., D.D., 1846
Briant, Samuel I., 1867
Bridgman, Henry M., 1860
Briggs, Charles A., D.D. 1864
Briggs, Marvin, 1855
Briscoe, John P., 1862
Brobston, William C., 1875
Brodhead, Harry, 1863
Brodt, John H., 1853

Brooks, Walter A., 1875
Brown, Allen H., 1842
Brown, Alonzo, 1856
Brown, Christopher R., 1867
Brown, Edmund W., 1858
Brown, Frederick A. M., 1863
Brown, Horatio W., 1858
Brown, John, 1870
Brown, John H., 1870
Brown, Josiah J., 1868
Brown, Justus N., 1871
Brown, Samuel R., D.D., 1838
Brown, Thomas J., 1868
Brown, William F., 1870
Browning, Joseph W., 1848
Brownson, Sidney J., 1876
Bruen, Arthur N., 1876
Bruen, Edward B., 1846
Bruen, James De H., 1871
Bruen, James M., 1842
Brundage, Israel, 1856
Brush, Jesse, 1869
Brush, Wilbur F., 1867
Bryan, Edward, 1876
Bryant, James P., 1874
Buck, Charles D., 1851
Buckland, Rabbi J. W., 1855
Buckley, Charles W., 1864
Buckner, John A., 1855
Bulkley, Charles H. A., 1842
Bulkley, Edwin A., D.D., 1847
Bull, Richard H., 1843
Bunstein, Henry L., 1872
Burbank, Lysander T., 1860
Burdick, Charles, 1871
Burke, Abel B., 1842
Burkhalter, Edward R., 1870
Burnett, Elijah L., 1865
Burnham, Edwin O., 1855
Burnham, Theodore F., 1874
Burns, Charles E., 1876
Burr, Almon W., 1871
Burr, J. Kelsey, 1849
Burrell, David J., 1870
Bush, Charles P., D.D., 1840
Bushnell, Albert, 1873
Bushnell, La Fayette, 1858
Butler, J. Glentworth, D.D., 1849
Butler, S. Russell, 1864
Butler, Wentworth S., 1855
Byington, George P., 1867
Byington, Theodore L., 1857

Cady, Chauncy M., 1854
Caldwell, George A., 1853
Caldwell, Isaac N., 1861
Caldwell, William E., 1854
Calkins, Lyman D., 1870
Calkins, Wolcott, 1861
Camp, Charles W., 1847
Camp, Samuel, 1861
Campbell, David H., 1875
Campbell, Robert, 1849
Canfield, Charles K., 1873
Carlile, Samuel, 1861
Carnes, John D., 1848
Carroll, George R., 1861
Carroll, James M., 1854
Cary, J. Addison, 1839
Cary, William B., 1871
Case, Francis W., 1858
Gaskey, Toliver F., 1868
Caswell, Enoch H., 1847
Cate, Charles N., 1875
Chalker, Richard A., 1842
Chalmers, William I., 1872
Chamberlain, Charles, 1839
Chamberlain, George W., 1862
Chamberlain, Joseph C., 1849
Chambers, Theodore F., 1871
Chapin, Aaron L., D.D., 1842
Chapin, George F., 1863
Chapin, Henry B., Ph.D., 1854
Chapin, L. Dwight, 1861
Chapin, Nathan C., 1849
Chapman, Chalmers D., 1872
Chapman, John L., 1841
Chapman, Joseph S., 1868
Charlier, Elisée, 1860
Chester, Edward W., M.D., 1857
Childs, Alexander C., 1849
Choate, Washington, 1875
Chrystie, Thomas M., 1874
Clapp, William T., 1862
Clark, Albert W., 1868
Clark, Allen, 1868
Clark, Asahel L., 1860
Clark, Edson L., 1858
Clark, Edward P., 1871
Clark, Elias, 1840
Clark, F. Gorham, D.D., 1845
Clark, George, 1848
Clark, George L., 1876
Clark, Isaac, 1861
Clark, John H., 1874
Clark, Patrick J., 1869
Clark, Royal W., 1861
Clark, Walter H., 1859
Clark, William H., 1863
Clarke, Edgar W., 1851
Clarke, Samuel T., 1865
Cleveland, William N., 1855
Clift, William A., 1843
Clizbe, Jay, 1864
Clymer, John M., 1858
Coan, G. Whitefield, 1849
Cobb, Elisha G., 1860
Cobb, Henry N., 1859
Cobb, Oliver E., 1857
Cobleigh, Nelson F., 1871
Cochran, Joseph G., 1847
Coe, Edward B., 1865
Coe, Philemon E., 1839
Coffey, George H., 1862
Coffing, Jackson G., 1856
Coit, Charles W., 1866
Coleman, James W., 1861
Collin, Henry P., 1869
Collins, Alfred S., 1860
Collins, Charles J., 1853
Collins, Charles T., 1871
Collins, Varnum D., 1854
Colton, Aaron M., 1838
Conant, Samuel M., 1847
Condict, Walter, 1867
Condit, Uzal W., 1850
Cone, Luther H., 1854
Coney, Archibald A., 1873
Conkling, Cornelius S., 1839
Cook, William W., 1876
Coon, Henry P., 1849
Cooper, Henry, 1866
Cornell, Howard, 1868
Corning, J. Leonard, 1852
Corwin, Eli, D.D., 1851
Cowan, John, 1875
Cowan, Perez D., 1869
Cowles, Augustus W., D.D., 1846
Coyle, John, 1869
Craighead, James G., D.D., 1847
Crane, Charles D., 1874
Crane, Edward P., 1855
Crane, Henry J., 1863
Crane, John J., 1865
Crane, Oliver, M.D., 1848
Crawford, Gideon S. W., 1874
Crawford, Levi P., 1853
Crawford, Robert, D.D., 1840
Crawford, William, 1860
Crawford, William A., 1848
Crittenden, Samuel W., 1855
Crocker, Rufus C., 1862
Cromwell, John, 1845
Crosby, Arthur, 1870
Cross, Roselle T., 1870
Crouse, Meigs V., 1874
Crowther, Thomas, 1866
Cumberland, William W., 1852
Cumings, Elbert W., 1874
Cumming, William J., 1871
Cummings, Seneca, 1847
Curtis, Edward H., 1867
Curtis, Smith, 1861
Curtis, Walter W., 1870
Curtiss, Samuel I., Jr., 1870
Cushman, John P., 1856
Cutler, Carroll, D.D., 1858
Cutler, James P., 1848
Cutler, William A., 1867

Dada, William B., 1856
Dale, Hervey S., 1841
Daly, James A., 1867
Dana, Malcolm McG., 1862
Dana, Stephen W., 1866
Daniels, Allen G., 1875
Daniels, Charles H., 1873
Danielson, Joseph, 1865
Danner, Edgar V., 1866
Danner, Julius L., 1867
Darling, Henry, D.D., 1845
Darling, Timothy G., 1869
Darlington, Newton W., 1855
Darwin, Charles C., 1871
Dashiell, Alfred H., 1847
Davenport, Henry A., 1873
Davenport, John G., 1867
Davenport, Silas A., 1871
Davis, George A., 1844
Davis, James W., 1865
Davis, J. Gardner, D.D., 1841
Day, Matthias, 1851
Deal, Lemuel J., 1864
Dean, Amos H., 1869
Dean, Benjamin A., 1865
Dearborn, Sylvanus S., 1862
Dechant, George B., 1860
De Forest, Henry S., 1862
De Long, Ira O., 1855
De Merit, John P., 1868
Dempsey, William, 1846
Denison, Andrew C., 1850
Denison, Daniel, 1864
Denison, Jesse W., 1847
Denniston, James O., 1865
Denny, Alfred N., 1860
Des Islets, Colbert M., 1872
Deuel, Silas W., 1848
Deyoe, Ephraim, 1842
Dexter, Newton, 1876
Dickerman, George A., 1858
Dickinson, Edward F., 1840
Dickinson, Richard S. S., 1848
Dickinson, William C., 1852
Dickinson, William E., 1858
Dickson, James M., 1857
Dilley, Alexander B., 1848
Diver, Charles F., 1842
Doane, Edward T., 1852
Dodd, Edward M., 1848
Dodd, Ira S., 1870
Dodd, Moses W., 1841
Dodge, David S., 1860
Doe, Walter P., 1847
Donaldson, James F., 1872
D'Oogé, Martin L., 1868
Dorland, Luke, 1845
Dorman, Lester M., 1858
Doubleday, William T., 1843
Dougherty, Michael A., 1867
Douglas, John W., 1848
Douglass, Eugene, 1859
Douglass, William A., 1875

Downs, Charles A., 1848
Draper, Gideon, 1858
Drennan, Manuel J., 1861
Drummond, James, 1841
Dudley, Daniel B., 1862
Dudley, Horace F., 1862
Dudley, La Fayette, 1854
Dudley, Myron S., 1869
Duffield, D. Bethune, 1845
Duffield, George, D.D., 1840
Dulles, John W., D.D., 1848
Dunham, Samuel, 1863
Dunmore, George W., 1849
Dunn, Ambrose, 1855
Dunn, Richard C., 1853
Dunning, Charles S., D.D., 1852
Dunning, Halsey, 1847
Dunning, Homer N., 1852
Dunning, William A., 1866
Durgin, Charles C., 1846
Durnett, William R., 1847
Dwight, James H., 1855
Dwight, Samuel G., 1847
Dwight, William B., 1857
Dwinell, Israel E., D.D., 1848
Dye, Charles B., 1860

Eagleton, George E., 1854
Earle, Cornelius, 1848
Earle, William W., 1859
Earnshaw, Joseph W.; 1876
Eastman, John H., 1875
Eastman, William R., 1862
Easton, Charles, 1863
Easton, Peter Z., 1870
Eaton, Horace, D.D., 1842
Eaton, Samuel W., 1845
Eddy, David R., 1863
Eddy, William W., D.D., 1850
Edson, Hanford A., D.D., 1861
Edson, Henry K., 1852
Edwards, John H., 1862
Edwards, George L., 1869
Egbert, James C., 1855
Elliott, Henry B., 1843
Elliott, Lester H., 1864
Ellis, John M., 1857
Ellsworth, Alfred A., 1861
Elmer, Nathaniel, 1843
Elmer, Oscar H., 1868
Emerson, Brown H., 1873
Emmons, Amzi B., 1873
Erdman, Albert, 1861
Erdman, William J., 1859
Evans, Daniel H., 1862
Evans, David W., 1866
Evans, Enoch K., 1857
Evans, James S., D.D., 1839
Evans, John G., 1858
Evans, Rees C., 1845
Everest, Asa E., 1850
Everest, Charles H., 1862
Everts, Josiah G., 1862
Ewing, Flavius L., 1862

Fairbank, John B., 1860
Fairbanks, Francis J., 1865
Fairchild, Charles G., 1869
Falkner, Bishop, 1863
Fanning, Charles, 1849
Fanning, James, 1844
Farwell, John E., 1839
Fay, Alonzo G., 1860
Fay, Barnabas M., 1839
Feltch, Joseph H., 1866
Ferguson, Daniel A., 1875
Ferguson, James A., 1869
Field, Justin, 1841
Finch, Horace W., 1849
Finch, James B., 1863
Findley, William L., 1873
Fish, Henry C., D.D., 1845
Fisher, Edward W., 1870
Fisher, James P., 1842
Fisher, Samuel V. 1872
Fisher, Samuel W., 1845
Fisher, Samuel W., D.D., 1839
Fisher, William P., 1870
Fitch, Albert. 1855
Fitch, Charles N., 1872
Fitch, Chester, 1840
Fitch, David, 1858
Fletcher, Donald, 1873
Fletcher, Patterson, 1844
Flichtner, George F., 1871
Folsom, George De F., 1849
Foote, Lewis R., 1872
Forbes, John M., 1860
Force, Charles H., 1849
Ford, Francis F., 1856
Ford, George A., 1876
Ford, Henry T., 1861
Ford, James T., 1874
Ford, J. Edwards, 1847
Ford, William H., 1873
Forrest, William, Jr., 1845
Foster, Bentley S., 1862
Foster, Stephen S., 1841
Foster, William C., 1844
Fowler, Francis, 1848
Fowler, John K., 1874
Fowler, William C., 1870
Fox, Daniel W., 1865
Fox, Jared W., 1839
Francis, Samuel A. K., 1865
Franklin, Morris J., 1858
Fraser, Horace, 1839
Fraser, John G., 1871
Fraser, Oris, 1839
Frazer, David R., 1864
Frear, Walter, 1854
Freeman, Amasa S., 1846
Freeman, Amzi W., 1847
Freeman, John C., 1875
French, Edward W., D.D., 1856
French, Herman A., 1871
French, J. Clement, D.D, 1856
French, William C., D.D., 1844
French, William T., 1844
French, Willison B., 1875
Frisbee, Edward S., 1865
Frizzell, William, 1875
Frost, D. Delavan, 1845
Fuller, Ashbel, 1842
Fuller, Homer T., 1869
Fulton, Edwin F., 1875

Gale, Sullivan F., 1869
Gallatin, Albert H., 1870
Gano, Lewis, 1851
Gardner, Edward P., 1862
Gardner, John S., 1875
Gardner, Theodore A., 1857
Gardner, Theodore Y., 1868
Garretson, Frederick V., 1868
Garretson, George R., 1875
Gates, Lorenzo M., 1860
Gates, William H., 1870
Gaylord, Joseph F., 1866
Gaylord, William L., 1861
Gaylord, Willis C., 1868
Geddes, Clarence. 1872
Gelston, Henry W., 1876
Gelston, Joseph M., 1873
Gemmel, George, 1841
Gerhard, James A., 1874
Gerould, Samuel L., 1861
Gibbs, Joseph F., 1875
Gibson, John, 1857
Giddings, William, 1869
Gidman, Richard H., 1866
Giles, James J., 1846
Giles, Walter H., 1864
Gillett, Ezra H., D.D., 1844
Gillette, Charles, 1842
Gillette, Charles B., 1873
Gillis, John, 1873
Gilman, Edward W., D.D., 1848
Gilson, Samuel S., 1871
Goldsmith, Benjamin M., 1842
Good, James I., 1875
Goodale, Alvin B., M.D., 1861
Goodell, Edwin, 1853
Goodell, Henry M., 1874
Goodman, Stephen S., 1850
Goodrich, Chauncy, 1864
Goodrich, Ezra W., 1849
Goodwin, Edward P., D.D., 1859
Goodwin, Hannibal, 1851
Goodwin, Henry M., 1846
Gordon, John O., 1871
Gordon, Matthew D., 1846
Gorham, W. Osman, 1842
Gould, George H., D.D., 1853
Gourley, John C., 1875
Granger, Henry C., 1875
Grandin, James L. S., 1841
Grant, Henry M., 1863
Graves, George A., 1869
Gray, George D., 1868
Gray, George S., 1860
Gray, Robert, 1847
Gray, Robert, 1851
Greene, Joseph K., 1858
Greene, Joseph M., 1868
Greene, William B., 1851
Greenough, J. Jay, 1839
Gregory, Lewis, 1867
Grieve, David G., 1866
Griffes, James A., 1860
Griffin, Edward H., 1867
Griffin, George H., 1864
Griggs, C. Edwin, 1859
Griswold, John V., 1868
Griswold, Wait R., 1852
Grout, Admatha, 1851
Grummon, Daniel N., 1870
Guernsey, Alfred H., 1846
Guild, Rufus B., 1862
Gulick, Alexander, 1839
Gulick, John T., 1862
Gulick, Theodore W., 1869
Gulick, Thomas L., 1868
Gutelius, Fisher, 1874

Hackley, Simeon, 1866
Hadden, Jacob W., 1873
Hageman, James W., 1875
Haines, Matthias L., 1874
Haire, John P., 1859
Hale, James R., 1856
Hale, John P., 1874
Haley, Charles T., 1858
Hall, Charles C., 1875
Hall, Charles L., 1874
Hall, Elliot C., 1865
Hall, Granville S., 1871
Hall, John G., 1839
Hall, John Q., 1862
Hall, Joshua B., 1858
Hall, Richard, 1850
Hall, Robert B., 1873
Hall, Russell T., 1870
Hall, Samuel H., D.D., 1843
Hall, William, Jr., 1840
Hallock, Luther C., 1848
Hallock, William A., 1859
Halsey, Samuel P., 1862
Hamilton, Edgar A., 1873
Hamilton, Henry H., 1871
Hamilton, Thomas J., 1875
Hamlin, Chauncey L., 1866
Hamlin, Cyrus, 1868

Hamlin, Teunis S., 1871
Hammond, Edward P., 1861
Hammond, Henry L., 1841
Hammond, James B., 1865
Hamner, James G., 1858
Hand, William A. M., 1841
Hanks, Stedman W., 1840
Hanna, John A., 1875
Hanna, Lyman E., 1875
Hardin, Oscar J., 1871
Harding, Charles, 1856
Harmon, Fisk, 1849
Harrah, Charles C., 1870
Harrington, Alfred L., 1855
Harris, John K., 1858
Harrison, Thomas, 1856
Harsen, John P., 1867
Hart, John M., 1876
Hart, Levi W., 1852
Hart, Theodore H., 1856
Hartley, Isaac S., D.D., 1856
Hartman, Aaron S., 1871
Harvey, Edward H., 1872
Harvey, W. Nye, 1850
Harwood, James H., 1864
Hascall, Theodore B., 1868
Haskell, Matthew W., 1856
Haskell, T. Nelson, 1854
Hastings, Eurotas P., 1846
Hastings, Henry, 1861
Hastings, Thomas S., D.D., 1851
Hatch, Junius L., 1852
Hathaway, Thomas E., 1844
Haven, Joseph, D.D., 1839
Hawks, John, 1850
Hawks, Theron H., D.D., 1851
Hawley, Charles, D.D., 1844
Hawley, Edwin H., 1840
Hawley, Giles P., 1876
Hay, Samuel C., 1864
Haydn, Hiram C., D.D., 1859
Hayes, Alonzo, 1842
Hayes, Charles G., 1857
Hayt, Samuel A., 1866
Haywood, Charles H., 1861
Hazeltine, Henry M., 1857
Hazelton, William A., 1863
Hazen, Timothy A., 1853
Hazlewood, Webster, 1866
Hebard, George D. A., 1857
Hedges, Henry C., 1852
Helfrich, Nicholas C., 1870
Helmer, Charles D., D.D., 1857
Henderson, James S. H., 1841
Hendrix, Eugene R., 1869
Henshaw, Marshall, LL.D., 1849
Herrick, Alanson C., 1866
Hervey, George W., 1849
Hetrick, Andrew J., 1864
Hickok, Henry, 1844
Hickok, Milo J., D.D., 1841
Hildreth, James, 1839
Hill, Charles J., 1856
Hill, Ellsworth J., 1863
Hill, Isaac N., 1852
Hill, Joshua A., 1874
Hill, Timothy, D.D., 1845
Hillman, James W., 1876
Hincks, Edward Y., 1869
Hoadley, James H., 1873
Hoar, William J., 1871
Hodgman, Edwin R., 1846
Holbrook, David A., Ph.D., 1847
Holland, George W., 1861
Hollister, Martin F., 1870
Holloway, Charles H., 1857
Holmes, Hamilton B., 1866
Holmes, Theodore J., 1859
Holt, Edmund D., 1849
Holton, Isaac F., 1839
Holyoke, William E., 1849
Hood, Edward C., 1874
Hood, J. Augustine, 1849
Hooper, Thomas W., 1858
Hoover, Thomas D., 1841
Hopkins, David, 1868
Hopkins, Henry, 1862
Hopkins, Judson H., 1853
Hopper, Edward, D.D., 1842
Hoppin, James M., D.D., 1845
Hopwood, Isaiah B., 1861
Hornbrooke, Francis B., 1874
Horton, Carlton S., 1857
Hosford, Frederic, 1866
Hoskins, Robert, 1869
Hotchkiss, William P., 1842
Hough, Jesse W., 1859
Hough, Joel J., 1863
Houghton, John C., 1864
House, John H., 1871
Howard, James B., 1852
Howard, John, 1849
Howard, Joseph D., 1856
Howe, Edward, 1845
Howe, Francis A., 1851
Howell, Horatio S., 1845
Howland, Harrison O., 1844
Howland, Samuel W., 1873
Howland, William W., 1845
Hoyt, James, 1844
Hoyt, James H., 1876
Hoyt, James S., 1858
Hoyt, Willard M., 1842
Hoyt, Zerah T., 1844
Hubbard, Joseph W., 1857
Hubbell, Henry L., 1859
Hubbell, James W., 1862
Hubbs, Isaac G., 1843
Hudson, Thomas D., 1852
Hughes, Thomas W., 1862
Hughitt, Emmons J., 1866
Hughson, Simeon S., 1850
Humphrey, Zeph. M., D.D., 1849
Humphreys, Richard G. E., 1849
Hunt, Myron W., 1873
Hunt, Theodore W., 1869
Hunter, Henry T., 1874
Huntington, Jedediah V., 1839
Hurd, Edwin L., D.D., 1856
Hurlbut, Everett B., 1856
Hurlbut, Joseph, Jr., 1852
Hurlbut, Samuel, 1845
Hutchins, Alexander, 1860
Hutchins, John C., 1876
Hutchins, Robert G., 1864
Hutchinson, Merrill N., 1869
Hutton, Mancius H., 1860
Hutton, William, 1867
Hyde, Charles M., D.D., 1856
Hyde, Henry F., 1863

Jackson, Samuel M., 1873
James, William A., 1865
Jenkins, Herman D., 1867
Jervis, Timothy B., 1842
Jessup, Henry H., D.D., 1855
Jessup, Lewis, 1849
Jessup, Samuel, 1861
Jessup, Samuel, Jr., 1858
Jessup, Silas, 1841
Jessup, Theodore F., 1868
Jesup, Henry G., 1853
Jester, Thomas D., 1873
Johnson, Alfred V., 1871
Johnson, Alonzo P., 1861
Johnson, Arthur, 1875
Johnson, Edwin, 1850
Johnson, Frank A., 1871
Johnson, John M., 1841
Johnson, Lyman H., 1857
Johnston, Cyrus A., 1868
Johnston, James, 1854
Johnston, John B., 1872
Jones, Caleb E., 1873
Jones, Charles J. K., 1873
Jones, Chester W., 1872
Jones, Martin P., 1864
Jones, Norman, 1860
Jones, Samuel J., 1846
Jones, William M., 1842
Judd, Frederick F., 1844
Judd, James S., 1839
Judd, John F., 1852
Judson, Elnathan, 1862
Julien, Matthew C., 1872
Junor, Kenneth F., 1873

Kalopothakes, Michael D., 1856
Karr, William S., D.D., 1854
Kedzie, John H., 1844
Kelley, John S., 1846
Kellogg, Charles, 1841
Kellogg, Henry M., 1876
Kellogg, Martin, 1854
Kellogg, Robert R., 1838
Kendall, Charles, 1842
Kendrick, William, 1859
Kenmore, Charles, 1839
Kerr, George, LL.D., 1843
Kershaw, John, 1868
Keyes, Richard G., 1851
Keyes, Russell M., 1865
Keyser, Calvin, 1875
Keyser, Sylvanus G., 1869
Kidder, Wenham, 1860
Kiehle, Amos A., 1874
Kiehle, David L., 1865
Kimball, Charles C., 1862
Kimball, George W., 1847
Kimball, Henry, 1859
Kimball, James M., 1847
Kimball, John, 1859
King, Albert B., 1858
King, Rufus, 1848
Kingsbury, Charles A., 1867
Kingsbury, Howard, 1869
Kingsbury, Oliver A., 1864
Kinney, Henry, 1847
Kirby, William Wallace, 1862
Kirkland, James, 1873
Kittredge, Josiah E., 1864
Kline, Robert H., 1875
Klink, Nathaniel B., 1850
Kloss, Daniel, 1861
Knouse, William H., 1858
Knowles, James F., 1870
Knox, Charles E., D.D., 1859
Kopf, John, 1871
Kruger, Theodore, 1861

Lador, Charles A., 1872
Lamar, Thomas J., 1852
Lambert, A. Bord., D.D., 1837
Lampe, Joseph J., 1867
Lampman, Lewis, 1870
Lamson, Ansel, 1866
Lanman, Joseph, 1867
Lane, John W., 1842
Lane, Saurin E., 1844
Larkin, Ethan P., 1854
Latham, Henry D., 1843
Laurie, Inglis, 1857
Lawrence, Amos E., 1844
Lawrence, William A., 1866
Leaman, Charles, 1874
Leavens, Philo F., 1866
Leavitt, William S., 1845
Ledoux, Louis P., D.D., 1851
Lee, Joseph T., 1843
Leeds, S. Penniman, D.D., 1846
Leftwich, James T., D.D., 1859
Lemert, George W., 1870
Leo, Patrick J., 1854

Leonard, Delavan L., 1862
Leonard, Joseph H., 1874
Leonard, Josiah, 1840
Lester, Timothy W., 1841
Lestrade, Joseph P., 1845
Lewis, Edwin R., 1871
Lewis, James, 1868
Lewis, John, 1843
Leyburn, George L., 1863
Liebenau, Michael F., 1841
Lillie, Ralph W., 1874
Lilly, Arunah H., 1851
Lilly, Henry M., M.D., 1856
Lindsay, John W., D.D., 1842
Lindsley, Aaron L., D.D., 1845
Linnell, Edward P., 1874
Linsley, Charles E., 1846
Linsley, Joel, 1859
Little, Charles H., 1873
Little, James, 1845
Little, James A., 1859
Littlejohn, Gilbert H., 1842
Livingston, Henry G. L., 1845
Livingstone, Charles, 1849
Lloyd, John T., 1876
Lobdell, Francis, 1861
Locke, Nathaniel C., D.D., 1844
Locke, William E., 1867
Lockwood, George A., 1870
Lockwood, V. Le Roy, 1853
Lockwood, William H., 1850
Loder, Achilles L., 1875
Long, John E., 1862
Loomis, Chauncy L., 1857
Loomis, Henry H., 1840
Loomis, Hezekiah H., 1840
Loomis, Samuel, 1853
Lord, Charles E., D.D., 1842
Lord, Francis E., 1840
Lord, Jeremiah S., D.D., 1839
Lounsbury, Henry A., 1854
Love, John, Jr., 1871
Low, Charles F., 1845
Ludden, Waldo W., 1854
Lum, Samuel Y., 1848
Lyman, Albert J., 1868
Lyman, Chester S., 1842
Lyman, Payson W., 1870
Lynch, William A., 1874
Lyon, Appleton P., 1873
Lyon, Daniel B., 1851
Lyons, Curtis J., 1861
Lyons, J. Lorenzo, 1854
Lyons, Jonathan, 1849

MacElroy, Patrick D., 1871
McAllister, David, 1863
McArthur, Henry G., 1859
McBride, Samuel, 1876
McCalla, Albert, 1870
McCallie, Thomas H., 1859
McCampbell, John, 1853
McCarer, William H., 1843
McChain, James, 1841
McClelland, Brainerd T., 1875
McConaughy, Nathaniel, 1858
McCord, Robert L., 1859
McCreery, Charles H., 1868
McCully, Charles G., 1859
McDevitt, John, 1851
McDonald, Clinton D., 1875
McDuffee, Samuel V., 1868
McElroy, H. Sneed, 1850
McElroy, William T., 1854
McGregor, Edwin R., 1846
McHarg, Charles K., 1846
McIntyre, Daniel C., 1876
McKean, John, 1855
McKechnie, Duncan L., 1874
McKee, Joseph, 1845
McKinney, Sabin, 1844
McLain, Henry Z., 1870
McLanahan, Samuel, 1876
McLaughlin, Daniel D. T., 1842
McLaughlin, James, 1861
McLean, Alexander, D.D. 1856
McLean, Charles B., 1840
McLean, James M., 1847
McLoud, Anson, 1841
McMahon, James J., 1853
McMonagle, John H., 1860
McMurran, John W., 1856
McMurran, Robert L., 1858
McNeil, Benjamin F., 1868
McNeill, George, 1849
McNeill, James H., 1848
McNinch, Thomas, 1876
McNulty, John, 1852
McQuesten, Rockwood, 1866
McVey, John, 1863
McVicar, Peter, D.D., 1860
Macbeth, William C., 1874
Macy, William C., 1863
Magee, Irving, D.D., 1860
Maguire, Hugh, 1875
Mallary, Raymond D., 1876
Mandell, William A., 1841
Mann, Joseph R., D.D., 1847
Mann, Matthew G., 1871
Mapes, Eugene L., 1876
Marble, William H 1848
Marcussohn, Jacob W., 1854
Marden, Augustus L., 1859
Margot, David, 1855
Marsh, Dwight W., D.D., 1849
Marsh, John T., 1849
Marsh, Joseph W., 1862
Marsh, Samuel D., 1847
Marsh, Sidney H., D.D., 1854
Marshall, Clifton G., 1871
Marshall, James, 1870
Marshall, J. Bryan, 1841
Marshall, Thomas, 1864
Martin, Charles F., 1853
Martin, Daniel S., 1866
Martin, George W., 1868
Martin, Joseph H., 1846
Martin, William M., 1842
Martin, William W., 1863
Marts, William G., 1872
Martyn, W. Carlos, 1869
Mason, James G., 1876
Mason, Rufus O., 1857
Mathews, Henry, 1847
Mathews, Israel G., 1863
Matthews, James T., 1859
Matthews, William F., 1874
Matthews, William H., 1846
Maxwell, J. Allen, 1860
May, Alonzo M., 1867
Maynard, Joshua L., 1841
Mayo, Warren, 1853
Meacham, John H., 1850
Meacham, John H., 1863
Means, Stewart, 1875
Meek, John B., 1846
Meeker, David C., 1846
Meerwein, Otto, 1869
Megie, Burtis C., D.D., 1838
Megie, Daniel E., 1839
Megie, William H., 1845
Meigs, Matthew, Ph.D., 1840
Mellis, S. Harvey, 1865
Merriam, Edwin E., 1863
Merriam, George F., 1864
Merrick, Lucius L., 1863
Merriman, Wm. E., D.D., 1854
Merwin, Almon B., 1863
Merwin, Miles T., 1841
Meteer, James H., 1870
Michael, George, 1874
Mighill, Nathaniel, 1864
Miles, Edward C., 1856
Milford, Mark L., 1869
Millard, Nelson, D.D., 1860
Millard, Watson B., 1874
Miller, George A., 1858
Miller, Benjamin F., 1868
Miller, Henry G., 1876
Miller, John C., 1874
Miller, Samuel, 1863
Miller, Victor, 1862
Mills, Cyrus T., D.D., 1847
Mills, Eugene R., 1873
Mills, John L., 1859
Mills, Robert C., D.D., 1840
Milner, Duncan C., 1869
Milton, George R., 1872
Mitchell, Arthur, D.D., 1859
Mitchell, Louis H., 1875
Mitchell, Samuel S., 1866
Mix, Eldridge, 1860
Mockridge, Emmons T. 1849
Monilaws, George, 1841
Montgomery, Alexander, 1840
Moore, Alexander D., 1860
Moore, Nathaniel S., 1865
Moore, William E. B., 1862
Morange, James P., 1843
Morgan, David S., 1866
Morgan, Hamilton, 1856
Morgan, H. Bartlett, 1850
Morris, George S., 1867
Morris, William F., 1869
Morrow, Corn. W. L. F., 1855
Morse, John H., 1847
Morse, Oliver C., 1874
Morse, Richard C., 1867
Morton, James, 1849
Morton, William D., 1863
Mosely, John W., 1854
Mosely, Samuel, 1839
Mudge, Thomas H., 1843
Murdoch, Alexander, 1854
Murdoch, David, D.D., 1848
Murdock, Samuel, 1862
Murphy, Elijah D., 1852
Murray, Thomas C., 1872
Mussey, Charles F., D.D., 1852
Myers, Alfred E., 1870
Myers, Joseph H., D.D., 1841
Myers, Peter J. H., 1850

Naff, Isaac N., 1849
Nazro, John C., 1843
Needham, George F., 1843
Nesbitt, Alexander, 1863
Newbanks, John, 1852
Newberry, Edwin D., 1855
Newcomb, George B., 1860
Newell, George B., 1872
Newell, William W., Jr., 1864
Newhall, Charles S., 1872
Newport, R. Marshall, 1863
Newton, Benjamin F., 1873
Newton, Oscar, 1852
Nichols, Henry F. C., 1864
Nichols, Thomas, 1861
Nickerson, Norman F., 1874
Nims, Granville W., 1876
Nitchie, Henry A., 1849
Noble, Charles, 1871
Noble, Franklin, 1861
Noble, George P., 1868
Noble, Mason, Jr., 1865
North, Josiah W., 1852
Northrop, George E., 1869
Northrop, Henry D., 1861
Norton, Charles H., 1856
Norton, Oliver W., 1841
Nott, Charles D., D.D., 1858
Noyes, Daniel T., 1851

Noyes, George C., D.D., 1858
Noyes, Gurdon W., 1849

Oakley, Charles M., 1841
Ogilvie, Charles B., 1872
Ogle, John, Jr., 1869
Olmstead, William, 1847
Olmsted, Alexander F., 1851
Olney, Alfonso R., 1869
Olney, Eugene C., 1872
Opdyke, Sylvester H., 1858
Osborn, Frederick W., 1861
Osborn, Henry, 1845
Osborn, Henry S., LL.D., 1845
Osborn, Thomas G., 1843
Osgood, Edward W., 1847
Ostrander, Luther A., 1870
Otis, Isaac N., 1871
Otis, Orin F., 1843
Ottinger, William, 1845
Overton, Floyd, 1854
Oviatt, Samuel N., 1872
Owen, David, 1859

Packard, Noah F., 1845
Paddock, Edward A., 1876
Page, Emery H., 1850
Page, Langford S., 1865
Page, William L., 1858
Page, William W., 1845
Paine, Bernard, 1866
Palmer, Charles M., 1867
Parish, Thomas H., 1847
Park, Andrew J., 1866
Parker, Charles, 1848
Parker, Charles C., D.D., 1846
Parker, Henry E., 1847
Parker, Samuel J., 1844
Parkhurst, Austin N., 1849
Parkins, Alexander, 1848
Parkinson, Royal, 1847
Parmelee, Howard R., 1872
Parmelee, Moses P., 1861
Parmly, Wheelock H., D.D., 1845
Parry, Samuel Jr., 1872
Parsons, Benjamin F., 1844
Parsons, Eben B., 1865
Parsons, James H., 1856
Parsons, Justin W., 1848
Parsons, Willard, 1871
Paton, Thomas, 1868
Patrick, Henry J., 1852
Patton, Jacob H., 1846
Patton, William W., D.D., 1842
Payson, Charles H., 1857
Payson, Edward P., 1864
Payson, George S., 1871
Peabody, Charles, 1845
Pearson, James B., 1860
Pease, Edmund M., 1860
Pease, Thomas H., 1864
Peck, Aaron, 1864
Peck, John, 1846
Peck, Thomas R. G., 1852
Peck, Whitman, 1841
Peck, William S., 1847
Peckham, Joseph, 1842
Peet, Edward, 1852
Peet, Isaac L., LL.D., 1849
Peffers, Aaron B., 1853
Peloubet, Alexander O., 1838
Penfield, Thornton B., 1859
Penland, Alfred M., 1862
Pennell, Joseph, 1842
Perkins, Frederick T., 1842
Perry, Cyrus M., 1865
Perry, David B., 1866
Perry, William D., 1874
Perryman, John D., 1841
Peters, Benjamin F., 1847
Peters, John W., 1867
Peterson, Walter S., 1875
Pettingell, John H., 1842
Pettinger, Isaac M., 1875
Phelps, J. Chester, 1849
Phelps, S. Wallace, 1851
Phelps, Winthrop H., 1845
Phelps, Zenas M., 1842
Phillips, Benjamin T., 1845
Phipps, William H., 1866
Phœnix, Sidney, 1861
Phraner, Wilson, 1850
Pick, Bernhard, 1868
Pierce, Epaminondas J., 1850
Pierce, Nehemiah, 1868
Pierce, Nehemiah P., D.D., 1846
Pierson, Arthur T., D.D., 1860
Pierson, George, Jr., 1859
Pierson, Ham. W., D.D. 1848
Pierson, Israel C., 1868
Pierson, Nathaniel E., 1845
Pingry, John F., Ph.D., 8843
Pinneo, Samuel L., 1861
Pitcher, Samuel L., 1843
Pitkin, S. Dwight, 1846
Pixley, Martin S., 1847
Plant, Alfred, 1850
Platt, William K., 1843
Platts, Lewis A., 1871
Plested, William, 1873
Plumley, Gardiner S., 1855
Pomeroy, Charles R., 1856
Pomeroy, Edward N., 1868
Pond, Theodore S., 1863
Porter, Timothy H., 1855
Porter, William, 1843
Porter, William H., 1844
Post, Edmund H., 1870
Post, George E., M.D., 1861
Post, Henry A., 1858
Potter, Aaron, 1850
Potter, Hiram, 1856
Potter, Ludlow D., D.D., 1846
Potter, Samuel S., 1845
Powell, Edward P., 1858
Powell, Henry A., 1876
Powell, Isaac P., 1867
Pratt, Almon B., 1842
Pratt, Andrew T., 1851
Pratt, Francis G., 1846
Preston, Marcus N., 1862
Priest, Josiah A., D.D., 1850
Prior, Isaac R., 1870
Pryse, William S., 1875
Putnam, Douglas P., 1870

Quick, Abram J., 1863
Quick, James, 1857

Ramsdell, Charles B., 1875
Rand, Edward A., 1863
Randall, Silas G., 1848
Rankin, Edward E., D.D., 1843
Ray, J. Wainwright, 1842
Redpath, John, 1872
Reeve, John B., D.D., 1861
Reid, John, 1853
Reid, J. Morrison, D.D., 1842
Reid, Joseph H., 1870
Reid, Lewis H., 1850
Reid, William H., 1867
Relyea, Benjamin J., 1845
Remick, Ninian B., 1869
Rhea, Samuel A., 1850
Rhodes, John T., 1862
Rice, Edwin W., 1858
Rice, George G., 1850
Rice, Henry H., 1870
Rich, Adoniram J., 1863
Rich, Alonzo B., D.D., 1845
Richards, Charles, 1845
Richards, Charles H., 1864
Richards, George J., 1876
Richards, J. DeFor., LL.D., 1840
Richards, Leonard E., 1863
Richards, William L., 1846
Richardson, Edgar M., 1852
Richardson, George P., 1858
Richardson, James M., 1852
Richardson, Robert H., 1863
Richardson, Sanford, 1854
Riggs, Alexander B., 1870
Riggs, Edward, 1869
Riggs, Herman C., 1856
Righter, Harris, 1843
Riley, Benjamin G., 1839
Riley, Isaac, 1861
Riley, J. Gamaliel, 1862
Robb, Edward C., 1850
Robbins, Alden B., D.D., 1843
Robert, James A., 1865
Robert, Joseph T., 1864
Roberts, Belville, 1855
Roberts, Edward, 1860
Robertson, Benjamin C., 1871
Robertson, James, 1861
Robertson, James D., 1869
Robinson, Charles S., D.D., 1855
Robinson, George C., 1859
Robinson, John J., 1849
Robinson, Moses, 1842
Roche, Spencer S., 1874
Rockwell, J. Edson, D.D., 1841
Rockwood, L. Burton, 1843
Rodgers, James, 1870
Roe, Sanford W., D.D., 1851
Rogers, Ambrose S., 1843
Rogers, Edson, 1861
Roof, Garret L., 1847
Root, James P., 1855
Rose, Henry T., 1869
Rose, William W., 1863
Rosenkrans, Cyrus E., 1842
Rosenkrans, Joseph, 1842
Rosenthal, Richard S., 1869
Ross, Edward F., 1851
Rossiter, Stealy B., 1869
Rouse, Thomas H., 1850
Rowell, Joseph, 1851
Rowley, Charles H., 1871
Roy, Joseph E., D.D., 1853
Ruggles, Henry E., 1850
Ruliffson, Albert G., 1862
Russell, Charles H., 1859
Russell, Frank, 1867
Russell, Robert C., 1862
Rust, Richard H., 1868
Ruston, William O., 1875
Rutherford, Collingwood, 1846

Sabin, Levi P., 1861
Sahagyan, Hohannes Der, 1847
Sailer, Randolph, 1860
Sailor, John, 1847
Salter, William, D.D., 1843
Samson, Thomas S., 1874
Sanders, Henry M., 1876
Savage, Frederick B., 1868
Sawyer, Leicester J., 1862
Sawyer, Rollin A., D.D., 1857
Sawyer, Samuel, 1848
Saxton, J. Addison, 1839
Scarritt, William R., 1872
Schaff, David S., 1876
Schauffler, Frederick A., 1871
Schell, James P., 1873
Schenck, Addison V. C., 1846
Schermerhorn, Henry O., 1842
Schermerhorn, John W., 1843
Schermerhorn, Martin K., 1868
Schlager, Adelbert J., 1872
Schoonmaker, Sylvester F., 1864
Schory, Peter D., 1843

Schultz, James A., 1865
Schuyler, George W., 1840
Scott, Walter, 1874
Scott, Walter Q., 1874
Scoville, Samuel, 1861
Scudder, Henry M., D.D., 1843
Seccombe, Charles, 1850
Seely, Abraham T., 1844
Seely, Raymond H., D.D., 1842
Selden, Silas R., 1865
Severance, Milton L., 1863
Sexton, Thomas L., 1872
Seymour, Bela N., 1855
Seymour, Erastus, 1860
Seymour, Henry, 1842
Seymour, John A., 1852
Seymour, Ova H., 1854
Shackford, Charles C., 1839
Shapleigh, Horace S., 1869
Sharp, Charles W., 1861
Shattuck, Amos F., 1862
Shattuck, Cortland W., 1846
Shaw, Alexander, 1869
Shaw, Charles D., 1862
Shaw, Ezra D., 1863
Shaw, Francis N., 1853
Sheeley, Homer, 1873
Sheldon, George W., 1867
Shepherd, Thos. J., D.D., 1843
Sherman, Lewis, 1868
Sherrill, Franklin G., 1850
Sherwood, Nathan M., 1864
Shoards, Joseph F., 1871
Shorey, Lyman M., 1868
Shuler, Lawrence T., 1873
Silber, William B., LL.D., 1853
Silcox, William L., 1849
Simpson, Charles, 1870
Sinclair, Angus, 1873
Sinclair, James, 1851
Skinner, James A., 1860
Skinner, Thomas E., 1854
Skinner, Thomas H., Jr., 1843
Slauson, Hiram, 1840
Sloan, Isaac O., 1852
Smart, David L., 1872
Smith, Arthur H., 1870
Smith, Edward C., 1863
Smith, Edward P., 1855
Smith, Edwin G., 1850
Smith, George H., 1876
Smith, George N., 1875
Smith, Henry A., 1856
Smith, Henry R., 1850
Smith, Horace P., 1859
Smith, I. Bryant, 1849
Smith, Jackson, 1840
Smith, James C., 1842
Smith, James M., 1840
Smith, James R., 1852
Smith, Judson, 1863
Smith, Matson M., D.D., 1847
Smith, Mortimer, 1868
Smith, Socrates, 1845
Smith, William A., 1859
Smith, William S., 1852
Smith, William T., 1864
Snow, Richard V. W., 1865
Snowden, R. Bayard, 1859
Snyder, George N., 1871
Snyder, Peter, 1839
Snyder, William H., 1871
Somerville, Robert J., 1868
Soule, George, 1851
Spalding, George B., 1861
Spellmeyer, Henry, 1870
Spencer, Franklin A., 1841
Spooner, Erastus C., 1842
Sprague, D. Jay, 1857
Squire, William W., 1859
Stanley, Frederick J., 1876
Stanley, Charles H., 1865
Starbuck, Charles C., 1854
Stark, James W., 1861
Starks, Henry A., 1872
Starkweather, Fred'k M., 1845
Staver, Daniel, 1875
Stead, Benjamin F., D.D., 1842
Stearns, Charles C., 1875
Stearns, Lewis F., 1872
Stebbins, Henry H., 1867
Steele, Thomas C., 1866
Stein, John P., 1864
Steiner, Nahum I., 1850
Sterling, George, 1873
Stevens, Moody A., 1862
Stevenson, Andrew J., 1846
Stewart, Alexander C., 1875
Stewart, David F., 1876
Stiles, Edmund R., 1863
Stimson, Henry A., 1869
Stockwell, Austin P., 1865
Stoddard, Charles A., D.D., 1859
Stoddard, Elijah W., 1852
Stoddard, Judson B., 1843
Stoddard, Samuel A., 1868
Stone, Andrew L., D.D., 1842
Stone, Mellen D., 1874
Stone, Seth B., 1850
Stoutenburgh, William J., 1862
Stowell, Alexander D., 1858
Stratton, Edward, 1855
Stratton, James P., 1868
Stroh, Charles R., 1874
Strong, Edward, D.D., 1842
Strong, Guy C., 1850
Strong, James W., D.D., 1862
Strong, John J., 1870
Strong, Stephen C., 1848
Sullivan, Edwin R., 1867
Sunderland, Byron, D.D., 1843
Suplee, Thomas D., 1873
Sutphen, Joseph W., 1851
Sutton, J. Ford, 1857
Swallow, J. Emerson, 1848
Swift, Alfred B., 1853
Swift, Henry M., 1855
Swift, Isaac, 1869
Swift, William H., 1873
Swinney, Lucius R., 1869
Swope, Luther A., 1875
Symington, Charles, 1876

Tabor, Rodney L., 1872
Taft, Don Carlos, 1855
Talbot, Howard A., 1875
Talbot, John W., 1873
Tallmadge, Leander, 1862
Tallmadge, Leander A., 1867
Tallmadge, William H., 1875
Tanner, Elias F., 1862
Taylor, David H., 1860
Taylor, George I., 1847
Taylor, James Henry, 1859
Taylor, John C., 1861
Taylor, Ransom, 1839
Taylor, Townsend E., 1847
Teal, John William, 1868
Teal, William H., 1867
Teller, Henry L., 1866
Tembrook, Isaac B., 1873
Tenney, Albert F., 1873
Tenney, Ephraim, 1844
Tenney, Henry M., 1867
Terrett, John C., 1845
Terry, Cassius M., 1870
Terry, Roderick, 1875
Tetley, Josiah, 1872
Thayer, D. Haven, 1852
Thomas, De Witt H., 1867
Thomas, James D., 1857
Thomas, Moses B., 1871
Thomas, William D., 1873
Thomas, William H., 1875
Thompson, Amherst L., 1859
Thompson, Everitt B., 1868
Thompson, Frank, 1868
Thompson, James M., 1872
Thompson, Lewis, 1857
Thompson, Lewis O., 1866
Thompson, William A., 1843
Thomson, John, 1868
Thomson, William, 1857
Thorne, William H., 1864
Thresher, James N., 1862
Thurber, Edward G., 1862
Thurston, Thomas G., 1865
Tibbals, Charles A., 1875
Tindall, George P., 1852
Titsworth, Adoniram J., 1873
Titus, Wicks S., 1850
Todd, Charles N., 1846
Todd, Elbert S., 1867
Todd, James E., 1870
Tolles, Cornelius W., 1852
Tolman, George B., 1861
Tompkins, James N., 1844
Torrey, David, D.D., 1846
Torrey, Henry A. P., 1864
Torrey, John P., 1863
Torrey, Watson W., 1868
Tower, J. Edwin, 1861
Townsend, James B., 1838
Tracy, Charles C., 1867
Traver, Allen, 1853
Trotter, Alexander, 1841
Trowbridge, James H., 1850
Trowbridge, Tillman C., 1855
Tucker, George L., 1856
Tupper, Henry M., 1856
Tuthill, George M., 1846
Twichell, Joseph H., 1862
Tyler, Charles M., 1858
Tyler, George P., D.D., 1840
Tyler, William E., 1848
Tyng, Morris A., 1870
Tyson, Ira C., 1862

Uglow, James, 1857
Uhl, Erskine, 1864
Uhler, George, 1847
Uhlfelder, Sigismund, 1853
Ulyat, William C., 1849
Underhill, John W., 1859
Underwood, Henry B., 1865
Upham, Albert G., 1843
Upham, Francis W., 1841
Utter, George B., 1843

Vail, Edward J., 1844
Vail, S. Montfort, D.D., 1842
Van Aken, Gulick, 1865
Van Cleef, George S., 1843
Van Derlip, George M., 1858
Van Deursen, Russell D., 1855
Van Dyck, Edward A., 1870
Van Norden, Charles, 1866
Van Nostrand, Jacob, 1842
Vance, Edward D., 1874
Very, Lorin, 1841

Wade, Matthew, 1873
Waite, Henry R., 1872
Waldo, Edmund F., 1840
Waldo, Levi F., 1844
Waldo, Theron L., 1866
Walker, Avery S., 1857
Walker, James, 1850
Walker, John, 1863
Walker, John A., 1846
Wallace, Charles C., 1856
Waller, David J., Jr., 1874
Walsworth, Ed. B., D.D., 1848

Walsworth, Lyman W., 1851
Walton, Robert H., 1860
Ward, Bradish C., 1857
Ward, Earl J., 1867
Ward, John, 1844
Ward, Samuel L., 1876
Ward, Thomas S., 1838
Ward, William H., D.D., 1859
Wardlaw, William, 1850
Warren, James H., 1850
Warriner, Francis, 1839
Washburn, Henry H., 1875
Waterman, Alfred T., 1860
Watson, Charles C., 1866
Watson, John P., 1861
Weed, Thomas A., 1847
Weitzel, Charles T., 1875
Welch, Josiah, 1871
Wells, Edward P., 1866
Wells, John L., 1874
Wells, Nathan D., 1860
Wells, Rufus P., 1845
Wells, Shepherd, 1845
Wenner, George U., 1868
Westerfield, William, Jr., 1868
Westgate, George L., 1868
Wetherby, Charles, 1860
Whallon, Edward P., 1872
Wharton, Charles D., 1844
Wheeler, Hiram, 1842
Whitaker, Epher, 1851
Whitaker, William F., 1876
Whitcomb, Cyrus B., 1869
White, Erskine N., D.D., 1857
White, George H., 1856
White, Samuel J., D.D., 1842
White, Theodore F., D.D., 1853
White, William C., 1856
Whitehead, J. Elias, M,D., 1848
Whitehead, Joseph H., 1872
Whitford, Oscar U., 1872
Whitford, William C., 1856
Whitman, John S., 1860
Whitney, Henry O., 1869
Whitney, Joseph C., 1849
Whittlesey, Eliphalet, 1843
Wicks, Emerson G., 1868
Wilder, Charles N., 1866
Wilder, Theodore, 1868
Willard, Livingston, 1844
Willcox, G. Buckingham, 1851
Willcox, William H., 1846
Willett, Marinus, 1856
Willey, Samuel H., D.D., 1848
Williams, Charles H. S., 1865
Williams, Frederick W., 1852
Williams, Horace R., 1864
Williams, Moseley H., 1867
Williams, Richard R., 1870
Williams, Samuel D., 1869
Williams, Thomas R., 1869
Williams, William W., 1863
Williamson, James D., 1875
Williamson, Joseph G., 1849
Williamson, Robert H., 1858
Williston, Martin L., 1869
Willoughby, Henry W., 1844
Wilson, Charles E., 1864
Wilson, James D., 1862
Wilson, John N., 1869
Winnie, Christian W., 1871
Winship, Charles F., 1859
Winslow, Horace, 1841
Winslow, Kenelm, 1867
Winters, David, 1872
Wisner, Christian, 1864
Wiswell, George F., D.D., 1844
Wittmeyer, Alfred V., 1870
Wolcott, John M., 1859
Wolcott, William H., 1868
Wolfe, Aaron R., 1851
Wood, Charles A., 1873
Wood, Frank A., 1871
Wood, Franklin P., 1871
Wood, George I., 1838
Wood, George W., Jr., 1869
Wood, James W., 1840
Wood, William, 1847
Woodbury, Francis P., 1864
Woodhull, George S., 1852
Woodin, Simeon F., 1859
Woodruff, Henry C., 1871
Woods, Robert M., 1872
Woodworth, Francis C., 1840
Woolley, Daniel M., 1875
Worcester, John H., Jr., 1871
Wrage, Hermann D., 1860
Wright, Albert A., 1870
Wright, Albert O., 1867
Wright, Allen, 1855
Wright, Cassius E., 1870
Wright, Charles C., 1865
Wright, E. Monroe, 1842
Wright, Edward B., D.D., 1867
Wright, John, 1866
Wright, Joseph H., 1875
Wright, Walter E. C., 1868
Wright, Wesley P., 1855
Wright, William J., Ph.D., 1862
Wyckoff, James D., 1859
Wyckoff, Samuel, 1861

Young, Abraham T., 1842
Young, Claiborne A., 1872
Young, John R., 1845

Zaraphonithes, Anas. D., 1876
Zelie, John S., 1854
Zielie, John J., 1847
Zivley, John H., 1847

THE

EARLY ANNALS

OF

UNION THEOLOGICAL SEMINARY

IN THE

CITY OF NEW-YORK.

By Rev. EDWIN F. HATFIELD, D.D.

NEW-YORK.
No. 30 Clinton Place.

1876.

The following Historical Discourse was prepared at the request of the Faculty of Union Theological Seminary, in the city of New-York, and delivered, at the Anniversary of the Seminary, in the Madison Square Presbyterian Church, on the evening of Monday, the 8th of May, 1876. It is now published at the request of the Board of Directors.

EARLY ANNALS.

"THESE forty years the Lord thy God hath been with thee; thou hast lacked nothing." To recall the past, and mark the hand of God in our varied experience, is both pleasant and profitable. The gracious dealings of the Father Almighty with us and ours, as seen in the review of life, should stimulate us to renewed zeal and effort, in our endeavors to promote and extend the kingdom of the Divine Redeemer. He, who, through all their weary pilgrimage of forty years in the Arabian desert, had fed and clothed, guarded and guided his people Israel, would surely be their shield and buckler in the dreaded conflict with the Amorite, and, in due season, put them in secure possession of Canaan, the land of promise. So reasoned Moses, on the borders of Edom.

We celebrate to-day the Fortieth Anniversary* of Union Theological Seminary in the city of New-York. Forty years of instruction in the science of God and the Gospel of Christ are now brought to a close. It is a fitting occasion for at least a brief review of the history of this favored institution. As in the case of Israel on their way to the promised land, that history has been marked by signal and repeated interpositions of Divine Providence, and is singularly illustrative of the special guardianship of the great Head of the Church. Having, by the good hand of God upon us, attained to a position of influence among the agencies for raising up and sending forth a godly and able ministry, second to none in the land, it will be both entertaining and instructive, to recall the way in which the Lord has led us hitherto, that so we may thank God as we ought, and take courage in the continued prosecution of the work that is given us to do.

* The first public anniversary was celebrated at the end of the second year of instruction.

To determine the paternity of a great benevolence—whose thought it was that gave it being, or that moulded it into form—is not always practicable. The grand cathedrals of the Old World took shape, mostly, in the brains of their respective architects, before a single stone was laid or plan expressed on paper. Most of the great charities that so happily characterize and adorn the present age, grew out of a perception, on the part of some devout and zealous mind, of a special want, and its appropriate relief. A comparison of views, it may be, in respect to some providential emergency, leads to something like a simultaneous thought, on the part of several persons, as to the requisite agency for the occasion. Such is ordinarily the case with our noble institutions of learning and benevolence.

The movement that issued in the founding of Union Seminary first took shape in the autumn of the year 1835. One of the most active originators of the enterprise, a venerable divine, now in the seventy-eighth year of his age,* says that a friend† called on him, one day, to advise with him as to the disposal of some funds, which a bookseller‡ of this city desired to appropriate to some good object. "Let him give the sum towards the founding of a Theological Seminary in New-York," was the reply. His friend remonstrated; raised objections to the project, and said, "It is no place for a Seminary." The matter was then argued at considerable length. It was affirmed that a large city was just the place for such an institution, furnishing, as it does, special means of support to the indigent in the way of teaching, singing, and playing the organ in churches, and other remunerative employment; also of greater usefulness to the young men while pursuing their studies, by withdrawing them from cloistered life, and introducing them, at an early stage of their course, to missionary work among the poor and degraded of a great city, and among the children and youth of its many Sunday-schools and Bible-classes; thus testing, in the outset, their piety and fidelity, as well as their general fitness for the work of the ministry, and training them for it.

This conference resulted in a consultation, first with the bookseller, and then with a few prominent merchants, whose generous

* Rev. William Patton, D.D., of New-Haven, Ct.

† Rev. Absalom Peters, D.D.

‡ Mr. Oliver Halsted, of the firm of Halsted & Voorhis, law-booksellers. The funds were never obtained.

benefactions had already given them prominence in the walks of benevolence. The project was received with favor. A meeting of a few ministers and laymen of kindred sympathies was informally called. It was held at the house of Mr. WILLIAM M. HALSTED, No. 60 Walker street. The more the matter was talked of and thought of, the more it seemed to be of God's ordering. At length a formal meeting was held, Saturday, October 10th, at the house of Mr. KNOWLES TAYLOR, No. 8 Bond street. In addition to Mr. TAYLOR, eight other persons were present: Messrs. WILLIAM M. HALSTED, RICHARD T. HAINES, ABIJAH FISHER, and MARCUS WILBUR; Rev. ABSALOM PETERS, D.D., Rev. HENRY WHITE, Rev. WILLIAM PATTON, and Rev. ERSKINE MASON. After a full interchange of views, it was then and there voted unanimously "That it is expedient, depending on the blessing of God, to attempt to establish a Theological Seminary in this city."

Other meetings followed weekly, at the same place, with a continual enlargement of the circle.* Inquiries were made as to the probable cost of the undertaking, and the means of providing for it. Recent developments had raised considerable opposition to permanent endowments. It was thought that the establishment of the Seminary would involve "an expense of sixty-five thousand dollars, or thirteen thousand dollars *per annum* for five years; supporting, during that period, all the Professors, and, at its expiration, leaving a building and a library free from debt." Thenceforward it was hoped that the annual expenditures would be met by voluntary contributions. At their meeting of November 9th, a subscription was called for, payable in five annual installments: the first on the first day of June, 1836, provided that not less than sixty thousand dollars had been subscribed. The sum of thirty-one thousand dollars was then assumed by those present; an additional subscription of ten thousand dollars was reported at the next meeting; and every encouragement was given that the whole sum would shortly be secured.

---

* Prominent among the additional attendants were the Rev. Drs. THOMAS MCAULEY and THOMAS H. SKINNER; the Rev. Messrs. JOHN C. BRIGHAM, ICHABOD S. SPENCER, WILLIAM ADAMS, ASA D. SMITH, ELIJAH P. BARROWS, HENRY A. ROWLAND, CHARLES HALL, and HENRY G. LUDLOW; and Messrs. FISHER HOWE, JOHN NITCHIE, LOWELL HOLBROOK, JAMES C. BLISS, M.D., CORNELIUS BAKER, ANSON G. PHELPS, RUFUS L. NEVINS, CHARLES BUTLER, CHARLES STARR, JOHN L. MASON, NORMAN WHITE, OLIVER WILCOX, and ALEXIS BAKER.

In a brief editorial notice of the movement, the *New-York Observer*, of November 14th, said: "The gentlemen connected with this undertaking, we believe, have the confidence of the great mass of the Presbyterian community." How came it to pass, it may well be asked, that these "wealthy citizens connected with the Presbyterian Church," as they were said to be, were induced to identify themselves with this enterprise, to give so freely of their substance for its establishment and support, and, without fee or earthly reward, to devote so much of their time, their influence, and their energies to its advancement? Not less than six other Theological Seminaries had been more or less permanently established within the bounds of the Presbyterian Church: at Princeton, N. J.; at Auburn, N. Y.; at Allegheny, Pa.; at Cincinnati, O.; at Columbia, S. C.; and at Hampden Sidney, Va. Only eight years before, a New-York professorship of twenty thousand dollars had been subscribed for Union Seminary in Virginia, chiefly by these very men. Princeton Seminary, established and sustained by the General Assembly, some fifty miles only from New-York, was sadly in need of funds. For twenty-three years "its whole existence had been a constant course of struggle with poverty." At that very date, a special agent, in accordance with the recommendations of the Assembly of 1835, was preparing to canvass the churches for the means to place it on a substantial and adequate basis. Why did these men deem it desirable to attempt a seventh enterprise? Was there not a noble institution of the kind in full operation at Andover, Mass.? And one nearer at hand, connected with the venerable college at New-Haven, Ct.? What need was there of a Seminary in the commercial metropolis?

On the occasion of the visit of the Rev. JOHN H. RICE, D.D., of Virginia, to obtain the funds just alluded to for the Hampden Sidney Seminary, this most excellent and able divine found himself subjected to a considerable scrutiny, both as to his doctrinal and ecclesiastical sympathies. Under date of June 5th, 1827, writing to Mrs. RICE, he says: "While all the brethren appear to regard me with great personal affection, neither of the parties are entirely cordial to me. The Princeton people apprehend that I am approximating to Auburn notions; and the zealous partisans of New-England divinity think me a thorough-going Princetonian. So it is! And, while there is much less of that unseemly bitterness and asperity which brought reproach on the Church in past times, I can see that the spirit of party has struck deeper than I had ever supposed. And I do fully expect that there will be either a strong effort to bring Princeton under different management, or to build up a new Seminary in the vicinity of New-York, to counteract the influence of Princeton. One or the other of these things will assuredly be done before long, unless the Lord interpose and turn the hearts of the ministers."

Ten days later (15th) he writes again, and says : "The people here are only waiting for me to get out of the way, to bring forward other enterprises. I should not be surprised if, next year, we should hear of a Seminary for the vicinity of New-York. I can not tell you all that I have learned here in a letter, but you shall know when I see you."

As early, therefore, as 1827, possibly earlier, it was in contemplation, and seriously talked of, to undertake the establishment of a Theological Seminary, to be located in the immediate vicinity of New-York, and to be sustained by a portion of the consecrated wealth of the great metropolis. Growing dissatisfaction with existing institutions of the kind, according to the reliable testimony of the judicious Dr. RICE, prompted the incipient thought. Questions theological, ecclesiastical, and partisan had already wrought contentions and divisions among the ministers and in the churches of the city. The leaven, that wrought so disastrously some ten years later, was even then at work.

From an early period of the century, and notably from the commencement of the War of 1812, a tide of desirable immigration had been pouring into the city of New-York from every part of New-England and the adjacent towns of New-Jersey. Full of enterprise, many of these new-comers speedily established themselves in lucrative trade and commerce. Many of them were the children of godly parents, had been early indoctrinated in the current theology of the times, and had become intelligent and active Christians. Of course they identified themselves at once with the church and its work in their new home. Congregationalism in the city took form not earlier than 1819, and was of the Unitarian type. Consequently the new-comers attached themselves mostly to Presbyterian churches. So large a portion of the members of the old Cedar-street Church (Dr. ROMEYN'S) were of this character, as to occasion its being called "The Federal Church"—the prevailing political type of the Eastern States. Most naturally, diversities of views in doctrine and polity, and consequent jealousies, were early developed, of which the series of essays known as "The Triangle," by the elder WHELPLEY, on the one hand, and "The Contrast," by EZRA STILES ELY, on the other, were the most obvious fruits. The friends of missions and of ministerial education were divided ere long into rival factions. The patrons of ecclesiastical boards were arrayed against the advocates of voluntary societies and co-operative benevolence. Such was the immediate occasion of that party spirit the exhibition of which had so sensibly affected Dr. RICE, and led to the ta k about a new Seminary for New-York.

These diversities of views and operations were further promoted by the controversy relative to revival measures, culminating in the New-Lebanon Convention of July, 1827; by the fierce and bitter agitation of the Anti-slavery and Colonization questions; by the numerous pamphlets, reviews, and essays, in newspapers, magazines, and other publications, that presently flooded the Church, in and out of New-England, pertaining to the controversy about the so-called "New-Haven Theology;" by the prosecution for heresy, persistently urged, of such useful and godly ministers as GEORGE DUFFIELD, ALBERT BARNES, and LYMAN BEECHER; by the division of churches, presbyteries, and synods into rival and zealous partisans; and by the unseemly struggles of the Old and New School parties, year by year, for the control of the General Assembly.

It is perfectly natural, and by no means surprising, that, after years of contention and strife, so absorbing and so embittered, measures should have been devised, and means sought, to obtain deliverance from these unhappy agitations, and a peaceful retreat from such unholy disturbances. The founding of a new Seminary, on an independent basis, not subject to the control of accidental majorities in ecclesiastical bodies, not committed to any of the parties in the various conflicts by which the churches of the day were distracted and likely to be convulsed, occupying ground on which good and faithful men, of all classes and parties in the Presbyterian Church, could meet and act together for the spread of the gospel and the glory of the Divine Redeemer, ruled by no ecclesiastical clique, and pledged to no faction, met, therefore, with peculiar favor.

It is further to be borne in mind that, during the previous eight or ten years, particularly in 1831, a large number of young men had connected themselves with the Presbyterian churches of New-York and Brooklyn, many of whom were desirous of entering the ministry, but were destitute of the requisite pecuniary means. A New-York Seminary was just what they needed. It would tend, moreover, to arrest the tendency, growing, in part, out of the agitations in the Presbyterian Church, towards the New-England Seminaries, and save these enterprising youth for the service of our own churches at home and abroad.

Furthermore, it was believed that an institution of this kind, planted in the city of New-York, would "enlist many young men of talent, piety, and missionary zeal, from these two flourishing cities, in the work of the ministry, who" would thus "have the opportunity of adding to solid learning enlightened experience, by means of the constant pastoral influence under which they" would "act, and the performance of the important duties of church members, in Sabbath-schools, Bible-classes, and prayer-meetings, in the several churches with which they" might "be connected, and through their acquaintance with the benevolent efforts of this location."

It was with such designs, moved thereto, doubtless, by the Spirit of God, that good men and true, in humble dependence on the great Head of the Church, laid the foundations of "the New-York Theological Seminary," as they proposed to call it. The guiding hand of Him who led Israel through the sea and the desert was seen also in timing the enterprise. The financial pressure of 1834 had passed away. The flush of 1835–6 had set in, and new enterprises were springing up on every hand. Speculation was rife. The new lands of the West were coming into the market. Fortunes were easily made in the purchase and sale of town lots in the newly-projected villages and cities everywhere attracting attention. The friends of the new Seminary were full of hope. They subscribed largely—four of them five thousand dollars each—and met with good encouragement from others. Five sixths of the sum required had been subscribed, when, on the memorable night of the sixteenth of December, 1835, a conflagration was kindled, in the providence of God, that, within twenty-four hours, laid the wealthiest section of the city in ashes, consuming more than five hundred buildings and seventeen millions of property. It was a day of consternation —a day of bankruptcy to hundreds, and of sore privations to thousands, many of whom were in affluence the day before. It was the beginning of darker days to come. Well was it that the enterprise had been undertaken so early in the autumn. Three months later, it would have been out of the question.

At a meeting of the subscribers, January 11th, 1836, less than a month after the great catastrophe, it was announced that a subscription of sixty-one thousand dollars had been obtained, and that the conditional clause had thus been fulfilled. A constitution, previously and carefully prepared, was adopted, a large and highly responsible Board of Directors was chosen, and order taken to procure, from the Legislature of the State, an act of incorporation. The Board met, for the first time, on the evening of Monday, January 18th, 1836, at the house of the American Tract Society, in Nassau street, proceeded to the choice of officers for the year, and so the organization of "the NEW-YORK THEOLOGICAL SEMINARY" was completed.

Measures were taken at once to procure a location, and to erect a suitable edifice for the Seminary. A plot of ground, two hundred feet square, between Sixth and Eighth streets, extending from Greene to Wooster streets, four full lots on each street, was selected. It formed a part of the property of "the Sailors' Snug Harbor," which shortly before had been located in the old Randall mansion, on Broadway, above Ninth street. It was subject to an annual ground rent of eight hundred dollars. The lease was purchased for eight thousand dollars. The locality was well up town—quite on the outskirts of the city. Population had been spreading from what was then familiarly known as "Greenwich Village," along the Hudson River, northward; and, in like manner, along the Third avenue, on the eastern side of the city. A few improvements had been made along the Bloomingdale Road from its junction with the Bowery Road, at Seventeenth street, to the House of Refuge, which stood at the starting-point of the old Boston Road, on the westerly side of the present Madison Square, extending to the present Broadway, and covering the site of the Worth Monument. Union Place, now "Union Square," had just been opened, at the forks of Broadway and the Bowery, but was still unimproved. Eighth street and a few of the parallel streets above, opened but a few years before, were beginning to exhibit some evidences of substantial improvement. With these exceptions, vacant lots, unpaved streets, primitive roads and lanes, open fields and country-seats, many of them highly cultivated and of considerable extent, covered the island to the north, as far as the ancient Dutch village of Harlem. The New-York of that day scarcely extended above Tenth street, the original terminus of Broadway. Beyond was the open country.

The General Theological Seminary of the Protestant Episcopal Church, some ten years before, had been erected far out of the city, and near it, on Twentieth street, an Episcopal chapel (St. Peter's), of small capacity, had been erected in 1832. Old "St. Mark's" occupied its present site on Tenth street, near the Second avenue. Two or three mission stations, in advance of the population, were struggling for a foothold in the outlying districts. Excepting these, not a church edifice of any description was to be found on the island, below the villages of Bloomingdale and Harlem, above Tenth street. A new Presbyterian church had just been erected in Mercer street, near Eighth street, which, for many subsequent years, was the "Up-town Church" of the denomination. The stately structure erected for the University of the City of New-York, on the block below the new purchase, had just been occupied in part, but was not fully completed. Wooster street had just been extended to Fourteenth street, and the part above the University widened and called "Jackson avenue"—a name shortly after exchanged for "University Place." The location was deemed quite eligible, near enough to the business portion of the city, and sufficiently remote for a quiet literary retreat.

A permanent corps of Instructors was now to be secured. The first choice of the Directors for the Chair of Theology was the Rev. JUSTIN EDWARDS, D.D., of Andover, Mass.; and for the Chair of Biblical Literature, Prof. JOSEPH ADDISON ALEXANDER, of Princeton, N. J.—a happy commingling of the prevalent theological tendencies of the age. Both appointments were declined. Professors Extraordinary* were appointed from among the ministerial members of the Board. On the last day of September, the Rev. HENRY WHITE, the pastor of the Allen-street Presbyterian Church of this city, was appointed to, and soon after accepted, the Chair of Theology. The Rev. THOMAS MCAULEY, D.D., the pastor of the Murray-street Presbyterian Church, and the first President of the Board, was chosen Professor of Pastoral Theology and Church Government, with the position of President of the institution. The Rev. Prof. GEORGE HOWE, of Columbia, S. C., was also chosen to

* Rev. Drs. THOMAS MCAULEY and THOMAS H. SKINNER, and Rev. Messrs. ICHABOD A. SPENCER, ERSKINE MASON, and HENRY WHITE.

the Chair of Biblical Literature. Dr. McAuley accepted, but Prof. Howe declined. The services of two regular Professors, and of several Professors Extraordinary, having thus been secured, the Recorder was authorized, November 24th, 1836, to announce, in the public prints, that the Seminary would be opened on the first Monday of December following.

Promptly, therefore, on the 5th day of December thirteen young men presented themselves at the house of the President, No. 112 Leonard street, and were duly enrolled as theological students. A fortnight later, Prof. Edward Robinson, D.D., late of Andover, Mass., was chosen to the Chair of Biblical Literature. At the end of a month he accepted, and entered upon his work. Ten additional students were enrolled during the first year.

The new Seminary had thus far acquired no "local habitation." The plans for the building had not yet been completed. The necessities of the case made the institution somewhat "peripatetic." Now the young gentlemen are seen wending their way to the house of the President in Leonard street; the day following they have gathered at the residence of Prof. White, No. 80 Eldridge street; the third day finds them at the rooms of the Presbyterian Education Society, No. 116 Nassau street, drinking in the erudition of Prof. Robinson; or, in the absence of the latter, profiting by the genial instructions of the scholarly George Bush, at his study, No. 115 Nassau street; and again they are to be found gathered about the polished and enthusiastic Skinner, in his quiet retreat in the chapel of the Mercer-street Church. No dormitories having yet been provided, the students came from every quarter of the city, as far away as the Deaf and Dumb Institution on Fiftieth street, and some from the other side of the river.

The plans having at length been completed and approved, contracts were made for the erection of a seminary building on University Place, and of four Professors' houses in the rear, on Greene street. Early in March, 1837, the work was fairly begun, but with utterly inadequate resources. The original subscription had reached nearly seventy thousand dollars; but the first installment, payable June 1st, 1836, had yielded scarcely more than ten thousand dollars, four fifths of which had been required for the purchase of the lease; the ground rent and assessments absorbed nearly three fourths of the small remainder, leaving almost no provision for the payment of the salaries of the three Professors, the purchase of books, and other current expenses. The great fire had crippled quite a number of the patrons of the Seminary, and the prospects for the second installment, in June, 1837, were anything but promising. Whence were the funds for building purposes to be derived? Only from loans. Further subscriptions, to any considerable extent, were out of the question.

The times were now adverse, in the extreme, for new enterprises. Mr. Van Buren had just succeeded to the Presidency. The exciting era of land speculations had come to an end. The commonwealth of trade and commerce had lost confidence in the policy of the general government. Credit was destroyed. Trade was prostrate. The great manufactories were suspended. The demand for labor ceased. An era of bankruptcy set in. Merchants and bankers, after a while, yielded to the storm. House after house went down into hopeless ruin. A tremendous panic ensued. The land was convulsed. Every bank in the city of New-York on the 10th of May, and immediately after every bank in the land, suspended specie payment. It was no time to borrow—no time to build. It is not strange, therefore, that the Directors of the Seminary resolved, April 26th, 1837, "to suspend the erection of the buildings until they shall possess the means which will encourage them to resume the task."

As if to add to the distractions of the times and the embarrassments of the Board, the Presbyterian General Assembly, at its meeting, in May, at Philadelphia, was led into heated and angry discussions, and convulsed with party strife. The excision of a portion of its constituency scattered the brands of discord all over the land, kindling the flames of contention throughout the denomination. The Church was rent in twain, and thenceforth became two bands, with small hope of reconciliation. The friends and founders of the Seminary, greatly to their grief, found themselves unwittingly on opposite sides of the dividing line, yet unwilling to identify themselves, or the enterprise in which they were embarked, with either of the opposing parties. It was a year of deep discouragement, and passed away with but little relief. The second installment of the subscription had produced less than eight thousand dollars, and the prospects for the following year were even less hopeful. From two of the warm friends of the Seminary, however, at the close of the year, loans amounting to twenty-seven thousand dollars, secured by mortgage on the grounds and prospective buildings, were obtained, and the work of construction resumed. The second year of instruction had commenced, and thirty new students had been enrolled.

Thus far very little had been, or could have been, done in the way of securing that indispensable acquisition, a Theological Library. An empty treasury, and heavy indebtedness for stone and mortar, gave small promise for the desired attainment. A kind Providence, long years before, however, had anticipated this very want. One result of the bloody conflicts that desolated the fairest portions of Europe, at the beginning of the present century, and particularly of the Peace of Luneville, February 9th, 1801, was the secularization of the territories of the prelates, and the sequestration of the property of religious houses, in Germany, taking effect early in 1803. Among the sufferers by this spoliation was the Benedictine Monastery of St. Mary, at Paderborn. Anticipating this event, the fraternity appropriated, individually, so much of the common property as could be divided among them. The monastic library had been the growth of centuries. At the time of the Reformation, a collection had been made of the controversial literature of the period, mostly in the original editions. Some six hundred works of this description, large and small, had thus found their way into a small apartment, the door of which was marked with the words "*Libri Prohibiti*," of which the key was kept by a monk whose family name was Leander Van Ess. This collection, with other volumes, fell to the share of this trusted brother, then about thirty years of age. Not long afterwards he became the Roman Catholic Professor of Divinity in the ancient University of Marburg. An ardent thirst for learning had characterized him from boyhood. To the study of the original Scriptures he gave himself with intense interest. He was thereby led, through divine grace, into the liberty of the children of God. He became a devout and devoted follower of the Lamb of God. Full of his new-found joy, he longed to impart of his spiritual wealth to his countrymen. He set himself, therefore, to make a careful and accurate version of the Bible, particularly of the New Testament, into the vernacular. He gathered Bibles, polyglots, lexicons, concordances, commentaries, the Latin and Greek Fathers, the decrees of councils and popes, church histories, and other similar literary treasures, including a large collection of *Incunabula*, the rare issues of the earliest period of the art of printing,—in all, with what he had saved from the wreck at Paderborn (more than 13,000 volumes), about 6000 separate works. He translated the New Testament into German, published it in 1810, and, by the aid of the British and Foreign Bible Society, put into circulation, principally among the Roman Catholics of Germany, with the happiest spiritual results, 523,000 copies of the New Testament and more than 10,000 Bibles. Grown old and infirm, he retired at length from the University of Marburg to the quiet little town of Alzey, in Hesse-Darmstadt, west of the Rhine, about equidistant from Mayence and Worms, and offered his great library for sale, for 11,000 florins.

Prof. Calvin E. Stowe, just returned from Europe, was advised of the fact. In a letter from Lane Seminary to Dr. Robinson, April 3d, 1837, he advised the purchase of this unique collection by the New-York Seminary. Terrible as were the times, Dr. Robinson, on his departure for Europe and the Holy Land, in July, was instructed to obtain the refusal of the Collection. After a careful examination of the books by Mr. Philipp Wolff, of Erlangen University (a brother of Mrs. Gordon Buck, of this city), the purchase was effected in April, 1838, for 10,000 florins. It had cost Dr. Van Ess 50,000 florins. Its whole cost to the Seminary, when it arrived in October, all charges paid, was $5070.08. It was received just in time to find its way into the alcoves of the library room of the new building. It has served as an invaluable nucleus around which to cluster the needful volumes of the more modern press. It is a treasure, rare and peculiar, whose riches have as yet been but partially explored. If lost, it could not possibly be replaced.

The second year of instruction had closed with an enrollment of fifty-six students. The first senior class, six in number, had graduated July 11th, 1838, with appropriate exercises in the Allen-street church. The third year had opened with a large accession. The Catalogue, now for the first time printed, presented a total of ninety-two students, thirty-two of them juniors. The new Seminary building was dedicated, with appropriate ceremonies, December 12th, 1838. Three years had now elapsed since the incipient movement. A "local habitation" had been secured; a large and rare library had been provided; a full and able Faculty inducted; and a position attained among the first three Seminaries of the land—Andover and Princeton alone ranking it, and the latter by six only in the regular classes. The enterprise had proved a marked success. It was no longer an experiment.

An Act of Incorporation * was obtained, March 27th, 1839, from

---

* Appendix A.

the Legislature of the State, the name "Union" having been given it at Albany, to distinguish it, probably, from the Episcopal Seminary on Twentieth street—a name not desired, much less chosen, by the Board, but prophetic of the position that the Institution has ever since maintained.

It now became evident to the Board that the original projectors of the Seminary had counted without their host. Not more than fifty thousand dollars of the original subscription had proved available; and more than this amount had already been expended at the end of the third year of instruction. To obtain the greater part of this sum, the buildings, and even "the Van Ess Library," had been mortgaged. The last installment of the subscription would scarcely avail to meet the current expenses. No provision had been made for the years beyond.

What was to be done? The thought of failure was not to be entertained for a moment. The promise of good was too pronounced to be at all problematical. The experiment had shown that New-York was just the place for a Theological Seminary. Young men of piety, talents, and culture had resorted hither for a ministerial education, not only from New-York and Brooklyn, but from every part of the United States. Personal expenses, it had been found, were no greater than elsewhere; while the means of self-support and usefulness were much superior. To place the enterprise on a firm foundation was worthy of an arduous effort and great sacrifices. It was determined to make an appeal to the churches. A Financial Agent* was appointed. Fifty-five new students had entered at the beginning of the fourth year, the most of whom could find no accommodations in the new building, fully occupied as it was by the two previous classes. Lodgings, at the expense of the Board, had to be provided elsewhere. The Catalogue for the new year showed a total of 129 students in attendance. Greatly encouraged, the Directors called together such of the pastors of the city and vicinity as sympathized with the movement. Invited thus to share the responsibility, these pastors resolved to open their pulpits to the Financial Agent, and to afford him all the aid in their power in his solicitations for funds.

In the course of the winter an attempt was made to raise the

---

* Rev. Gideon N. Judd D.D., of Bloomfield, N. J., and subsequently of Catskill, N. Y.

sum of $50,000, but nothing came of it. In February, 1840, the Treasurer had advanced, over and above the loans, more than $16,000, although one of the four houses had been sold for $8500. Every expedient had been exhausted, and no provision had been made, or apparently could be made, for the payment of the Professors' salaries and other current expenses. The prospects were exceedingly dark. To carry forward the enterprise, in circumstances so adverse, was indeed a "work of faith and labor of love," demanding great "patience of hope in our Lord Jesus Christ." It was determined to make still more strenuous efforts; and, at the close of the year, May, 1840, the work of solicitation having been more vigorously pressed, it was found that a sufficient sum had been raised by subscription to justify the Board "in continuing the Seminary in operation for the ensuing year." None but the Board knew how precarious an existence was at that date accorded to the Seminary, overflowing though it was with students. The salaries of the Professors for two years had been mostly unpaid, and the incumbents subjected to severe trials. One of them at least, the Professor of Theology, was compelled to borrow nearly a year's salary, then to convert his home into a boarding-house, to become the stated supply of a pulpit, and, at length, to enter upon a voluntary agency for the solicitation of means to pay his very moderate salary. All honor to the men that endured such tribulations to perpetuate the work so auspiciously begun, in the founding of Union Seminary! Late in the year a strenuous effort was made to retrieve the original error. A Permanent Fund was imperatively demanded. A large floating debt had been incurred. To meet these demands, a subscription, payable on the attainment of pledges to the amount of $140,000, was opened. One subscription of $25,000, two of $12,500 each, eleven of $1000 each, and others amounting in all to $90,000, were obtained, but nothing more could be had, and the whole was lost.

Still they pressed on—those men of faith and prayer. Collections were made in an increasing number of churches annually. Agents were sent through the country, soliciting funds, in gifts of one dollar and upwards, from the people at their homes, in their warehouses and workshops, on their farms and in their factories, to meet current expenses. Thus the struggle for life was kept up during the next two or three years. The project of sustaining the Seminary by annual contributions was effectually tried, and found to be utterly unreliable. It now became evident that the enterprise must be abandoned, unless some permanent provision was made for the support of the Professors. Their services were sought elsewhere, and they seriously thought of resigning their positions. One of them resigned conditionally. A public meeting was called in September, 1843, and an appeal was made for the sum of $25,000, to endow the Professorship of Theology. The appeal was sustained, and the first Permanent Fund subscribed. To secure the payment of these subscriptions, to pay off a floating debt of nearly $20,000, and to meet current expenses, required diligent and laborious exertions for the next three years. Dr. McAuley had retired from the Faculty in 1840, and the Rev. Joel Parker, D.D., had succeeded him as President, and served as Financial Agent, retiring in 1842. The Rev. Absalom Peters, D.D., had in 1842 been elected Professor of Pastoral Theology, and, without entering on the duties of the professorship, had served as Financial Agent about one year, when he, too, retired, leaving only Professors White and Robinson in the Faculty. Partial provision, through the beneficence of a personal friend,* had been made for the support of the Professor of Biblical Literature. A generous proposal, on the part of several residents of Brooklyn, to contribute ample grounds, and to build thereon a seminary edifice and three dwelling-houses for the Professors, made early in the year 1844, had, after mature consideration, been gratefully declined. Such was the condition of affairs at the close of the first ten years of instruction.

A special providence, at the beginning of the next ten years, contributing materially to the relief of the Seminary, should not be overlooked. A grandson of an eminent citizen,† connected with one of our Presbyterian churches, had been carefully trained for the priesthood of the Episcopal Church, and duly ordained. Having served in the ministry, first at Harlem, N. Y., and then at Hagerstown, Md., he became so thorough a Ritualist that nothing would content him but the Papacy, which presently he espoused. After a brief novitiate at St. Sulpice, in Paris, he was ordained, in 1842, to the Roman Catholic priesthood by the late Archbishop Hughes, whose secretary he became in 1846. Shortly after this latter date his venerable grandfather died, and it was found that, in consequence of this change of faith, the inheritance, valued at about $30,000, originally

---

* Mr. James Boorman, of New-York City. † Mr. James Roosevelt.

designed for the grandson, had been devised to "Union Theological Seminary, in the city of New-York." This bequest was contested, successfully at first; but the provisions of the will were finally sustained by the Court of Appeals. The contestant is now the Roman Catholic Archbishop of Baltimore,* and his forfeited patrimony has done excellent service in sustaining this Protestant Seminary.

The day had now fairly dawned. A gracious Providence had kindly interposed, and rescued the enterprise from impending bankruptcy. Early in 1848 the Rev. THOMAS H. SKINNER, D.D., of precious memory, a devoted friend and patron of the Seminary from the beginning, was chosen to the newly-created Professorship of Sacred Rhetoric, Pastoral Theology, and Church Government,—a position for which he was pre-eminently fitted,—and permanent provision was made, by a few personal friends, for his support.

The Professorship of Theology was made vacant in August, 1850, by the decease of Professor HENRY WHITE, in the full maturity of his powers—greatly to the grief of the Board and Faculty. The Rev. HENRY B. SMITH, a Professor in Amherst College, Mass., entered, in December, 1850, upon the duties of the Professorship of Ecclesiastical History, to which he had been elected in July. To the Chair of Theology the Rev. JAMES P. WILSON, D.D., of Philadelphia, succeeded in May of the following year.

The time had now come for enlargement. The annual expenses of the institution were about $12,000. Its annual income, from the legacy of Mr. ROOSEVELT, from individual subscriptions, and from all other sources, was only about $5000. An annual deficiency of $7000 had to be supplied by voluntary contributions. In February, 1852, it was determined to attempt the obtaining of an additional investment of $150,000, subscriptions to be binding on the first of May, 1853, if at that time $100,000 should have been pledged. A few members of the Board, at a meeting in March, 1852, pledged themselves for $42,367 of the sum, the services of the Rev. JOSEPH S. GALLAGHER, of Bloomfield, N. J., were happily obtained for the agency, and the requisite $100,000 secured within the specified period. The further prosecution of the endowment effort was providentially postponed to a more favorable season.

From the first it had been evident that the accommodations for students were entirely inadequate. A fourth story and an attic story,

* Most Rev. JAMES R. BAYLEY, D.D.

therefore, were added to the original building, in the summer of 1852, at an expense of $12,524, for the payment of which, in part, the building was mortgaged for $10,500. Provision was thus made for forty-eight additional students, the new rooms having been gratuitously furnished, at an expense of $2000, by that genuine servant of Christ and most devoted friend of the Seminary, the late lamented ANSON G. PHELPS, Jr.

The Chair of Theology was again made vacant by the resignation, in October, 1853, of Prof. JAMES P. WILSON. Prof. SMITH was transferred to the vacant Professorship, in March, 1854. The funds were further enlarged, in 1854, by a legacy, received from the estate of MARY FASSITT, deceased, of Philadelphia, amounting eventually to about $20,000; and by a subscription, in 1855, of $25,000, by a lady of this city,* to found the Professorship of Ecclesiastical History. The Rev. ROSWELL D. HITCHCOCK, a Professor in Bowdoin College, was chosen to the vacant chair in July, 1855, and entered upon its duties at the commencement of the next term. The second period of ten years closed under the happiest auspices. The days of doubt and perplexity had passed. The question of a permanent existence had been solved. Progress had been made, with good promise for the future, towards a complete endowment of the Professorships. The Seminary had secured a full and able Faculty, and now occupied a position of influence, second to no similar institution of the kind in the whole land. Great as had been the effort, the struggle, and the sacrifices of the founders, they were amply repaid. Much remained to be accomplished, a far greater amount of funds was still needed; but the past success fully warranted the assurance of better days to come.

The early story has now been told. A brief glance at the salient points of the later story must suffice. The subscription begun in 1852, and suspended the following year because of financial pressure resulting in the wide-spread bankruptcy of 1857, was, in 1859, resumed, and increased to $200,000. Hitherto the pecuniary affairs of the institution had necessarily been administered on principles of the most rigid economy, almost approximating to parsimony. The burden of heavy indebtedness, incurred by the erection of buildings, and the meagre provision for current expenses, had kept the corps of

* Mrs. JACOB BELL. The chair was named for her deceased brother, the Rev. SAMUEL WASHBURN, of Baltimore, Md.

instruction and the salaries of the Professors inadequately small, with but little prospect of advancement. And now the Civil War of 1861–5 still further aggravated the difficulty. Specie was withdrawn from circulation. The land was flooded with irredeemable paper money. Prices of all commodities were greatly enhanced. The purchasing power of a fixed salary was reduced from fifty to a hundred per cent. The Professorships, originally rated at $25,000, had never yielded enough to pay the salaries of the incumbents. As prices advanced, the income proved but little more than enough to pay the rent of a respectable dwelling-house.

It became necessary, therefore, to make another appeal, for $150,000, for endowment and scholarships. The Rev. Edwin F. Hatfield, D.D., was appointed Financial Agent. The churches generously responded to the appeal, and the sum was secured in 1865. The inadequacy of the original accommodations for the Seminary, and the need of a fire-proof building for the Library, had long been apparent. A whole generation had passed, and a new city, vastly more substantial and elegant, had grown up above Tenth street. The churches had mostly migrated with the advancing population. The old city was fast becoming simply a mart of trade and commerce. It was judged expedient to secure a more eligible site for the Seminary, and to erect thereon more commodious and suitable buildings. The old feuds of the Presbyterian Church had died out, and the dissevered parts were soon to be reunited. The times were favorable—never more so. Early in 1870 an appeal was, therefore, made, through the same agency, for a subscription of $300,000. The appeal was, in the course of the following year, sustained. Ground was secured, but, owing to the changed aspect of the times, has not yet been occupied.

The Chair of Biblical Literature, by the lamented decease, in 1863, of that eminent scholar, of world-wide fame, Prof. Edward Robinson, D.D., LL.D., was made vacant. Prof. William G. T. Shedd, D.D., then the pastor of the Brick Church of this city, was induced to accept the position. Prof. Philip Schaff, D.D., was added to the Faculty in 1870, and the revered and greatly-beloved Thomas H. Skinner, D.D., LL.D., taken to his rest and reward early in 1871. Subsequently, in 1873, the Rev. William Adams, D.D.,* and Rev. George L. Prentiss, D.D., were added to the

* The office of President of the Institution, without an incumbent for thirty years, was now filled by the appointment of the Rev. Dr. Adams to the responsible post.

corps of Professors. The following year, by reason of the prolonged illness of Prof. SMITH, Dr. SHEDD was transferred to the Chair of Theology; and Dr. SCHAFF to the Chair of Sacred Literature. The Rev. CHARLES A. BRIGGS was made Provisional Professor of Hebrew and the Cognate Languages. The original corps of instruction was thus extended from three to seven Professors; and, to crown the whole, the most ample provision was made for their support by the princely gift, on the part of Mr. JAMES BROWN, of this city, of *three hundred thousand dollars*,— the endowment of each of the six regular Professorships being thus extended from $25,000 to $80,000. To furnish proper accommodations for the overflow of students, two of the four houses originally owned by the Seminary, and sold, have been repurchased, together with a third house on the corner of Clinton Place. The latter building has been connected with one of the former by an additional edifice, erected last summer. The Seminary building, at the same time, was rendered much more commodious and attractive by a large addition on its northern side, and by a refurnishing of the chapel and students' rooms; providing thus much larger space, also, for the Library, which has grown to more than 33,000 volumes. The new building and the repairs of the Seminary have involved an expenditure of about $45,000, seven ninths of which sum have been furnished for the purpose by the munificence of a noble friend* of the Institution.

The last Catalogue shows a total of students, for the year now ending, of 142, the largest number reported for any one year, save in 1859–60, when, owing to the great revival of the previous year, the number reached 146. In this respect Union Seminary now ranks every other in the land. By the grace of God, it has, through much and severe tribulation, attained to a position of influence excelled by none other. During the forty years of its operations, it has sent forth 1778 students, of whom 1070 have graduated here. Of the whole number, about 267 have finished their course, and entered the rest prepared for the people of God. With few exceptions, the remaining 1511 are doing yeoman service in the Master's vineyard. They are found in every section, in nearly every State, of the Union. They are occupying influential pulpits in our largest towns and cities. In all the newer States, and in the outlying hamlets of the older States, they are laboring, with apostolic zeal, to " build the

* Mr. FREDERICK MARQUAND, of the city of New-York.

old waste places" and "raise up the foundations of many generations." They are found in our academies, colleges, and seminaries, forming the minds and cultivating the hearts of the rising generation. On every continent and ocean group of islands they are toiling to raise the heathen from their degradation and corruption, and train them for God and glory. Union Seminary is a mighty power in the world—a grand instrumentality for building up the kingdom of our Lord Jesus Christ among men.

It was not in vain that its founders toiled and prayed, and gave, in many instances most liberally, of their substance, to build up an institution that should "commend itself to all men of moderate views and feelings, who desire to live free from party strife, and to stand aloof from all extremes of doctrine or of practice," in the attempt to raise up a learned and godly ministry for the Church. All honor to such men as RICHARD T. HAINES, for nearly thirty years the efficient and generous President of the Board, and WILLIAM M. HALSTED and ANTHONY P. HALSEY, the two deceased Treasurers. They are to be held in lasting remembrance for their untiring and unswerving devotion to the work of building up this dearly-cherished institution. Among those who have served as members of the Board of Directors, and who have finished their course on earth, grateful mention should be made, also, of Messrs. CALEB O. HALSTED, ABIJAH FISHER, FISHER HOWE, ANSON G. PHELPS (father and son), JAMES BOORMAN, DAVID HOADLEY, and that princely giver, JOHN C. BALDWIN. Their record is on high, and we, to-day, are reaping the fruits of their labors.

The friends and patrons of Union Seminary have been found in the most of the Presbyterian churches of the city; but it is due to historic justice to recall the fact, that it is owing to the large-hearted sympathies and noble benefactions, chiefly, of the late "Mercer-street Church," and its offspring, the "Church of the Covenant," together with the "Madison-square Church," that this beloved Seminary has been sustained these forty years, and elevated to its present commanding position among the agencies of the Church.* To their honor, and to the glory of the Master, be it said, they have never faltered in their love and devotion to this work. Neither they nor their beloved pastors ever failed to respond promptly, heartily, and nobly to the numerous appeals of the Board for help in

---

* Appendix B.

time of need. But for them, the enterprise must long since have been abandoned. They may well rejoice, to-day, in what their own hands have wrought.

In conclusion, before all and above all, we render most hearty and devout thanks to the God of Israel, the God and Father of our Lord Jesus Christ, who, through all these forty years of peril and perplexity, of sowing and reaping, of sadness and joy, has been with us, and made the work of our hands to prosper. "Now unto the King eternal, immortal, invisible, the only wise God, be honor and glory for ever and ever. Amen."

APPENDIX.

A.

ACT OF INCORPORATION.

An Act to incorporate the Union Theological Seminary in the City of New York. —Passed March 27th, 1839.

The People of the State of New York, represented in Senate and Assembly, do enact as follows:

§ 1. Thomas McAuley, Henry White, Samuel H. Cox, Thomas H. Skinner, William Patton, Erskine Mason, Ichabod S. Spencer, Absalom Peters, William Adams, Nathanael E. Johnson, Henry A. Rowland, David Magie, Ansel D. Eddy, Selah B. Treat, Zechariah Lewis, Micah Baldwin, Charles Butler, Leonard Corning, Abijah Fisher, William M. Halsted, Caleb O. Halsted, Fisher Howe, Richard T. Haines, Joseph Otis, Anson G. Phelps, Pelatiah Perit, Cornelius Baker, and Knowles Taylor, and their associates, who are the present Directors, and their successors, are hereby constituted a body corporate by the name of "The Union Theological Seminary in the City of New-York;" and by that name shall have succession, and be capable in law of taking and holding by gift, grant and devise, or otherwise, and of purchasing and holding and conveying, both in law and equity, any estate, real or personal; provided that the clear annual value or income of their real estate should not exceed the sum of fifteen thousand dollars; and their personal estate shall not exceed the sum of fifty thousand dollars,* exclusive of such Professorships as may be from time to time endowed.

§ 2. The government of the Seminary shall at all times be vested in a Board of Directors, which shall consist of twenty-eight members;† one half of whom shall be clergymen, and the other half laymen.

---

* By act of the Legislature, May 11, 1874, increased to "five hundred thousand dollars, exclusive of the Library, and of such Professorships, Scholarships, and Lectureships, or other offices connected with the Educational Department of the Seminary as are now or may hereafter be, from time to time, endowed."

† By Act of the Legislature, April 1, 1870, this was altered, so as to read—"*not less than* twenty-eight members."

§ 3. The Board of Directors already chosen shall be divided into four classes, to be numbered one, two, three and four; the term of the first class shall expire in one, the second in two, the third in three, and the fourth in four years from the eighteenth of January last. The following persons shall be Directors of the first class: Thomas H. Skinner, William Adams, Samuel H. Cox, Selah B. Treat, Abijah Fisher, Joseph Otis, Caleb O. Halsted, and Leonard Corning. Of the second class: William Patton, Ichabod S. Spencer, Henry White, David Magie, Pelatiah Perit, Charles Butler, and Micah Baldwin. Of the third class: Henry A. Rowland, Absalom Peters, Nathanael E. Johnson, Fisher Howe, Richard T. Haines, William M. Halsted, and Anson G. Phelps. Of the fourth class: Thomas McAuley, Ansel D. Eddy, Erskine Mason, Zechariah Lewis, Knowles Taylor, and Cornelius Baker. Each class of Directors shall hereafter be chosen for, and hold their offices during, four years, and until a new election to supply the places of such class.

§ 4. The members of any class of Directors may be eligible to a re-election; and each election shall take place at least one week previous to the expiration of the term of office of the class to be supplied. And the said Directors shall have power to fill all vacancies in their own Board, which may happen from year to year; and the appointment to fill such vacancy shall be valid for the unexpired term of the Director whose office shall be vacant.

§ 5. Equal privileges of admission and instruction, with all the advantages of the Institution, shall be allowed to students of every denomination of Christians.

§ 6. The Legislature may at any time alter or repeal this act.

B.

It appears from these Annals, that this Seminary was "founded before the disruption of the Presbyterian Church," that it "belonged exclusively to neither of its branches," and was "administered upon its own independent charter." On the occasion of the union of the two branches of the Church, the Board of Directors memorialized the General Assembly of 1870 "to the following effect—namely: That the General Assembly may be pleased to adopt it as a rule and plan, in the exercise of the proprietorship and control over the several Theological Seminaries, that, so far as the election of Professors is concerned, the Assembly will commit the same to their respective Boards of Directors, on the following terms and conditions:

"*First*, That the Board of Directors of each Theological Seminary shall be authorized to appoint all Professors for the same.

"*Second*, That all such appointments shall be reported to the General Assembly, and no such appointment of Professor shall be considered as a complete election, if disapproved by a majority vote of the Assembly."

The Directors further declared, "if the said plan shall be adopted by the General Assembly, that they will agree to conform to the same, the Union Seminary in New-York being, in this respect, on the same ground with other Theological Seminaries of the Presbyterian Church."

The plan was adopted by the Assembly June 1, 1870, and Union Seminary was thus brought into ecclesiastical connection with the Presbyterian Church, on the same footing as that of the other Seminaries of the Church.

The utmost care, however, had been taken, from the first, to provide for such instruction, and such only, in the Seminary, as would command the approbation and confidence of the Presbyterian Church in the United States of America. It was made an irrevocable part of the Constitution, that

"Every Director, on entering upon his office and also after each re-election, shall make the following declaration in the presence of the Board, namely:

"'Approving of the plan and Constitution of the Union Theological Seminary in the City of New-York, and of the Westminster Confession of Faith, and the Presbyterian Form of Church Government, I do solemnly promise to maintain the same, so long as I shall continue to be a member of the Board of Directors.'"

The following rules were, also, in like manner, adopted in reference to the Professors:

"Every member of the Faculty shall, on entering upon his office, and triennially thereafter, or when required by the Board, so long as he remains in office, make and subscribe the following declaration in the presence of the Board—namely:

"'I believe the Scriptures of the Old and New Testament to be the Word of God, the only infallible rule of faith and practice; and I do now, in the presence of God and the Directors of this Seminary, solemnly and sincerely receive and adopt the Westminster Confession of Faith, as containing the system of doctrine taught in the Holy Scriptures. I do also, in like manner, approve of the Presbyterian Form of Government; and I do solemnly promise, that I will not teach or inculcate any thing which shall appear to me to be subversive of the said system of doctrine, or of the principles of said Form of Government, so long as I shall continue to be a Professor in the Seminary.'

"If any Professor shall refuse, at the stated time, or when required by the Board, to repeat the above declaration, he shall forthwith cease to be a Professor in the Institution."

No amendments can be made to the Constitution that are "inconsistent with the doctrinal basis contained in" these declarations.

www.ingramcontent.com/pod-product-compliance
Lightning Source LLC
LaVergne TN
LVHW011219110826
845150LV00006B/1472

* 9 7 8 1 4 2 5 5 1 6 6 5 9 *